LEGAL PRACTICE COURSE

CORE STATUTES ON
PROPERTY LAW

CORE STATUTES ON PROPERTY LAW

Alan Moran and Peter Luther

Law Matters Publishing

Published by Law Matters Publishing

Law Matters Limited
33 Southernhay East
Exeter EX1 1NX
Tel: 01392 215577
www.lawmatterspublishing.co.uk

British Library Cataloguing-in-Publication Data

A catalogue record for this book is available from the British Library.

Crown copyright material is reproduced with the permission of the Controller of HMSO.

ISBN 10: 1 84641 033 9
ISBN 13: 978 1 84641 033 8

Typeset by Style Photosetting Ltd, Mayfield, East Sussex

Printed in Great Britain by Ashford Colour Press Ltd, Gosport, Hampshire

PREFACE

We are grateful that so many have responded positively to the first edition of our book. The aim of this second edition remains the same: to make available the essential statutory material required by students on most property law courses. With two exceptions, we have included only statutory material that is in force at the time of publication. The first of these exceptions is the Land Registration Act 1925 which, though repealed, is likely to remain relevant to students of property law for some time to come; as in the first edition of this collection, we have included key sections. We have also included clauses 1 to 5 of the Charities Bill which is currently under consideration by Parliament.

Our thanks go to those who have made suggestions for the improvement of the book, even if we have not, on this occasion, taken up their suggestions.

As ever, we express our gratitude to the publishers for their help to us. We have tried to state the law as at 31 July 2006.

Alan Moran
Peter Luther

CONTENTS

ALPHABETICAL LIST OF CONTENTS

PRESCRIPTION ACT 1832
(1832, c. 71)

1. **Claims to right of common and other profits à prendre, not to be defeated after thirty years enjoyment by merely showing the commencement; after sixty years enjoyment the right to be absolute, unless had by consent or agreement**

   No claim which may be lawfully made at the common law, by custom, prescription, or grant, to any right of common or other profit or benefit to be taken and enjoyed from or upon any land of our sovereign lord the King, . . . or any land being parcel of the duchy of Lancaster or of the duchy of Cornwall, or of any ecclesiastical or lay person, or body corporate, except such matters and things as are herein specially provided for, and except tithes, rent, and services, shall, where such right, profit, or benefit shall have been actually taken and enjoyed by any person claiming right thereto without interruption for the full period of thirty years, be defeated or destroyed by showing only that such right, profit, or benefit was first taken or enjoyed at any time prior to such period of thirty years, but nevertheless such claim may be defeated in any other way by which the same is now liable to be defeated; and when such right, profit, or benefit shall have been so taken and enjoyed as aforesaid for the full period of sixty years, the right thereto shall be deemed absolute and indefeasible, unless it shall appear that the same was taken and enjoyed by some consent or agreement expressly made or given for that purpose by deed or writing.

2. **In claims of right of way or other easement the periods to be twenty years and forty years**

   No claim which may be lawfully made at the common law, by custom, prescription, or grant, to any way or other easement, or to any watercourse, or the use of any water, to be enjoyed or derived upon, over, or from any land or water of our said lord the King, . . . or being parcel of the duchy of Lancaster or of the duchy of Cornwall, or being the property of any ecclesiastical or lay person, or body corporate, when such way or other matter as herein last before mentioned shall have been actually enjoyed by any person claiming right thereto without interruption for the full period of twenty years, shall be defeated or destroyed by showing only that such way or other matter was first enjoyed at any time prior to such period of twenty years, but nevertheless such claim may be defeated in any other way by which the same is now liable to be defeated; and where such way or other matter as herein last before mentioned shall have been so enjoyed as aforesaid for the full period of forty years, the right thereto shall be deemed absolute and indefeasible, unless it shall appear that the same was enjoyed by some consent or agreement expressly given or made for that purpose by deed or writing.

3. **Claim to the use of light enjoyed for 20 years**

   When the access and use of light to and for any dwelling house, workshop, or other building shall have been actually enjoyed therewith for the full period of twenty years without interruption, the right thereto shall be deemed absolute and indefeasible, any local usage or custom to the contrary notwithstanding, unless it shall appear that the same was enjoyed by some consent or agreement expressly made or given for that purpose by deed or writing.

4. **Before mentioned periods to be deemed those next before suits**

   Each of the respective periods of years hereinbefore mentioned shall be deemed and taken to be the period next before some suit or action wherein the claim or matter to which such period may relate shall have been or shall be brought into question and that no act or other matter shall be deemed to be an interruption, within the meaning of this statute, unless the same shall have been or shall be submitted to or acquiesced in for one year after the party interrupted shall have had or shall have notice thereof, and of the person making or authorizing the same to be made.

5.   **In actions on the case, the claimant may allege his right generally, as at present. In pleas to trespass and certain other pleadings, the period mentioned in this Act may be alleged. Exceptions, etc. to be replied to specially**

In all actions upon the case and other pleadings, wherein the party claiming may now by law allege his right generally, without averring the existence of such right from time immemorial, such general allegation shall still be deemed sufficient, and if the same shall be denied all and every the matters in this Act mentioned and provided, which shall be applicable to the case, shall be admissible in evidence to sustain or rebut such allegation; and that in all pleadings to actions of trespass, and in all other pleadings wherein before the passing of this Act it would have been necessary to allege the right to have existed from time immemorial, it shall be sufficient to allege the enjoyment thereof as of right by the occupiers of the tenement in respect whereof the same is claimed for and during such of the periods mentioned in this Act as may be applicable to the case, and without claiming in the name or right of the owner of the fee, as is now usually done; and if the other party shall intend to rely on any proviso, exception, incapacity, disability, contract, agreement, or other matter herein-before mentioned, or on any cause or matter of fact or of law not inconsistent with the simple fact of enjoyment, the same shall be specially alleged and set forth in answer to the allegation of the party claiming, and shall not be received in evidence on any general traverse or denial of such allegation.

6.   **Presumption to be allowed in claims herein provided for**

In the several cases mentioned in and provided for by this Act, no presumption shall be allowed or made in favour or support of any claim, upon proof of the exercise or enjoyment of the right or matter claimed for any less period of time or number of years than for such period or number mentioned in this Act as may be applicable to the case and to the nature of the claim.

7.   **Proviso for infants, etc.**

Provided also, that the time during which any person otherwise capable of resisting any claim to any of the matters before mentioned shall have been or shall be an infant, idiot, non compos mentis, feme covert, or tenant for life, or during which any action or suit shall have been pending, and which shall have been diligently prosecuted, until abated by the death of any party or parties thereto, shall be excluded in the computation of the periods herein-before mentioned, except only in cases where the right or claim is hereby declared to be absolute and indefeasible.

8.   **What time to be excluded in computing the term of forty years appointed by this Act**

Provided always, that when any land or water upon, over, or from which any such way or other convenient watercourse or use of water shall have been or shall be enjoyed or derived hath been or shall be held under or by virtue of any term of life, or any term of years exceeding three years from the granting thereof, the time of the enjoyment of any such way or other matter as herein last before mentioned, during the continuance of such terms, shall be excluded in the computation of the said period of forty years, in case the claim shall within three years next after the end or sooner determination of such term be resisted by any person entitled to any reversion expectant on the determination thereof.

WILLS ACT 1837
1837 (7 Will. 4 and 1 Vict. C. 26)

3.   **All property may be disposed of by will**

It shall be lawful for every person to devise, bequeath, or dispose of, by his will executed in manner herein-after required, all real estate and all personal estate which he shall be entitled to, either at law or in equity, at the time of his death, and which, if not so devised, bequeathed, or disposed of, would devolve . . . upon his executor or administrator; and the power hereby given shall extend . . . to all contingent, executory or other future interests in any real or personal estate, whether the testator may or may not be ascertained as the person or one of the persons in whom the same respectively may become vested, and whether he may be entitled thereto under the instrument by which the same respectively were created, or under any disposition thereof by deed or will; and also to all rights of entry for conditions broken, and other rights of entry; and also to such of the same estates, interests, and rights respectively, and other real and personal estate, as the testator may be entitled to at the time of his death, notwithstanding that he may become entitled to the same subsequently to the execution of his will.

7. **No will of a person under age valid**

No will made by any person under the age of eighteen years shall be valid.

9. **Signing and attestation of wills**

No will shall be valid unless—

(a) it is in writing, and signed by the testator, or by some other person in his presence and by his direction; and

(b) it appears that the testator intended by his signature to give effect to the will; and

(c) the signature is made or acknowledged by the testator in the presence of two or more witnesses present at the same time; and

(d) each witness either—

    (i) attests and signs the will; or

    (ii) acknowledges his signature, in the presence of the testator (but not necessarily in the presence of any other witness), but no form of attestation shall be necessary.

11. **Soldiers and mariners wills excepted**

Provided always, that any soldier being in actual military service, or any mariner or seaman being at sea, may dispose of his personal estate as he might have done before the making of this Act.

14. **Will not to be void on account of incompetency of attesting witness**

If any person who shall attest the execution of a will shall at the time of the execution thereof or at any time afterwards be incompetent to be admitted a witness to prove the execution thereof, such will shall not on that account be invalid.

15. **Gifts to an attesting witness to be void**

If any person shall attest the execution of any will to whom or to whose wife or husband any beneficial devise, legacy, estate, interest, gift, or appointment, of or affecting any real or personal estate (other than and except charges and directions for the payment of any debt or debts), shall be thereby given or made, such devise, legacy, estate, interest, gift; or appointment shall, so far only as concerns such person attesting the execution of such will, or the wife or husband of such person, or any person claiming under such person or wife or husband, be utterly null and void, and such person so attesting shall be admitted as a witness to prove the execution of such will, or to prove the validity or invalidity thereof, notwithstanding such devise, legacy, estate, interest, gift, or appointment mentioned in such will.

18. **Wills to be revoked by marriage, except in certain cases**

(1) Subject to subsections (2) to (4) below, a will shall be revoked by the testator's marriage.

(2) A disposition in a will in exercise of a power of appointment shall take effect notwithstanding the testator's subsequent marriage unless the property so appointed would in default of appointment pass to his personal representatives.

(3) Where it appears from a will that at the time it was made the testator was expecting to be married to a particular person and that he intended that the will should not be revoked by the marriage, the will shall not be revoked by his marriage to that person.

(4) Where it appears from a will that at the time it was made the testator was expecting to be married to a particular person and that he intended that a disposition in the will should not be revoked by his marriage to that person,—

(a) that disposition shall take effect notwithstanding the marriage; and

(b) any other disposition in the will shall take effect also, unless it appears from the will that the testator intended the disposition to be revoked by the marriage.

18B   Will to be revoked by civil partnership

(1)   Subject to subsections (2) to (6), a will is revoked by the formation of a civil partnership between the testator and another person.

(2)   A disposition in a will in exercise of a power of appointment takes effect despite the formation of a subsequent civil partnership between the testator and another person unless the property so appointed would in default of appointment pass to the testator's personal representatives.

(3)   If it appears from a will

    (a)   that at the time it was made the testator was expecting to form a civil partnership with a particular person, and

    (b)   that he intended that the will should not be revoked by the formation of the civil partnership,

the will is not revoked by its formation.

(4)   Subsections (5) and (6) apply if it appears from a will

    (a)   that at the time it was made the testator was expecting to form a civil partnership with a particular person, and

    (b)   that he intended that a disposition in the will should not be revoked by the formation of the civil partnership.

(5)   The disposition takes effect despite the formation of the civil partnership.

(6)   Any other disposition in the will also takes effect, unless it appears from the will that the testator intended the disposition to be revoked by the formation of the civil partnership.

20.   No will to be revoked but by another will or codicil, or by a writing executed like a will, or by destruction

No will or codicil, or any part thereof, shall be revoked otherwise than as aforesaid, or by another will or codicil executed in manner herein-before required, or by some writing declaring an intention to revoke the same, and executed in the manner in which a will is herein-before required to be executed, or by the burning, tearing, or otherwise destroying the same by the testator, or by some person in his presence and by his direction, with the intention of revoking the same.

21.   No alteration in a will shall have any effect unless executed as a will

No obliteration, interlineation, or other alteration made in any will after the execution thereof shall be valid or have any effect, except so far as the words or effect of the will before such alteration shall not be apparent, unless such alteration shall be executed in like manner as herein-before is required for the execution of the will; but the will, with such alteration as part thereof, shall be deemed to be duly executed if the signature of the testator and the subscription of the witnesses be made in the margin or on some other part of the will opposite or near to such alteration, or at the foot or end of or opposite to a memorandum referring to such alteration, and written at the end or some other part of the will.

24.   A will shall be construed to speak from the death of the testator

Every will shall be construed, with reference to the real estate and personal estate comprised in it, to speak and take effect as if it had been executed immediately before the death of the testator, unless a contrary intention shall appear by the will.

33.   Gifts to children or other issue who leave issue living as the testator's death shall not lapse

(1)   Where—

    (a)   a will contains a devise or bequest to a child or remoter descendant of the testator; and

    (b)   the intended beneficiary dies before the testator, leaving issue; and

    (c)   issue of the intended beneficiary are living at the testator's death, then, unless a contrary intention appears by the will, the devise or bequest shall take effect as a devise or bequest to the issue living at the testator's death.

(2)   Where—

    (a)   a will contains a devise or bequest to a class of persons consisting of children or remoter descendants of the testator; and

    (b)   a member of the class dies before the testator, leaving issue; and

(c)   issue of that member are living at the testator's death, then, unless a contrary intention appears by the will, the devise or bequest shall take effect as if the class included the issue of its deceased member living at the testator's death.

(3)   Issue shall take under this section through all degrees, according to their stock, in equal shares if more than one, any gift or share which their parent would have taken and so that no issue shall take whose parent is living at the testator's death and so capable of taking.

(4)   For the purposes of this section—

(a)   the illegitimacy of any person is to be disregarded; and

(b)   a person conceived before the testator's death and born living thereafter is to be taken to have been living at the testator's death.

TRUSTEE ACT 1925
(1925, c. 19)

PART II
GENERAL POWERS OF TRUSTEES AND PERSONAL REPRESENTATIVES

General Powers

12.   Power of trustees for sale to sell by auction, etc.

(1)   Where a trustee has a duty or power to sell property, he may sell or concur with any other person in selling all or any part of the property, either subject to prior charges or not, and either together or in lots, by public auction or by private contract, subject to any such conditions respecting title or evidence of title or other matter as the Trustee thinks fit, with power to vary any contract for sale, and to buy in at any auction, or to rescind any contract for sale and to re-sell, without being answerable for any loss.

(2)   A duty or power to sell or dispose of land includes a duty or power to sell or dispose of part thereof, whether the division is horizontal, vertical, or made in any other way.

(3)   This section does not enable an express power to sell settled land to be exercised where the power is not vested in the tenant for life or statutory owner.

13.   Power to sell subject to depreciatory conditions

(1)   No sale made by a trustee shall be impeached by any beneficiary upon the ground that any of the conditions subject to which the sale was made have been unnecessarily depreciatory, unless it also appears that the consideration for the sale was thereby rendered inadequate.

(2)   No sale made by a trustee shall, after the execution of the conveyance, be impeached as against the purchaser upon the ground that any of the conditions subject to which the sale was made may have been unnecessarily depreciatory, unless it appears that the purchaser was acting in collusion with the trustee at the time when the contract for sale was made.

(3)   No purchaser, upon any sale made by a trustee, shall be at liberty to make any objection against the title upon any of the grounds aforesaid.

(4)   This section applies to sales made before or after the commencement of this Act.

14.   Power of trustees to give receipts

(1)   The receipt in writing of a trustee for any money, securities, investments or other personal property or effects payable, transferable, or deliverable to him under any trust or power shall be a sufficient discharge to the person paying, transferring, or delivering the same and shall effectually exonerate him from seeing to the application or being answerable for any loss or misapplication thereof.

(2)   This section does not, except where the trustee is a trust corporation, enable a sole trustee to give a valid receipt for—

(a)   proceeds of sale or other capital money arising under a trust of land;

(b)   capital money arising under the Settled Land Act, 1925.

(3)   This section applies notwithstanding anything to the contrary in the instrument, if any, creating the trust.

15.   Power to compound liabilities

A personal representative, or two or more trustees acting together, or, subject to the restrictions imposed in regard to receipts by a sole trustee not being a trust corporation, a sole acting trustee where by the instrument, if any, creating the trust, or by statute, a sole trustee is authorised to execute the trusts and powers reposed in him, may, if and as he or they think fit—

(a)   accept any property, real or personal, before the time at which it is made transferable or payable; or

(b)   sever and apportion any blended trust funds or property; or

(c)   pay or allow any debt or claim on any evidence that he or they think sufficient; or

(d)   accept any composition or any security, real or personal, for any debt or for any property, real or personal claimed; or

(e)   allow any time of payment of any debt; or

(f)   compromise, compound, abandon, submit to arbitration, or otherwise settle any debt, account, claim, or thing whatever relating to the testator's or intestate's estate or to the trust;

and for any of those purposes may enter into, give, execute, and do such agreements, instruments of composition or arrangement, releases, and other things as to him or them seem expedient, without being responsible for any loss occasioned by any act or thing so done by him or them if he has or they have discharged the duty of care set out in section 1(1) of the Trustee Act 2000.

16.   Power to raise money by sale, mortgage, etc.

(1)   Where trustees are authorised by the instrument, if any, creating the trustor by law to pay or apply capital money subject to the trust for any purpose or in any manner, they shall have and shall be deemed always to have had power to raise the money required by sale, conversion, calling in, or mortgage of all or any part of the trust property for the time being in possession.

(2)   This section applies notwithstanding anything to the contrary contained in the instrument, if any, creating the trust, but does not apply to trustees of property held for charitable purposes, or to trustees of a settlement for the purposes of the Settled Land Act, 1925, not being also the statutory owners.

17.   Protection to purchasers and mortgagees dealing with trustees

No purchaser or mortgagee, paying or advancing money on a sale or mortgage purporting to be made under any trust or power vested in trustees, shall be concerned to see that such money is wanted, or that no more than is wanted is raised, or otherwise as to the application thereof.

18.   Devolution of powers or trusts

(1)   Where a power or trust is given to or imposed on two or more trustees jointly, the same may be exercised or performed by the survivors or survivor of them for the time being.

(2)   Until the appointment of new trustees, the personal representatives or representative for the time being of a sole trustee, or, where there were two or more trustees of the last surviving or continuing trustee, shall be capable of exercising or performing any power or trust which was given to, or capable of being exercised by, the sole or last surviving or continuing trustee, or other the trustees or trustee for the time being of the trust.

(3)   This section takes effect subject to the restrictions imposed in regard to receipts by a sole trustee, not being a trust corporation.

(4)   In this section 'personal representative' does not include an executor who has renounced or has not proved.

19.   Power to insure

(1)   A trustee may—

(a)   insure any property which is subject to the trust against risks of loss or damage due to any event, and

(b)   pay the premiums out of the trust funds.

(2)   In the case of property held on a bare trust, the power to insure is subject to any direction given by the beneficiary or each of the beneficiaries—

(a)   that any property specified in the direction is not to be insured;

(b) that any property specified in the direction is not to be insured except on such conditions as may be so specified.

(3) Property is held on a bare trust if it is held on trust for—

    (a) a beneficiary who is of full age and capacity and absolutely entitled to the property subject to the trust, or

    (b) beneficiaries each of whom is of full age and capacity and who (taken together) are absolutely entitled to the property subject to the trust.

(4) If a direction under subsection (2) of this section is given, the power to insure, so far as it is subject to the direction, ceases to be a delegable function for the purposes of section 11 of the Trustee Act 2000 (power to employ agents).

(5) In this section 'trust funds' means any income or capital funds of the trust.

20. Application of insurance money where policy kept up under any trust, power or obligation

(1) Money receivable by trustees or any beneficiary under a policy of insurance against the loss or damage of any property subject to a trust or to a settlement within the meaning of the Settled Land Act, 1925, . . . shall, where the policy has been kept up under any trust in that behalf or under any power statutory or otherwise, or in performance of any covenant or of any obligation statutory or otherwise, or by a tenant for life impeachable for waste, be capital money for the purposes of the trust or settlement, as the case may be.

(2) If any such money is receivable by any person, other than the trustees of the trust or settlement, that person shall use his best endeavours to recover and receive the money, and shall pay the net residue thereof, after discharging any costs of recovering and receiving it, to the trustees of the trust or settlement, or, if there are no trustees capable of giving a discharge therefor, into court.

(3) Any such money—

    (a) if it was receivable in respect of settled land within the meaning of the Settled Land Act, 1925, or any building or works thereon, shall be deemed to be capital money arising under that Act from the settled land, and shall be invested or applied by the trustees, or, if in court, under the direction of the court, accordingly;

    (b) if it was receivable in respect of personal chattels settled as heirlooms within the meaning of the Settled Land Act, 1925, shall be deemed to be capital money arising under that Act, and shall be applicable by the trustees, or, if in court, under the direction of the court, in like manner as provided by that Act with respect to money arising by a sale of chattels settled as heirlooms as aforesaid;

    (c) if it was receivable in respect of land subject to a trust of land or personal property held on trust for sale, shall be held upon the trusts and subject to the powers and provisions applicable to money arising by a sale under such trust;

    (d) in any other case, shall be held upon trusts corresponding as nearly as may be with the trusts affecting the property in respect of which it was payable.

(4) Such money, or any part thereof, may also be applied by the trustees, or, if in court, under the direction of the court, in rebuilding, reinstating, replacing, or repairing the property lost or damaged, but any such application by the trustees shall be subject to the consent of any person whose consent is required by the instrument, if any, creating the trust to the investment of money subject to the trust, and, in the case of money which is deemed to be capital money arising under the Settled Land Act, 1925, be subject to the provisions of that Act with respect to the application of capital money by the trustees of the settlement.

(5) Nothing contained in this section prejudices or affects the right of any person to require any such money or any part thereof to be applied in rebuilding, reinstating, or repairing the property lost or damaged, or the rights of any mortgagee, lessor, or lessee, whether under any statute or otherwise.

(6) This section applies to policies effected either before or after the commencement of this Act, but only to money received after such commencement.

22.   Reversionary interests, valuations and audit

(1)   Where trust property includes any share or interest in property not vested in the trustees, or the proceeds of the sale of any such property, or any other thing in action, the trustees on the same falling into possession, or becoming payable or transferable may—

(a)   agree or ascertain the amount or value thereof or any part thereof in such manner as they may think fit;

(b)   accept in or towards satisfaction thereof, at the market or current value, or upon any valuation or estimate of value which they may think fit, any authorised investments;

(c)   allow any deductions for duties, costs, charges and expenses which they may think proper or reasonable;

(d)   execute any release in respect of the premises so as effectually to discharge all accountable parties from all liability in respect of any matters coming within the scope of such release;

without being responsible in any such case for any loss occasioned by any act or thing so done by them if they have discharged the duty of care set out in section 1(1) of the Trustee Act 2000.

(2)   The trustees shall not be under any obligation and shall not be chargeable with any breach of trust by reason of any omission—

(a)   to place any distringas notice or apply for any stop or other like order upon any securities or other property out of or on which such share or interest or other thing in action as aforesaid is derived, payable or charged; or

(b)   to take any proceedings on account of any act, default, or neglect on the part of the persons in whom such securities or other property or any of them or any part thereof are for the time being, or had at any time been, vested; unless and until required in writing so to do by some person, or the guardian of some person, beneficially interested under the trust, and unless also due provision is made to their satisfaction for payment of the costs of any proceedings required to be taken:

Provided that nothing in this subsection shall relieve the trustees of the obligation to get in and obtain payment or transfer of such share or interest or other thing in action on the same falling into possession.

(3)   Trustees may, for the purpose of giving effect to the trust, or any of the provisions of the instrument, if any, creating the trust or of any statute, from time to time (by duly qualified agents) ascertain and fix the value of any trust property in such manner as they think proper, and any valuation so made . . . shall be binding upon all persons interested under the trust if the trustees have discharged the duty of care set out in section 1(1) of the Trustee Act 2000.

(4)   Trustees may, in their absolute discretion, from time to time, but not more than once in every three years unless the nature of the trust or any special dealings with the trust property make a more frequent exercise of the right reasonable, cause the accounts of the trust property to be examined or audited by an independent accountant, and shall, for that purpose, produce such vouchers and give such information to him as he may require; and the costs of such examination or audit, including the fee of the auditor, shall be paid out of the capital or income of the trust property, or partly in one way and partly in the other, as the trustees, in their absolute discretion, think fit, but, in default of any direction by the trustees to the contrary in any special case, costs attributable to capital shall be borne by capital and those attributable to income by income.

24.   Power to concur with others

Where an undivided share in any property, is subject to a trust, or forms part of the estate of a testator or intestate, the trustees or personal representatives may (without prejudice to the trust affecting the entirety of the land and the powers of the trustees in reference thereto) execute or exercise any duty or power vested in them in relation to such share in conjunction with the persons entitled to or having power in that behalf over the other share or shares, and notwithstanding that any one or more of the trustees or personal representatives may be entitled to or interested in any such other share, either in his or their own right or in a fiduciary capacity.

25. Delegation of trustee's functions by power of attorney

(1) Notwithstanding any rule of law or equity to the contrary, a trustee may, by power of attorney, delegate the execution or exercise of all or any of the trusts, powers and discretions vested in him as trustee either alone or jointly with any other person or persons.

(2) A delegation under this section—

    (a) commences as provided by the instrument creating the power or, if the instrument makes no provision as to the commencement of the delegation, with the date of the execution of the instrument by the donor; and

    (b) continues for a period of twelve months or any shorter period provided by the instrument creating the power.

(3) The persons who may be donees of a power of attorney under this section include a trust corporation.

(4) Before or within seven days after giving a power of attorney under this section the donor shall give written notice of it (specifying the date on which the power comes into operation and its duration, the donee of the power, the reason why the power is given and, where some only are delegated, the trusts, powers and discretions delegated) to—

    (a) each person (other than himself), if any, who under any instrument creating the trust has power (whether alone or jointly) to appoint a new trustee; and

    (b) each of the other trustees, if any;

but failure to comply with this subsection shall not, in favour of a person dealing with the donee of the power, invalidate any act done or instrument executed by the donee.

(5) A power of attorney given under this section by a single donor—

    (a) in the form set out in subsection (6) of this section; or

    (b) in a form to the like effect but expressed to be made under this subsection,

shall operate to delegate to the person identified in the form as the single donee of the power the execution and exercise of all the trusts, powers and discretions vested in the donor as trustee (either alone or jointly with any other person or persons) under the single trust so identified.

(6) The form referred to in subsection (5) of this section is as follows—

'THIS GENERAL TRUSTEE POWER OF ATTORNEY is made on *date* by *name of one donor* of *address of donor* as trustee of *name or details of one trust*.

I appoint *name of one donee* of *address of donee* to be my attorney *if desired, the date on which the delegation commences or the period for which it continues (or both)* in accordance with section 25(5) of the Trustee Act 1925. *To be executed as a deed'*.

(7) The donor of a power of attorney given under this section shall be liable for the acts or defaults of the donee in the same manner as if they were the acts or defaults of the donor.

(8) For the purpose of executing or exercising the trusts or powers delegated to him, the donee may exercise any of the powers conferred on the donor as trustee by statute or by the instrument creating the trust, including power, for the purpose of the transfer of any inscribed stock, himself to delegate to an attorney power to transfer, but not including the power of delegation conferred by this section.

(9) The fact that it appears from any power of attorney given under this section, or from any evidence required for the purposes of any such power of attorney or otherwise, that in dealing with any stock the donee of the power is acting in the execution of a trust shall not be deemed for any purpose to affect any person in whose books the stock is inscribed or registered with any notice of the trust.

(10) This section applies to a personal representative, tenant for life and statutory owner as it applies to a trustee except that subsection (4) shall apply as if it required the notice there mentioned to be given—

    (a) in the case of a personal representative, to each of the other personal representatives, if any, except any executor who has renounced probate;

    (b) in the case of a tenant for life, to the trustees of the settlement and to each person, if any, who together with the person giving the notice constitutes the tenant for life; and

    (c) in the case of a statutory owner, to each of the persons, if any, who together with the person giving the notice constitute the statutory owner and, in the case of a statutory owner by virtue of section 23(1)(a) of the Settled Land Act 1925, to the trustees of the settlement.

Indemnities

26.   Protection against liability in respect of rents and convenants

(1)   Where a personal representative or trustee liable as such for—

(a)   any rent, covenant, or agreement reserved by or contained in any lease; or

(b)   any rent, covenant or agreement payable under or contained in any grant made in consideration of a rentcharge; or

(c)   any indemnity given in respect of any rent, covenant or agreement referred to in either of the foregoing paragraphs;

satisfies all liabilities under the lease or grant which may have accrued and been claimed up to the date of the conveyance hereinafter mentioned, and, where necessary, sets apart a sufficient fund to answer any future claim that may be made in respect of any fixed and ascertained sum which the lessee or grantee agreed to lay out on the property demised or granted, although the period for laying out the same may not have arrived, then and in any such case the personal representative or trustee may convey the property demised or granted to a purchaser, legatee, devisee, or other person entitled to call for a conveyance thereof and thereafter—

(i)   he may distribute the residuary real and personal estate of the deceased testator or intestate, or, as the case may be, the trust estate (other than the fund, if any, set apart as aforesaid) to or amongst the persons entitled thereto, without appropriating any part, or any further part, as the case may be, of the estate of the deceased or of the trust estate to meet any future liability under the said lease or grant;

(ii)   notwithstanding such distribution, he shall not be personally liable in respect of any subsequent claim under the said lease or grant.

(1A) Where a personal representative or trustee has as such entered into, or may as such be required to enter into, an authorised guarantee agreement with respect to any lease comprised in the estate of a deceased testator or intestate or a trust estate (and, in a case where he has entered into such an agreement, he has satisfied all liabilities under it which may have accrued and been claimed up to the date of distribution)—

(a)   he may distribute the residuary real and personal estate of the deceased testator or intestate, or the trust estate, to or amongst the persons entitled thereto—

(i)   without appropriating any part of the estate of the deceased, or the trust estate, to meet any future liability (or, as the case may be, any liability) under any such agreement, and

(ii)   notwithstanding any potential liability of his to enter into any such agreement; and

(b)   notwithstanding such distribution, he shall not be personally liable in respect of any subsequent claim (or, as the case may be, any claim) under any such agreement.

In this subsection 'authorised guarantee agreement' has the same meaning as in the Landlord and Tenant (Covenants) Act 1995.

(2)   This section operates without prejudice to the right of the lessor or grantor, or the persons deriving title under the lessor or grantor, to follow the assets of the deceased or the trust property into the hands of the persons amongst whom the same may have been respectively distributed, and applies notwithstanding anything to the contrary in the will or other instrument, if any, creating the trust.

(3)   In this section 'lease' includes an underlease and an agreement for a lease or underlease and any instrument giving any such indemnity as aforesaid or varying the liabilities under the lease; 'grant' applies to a grant whether the rent is created by limititation, grant, reservation or otherwise, and includes an agreement for a grant and any instrument giving any such indemnity as aforesaid or varying the liabilities under the grant; 'lessee' and 'grantee' include persons respectively deriving title under them.

27.   Protection by means of advertisements

(1)   With a view to the conveyance to or distribution among the persons entitled to any real or personal property, the trustees of a settlement, trustees of land, trustees for sale of personal property or personal representatives, may give notice by advertisement in the Gazette, and in a newspaper circulating in the district in which the land is situated and such other like notices, including notices elsewhere than in England and Wales, as would, in any special case, have been directed by a court of competent jurisdiction in an action for administration, of their intention to make such conveyance or distribution as aforesaid, and requiring any person interested to send to the trustees or personal representatives within the time, not being less than two months, fixed in the notice or, where more than one notice is given, in the last of the notices, particulars of his claim in respect of the property or any part thereof to which the notice relates.

(2)   At the expiration of the time fixed by the notice the trustees or personal representatives may convey or distribute the property or any part thereof to which the notice relates, to or among the persons entitled thereto, having regard only to the claims, whether formal or not, of which the trustees or personal representatives then had notice and shall not, as respects the property so conveyed or distributed, be liable to any person of whose claim the trustees or personal representatives have not had notice at the time of conveyance or distribution; but nothing in this section—

(a)   prejudices the right of any person to follow the property, or any property representing the same, into the hands of any person, other than a purchaser, who may have received it; or

(b)   frees the trustees or personal representatives from any obligation to make searches or obtain official certificates of search similar to those which an intending purchaser would be advised to make or obtain.

(3)   This section applies notwithstanding anything to the contrary in the will or other instrument, if any, creating the trust.

28.   Protection in regard to notice

A trustee or personal representative acting for the purposes of more than one trust or estate shall not, in the absence of fraud, be affected by notice of any instrument, matter, fact or thing in relation to any particular trust or estate if he has obtained notice thereof merely by reason of his acting or having acted for the purposes of another trust or estate.

Maintenance, Advancement and Protective Trusts

31.   Power to apply income for maintenance and to accumulate surplus income during a minority

(1)   Where any property is held by trustees in trust for any person for any interest whatsoever, whether vested or contingent, then, subject to any prior interests or charges affecting that property—

(i)   during the infancy of any such person, if his interest so long continues, the trustees may, at their sole discretion, pay to his parent or guardian, if any, or otherwise apply for or towards his maintenance, education, or benefit, the whole or such part, if any, of the income of that property as may, in all the circumstances, be reasonable, whether or not there is—

(a)   any other fund applicable to the same purpose: or

(b)   any person bound by law to provide for his maintenance or education; and

(ii)   if such person on attaining the age of eighteen years has not a vested interest in such income, the trustees shall thenceforth pay the income of that property and of any accretion thereto under subsection (2) of this section to him, until he either attains a vested interest therein or dies, or until failure of his interest:

Provided that, in deciding whether the whole or any part of the income of the property is during a minority to be paid or applied for the purposes aforesaid, the trustees shall have regard to the age of the infant and his requirements and generally to the circumstances of the case, and in particular to what other income, if any, is applicable for the same purposes; and where trustees have notice that the income of more than one fund is applicable for those purposes, then, so far as practicable, unless the entire income of the funds is paid or applied as aforesaid or the court otherwise directs, a proportionate part only of the income of each fund shall be so paid or applied.

(2) During the infancy of any such person, if his interest so long continues, the trustees shall accumulate all the residue of that income by investing it, and any profits from so investing it from time to time in authorised investments, and shall hold those accumulations as follows:—

(i) If any such person—

(a) attains the age of eighteen years, or marries under that age or forms a civil partnership under that age, and his interest in such income during his infancy, or until his marriage or his formation of a civil partnership, is a vested interest or;

(b) on attaining the age of eighteen years or on marriage, or formation of a civil partnership, under that age becomes entitled to the property from which such income arose in fee simple, absolute or determinable, or absolutely, or for an entailed interest;

the trustees shall hold the accumulations in trust for such person absolutely, but without prejudice to any provision with respect thereto contained in any settlement by him made under any statutory powers during his infancy, and so that the receipt of such person after marriage or formation of a civil partnership, and though still an infant shall be a good discharge; and

(ii) In any other case the trustees shall, notwithstanding that such person had a vested interest in such income, hold the accumulations as an accretion to the capital of the property from which such accumulations arose, and as one fund with such capital for all purposes, and so that, if such property is settled land, such accumulations shall be held upon the same trusts as if the same were capital money arising therefrom;

but the trustees may, at any time during the infancy of such person if his interest so long continues, apply those accumulations, or any part thereof, as if they were income arising in the then current year.

(3) This section applies in the case of a contingent interest only if the limitation or trust carries the intermediate income of the property, but it applies to a future or contingent legacy by the parent of, or a person standing in loco parentis to, the legatee, if and for such period as, under the general law, the legacy carries interest for the maintenance of the legatee, and in any such case as last aforesaid the rate of interest shall (if the income available is sufficient, and subject to any rules of court to the contrary) be five pounds per centum per annum.

(4) This section applies to a vested annuity in like manner as if the annuity were the income of property held by trustees in trust to pay the income thereof to the annuitant for the same period for which the annuity is payable, save that in any case accumulations made during the infancy of the annuitant shall be held in trust for the annuitant or his personal representatives absolutely.

(5) This section does not apply where the instrument, if any, under which the interest arises came into operation before the commencement of this Act.

32.   Power of advancement

(1) Trustees may at any time or times pay or apply any capital money subject to a trust, for the advancement or benefit, in such manner as they may, in their absolute discretion, think fit, of any person entitled to the capital of the trust property or of any share thereof, whether absolutely or contingently on his attaining any specified age or on the occurrence of any other event, or subject to a gift over on his death under any specified age or on the occurrence of any other event, and whether in possession or in remainder or reversion, and such payment or application may be made notwithstanding that the interest of such person is liable to be defeated by the exercise of a power of appointment or revocation, or to be diminished by the increase of the class to which he belongs:

Provided that—

(a) the money so paid or applied for the advancement or benefit of any person shall not exceed altogether in amount one-half of the presumptive or vested share or interest of that person in the trust property; and

(b) if that person is or becomes absolutely and indefeasibly entitled to a share in the trust property the money so paid or applied shall be brought into account as part of such share; and

(c) no such payment or application shall be made so as to prejudice any person entitled to any prior life or other interest, whether vested or contingent, in the money paid or applied unless such person is in existence and of full age and consents in writing to such payment or application.

(2) This section does not apply to capital money arising under the Settled Land Act 1925.

(3) This section does not apply to trusts constituted or created before the commencement of this Act.

33. Protective trusts

(1) Where any income, including an annuity or other periodical income payment, is directed to be held on protective trusts for the benefit of any person (in this section called 'the principal beneficiary') for the period of his life or for any less period, then, during that period (in this section called the 'trust period') the said income shall, without prejudice to any prior interest, be held on the following trusts, namely:—

(i) Upon trust for the principal beneficiary during the trust period or until he, whether before or after the termination of any prior interest, does or attempts to do or suffers any act or thing, or until any event happens, other than an advance under any statutory or express power, whereby, if the said income were payable during the trust period to the principal beneficiary absolutely during that period, he would be deprived of the right to receive the same or any part thereof, in any of which cases, as well as on the termination of the trust period, whichever first happens, this trust of the said income shall fail or determine;

(ii) If the trust aforesaid fails or determines during the subsistence of the trust period, then, during the residue of that period, the said income shall be held upon trust for the application thereof for the maintenance or support, or otherwise for the benefit, of all or any one or more exclusively of the other or others of the following persons (that is to say)—

(a) the principal beneficiary and his or her spouse or civil partner, if any, and his or her children or more remote issue, if any; or

(b) if there is no spouse or civil partner or issue of the principal beneficiary in existence, the principal beneficiary and the persons who would, if he were actually dead, be entitled to the trust property or the income thereof or to the annuity fund, if any, or arrears of the annuity, as the case may be;

as the trustees in their absolute discretion, without being liable to account for the exercise of such discretion, think fit.

(2) This section does not apply to trusts coming into operation before the commencement of this Act, and has effect subject to any variation of the implied trusts aforesaid contained in the instrument creating the trust.

(3) Nothing in this section operates to validate any trust which would, if contained in the instrument creating the trust, be liable to be set aside.

(4) In relation to the dispositions mentioned in section 19(1) of the Family Law Reform Act 1987, this section shall have effect as if any reference (however expressed) to any relationship between two persons were construed in accordance with section 1 of that Act.

PART III
APPOINTMENT AND DISCHARGE OF TRUSTEES

34. Limitation of the number of trustees

(1) Where, at the commencement of this Act, there are more than four trustees of a settlement of land, or more than four trustees holding land on trust for sale, no new trustees shall (except

where as a result of the appointment the number is reduced to four or less) be capable of being appointed until the number is reduced to less than four, and thereafter the number shall not be increased beyond four.

(2)   In the case of settlements and dispositions creating trusts of land made or coming into operation after the commencement of this Act—

(a)   the number of trustees thereof shall not in any case exceed four, and where more than four persons are named as such trustees, the four first named (who are able and willing to act) shall alone be the trustees, and the other persons named shall not be trustees unless appointed on the occurrence of a vacancy;

(b)   the number of the trustees shall not be increased beyond four.

(3)   This section only applies to settlements and dispositions of land, and the restrictions imposed on the number of trustees do not apply—

(a)   in the case of land vested in trustees for charitable, ecclesiastical, or public purposes; or

(b)   where the net proceeds of the sale of the land are held for like purposes; or

(c)   to the trustees of a term of years absolute limited by a settlement on trusts for raising money, or of a like term created under the statutory remedies relating to annual sums charged on land.

35.   Appointments of trustees of settlements and trustees of land

(1)   Appointments of new trustees of land and of new trustees of any trust of the proceeds of sale of the land shall, subject to any order of the court, be effected by separate instruments, but in such manner as to secure that the same persons become trustees of land and trustees of the trust of the proceeds of sale.

(2)   Where new trustees of a settlement are appointed, a memorandum of the names and addresses of the persons who are for the time being the trustees thereof for the purposes of the Settled Land Act, 1925, shall be endorsed on or annexed to the last or only principal vesting instrument by or on behalf of the trustees of the settlement, and such vesting instrument shall, for that purpose, be produced by the person having the possession thereof to the trustees of the settlement when so required.

(3)   Where new trustees of land are appointed, a memorandum of the persons who are for the time being the trustees of the land shall be endorsed on or annexed to the conveyance by which the land was vested in trustees of land; and that conveyance shall be produced to the persons who are for the time being the trustees of the land by the person in possession of it in order for that to be done when the trustees require its production.

(4)   This section applies only to settlements and dispositions of land.

36.   Power of appointing new or additional trustees

(1)   Where a trustee, either original or substituted, and whether appointed by a court or otherwise, is dead, or remains out of the United Kingdom for more than twelve months, or desires to be discharged from all or any of the trusts or powers reposed in or conferred on him, or refuses or is unfit to act therein, or is incapable of acting therein, or is an infant, then, subject to the restrictions imposed by this Act on the number of trustees,—

(a)   the person or persons nominated for the purpose of appointing new trustees by the instrument, if any, creating the trust; or

(b)   if there is no such person, or no such person able and willing to act, then the surviving or continuing trustees or trustee for the time being, or the personal representatives of the last surviving or continuing trustee;

may, by writing, appoint one or more other persons (whether or not being the persons exercising the power) to be a trustee or trustees in the place of the trustee so deceased remaining out of the United Kingdom, desiring to be discharged, refusing, or being unfit or being incapable, or being an infant, as aforesaid.

(2)   Where a trustee has been removed under a power contained in the instrument creating the trust, a new trustee or new trustees may be appointed in the place of the trustee who is removed, as if he were dead, or, in the case of a corporation, as if the corporation desired to

be discharged from the trust, and the provisions of this section shall apply accordingly, but subject to the restrictions imposed by this Act on the number of trustees.

(3)   Where a corporation being a trustee is or has been dissolved, either before or after the commencement of this Act, then, for the purposes of this section and of any enactment replaced thereby, the corporation shall be deemed to be and to have been from the date of the dissolution incapable of acting in the trusts or powers reposed in or conferred on the corporation.

(4)   The power of appointment given by subsection (1) of this section or any similar previous enactment to the personal representatives of last surviving or continuing trustee shall be and shall be deemed always to have been exercisable by the executors for the time being (whether original or by representation) of such surviving or continuing trustee who have proved the will of their testator or by the administrators for the time being of such trustee without the concurrence of any executor who has renounced or has not proved.

(5)   But a sole or last surviving executor intending to renounce, or all the executors where they all intend to renounce, shall have and shall be deemed always to have had power, at any time before renouncing probate, to exercise the power of appointment given by this section, or by any similar previous enactment, if willing to act for that purpose and without thereby accepting the office of executor.

(6)   Where, in the case of any trust, there are not more than three trustees—

(a)   the person or persons nominated for the purpose of appointing new trustees by the instrument, if any, creating the trust; or

(b)   if there is no such person, or no such person able and willing to act, then the trustee or trustees for the time being;

may, by writing, appoint another person or other persons to be an additional trustee or additional trustees, but it shall not be obligatory to appoint any additional trustee, unless the instrument, if any, creating the trust, or any statutory enactment provides to the contrary, nor shall the number of trustees be increased beyond four by virtue of any such appointment.

(6A) A person who is either—

(a)   both a trustee and attorney for the other trustee (if one other), or for both of the other trustees (if two others), under a registered power; or

(b)   attorney under a registered power for the trustee (if one) or for both or each of the trustees (if two or three),

may, if subsection (6B) of this section is satisfied in relation to him, make an appointment under subsection (6)(b) of this section on behalf of the trustee or trustees.

(6B) This subsection is satisfied in relation to an attorney under a registered power for one or more trustees if (as attorney under the power)—

(a)   he intends to exercise any function of the trustee or trustees by virtue of section 1(1) of the Trustee Delegation Act 1999; or

(b)   he intends to exercise any function of the trustee or trustees in relation to any land, capital proceeds of a conveyance of land or income from land by virtue of its delegation to him under section 25 of this Act or the instrument (if any) creating the trust.

(6C) In subsections (6A) and (6B) of this section 'registered power' means a power of attorney created by an instrument which is for the time being registered under section 6 of the Enduring Powers of Attorney Act 1985.

(6D) Subsection (6A) of this section—

(a)   applies only if and so far as a contrary intention is not expressed in the instrument creating the power of attorney (or, where more than one, any of them) or the instrument (if any) creating the trust; and

(b)   has effect subject to the terms of those instruments.

(7)   Every new trustee appointed under this section as well before as after all the trust property becomes by law, or by assurance, or otherwise, vested in him, shall have the same powers, authorities, and discretions, and may in all respects act as if he had been originally appointed a trustee by the instrument, if any, creating the trust.

(8) The provisions of this section relating to a trustee who is dead include the case of a person nominated trustee in a will but dying before the testator, and those relative to a continuing trustee include a refusing or retiring trustee, if willing to act in the execution of the provisions of this section.

(9) Where a trustee is incapable, by reason of mental disorder within the meaning of the Mental Health Act 1983 of exercising his functions as trustee and is also entitled in possession to some beneficial interest in the trust property, no appointment of a new trustee in his place shall be made by virtue of paragraph (b) of subsection (1) of this section unless leave to make the appointment has been given by the authority having jurisdiction under Part VII of the Mental Health Act 1983.

37.   Supplemental provisions as to appointment of trustees

(1) On the appointment of a trustee for the whole or any part of trust property—

   (a) the number of trustees may, subject to the restrictions imposed by this Act on the number of trustees, be increased; and

   (b) a separate set of trustees, not exceeding four, may be appointed for any part of the trust property held on trusts distinct from those relating to any other part or parts of the trust property, notwithstanding that no new trustees or trustee are or is to be appointed for other parts of the trust property, and any existing trustee may be appointed or remain one of such separate set of trustees, or, if only one trustee was originally appointed, then, save as hereinafter provided, one separate trustee may be so appointed; and

   (c) it shall not be obligatory, save as hereinafter provided, to appoint more than one new trustee where only one trustee was originally appointed, or to fill up the original number of trustees where more than two trustees were originally appointed, but, except where only one trustee was originally appointed, and a sole trustee when appointed will be able to give valid receipts for all capital money, a trustee shall not be discharged from his trust unless there will be either a trust corporation or at least two persons to act as trustees to perform the trust; and

   (d) any assurance or thing requisite for vesting the trust property, or any part thereof, in a sole trustee, or jointly in the persons who are the trustees, shall be executed or done.

(2) Nothing in this Act shall authorise the appointment of a sole trustee, not being a trust corporation, where the trustee, when appointed, would not be able to give valid receipts for all capital money arising under the trust.

38.   Evidence as to a vacancy in a trust

(1) A statement, contained in any instrument coming into operation after the commencement of this Act by which a new trustee is appointed for any purpose connected with land, to the effect that a trustee has remained out of the United Kingdom for more than twelve months or refuses or is unfit to act, or is incapable of acting, or that he is not entitled to a beneficial interest in the trust property in possession, shall, in favour of a purchaser of a legal estate, be conclusive evidence of the matter stated.

(2) In favour of such purchaser any appointment of a new trustee depending on that statement, and any vesting declaration, express or implied, consequent on the appointment, shall be valid.

39.   Retirement of trustee without a new appointment

(1) Where a trustee is desirous of being discharged from the trust, and after this discharge there will be either a trust corporation or at least two persons to act as trustees to perform the trust, then, if such trustee as aforesaid by deed declares that he is desirous of being discharged from the trust, and if his co-trustees and such other person, if any, as is empowered to appoint trustees, by deed consent to the discharge of the trustee, and to the vesting in the co-trustees alone of the trust property, the trustee desirous of being discharged shall be deemed to have retired from the trust, and shall, by the deed, be discharged therefrom under this Act, without any new trustee being appointed in his place.

(2) Any assurance or thing requisite for vesting the trust property in the continuing trustees alone shall be executed or done.

40.   Vesting of trust property in new or continuing trustees

(1)   Where by a deed a new trustee is appointed to perform any trust, then—

(a)   if the deed contains a declaration by the appointor to the effect that any estate or interest in any land subject to the trust, or in any chattel so subject, or the right to recover or receive any debt or other thing in action so subject, shall vest in the persons who by virtue of the deed become or are the trustees for performing the trust, the deed shall operate, without any conveyance or assignment, to vest in those persons as joint tenants and for the purposes of the trust the estate interest or right to which the declaration relates; and

(b)   if the deed is made after the commencement of this Act and does not contain such a declaration, the deed shall, subject to any express provision to the contrary therein contained, operate as if it had contained such a declaration by the appointor extending to all the estates interests and rights with respect to which a declaration could have been made.

(2)   Where by a deed a retiring trustee is discharged under section 39 of this Act or section 19 of the Trusts of Land and Appointment of Trustees Act 1996 without a new trustee being appointed, then—

(a)   if the deed contains such a declaration as aforesaid by the retiring and continuing trustees, and by the other person, if any, empowered to appoint trustees, the deed shall, without any conveyance or assignment, operate to vest in the continuing trustees alone, as joint tenants, and for the purposes of the trust, the estate, interest, or right to which the declaration relates; and

(b)   if the deed is made after the commencement of this Act and does not contain such a declaration, the deed shall, subject to any express provision to the contrary therein contained, operate as if it had contained such a declaration by such persons as aforesaid extending to all the estates, interests and rights with respect to which a declaration could have been made.

(3)   An express vesting declaration, whether made before or after the commencement of this Act, shall, notwithstanding that the estate, interest or right to be vested is not expressly referred to, and provided that the other statutory requirements were or are complied with, operate and be deemed always to have operated (but without prejudice to any express provision to the contrary contained in the deed of appointment or discharge) to vest in the persons respectively referred to in subsections (1) and (2) of this section, as the case may require, such estates, interests and rights as are capable of being and ought to be vested in those persons.

(4)   This section does not extend—

(a)   to land conveyed by way of mortgage for securing money subject to the trust, except land conveyed on trust for securing debentures or debenture stock;

(b)   to land held under a lease which contains any covenant, condition or agreement against assignment or disposing of the land without licence or consent, unless, prior to the execution of the deed containing expressly or impliedly the vesting declaration, the requisite licence or consent has been obtained, or unless, by virtue of any statute or rule of law, the vesting declaration, express or implied, would not operate as a breach of covenant or give rise to a forfeiture;

(c)   to any share, stock, annuity or property which is only transferable in books kept by a company or other body, or in manner directed by or under an Act of Parliament.

In this subsection 'lease' includes an underlease and an agreement for a lease or underlease.

(5)   For purposes of registration of the deed in any registry, the person or persons making the declaration expressly or impliedly, shall be deemed the conveying party or parties, and the conveyance shall be deemed to be made by him or them under a power conferred by this Act.

(6)   This section applies to deeds of appointment or discharge executed on or after the first day of January, eighteen hundred and eighty-two.

PART IV
POWERS OF THE COURT

Appointment of new Trustees

41.   Power of court to appoint new trustees

(1)   The court may, whenever it is expedient to appoint a new trustee or new trustees, and it is found inexpedient difficult or impracticable so to do without the assistance of the court, make an order appointing a new trustee or new trustees either in substitution for or in addition to any existing trustees, or although there is no existing trustee.

In particular and without prejudice to the generality of the foregoing provision, the court may make an order appointing a new trustee in substitution for a trustee who . . . is incapable, by reason of mental disorder within the meaning of the Mental Health Act 1983 of exercising his functions as trustee, or is a bankrupt, or is a corporation which is in liquidation or has been dissolved.

(2)   The power conferred by this section may, in the case of a deed of arrangement within the meaning of the Deeds of Arrangement Act, 1914, be exercised either by the High Court or by the court having jurisdiction in the bankruptcy in the district in which the debtor resided or carried on business at the date of the execution of the deed.

(3)   An order under this section, and any consequential vesting order or conveyance, shall not operate further or otherwise as a discharge to any former or continuing trustee than an appointment of new trustees under any power for that purpose contained in any instrument would have operated.

(4)   Nothing in this section gives power to appoint an executor or administrator.

42.   Power to authorise remuneration

Where the court appoints a corporation, other than the Public Trustee, to be a trustee either solely or jointly with another person, the court may authorise the corporation to charge such remuneration for its services as trustee as the court may think fit.

43.   Powers of new trustee appointed by the court

Every trustee appointed by a court of competent jurisdiction shall, as well before as after the trust property becomes by law, or by assurance, or otherwise, vested in him, have the same powers, authorities, and discretions, and may in all respects act as if he had been originally appointed a trustee by the instrument, if any, creating the trust.

Vesting Orders

44.   Vesting orders of land

In any of the following cases, namely:—

(i)   Where the court appoints or has appointed a trustee, or where a trustee has been appointed out of court under any statutory or express power;

(ii)   Where a trustee entitled to or possessed of any land or interest therein, whether by way of mortgage or otherwise, or entitled to a contingent right therein, either solely or jointly with any other person—

(a)   is under disability; or

(b)   is out of the jurisdiction of the High Court; or

(c)   cannot be found, or, being a corporation, has been dissolved.

(iii)   Where it is uncertain who was the survivor of two or more trustees jointly entitled to or possessed of any interest in land;

(iv)   Where it is uncertain whether the last trustee known to have been entitled to or possessed of any interest in land is living or dead;

(v)   Where there is no personal representative of a deceased trustee who was entitled to or possessed of any interest in land, or where it is uncertain who is the personal representative of a deceased trustee who was entitled to or possessed of any interest in land;

(vi)   Where a trustee jointly or solely entitled to or possessed of any interest in land, or entitled to a contingent right therein, has been required, by or on behalf of a person entitled to require a conveyance of the land or interest or a release of the right, to convey the land or interest or to release the right, and has wilfully refused or neglected to convey the land or interest or release the right for twenty-eight days after the date of the requirement;

(vii) Where land or any interest therein is vested in a trustee whether by way of mortgage or otherwise, and it appears to the court to be expedient;

the court may make an order (in this Act called a vesting order) vesting the land or interest therein in any such person in any such manner and for any such estate or interest as the court may direct, or releasing or disposing of the contingent right to such person as the court may direct:

Provided that—

(a) Where the order is consequential on the appointment of a trustee the land or interest therein shall be vested for such estate as the court may direct in the persons who on the appointment are the trustees; and

(b) Where the order relates to a trustee entitled or formerly entitled jointly with another person, and such trustee is under disability or out of the jurisdiction of the High Court or cannot be found, or being a corporation has been dissolved, the land interest or right shall be vested in such other person who remains entitled, either alone or with any other person the court may appoint.

45.   Orders as to contingent rights of unborn persons

Where any interest in land is subject to a contingent right in an unborn person or class of unborn persons who, on coming into existence would, in respect thereof, become entitled to or possessed of that interest on any trust, the court may make an order releasing the land or interest therein from the contingent right, or may make an order vesting in any person the estate or interest to or of which the unborn person or class of unborn persons would, on coming into existence, be entitled or possessed in the land.

46.   Vesting order in place of conveyance by infant mortgagee

Where any person entitled to or possessed of any interest in land, or entitled to a contingent right in land, by way of security for money, is an infant, the court may make an order vesting or releasing or disposing of the interest in the land or the right in like manner as in the case of a trustee under disability.

47.   Vesting order consequential on order for sale or mortgage of land

Where any court gives a judgment or makes an order directing the sale or mortgage of any land, every person who is entitled to or possessed of any interest in the land, or entitled to a contingent right therein, and is a party to the action or proceeding in which the judgment or order is given or made or is otherwise bound by the judgment or order, shall be deemed to be so entitled or possessed, as the case may be, as a trustee for the purpose of this Act, and the court may, if it thinks expedient, make an order vesting the land or any part thereof for such estate or interest as that court thinks fit in the purchaser or mortgagee or in any other person:

Provided that, in the case of a legal mortgage, the estate to be vested in the mortgagee shall be a term of years absolute.

48.   Vesting order consequential on judgment for specific performance, etc.

Where a judgment is given for the specific performance of a contract concerning any interest in land, or for sale or exchange of any interest in land, or generally where any judgment is given for the conveyance of any interest in land either in cases arising out of the doctrine of election or otherwise, the court may declare—

(a) that any of the parties to the action are trustees of any interest in the land or any part thereof within the meaning of this Act; or

(b) that the interests of unborn persons who might claim under any party to the action, or under the will or voluntary settlement of any deceased person who was during his lifetime a party to the contract or transaction concerning which the judgment is given, are the interests of persons who, on coming into existence, would be trustees within the meaning of this Act;

and thereupon the court may make a vesting order relating to the rights of those persons, born and unborn, as if they had been trustees.

49.   Effect of vesting order

A vesting order under any of the foregoing provisions shall in the case of a vesting order consequential on the appointment of a trustee, have the same effect—

(a)   as if the persons who before the appointment were the trustees, if any, had duly executed all proper conveyances of the land for such estate or interest as the court directs; or

(b)   if there is no such person, or no such person of full capacity, as if such person had existed and been of full capacity and had duly executed all proper conveyances of the land for such estate or interest as the court directs;

and shall in every other case have the same effect as if the trustee or other person or description or class of persons to whose rights or supposed rights the said provisions respectively relate had been an ascertained and existing person of full capacity, and had executed a conveyance or release to the effect intended by the order.

50.   Power to appoint person to convey

In all cases where a vesting order can be made under any of the foregoing provisions, the court may, if it is more convenient, appoint a person to convey the land or any interest therein or release the contingent right, and a conveyance or release by that person in conformity with the order shall have the same effect as an order under the appropriate provision.

51.   Vesting orders as to stock and things in action

(1)   In any of the following cases, namely:—

(i)   Where the court appoints or has appointed a trustee, or where a trustee has been appointed out of court under any statutory or express power;

(ii)   Where a trustee entitled, whether by way of mortgage or otherwise, alone or jointly with another person to stock or to a thing in action—

(a)   is under disability; or

(b)   is out of the jurisdiction of the High Court; or

(c)   cannot be found, or, being a corporation, has been dissolved; or

(d)   neglects or refuses to transfer stock or receive the dividends or income thereof, or to sue for or recover a thing in action, according to the direction of the person absolutely entitled thereto for twenty-eight days next after a request in writing has been made to him by the person so entitled; or

(e)   neglects or refuses to transfer stock or receive the dividends or income thereof, or to sue for or recover a thing in action for twenty-eight days next after an order of the court for that purpose has been served on him;

(iii)   Where it is uncertain whether a trustee entitled alone or jointly with another person to stock or to a thing in action is alive or dead;

(iv)   Where stock is standing in the name of a deceased person whose personal representative is under disability;

(v)   Where stock or a thing in action is vested in a trustee whether by way of mortgage or otherwise and it appears to the court to be expedient;

the court may make an order vesting the right to transfer or call for a transfer of stock, or to receive the dividends or income thereof, or to sue for or recover the thing in action, in any such person as the court may appoint:

Provided that—

(a)   Where the order is consequential on the appointment of a trustee, the right shall be vested in the persons who, on the appointment, are the trustees; and

(b)   Where the person whose right is dealt with by the order was entitled jointly with another person, the right shall be vested in that last-mentioned person either alone or jointly with any other person whom the court may appoint.

(2)   In all cases where a vesting order can be made under this section, the court may, if it is more convenient, appoint some proper person to make or join in making the transfer:

Provided that the person appointed to make or join in making a transfer of stock shall be some proper officer of the bank, or the company or society whose stock is to be transferred.

(3)   The person in whom the right to transfer or call for the transfer of any stock is vested by an order of the court under this Act, may transfer the stock to himself or any other person,

according to the order, and the Bank of England and all other companies shall obey every order under this section according to its tenor.

(4)   After notice in writing of an order under this section it shall not be lawful for the Bank of England or any other company to transfer any stock to which the order relates or to pay any dividends thereon except in accordance with the order.

(5)   The court may make declarations and give directions concerning the manner in which the right to transfer any stock or thing in action vested under the provisions of this Act is to be exercised.

(6)   The provisions of this Act as to vesting orders shall apply to shares in ships registered under the Merchant Shipping Act 1995 as if they were stock.

52.   Vesting orders of charity property

The powers conferred by this Act as to vesting orders may be exercised for vesting any interest in land, stock, or thing in action in any trustee of a charity or society over which the court would have jurisdiction upon action duly instituted, whether the appointment of the trustee was made by instrument under a power or by the court under its general or statutory jurisdiction.

53.   Vesting orders in relation to infant's beneficial interests

Where an infant is beneficially entitled to any property the court may, with a view to the application of the capital or income thereof for the maintenance, education, or benefit of the infant, make an order—

(a)   appointing a person to convey such property; or

(b)   in the case of stock, or a thing in action, vesting in any person the right to transfer or call for a transfer of such stock, or to receive the dividends or income thereof, or to sue for and recover such thing in action, upon such terms as the court may think fit.

54.   Jurisdiction in regard to mental patients

(1)   Subject to the provisions of this section, the authority having jurisdiction under Part VII of the Mental Health Act 1983 shall not have power to make any order, or give any direction or authority, in relation to a patient who is a trustee if the High Court has power under this Act to make an order to the like effect.

(2)   Where a patient is a trustee and a receiver appointed by the said authority is acting for him or an application for the appointment of a receiver has been made but not determined, then, except as respects a trust which is subject to an order for administration made by the High Court, the said authority shall have concurrent jurisdiction with the High Court in relation to—

(a)   mortgaged property of which the patient has become a trustee merely by reason of the mortgage having been paid off;

(b)   matters consequent on the making of provision by the said authority for the exercise of a power of appointing trustees or retiring from a trust;

(c)   matters consequent on the making of provision by the said authority for the carrying out of any contract entered into by the patient;

(d)   property to some interest in which the patient is beneficially entitled but which, or some interest in which, is held by the patient under an express, implied or constructive trust.

The Lord Chancellor may make rules with respect to the exercise of the jurisdiction referred to in this subsection.

(3)   In this section 'patient' means a patient as defined by section 94 of the Mental Health Act 1983, or a person as to whom powers are exercisable under section 98 of that Act and have been exercised under that section or under section 104 of the Mental Health Act 1959.

55.   Orders made upon certain allegations to be conclusive evidence

Where a vesting order is made as to any land under this Act or under Part VII of the Mental Health Act 1983, as amended by any subsequent enactment, or under any Act relating to lunacy in Northern Ireland, founded on an allegation of any of the following matters namely—

(a)   the personal incapacity of a trustee or mortgage; or

(b)   that a trustee or mortgagee or the personal representative of or other person deriving title under a trustee or mortgagee is out of the jurisdiction of the High Court or cannot be found, or being a corporation has been dissolved; or

(c) that it is uncertain which of two or more trustees, or which of two or more persons interested in a mortgage, was the survivor, or

(d) that it is uncertain whether the last trustee or the personal representative of or other person deriving title under a trustee or mortgagee, or the last surviving person interested in a mortgage is living or dead; or

(e) that any trustee or mortgagee has died intestate without leaving a person beneficially interested under the intestacy or has died and it is not known who is his personal representative or the person interested;

the fact that the order has been so made shall be conclusive evidence of the matter so alleged in any court upon any question as to the validity of the order; but this section does not prevent the court from directing a reconveyance or surrender or the payment of costs occasioned by any such order if improperly obtained.

Jurisdiction to make other Orders

57. Power of court to authorise dealings with trust property

(1) Where in the management or administration of any property vested in trustees, any sale, lease, mortgage, surrender, release, or other disposition, or any purchase, investment, acquisition, expenditure or other transaction, is in the opinion of the court expedient, but the same cannot be effected by reason of the absence of any power for that purpose vested in the trustees by the trust instrument, if any, or by law, the court may by order confer upon the trustees, either generally or in any particular instance, the necessary power for the purpose, on such terms, and subject to such provisions and conditions, if any, as the court may think fit and may direct in what manner any money authorised to be expended, and the costs of any transaction, are to be paid or borne as between capital and income.

(2) The court may, from time to time, rescind or vary any order made under this section, or may make any new or further order.

(3) An application to the court under this section may be made by the trustees, or by any of them, or by any person beneficially interested under the trust.

(4) This section does not apply to trustees of a settlement for the purposes of the Settled Land Act, 1925.

58. Persons entitled to apply for orders

(1) An order under this Act for the appointment of a new trustee or concerning any interest in land, stock, or thing in action subject to a trust, may be made on the application of any person beneficially interested in the land, stock, or thing in action, whether under disability or not, or on the application of any person duly appointed trustee thereof.

(2) An order under this Act concerning any interest in land, stock, or thing in action subject to a mortgage may be made on the application of any person beneficially interested in the equity of redemption, whether under disability or not, or of any person interested in the money secured by the mortgage.

59. Power to give judgment in absence of a trustee

Where in any action the court is satisfied that diligent search has been made for any person who, in the character of trustee, is made a defendant in any action, to serve him with a process of the court, and that he cannot be found, the court may hear and determine the action and give judgment therein against that person in his character of a trustee as if he had been duly served, or had entered an appearance in the action, and had also appeared by his counsel and solicitor at the hearing, but without prejudice to any interest he may have in the matters in question in the action in any other character.

60. Power to charge costs on trust estate

The court may order the costs and expenses of and incident to any application for an order appointing a new trustee, or for a vesting order, or of and incident to any such order, or any transfer in pursuance thereof, to be raised and paid out of the property in respect whereof the same is made, or out of the income thereof, or to be borne and paid in such manner and by such persons as to the court may seem just.

61. Power to relieve trustee from personal liability

If it appears to the court that a trustee, whether appointed by the court or otherwise, is or may be personally liable for any breach of trust, whether the transaction alleged to be a breach of trust occurred before or after the commencement of this Act, but has acted honestly and reasonably, and ought fairly to be excused for the breach of trust and for omitting to obtain the directions of the court in the matter in which he committed such breach, then the court may relieve him either wholly or partly from personal liability for the same.

62. Power to make beneficiary indemnify for breach of trust

(1)   Where a trustee commits a breach of trust at the instigation or request or with the consent in writing of a beneficiary, the court may, if it thinks fit, . . . make such order as to the court seems just, for impounding all or any part of the interest of the beneficiary in the trust estate by way of indemnity to the trustee or persons claiming through him.

(2)   This section applies to breaches of trust committed as well before as after the commencement of this Act.

Payment into Court

63. Payment into court by trustees

(1)   Trustees, or the majority of trustees, having in their hands or under their control money or securities belonging to a trust, may pay the same into court; . . .

(2)   The receipt or certificate of the proper officer shall be a sufficient discharge to trustees for the money or securities so paid into court.

(3)   Where money or securities are vested in any persons as trustees, and the majority are desirous of paying the same into court, but the concurrence of the other or others cannot be obtained, the court may order the payment into court to be made by the majority without the concurrence of the other or others.

(4)   Where any such money or securities are deposited with any banker, broker, or other depositary, the court may order payment or delivery of the money or securities to the majority of the trustees for the purpose of payment into court.

(5)   Every transfer payment and delivery made in pursuance of any such order shall be valid and take effect as if the same had been made on the authority or by the act of all the persons entitled to the money and securities so transferred, paid, or delivered.

PART V
GENERAL PROVISIONS

64. Application of Act to Settled Land Act Trustees

(1)   All the powers and provisions contained in this Act with reference to the appointment of new trustees, and the discharge and retirement of trustees, apply to and include trustees for the purposes of the Settled Land Act, 1925, and trustees for the purpose of the management of land during a minority, whether such trustees are appointed by the court or by the settlement, or under provisions contained in any instrument.

(2)   Where, either before or after the commencement of this Act, trustees of a settlement have been appointed by the court for the purposes of the Settled Land Acts, 1882 to 1890, or of the Settled Land Act, 1925, then, after the commencement of this Act—

(a)   the person or persons nominated for the purpose of appointing new trustees by the instrument, if any, creating the settlement, though no trustees for the purposes of the said Acts were thereby appointed; or

(b)   if there is no such person, or no such person able and willing to act, the surviving or continuing trustees or trustee for the time being for the purposes of the said Acts, or the personal representatives of the last surviving or continuing trustee for those purposes,

shall have the powers conferred by this Act to appoint new or additional trustees of the settlement for the purposes of the said Acts.

(3)   Appointments of new trustees for the purposes of the said Acts made or expressed to be made before the commencement of this Act by the trustees or trustee or personal

representatives referred to in paragraph (b) of the last preceding subsection or by the persons referred to in paragraph (a) of that subsection are, without prejudice to any order of the court made before such commencement, hereby confirmed.

66.   Indemnity to banks, etc.
This Act, and every order purporting to be made under this Act, shall be a complete indemnity to the Bank of England, and to all persons for any acts done pursuant thereto, and it shall not be necessary for the Bank or for any person to inquire concerning the propriety of the order, or whether the court by which the order was made had jurisdiction to make it.

67.   Jurisdiction of the 'court'
(1)   In this Act 'the court' means the High Court, . . . or the county court, where those courts respectively have jurisdiction.
(2)   The procedure under this Act in . . . county courts shall be in accordance with the Acts and rules regulating the procedure of those courts.

68.   Definitions
(1)   In this Act, unless the context otherwise requires, the following expressions have the meanings hereby assigned to them respectively, that is to say: —
    (1)   'Authorised investments' mean investments authorised by the instrument, if any, creating the trust for the investment of money subject to the trust, or by law;
    (2)   'Contingent right' as applied to land includes a contingent or executory interest, a possibility coupled with an interest, whether the object of the gift or limitation of the interest, or possibility is or is not ascertained, also a right of entry, whether immediate or future, and whether vested or contingent;
    (3)   'Convey' and 'conveyance' as applied to any person include the execution by that person of every necessary or suitable assurance (including an assent) for conveying, assigning, appointing, surrendering, or otherwise transferring or disposing of land whereof he is seised or possessed, or wherein he is entitled to a contingent right, either for his whole estate or for any less estate, together with the performance of all formalities required by law for the validity of the conveyance; 'sale' includes an exchange;
    (4)   'Gazette' means the London Gazette;
    (5)   'Instrument' includes Act of Parliament;
    (6)   'Land' includes land of any tenure, and mines and minerals, whether or not severed from the surface, buildings or parts of buildings, whether the division is horizontal, vertical or made in any other way, and other corporeal hereditaments; also a manor, an advowson, and a rent and other incorporeal hereditaments, and an easement, right, privilege, or benefit in, over, or derived from land . . . ; and in this definition 'mines and minerals' include any strata or seam of minerals or substances in or under any land, and powers of working and getting the same . . . ; and 'hereditaments' mean real property which under an intestacy occurring before the commencement of this Act might have devolved on an heir;
    (7)   'Mortgage' and 'mortgagee' include a charge or chargee by way of legal mortgage, and relate to every estate and interest regarded in equity as merely a security for money, and every person deriving title under the original mortgagee;
    (8)   . . .
    (9)   'Personal representative' means the executor, original or by representation, or administrator for the time being of a deceased person;
    (10)   'Possession' includes receipt of rents and profits or the right to receive the same, if any; 'income' includes rents and profits; and 'possessed' applies to receipt of income of and to any vested estate less than a life interest in possession or in expectancy in any land;
    (11)   'Property' includes real and personal property, and any estate share and interest in any property, real or personal, and any debt, and any thing in action, and any other right or interest, whether in possession or not;

(12) 'Rights' include estates and interests;

(13) 'Securities' include stocks, funds, and shares; . . . and 'securities payable to bearer' include securities transferable by delivery or by delivery and endorsement;

(14) 'Stock' includes fully paid up shares, and so far as relates to vesting orders made by the court under this Act, includes any fund, annuity, or security transferable in books kept by any company or society, or by instrument of transfer either alone or accompanied by other formalities, and any share of interest therein;

(15) 'Tenant for life,' 'statutory owner,' 'settled land,' 'settlement,' 'trust instrument,' 'trustees of the settlement' . . . 'term of years absolute' and 'vesting instrument' have the same meanings as in the Settled Land Act, 1925, and 'entailed interest' has the same meaning as in the Law of Property Act, 1925;

(16) 'Transfer' in relation to stock or securities, includes the performance and execution of every deed, power of attorney, act, and thing on the part of the transferor to effect and complete the title in the transferee;

(17) 'Trust' does not include the duties incident to an estate conveyed by way of mortgage, but with this exception the expressions 'trust' and 'trustee' extend to implied and constructive trusts, and to cases where the trustee has a beneficial interest in the trust property, and to the duties incident to the office of a personal representative, and 'trustee' where the context admits, includes a personal representative, and 'new trustee' includes an additional trustee;

(18) 'Trust corporation' means the Public Trustee or a corporation either appointed by the court in any particular case to be a trustee, or entitled by rules made under subsection (3) of section four of the Public Trustee Act, 1906, to act as custodian trustee;

(19) 'Trust for sale' in relation to land means an immediate . . . trust for sale, whether or not exercisable at the request or with the consent of any person . . . ;

(20) 'United Kingdom' means Great Britain and Northern Ireland.

(2) Any reference in this Act to paying money or securities into court shall be construed as referring to paying the money or transferring or depositing the securities into or in the Supreme Court or into or in any other court that has jurisdiction, and any reference in this Act to payment of money or securities into court shall be construed—

(a) with reference to an order of the High Court, as referring to payment of the money or transfer or deposit of the securities into or in the Supreme Court; and

(b) with reference to an order of any other court, as referring to payment of the money or transfer or deposit of the securities into or in that court.

69. Application of Act

(1) This Act, except where otherwise expressly provided, applies to trusts including, so far as this Act applies thereto, executorships and administratorships constituted or created either before or after the commencement of this Act.

(2) The powers conferred by this Act on trustees are in addition to the powers conferred by the instrument, if any, creating the trust, but those powers, unless otherwise stated, apply if and so far only as a contrary intention is not expressed in the instrument, if any, creating the trust, and have effect subject to the terms of that instrument.

(3) . . .

70. Enactments repealed

. . . without prejudice to the provisions of section thirty-eight of the Interpretation Act, 1889:

(a) Nothing in this repeal shall affect any vesting order or appointment made or other thing done under any enactment so repealed, and any order or appointment so made may be revoked or varied in like manner as if it had been made under this Act;

(b) References in any document to any enactment repealed by this Act shall be construed as references to this Act or to the corresponding enactment in this Act.

LAW OF PROPERTY ACT 1925
(1925, c. 20)

Note. References to the Land Charges Act, 1925 should be read as references to the Land Charges Act, 1972.

PART I

GENERAL PRINCIPLES AS TO LEGAL ESTATES, EQUITABLE INTERESTS AND POWERS

1.   Legal estates and equitable interests

(1)   The only estates in land which are capable of subsisting or of being conveyed or created at law are—

(a)   An estate in fee simple absolute in possession;

(b)   A term of years absolute.

(2)   The only interests or charges in or over land which are capable of subsisting or of being conveyed or created at law are—

(a)   An easement, right, or privilege in or over land for an interest equivalent to an estate in fee simple absolute in possession or a term of years absolute;

(b)   A rentcharge in possession issuing out of or charged on land being either perpetual or for a term of years absolute;

(c)   A charge by way of legal mortgage;

(d)   . . . and any other similar charge on land which is not created by an instrument;

(e)   Rights of entry exercisable over or in respect of a legal term of years absolute, or annexed, for any purpose, to a legal rentcharge.

(3)   All other estates, interests, and charges in or over land take effect as equitable interests.

(4)   The estates, interests, and charges which under this section are authorised to subsist or to be conveyed or created at law are (when subsisting or conveyed or created at law) in this Act referred to as 'legal estates', and have the same incidents as legal estates subsisting at the commencement of this Act; and the owner of a legal estate is referred to as an 'estate owner' and his legal estate is referred to as his estate.

(5)   A legal estate may subsist concurrently with or subject to any other legal estate in the same land in like manner as it could have done before the commencement of this Act.

(6)   A legal estate is not capable of subsisting or of being created in an undivided share in land or of being held by an infant.

(7)   Every power of appointment over, or power to convey or charge land or any interest therein, whether created by a statute or other instrument or implied by law, and whether created before or after the commencement of this Act (not being a power vested in a legal mortgagee or an estate owner in right of his estate and exercisable by him or by another person in his name and on his behalf), operates only in equity.

(8)   Estates, interests, and charges in or over land which are not legal estates are in this Act referred to as 'equitable interests,' and powers which by this Act are to operate in equity only are in this Act referred to as 'equitable powers.'

(9)   The provisions in any statute or other instrument requiring land to be conveyed to uses shall take effect as directions that the land shall (subject to creating or reserving thereout any legal estate authorised by this Act which may be required) be conveyed to a person of full age upon the requisite trusts.

(10) The repeal of the Statute of Uses (as amended) does not affect the operation thereof in regard to dealings taking effect before the commencement of this Act.

2.   Conveyances overreaching certain equitable interests and powers

(1)   A conveyance to a purchaser of a legal estate in land shall overreach any equitable interest or power affecting that estate, whether or not he has notice thereof, if—

(i)   the conveyance is made under the powers conferred by the Settled Land Act 1925, or any additional powers conferred by a settlement, and the equitable interest or power is capable of being overreached thereby, and the statutory requirements respecting the payment of capital money arising under the settlement are complied with;

(ii)   the conveyance is made by trustees of land and the equitable interest or power is at the date of the conveyance capable of being overreached by such trustees under the provisions of subsection (2) of this section or independently of that subsection, and the requirements of section 27 of this Act respecting the payment of capital money arising on such a conveyance are complied with;

(iii) the conveyance is made by a mortgagee or personal representative in the exercise of his paramount powers, and the equitable interest or power is capable of being overreached by such conveyance, and any capital money arising from the transaction is paid to the mortgagee or personal representative;

(iv) the conveyance is made under an order of the court and the equitable interest or power is bound by such order, and any capital money arising from the transaction is paid into, or in accordance with the order of, the court.

(1A) An equitable interest in land subject to a trust of land which remains in, or is to revert to, the settlor shall (subject to any contrary intention) be overreached by the conveyance if it would be so overreached were it an interest under the trust.

(2) Where the legal estate affected is subject to a trust of land, then if at the date of a conveyance made after the commencement of this Act by the trustees, the trustees (whether original or substituted) are either—

(a) two or more individuals approved or appointed by the court or the successors in office of the individuals so approved or appointed; or

(b) a trust corporation,

any equitable interest or power having priority to the trust shall, notwithstanding any stipulation to the contrary, be overreached by the conveyance, and shall, according to its priority, take effect as if created or arising by means of a primary trust affecting the proceeds of sale and the income of the land until sale.

(3) The following equitable interests and powers are excepted from the operation of subsection (2) of this section, namely—

(i) Equitable interest protected by a deposit of documents relating to the legal estate affected;

(ii) The benefit of any covenant or agreement restrictive of the user of land;

(iii) Any easement, liberty, or privilege over or affecting land and being merely an equitable interest (in this Act referred to as an 'equitable easement');

(iv) The benefit of any contract (in this Act referred to as an 'estate contract') to convey or create a legal estate, including a contract conferring either expressly or by statutory implication a valid option to purchase, a right of preemption, or any other like right;

(v) Any equitable interest protected by registration under the Land Charges Act, 1925, other than—

(a) an annuity within the meaning of Part II of that Act;

(b) a limited owner's charge or a general equitable charge within the meaning of that Act.

(4) Subject to the protection afforded by this section to the purchaser of a legal estate, nothing contained in this section shall deprive a person entitled to an equitable charge of any of his rights or remedies for enforcing the same.

(5) So far as regards the following interests, created before the commencement of this Act (which accordingly are not within the provisions of the Land Charges Act, 1925), namely—

(a) the benefit of any covenant or agreement restrictive of the user of the land;

(b) any equitable easement;

(c) the interest under a puisne mortgage within the meaning of the Land Charges Act, 1925, unless and until acquired under a transfer made after the commencement of this Act;

(d) the benefit of an estate contract, unless and until the same is acquired under a conveyance made after the commencement of this Act;

a purchaser of a legal estate shall only take subject thereto if he has notice thereof, and the same are not overreached under the provisions contained or in the manner referred to in this section.

3.   **Manner of giving effect to equitable interests and powers**

(1)   All equitable interests and powers in or over land shall be enforceable against the estate owner of the legal estate affected in manner following (that is to say):—

     (a)   Where the legal estate affected is settled land, the tenant for life or statutory owner shall be bound to give effect to the equitable interests and powers in manner provided by the Settled Land Act, 1925;

     (b)   . . .

     (c)   In any other case, the estate owner shall be bound to give effect to the equitable interests and powers affecting his estate of which he has notice according to their respective priorities. This provision does not affect the priority or powers of a legal mortgagee, or the powers of personal representatives for purposes of administration.

(2)   . . .

(3)   Where, by reason . . . of an equitable right of entry taking effect, or for any other reason, a person becomes entitled to require a legal estate to be vested in him, then and in any such case the estate owner whose estate is affected shall be bound to convey or create such legal estate as the case may require.

(4)   If any question arises whether any and what legal estate ought to be transferred or created as aforesaid, any person interested may apply to the court for directions in the manner provided by this Act.

(5)   If the . . . estate owners refuse or neglect for one month after demand to transfer or create any such legal estate, or if by reason of their being out of the United Kingdom or being unable to be found, or by reason of the dissolution of a corporation, or for any other reason, the court is satisfied that the transaction cannot otherwise be effected, or cannot be effected without undue delay or expense, the court may, on the application of any person interested, make a vesting order transferring or creating a legal estate in the manner provided by this Act.

(6)   This section does not affect a purchaser of a legal estate taking free from an equitable interest or power.

(7)   The county court has jurisdiction under this section where the land which is to be dealt with in the court does not exceed £30,000 in capital value. . . .

4.   **Creation and disposition of equitable interests**

(1)   Interests in land validly created or arising after the commencement of this Act, which are not capable of subsisting as legal estates, shall take effect as equitable interests, and, save as otherwise expressly provided by statute, interests in land which under the Statute of Uses or otherwise could before the commencement of this Act have been created as legal interests, shall be capable of being created as equitable interests:

      Provided that, after the commencement of this Act (and save as hereinafter expressly enacted), an equitable interest in land shall only be capable of being validly created in any case in which an equivalent equitable interest in property real or personal could have been validly created before such commencement.

(2)   All rights and interests in land may be disposed of, including—

     (a)   a contingent, executory or future equitable interest in any land, or a possibility coupled with an interest in any land, whether or not the object of the gift or limitation of such interest or possibility be ascertained;

     (b)   a right of entry, into or upon land whether immediate or future, and whether vested or contingent.

(3)   All rights of entry affecting a legal estate which are exercisable on condition broken or for any other reason may, after the commencement of this Act, be made exercisable by any person and the persons deriving title under him, but, in regard to an estate in fee simple (not being a rentcharge held for a legal estate) only within the period authorised by the rule relating to perpetuities.

5. Satisfied terms, whether created out of freehold or leasehold land to cease

(1) Where the purposes of a term of years created or limited at any time out of freehold land, become satisfied either before or after the commencement of this Act (whether or not that term either by express declaration or by construction of law becomes attendant upon the freehold reversion) it shall merge in the reversion expectant thereon and shall cease accordingly.

(2) Where the purposes of a term of years created or limited, at any time, out of leasehold land, become satisfied after the commencement of this Act, that term shall merge in the reversion expectant thereon and shall cease accordingly.

(3) Where the purposes are satisfied only as respects part of the land comprised in a term, this section shall have effect as if a separate term had been created in regard to that part of the land.

6. Saving of lessors' and lessees' covenants

(1) Nothing in this Part of this Act affects prejudicially the right to enforce any lessor's or lessee's covenants, agreements or conditions (including a valid option to purchase or right of preemption over the reversion), contained in any such instrument as is in this section mentioned, the benefit or burden of which runs with the reversion or the term.

(2) This section applies where the covenant, agreement or condition is contained in any instrument—

(a) creating a term of years absolute, or

(b) varying the rights of the lessor or lessee under the instrument creating the term.

7. Saving of certain legal estates and statutory powers

(1) A fee simple which, by virtue of the Lands Clauses Acts, . . . or any similar statute, is liable to be divested, is for the purposes of this Act a fee simple absolute, and remains liable to be divested as if this Act had not been passed, and a fee simple subject to a legal or equitable right of entry or re-entry is for the purposes of this Act a fee simple absolute.

(2) A fee simple vested in a corporation which is liable to determine by reason of the dissolution of the corporation is, for the purposes of this Act, a fee simple absolute.

(3) The provisions of—

(a) . . .

(b) the Friendly Societies Act 1896, in regard to land to which that Act applies;

(c) any other statutes conferring special facilities or prescribing special modes (whether by way of registered memorial or otherwise) for disposing of or acquiring land, or providing for the vesting (by conveyance or otherwise) of the land in trustees or any person, or the holder for the time being of an office or any corporation sole or aggregate (including the Crown);

shall remain in full force.

. . .

(4) Where any such power for disposing of or creating a legal state is exercisable by a person who is not the estate owner, the power shall, when practicable, be exercised in the name and on behalf of the estate owner.

8. Saving of certain legal powers to lease

(1) All leases or tenancies at a rent for a term of years absolute authorised to be granted by a mortgagor or mortgagee or by the Settled Land Act, 1925, or any other statute (whether or not extended by any instrument) may be granted in the name and on behalf of the estate owner by the person empowered to grant the same, whether being an estate owner or not, with the same effect and priority as if this Part of this Act had not been passed; but this section does not (except as respects the usual qualified covenant for quiet enjoyment) authorise any person granting a lease in the name of an estate owner to impose any personal liability on him.

(2) Where a rentcharge is held for a legal estate, the owner thereof may under the statutory power or under any corresponding power, create a legal term of years absolute for securing or compelling payment of the same; but in other cases terms created under any such power

shall, unless and until the estate owner of the land charged gives legal effect to the transaction, take effect only as equitable interests.

9.   Vesting orders and dispositions of legal estates operating as conveyances by an estate owner

(1)   Every such order, declaration, or conveyance as is hereinafter mentioned, namely—

   (a)   every vesting order made by any court or other competent authority;

   (b)   every vesting declaration (express or implied) under any statutory power;

   (c)   every vesting instrument made by the trustees of a settlement or other persons under the provisions of the Settled Land Act, 1925;

   (d)   every conveyance by a person appointed for the purpose under an order of the court or authorised under any statutory power to convey in the name or on behalf of an estate owner;

   (e)   every conveyance made under any power reserved or conferred by this Act,

   which is made or executed for the purpose of vesting, conveying, or creating a legal estate, shall operate to convey or create the legal estate disposed of in like manner as if the same had been a conveyance executed by the estate owner of the legal estate to which the order, declaration, vesting instrument, or conveyance relates.

(2)   Where the order, declaration, or conveyance is made in favour of a purchaser, the provisions of this Act relating to a conveyance of a legal estate to a purchaser shall apply thereto.

(3)   The provisions of the Trustee Act, 1925, relating to vesting orders and orders appointing a person to convey shall apply to all vesting orders authorised to be made by this Part of this Act.

10.   Title to be shown to legal estates

(1)   Where title is shown to a legal estate in land, it shall be deemed not necessary or proper to include in the abstract of title an instrument relating only to interests or powers which will be overreached by the conveyance of the estate to which title is being shown; but nothing in this Part of this Act affects the liability of any person to disclose an equitable interest or power which will not be so overreached, or to furnish an abstract of any instrument creating or affecting the same.

(2)   A solicitor delivering an abstract framed in accordance with this Part of this Act shall not incur any liability on account of an omission to include therein an instrument which, under this section, is to be deemed not necessary or proper to be included, nor shall any liability be implied by reason of the inclusion of any such instrument.

12.   Limitation and Prescription Acts

Nothing in this Part of this Act affects the operation of any statute, or of the general law for the limitation of actions or proceedings relating to land or with reference to the acquisition of easements or rights over or in respect of land.

13.   Effect of possession of documents

This Act shall not prejudicially affect the right or interest of any person arising out of or consequent on the possession by him of any documents relating to a legal estate in land, nor affect any question arising out of or consequent upon any omission to obtain or any other absence of possession by any person of any documents relating to a legal estate in land.

14.   Interests of persons in possession

This Part of this Act shall not prejudicially affect the interest of any person in possession or in actual occupation of land to which he may be entitled in right of such possession or occupation.

15.   Presumption that parties are of full age

The persons expressed to be parties to any conveyance shall, until the contrary is proved, be presumed to be of full age at the date thereof.

Infants and Lunatics

20. Infants not to be appointed trustees

The appointment of an infant to be a trustee in relation to any settlement or trust shall be void, but without prejudice to the power to appoint a new trustee to fill the vacancy.

21. Receipts by married infants

A married infant shall have power to give valid receipts for all income (including statutory accumulations of income made during the minority) to which the infant may be entitled in like manner as if the infant were of full age.

22. Conveyances on behalf of persons suffering from mental disorder and as to land held by them in trust

(1) Where a legal estate in land (whether settled or not) is vested in a person suffering from mental disorder, either solely or jointly with any other person or persons, his receiver or (if no receiver is acting for him) any person authorised in that behalf shall, under an order of the authority having jurisdiction under Part VII of the Mental Health Act, 1983, or of the court, or under any statutory power, make or concur in making all requisite dispositions for conveying or creating a legal estate in his name and on his behalf.

(2) If land subject to a trust of land is vested, either solely or jointly with any other person or persons, in a person who is incapable, by reason of mental disorder, of exercising his functions as trustee, a new trustee shall be appointed in the place of that person, or he shall be otherwise discharged from the trust, before the legal estate is dealt with by the trustees.

(3) Subsection (2) of this section does not prevent a legal estate being dealt with without the appointment of a new trustee, or the discharge of the incapable trustee, at a time when the donee of an enduring power (within the meaning of the Enduring Powers of Attorney Act 1985) is entitled to act for the incapable trustee in the dealing.

Trusts of land

24. Appointment of trustees of land

(1) The persons having power to appoint new trustees of land shall be bound to appoint the same persons (if any) who are for the time being trustees of any trust of the proceeds of sale of the land.

(2) A purchaser shall not be concerned to see that subsection (1) of this section has been complied with.

(3) This section applies whether the trust of land and the trust of proceeds of sale are created, or arise, before or after the commencement of this Act.

27. Purchaser not to be concerned with the trusts of the proceeds of sale which are to be paid to two or more trustees or to a trust corporation

(1) A purchaser of a legal estate from trustees of land shall not be concerned with the trusts affecting the land, the net income of the land or the proceeds of sale of the land whether or not those trusts are declared by the same instrument as that by which the trust of land is created.

(2) Notwithstanding anything to the contrary in the instrument (if any) creating a trust of land or in any trust affecting the net proceeds of sale of the land if it is sold, the proceeds of sale or other capital money shall not be paid to or applied by the direction of fewer than two persons as trustees, except where the trustee is a trust corporation, but this subsection does not affect the right of a sole personal representative as such to give valid receipts for, or direct the application of, proceeds of sale or other capital money, nor, except where capital money arises on the transaction, render it necessary to have more than one trustee.

31. Trust of mortgaged property where right of redemption is barred

(1) Where any property, vested in trustees by way of security, becomes, by virtue of the statutes of limitation, or of an order for foreclosure or otherwise, discharged from the right of redemption, it shall be held by them . . . in trust—

   (a) to apply the income from the property in the same manner as interest paid on the mortgage debt would have been applicable; and

   (b) if the property is sold, to apply the net proceeds of sale, after payment of costs and expenses, in the same manner as repayment of the mortgage debt would have been applicable.

 (2) Subsection (1) of this section operates without prejudice to any rule of law relating to the apportionment of capital and income between tenant for life and remainderman.

 (3) . . .

 (4) Where—

   (a) the mortgage money is capital money for the purposes of the Settled Land Act 1925;

   (b) land other than any forming the whole or part of the property mentioned in subsection (1) of this section is, or is deemed to be, subject to the settlement; and

   (c) the tenant for life or statutory owner requires the trustees to execute with respect to land forming the whole or part of that property a vesting deed such as would have been required in relation to the land if it had been acquired and purchased with capital money,

  the trustees shall execute such a vesting deed.

 (5) This section applies whether the right of redemption was discharged before or after the first day of January, nineteen hundred and twelve, but has effect without prejudice to any dealings or arrangements made before that date.

33. **Application of Part I to personal representatives**

The provisions of this Part of this Act relating to trustees of land apply to personal representatives holding land in trust, but without prejudice to their rights and powers for purposes of administration.

Undivided Shares and Joint Ownership

34. **Effect of future dispositions to tenants in common**

 (1) An undivided share in land shall not be capable of being created except as provided by the Settled Land Act, 1925, or as hereinafter mentioned.

 (2) Where, after the commencement of this Act, land is expressed to be conveyed to any persons in undivided shares and those persons are of full age, the conveyance shall (notwithstanding anything to the contrary in this Act) operate as if the land had been expressed to be conveyed to the grantees, or, if there are more than four grantees, to the four first named in the conveyance, as joint tenants in trust for the persons interested in the land:

  Provided that, where the conveyance is made by way of mortgage the land shall vest in the grantees or such four of them as aforesaid for a term of years absolute (as provided by this Act) as joint tenants subject to cesser on redemption in like manner as if the mortgage money had belonged to them on a joint account, but without prejudice to the beneficial interests in the mortgage money and interest.

 (3) A devise bequest or testamentary appointment, coming into operation after the commencement of this Act, of land to two or more persons in undivided shares shall operate as a devise bequest or appointment of the land . . . to the personal representatives of the testator, and . . . (but without prejudice to the rights and powers of the personal representatives for purposes of administration) in trust for the persons interested in the land.

 (3A) In subsections (2) and (3) of this section references to the persons interested in the land include persons interested as trustees or personal representatives (as well as persons beneficially interested).

36. **Joint tenancies**

 (1) Where a legal estate (not being settled land) is beneficially limited to or held in trust for any persons as joint tenants, the same shall be held in trust in like manner as if the persons beneficially entitled were tenants in common, but not so as to sever their joint tenancy in equity.

(2)   No severance of a joint tenancy of a legal estate, so as to create a tenancy in common in land, shall be permissible, whether by operation of law or otherwise, but this subsection does not affect the right of a joint tenant to release his interest to the other joint tenants, or the right to sever a joint tenancy in an equitable interest whether or not the legal estate is vested in the joint tenants:

Provided that, where a legal estate (not being settled land) is vested in joint tenants beneficially, and any tenant desires to sever the joint tenancy in equity, he shall give to the other joint tenants a notice in writing of such desire or do such other acts or things as would, in the case of personal estate, have been effectual to sever the tenancy in equity, and thereupon the land shall be held in trust on terms which would have been requisite for giving effect to the beneficial interests if there had been an actual severance.

Nothing in this Act affects the right of a survivor of joint tenants, who is solely and beneficially interested, to deal with his legal estate as if it were not held in trust.

(3)   Without prejudice to the right of a joint tenant to release his interest to the other joint tenants no severance of a mortgage term or trust estate, so as to create a tenancy in common, shall be permissible.

37.   Rights of husband and wife

A husband and wife shall, for all purposes of acquisition of any interest in property, under a disposition made or coming into operation after the commencement of this Act, be treated as two persons.

38.   Party structures

(1)   Where under a disposition or other arrangement which, if a holding in undivided shares had been permissible, would have created a tenancy in common, a wall or other structure is or is expressed to be made a party wall or structure, that structure shall be and remain severed vertically as between the respective owners, and the owner of each part shall have such rights to support and user over the rest of the structure as may be requisite for conferring rights corresponding to those which would have subsisted if a valid tenancy in common had been created.

(2)   Any person interested may, in case of dispute, apply to the court for an order declaring the rights and interests under this section of the persons interested in any such party structure, and the court may make such order as it thinks fit.

Transitional Provisions

39.   Transitional provisions in First Schedule

For the purpose of effecting the transition from the law existing prior to the commencement of the Law of Property Act, 1922, to the law enacted by that Act (as amended), the provisions set out in the First Schedule to this Act shall have effect—

(1)   for converting existing legal estates, interests and charges not capable under the said Act of taking effect as legal interests into equitable interests;

(2)   for discharging, getting in or vesting outstanding legal estates;

(3)   for making provision with respect to legal estates vested in infants;

(4)   for subjecting land held in undivided shares to trusts;

(5)   for dealing with party structures and open spaces held in common;

(6)   . . .

(7)   for converting existing freehold mortgages into mortgages by demise;

(8)   for converting existing leasehold mortgages into mortgages by sub-demise.

PART II
CONTRACTS, CONVEYANCES AND OTHER INSTRUMENTS
Contracts

41.   Stipulations not of the essence of a contract

Stipulations in a contract, as to time or otherwise, which according to rules of equity are not deemed to be or to have become of the essence of the contract, are also construed and have effect at law in accordance with the same rules.

42.   Provisions as to contracts

(1)   A stipulation that a purchaser of a legal estate in land shall accept a title made with the concurrence of any person entitled to an equitable interest shall be void, if a title can be made discharged from the equitable interest without such concurrence—

(a)   under a trust of land; or

(b)   under this Act, or the Settled Land Act, 1925, or any other statute.

(2)   A stipulation that a purchaser of a legal estate in land shall pay or contribute towards the costs of or incidental to—

(a)   obtaining a vesting order, or the appointment of trustees of a settlement, or the appointment of trustees of land; or

(b)   the preparation stamping or execution of a conveyance in trust, or of a vesting instrument for bringing into force the provisions of the Settled Land Act, 1925; shall be void.

(3)   A stipulation contained in any contract for the sale or exchange of land made after the commencement of this Act, to the effect that an outstanding legal estate is to be traced or got in by or at the expense of a purchaser or that no objection is to be taken on account of an outstanding legal estate, shall be void.

(4)   If the subject matter of any contract for the sale or exchange of land—

(i)   is a mortgage term and the vendor has power to convey the fee simple in the land, or, in the case of a mortgage of a term of years absolute, the leasehold reversion affected by the mortgage, the contract shall be deemed to extend to the fee simple in the land or such leasehold reversion;

(ii)   is an equitable interest capable of subsisting as a legal estate, and the vendor has power to vest such legal estate in himself or in the purchaser or to require the same to be so vested, the contract shall be deemed to extend to such legal estate;

(iii)   is an entailed interest in possession and the vendor has power to vest in himself or in the purchaser the fee simple in the land, (or, if the entailed interest is an interest in a term of years absolute, such term,) or to require the same to be so vested, the contract shall be deemed to extend to the fee simple in the land or the term of years absolute.

(5)   This section does not affect the right of a mortgagee of leasehold land to sell his mortgage term only if he is unable to convey or vest the leasehold reversion expectant thereon.

(6)   . . .

(7)   Where a purchaser has power to acquire land compulsorily, and a contract, whether by virtue of a notice to treat or otherwise, is subsisting under which title can be made without payment of the compensation money into court, title shall be made in that way unless the purchaser, to avoid expense or delay or for any special reason, considers it expedient that the money should be paid into court.

(8)   A vendor shall not have any power to rescind a contract by reason only of the enforcement of any right under this section.

(9)   This section only applies in favour of a purchaser for money or money's worth.

43.   Rights protected by registration

(1)   Where a purchaser of a legal estate is entitled to acquire the same discharged from an equitable interest which is protected by registration as a pending action, annuity, writ, order, deed of arrangement or land charge, and which will not be overreached by the conveyance to him, he may notwithstanding any stipulation to the contrary, require—

(a)   that the registration shall be cancelled; or

(b)   that the person entitled to the equitable interest shall concur in the conveyance; and in either case free of expense to the purchaser.

(2)   Where the registration cannot be cancelled or the person entitled to the equitable interest refuses to concur in the conveyance, this section does not affect the right of any person to rescind the contract.

44.   Statutory commencements of title

(1)   After the commencement of this Act fifteen years shall be substituted for forty years as the period of commencement of title which a purchaser of land may require; nevertheless earlier title than fifteen years may be required in cases similar to those in which earlier title than forty years might immediately before the commencement of this Act be required.

(2)   Under a contract to grant or assign a term of years, whether derived or to be derived out of freehold or leasehold land, the intended lessee or assign shall not be entitled to call for the title to the freehold.

(3)   Under a contract to sell and assign a term of years derived out of a leasehold interest in land, the intended assign shall not have the right to call for the title to the leasehold reversion.

(4)   On a contract to grant a lease for a term of years to be derived out of a leasehold interest, with a leasehold reversion, the intended lessee shall not have the right to call for the title to that reversion.

(4A) Subsections (2) and (4) of this section do not apply to a contract to grant a term of years if the grant will be an event within section 4(1) of the Land Registration Act 2002 (events which trigger first registration of title).

(5)   Where by reason of any of the subsections (2) to (4) of this section, an intending lessee or assign is not entitled to call for the title to the freehold or to a leasehold reversion, as the case may be, he shall not, where the contract is made after the commencement of this Act, be deemed to be affected with notice of any matter or thing of which, if he had contracted that such title should be furnished, he might have had notice.

(6)   Where land of copyhold or customary tenure has been converted into freehold by enfranchisement, then, under a contract to sell and convey the freehold, the purchaser shall not have the right to call for the title to make the enfranchisement.

(7)   Where the manorial incidents formerly affecting any land have been extinguished, then, under a contract to sell and convey the freehold, the purchaser shall not have the right to call for the title of the person entering into any compensation agreement or giving a receipt for the compensation money to enter into such agreement or to give such receipt, and shall not be deemed to be affected with notice of any matter or thing of which, if he had contracted that such title should be furnished, he might have had notice.

(8)   A purchaser shall not be deemed to be or ever to have been affected with notice of any matter or thing of which, if he had investigated the title or made enquiries in regard to matters prior to the period of commencement of title fixed by this Act, or by any other statute, or by any rule of law, he might have had notice, unless he actually makes such investigation or enquiries.

(9)   Where a lease whether made before or after the commencement of this Act, is made under a power contained in a settlement, will, Act of Parliament, or other instrument, any preliminary contract for or relating to the lease shall not, for the purpose of the deduction of title to an intended assign, form part of the title, or evidence of the title, to the lease.

(10) This section, save where otherwise expressly provided, applies to contracts for sale whether made before or after the commencement of this Act, and applies to contracts for exchange in like manner as to contracts for sale, save that it applies only to contracts for exchange made after such commencement.

(11) This section applies only if and so far as a contrary intention is not expressed in the contract.

(12) Nothing in this section applies in relation to registered land or to a term of years to be derived out of registered land.

45.　Other statutory conditions of sale

(1)　A purchaser of any property shall not—

(a)　require the production, or any abstract or copy, of any deed, will, or other document, dated or made before the time prescribed by law, or stipulated, for the commencement of the title, even though the same creates a power subsequently exercised by an instrument abstracted in the abstract furnished to the purchaser; or

(b)　require any information, or make any requisition, objection, or inquiry, with respect to any such deed, will, or document, or the title prior to that time, notwithstanding that any such deed, will, or other document, or that prior title, is recited, agreed to be produced, or noticed;

and he shall assume, unless the contrary appears, that the recitals, contained in the abstracted instruments, of any deed, will, or other document, forming part of that prior title, are correct, and give all the material contents of the deed, will, or other document so recited, and that every document so recited was duly executed by all necessary parties, and perfected, if and as required, by fine, recovery, acknowledgment, inrolment, or otherwise:

Provided that this subsection shall not deprive a purchaser of the right to require the production, or an abstract or copy of—

(i)　any power of attorney under which any abstracted document is executed; or

(ii)　any document creating or disposing of an interest, power or obligation which is not shown to have ceased or expired, and subject to which any part of the property is disposed of by an abstracted document; or

(iii)　any document creating any limitation or trust by reference to which any part of the property is disposed of by an abstracted document.

(2)　Where land sold is held by lease (other than an under-lease), the purchaser shall assume, unless the contrary appears, that the lease was duly granted; and, on production of the receipt for the last payment due for rent under the lease before the date of actual completion of the purchase, he shall assume, unless the contrary appears, that all the covenants and provisions of the lease have been duly performed and observed up to the date of actual completion of the purchase.

(3)　Where land sold is held by under-lease, the purchaser shall assume, unless the contrary appears, that the under-lease and every superior lease were duly granted; and, on production of the receipt for the last payment due for rent under the under-lease before the date of actual completion of the purchase, he shall assume, unless the contrary appears, that all the covenants and provisions of the under-lease have been duly performed and observed up to the date of actual completion of the purchase, and further that all rent due under every superior lease, and all the covenants and provisions of every superior lease, have been paid and duly performed and observed up to that date.

(4)　On a sale of any property, the following expenses shall be borne by the purchaser where he requires them to be incurred for the purpose of verifying the abstract or any other purpose, that is to say—

(a)　the expenses of the production and inspection of all Acts of Parliament, inclosure awards, records, proceedings of courts, court rolls, deeds, wills, probates, letters of administration, and other documents, not in the possession of the vendor or his mortgagee or trustee, and the expenses of all journeys incidental to such production or inspection; and

(b)　the expenses of searching for, procuring, making, verifying, and producing all certificates, declarations, evidences, and information not in the possession of the vendor or his mortgagee or trustee, and all attested, stamped, office, or other copies or abstracts of, or extracts from, any Acts of Parliament or other documents aforesaid, not in the possession of the vendor or his mortgagee or trustee,

and where the vendor or his mortgagee or trustee retains possession of any document, the expenses of making any copy thereof, attested or unattested, which a purchaser requires to be delivered to him, shall be borne by that purchaser.

(5)   On a sale of any property in lots, a purchaser of two or more lots, held wholly or partly under the same title, shall not have a right to more than one abstract of the common title, except at his own expense.

(6)   Recitals, statements, and descriptions of facts, matters, and parties contained in deeds, instruments, Acts of Parliament, or statutory declarations, twenty years old at the date of the contract, shall, unless and except so far as they may be proved to be inaccurate, be taken to be sufficient evidence of the truth of such facts, matters, and descriptions.

(7)   The inability of a vendor to furnish a purchaser with an acknowledgment of his right to production and delivery of copies of documents of title or with a legal covenant to produce and furnish copies of documents of title shall not be an objection to title in case the purchaser will, on the completion of the contract, have an equitable right to the production of such documents.

(8)   Such acknowledgments of the right of production or covenants for production and such undertakings or covenants for safe custody of documents as the purchaser can and does require shall be furnished or made at his expense, and the vendor shall bear the expense of perusal and execution on behalf of and by himself, and on behalf of and by necessary parties other than the purchaser.

(9)   A vendor shall be entitled to retain documents of title where—

      (a)   he retains any part of the land to which the documents relate; or

      (b)   the document consists of a trust instrument or other instrument creating a trust which is still subsisting, or an instrument relating to the appointment or discharge of a trustee of a subsisting trust.

(10)   This section applies to contracts for sale made before or after the commencement of this Act, and applies to contracts for exchange in like manner as to contracts for sale, except that it applies only to contracts for exchange made after such commencement:

      Provided that this section shall apply subject to any stipulation or contrary intention expressed in the contract.

(11)   Nothing in this section shall be construed as binding a purchaser to complete his purchase in any case where, on a contract made independently of this section, and containing stipulations similar to the provisions of this section, or any of them, specific performance of the contract would not be enforced against him by the court.

46.   Forms of contracts and conditions of sale

The Lord Chancellor may from time to time prescribe and publish forms of contracts and conditions of sale of land, and the forms so prescribed shall, subject to any modification, or any stipulation or intention to the contrary, expressed in the correspondence, apply to contracts by correspondence, and may, but only by express reference thereto, be made to apply to any other cases for which the forms are made available.

47.   Application of insurance money on completion of a sale or exchange

(1)   Where after the date of any contract for sale or exchange of property, money becomes payable under any policy of insurance maintained by the vendor in respect of any damage to or destruction of property included in the contract, the money shall, on completion of the contract, be held or receivable by the vendor on behalf of the purchaser and paid by the vendor to the purchaser on completion of the sale or exchange, or so soon thereafter as the same shall be received by the vendor.

(2)   This section applies only to contracts made after the commencement of this Act, and has effect subject to—

      (a)   any stipulation to the contrary contained in the contract,

      (b)   any requisite consents of the insurers,

      (c)   the payment by the purchaser of the proportionate part of the premium from the date of the contract.

(3)   This section applies to a sale or exchange by an order of the court, as if—

      (a)   for references to the 'vendor' there were substituted references to the 'person bound by the order';

(b)	for the reference to the completion of the contract there were substituted a reference to the payment of the purchase or equality money (if any) into court;

(c)	for the reference to the date of the contract there were substituted a reference to the time when the contract becomes binding.

**48.	Stipulations preventing a purchaser, lessee, or underlessee from employing his own solicitor to be void**

(1)	Any stipulation made on the sale of any interest in land after the commencement of this Act to the effect that the conveyance to, or the registration of the title of, the purchaser shall be prepared or carried out at the expense of the purchaser by a solicitor appointed by or acting for the vendor, and any stipulation which might restrict a purchaser in the selection of a solicitor to act on his behalf in relation to any interest in land agreed to be purchased, shall be void; and, if a sale is effected by demise or subdemise, then, for the purposes of this subsection, the instrument required for giving effect to the transaction shall be deemed to be a conveyance:

Provided that nothing in this subsection shall affect any right reserved to a vendor to furnish a form of conveyance to a purchaser from which the draft can be prepared, or to charge a reasonable fee therefor, or, where a perpetual rentcharge is to be reserved as the only consideration in money or money's worth, the right of a vendor to stipulate that the draft conveyance is to be prepared by his solicitor at the expense of the purchaser.

(2)	Any covenant or stipulation contained in, or entered into with reference to any lease or underlease made before or after the commencement of this Act—

(a)	whereby the right of preparing, at the expense of a purchaser, any conveyance of the estate or interest of the lessee or underlessee in the demised premises or in any part thereof, or of otherwise carrying out, at the expense of the purchaser, any dealing with such estate or interest, is expressed to be reserved to or vested in the lessor or underlessor or his solicitor; or

(b)	which in any way restricts the right of the purchaser to have such conveyance carried out on his behalf by a solicitor appointed by him;

shall be void:

Provided that, where any covenant or stipulation is rendered void by this subsection, there shall be implied in lieu thereof a covenant or stipulation that the lessee or underlessee shall register with the lessor or his solicitor within six months from the date thereof, or as soon after the expiration of that period as may be practicable, all conveyances and devolutions (including probates or letters of administration) affecting the lease or under-lease and pay a fee of one guinea in respect of each registration, and the power of entry (if any) on breach of any convenant contained in the lease or underlease shall apply and extend to the breach of any covenant so to be implied.

(3)	Save where a sale is effected by demise or sub-demise, this section does not affect the law relating to the preparation of a lease or underlease or the draft thereof.

(4)	In this section 'lease' and 'underlease' include any agreement therefor or other tenancy, and 'lessee' and 'underlessee' and 'lessor' and 'underlessor' have corresponding meanings.

**49.	Applications to the court by vendor and purchaser**

(1)	A vendor or purchaser of any interest in land, or their representatives respectively, may apply in a summary way to the court, in respect of any requisitions or objections, or any claim for compensation, or any other question arising out of or connected with the contract (not being a question affecting the existence or validity of the contract), and the court may make such order upon the application as to the court may appear just, and may order how and by whom all or any of the costs of and incident to the application are to be borne and paid.

(2)	Where the court refuses to grant specific performance of a contract, or in any action for the return of a deposit, the court may, if it thinks fit, order the repayment of any deposit.

(3)	This section applies to a contract for the sale or exchange of any interest in land.

(4)   The county court has jurisdiction under this section where land which is to be dealt with in the court does not exceed £30,000 in capital value . . . .

50.   Discharge of incumbrances by the court on sales or exchanges

(1)   Where land subject to any incumbrance, whether immediately realisable or payable or not, is sold or exchanged by the court, or out of court, the court may, if it thinks fit, on the application of any party to the sale or exchange, direct or allow payment into court of such sum as is hereinafter mentioned, that is to say—

(a)   in the case of an annual sum charged on the land, or of a capital sum charged on a determinable interest in the land, the sum to be paid into court shall be of such amount as, when invested in Government securities, the court considers will be sufficient, by means of the dividends thereof, to keep down or otherwise provide for that charge; and

(b)   in any other case of capital money charged on the land, the sum to be paid into court shall be of an amount sufficient to meet the incumbrance and any interest due thereon;

but in either case there shall also be paid into court such additional amount as the court considers will be sufficient to meet the contingency of further costs, expenses and interest, and any other contingency, except depreciation of investments, not exceeding one-tenth part of the original amount to be paid in, unless the court for special reason thinks fit to require a larger additional amount.

(2)   Thereupon, the court may, if it thinks fit, and either after or without any notice to the incumbrancer, as the court thinks fit, declare the land to be freed from the incumbrance, and make any order for conveyance, or vesting order, proper for giving effect to the sale or exchange, and give directions for the retention and investment of the money in court and for the payment or application of the income thereof.

(3)   The court may declare all other land, if any, affected by the incumbrance (besides the land sold or exchanged) to be freed from the incumbrance, and this power may be exercised either after or without notice to the incumbrancer, and notwithstanding that on a previous occasion an order, relating to the same incumbrance, has been made by the court which was confined to the land then sold or exchanged.

(4)   On any application under this section the court may, if it thinks fit, as respects any vendor or purchaser, dispense with the service of any notice which would otherwise be required to be served on the vendor or purchaser.

(5)   After notice served on the persons interested in or entitled to the money or fund in court, the court may direct payment or transfer thereof to the persons entitled to receive or give a discharge for the same, and generally may give directions respecting the application or distribution of the capital or income thereof.

(6)   This section applies to sales or exchanges whether made before or after the commencement of this Act, and to incumbrances whether created by statute or otherwise.

Conveyances and other Instruments

51.   Lands lie in grant only

(1)   All lands and all interests therein lie in grant and are incapable of being conveyed by livery or livery and seisin, or by feoffment, or by bargain and sale; and a conveyance of an interest in land may operate to pass the possession or right to possession thereof, without actual entry, but subject to all prior rights thereto.

(2)   The use of the word grant is not necessary to convey land or to create any interest therein.

52.   Conveyances to be by deed

(1)   All conveyances of land or of any interest therein are void for the purpose of conveying or creating a legal estate unless made by deed.

(2)   This section does not apply to—

(a)   assents by a personal representative;

(b)   disclaimers made in accordance with sections 178 to 180 or sections 315 to 319 of the Insolvency Act 1986 or not required to be evidenced in writing;

     (c)   surrenders by operation of law, including surrenders which may, by law, be effected without writing;

     (d)   leases or tenancies or other assurances not required by law to be made in writing;

     (e)   receipts other than those falling within section 115 below;

     (f)   vesting orders of the court or other competent authority;

     (g)   conveyances taking effect by operation of law.

53.   Instruments required to be in writing

(1)   Subject to the provision hereinafter contained with respect to the creation of interests in land by parol—

     (a)   no interest in land can be created or disposed of except by writing signed by the person creating or conveying the same, or by his agent thereunto lawfully authorised in writing, or by will, or by operation of law;

     (b)   a declaration of trust respecting any land or any interest therein must be manifested and proved by some writing signed by some person who is able to declare such trust or by his will;

     (c)   a disposition of an equitable interest or trust subsisting at the time of the disposition, must be in writing signed by the person disposing of the same, or by his agent thereunto lawfully authorised in writing or by will.

(2)   This section does not affect the creation or operation of resulting, implied or constructive trusts.

54.   Creation of interests in land by parol

(1)   All interests in land created by parol and not put in writing and signed by the persons so creating the same, or by their agents thereunto lawfully authorised in writing, have, notwithstanding any consideration having been given for the same, the force and effect of interests at will only.

(2)   Nothing in the foregoing provisions of this Part of this Act shall affect the creation by parol of leases taking effect in possession for a term not exceeding three years (whether or not the lessee is given power to extend the term) at the best rent which can be reasonably obtained without taking a fine.

55.   Savings in regard to last two sections

Nothing in the last two foregoing sections shall—

(a)   invalidate dispositions by will; or

(b)   affect any interest validly created before the commencement of this Act; or

(c)   affect the right to acquire an interest in land by virtue of taking possession; or

(d)   affect the operation of the law relating to part performance.

56.   Persons taking who are not parties and as to indentures

(1)   A person may take an immediate or other interest in land or other property, or the benefit of any condition, right of entry, covenant or agreement over or respecting land or other property, although he may not be named as a party to the conveyance or other instrument.

(2)   A deed between parties, to effect its objects, has the effect of an indenture though not indented or expressed to be an indenture.

57.   Description of deeds

Any deed, whether or not being an indenture, may be described (at the commencement thereof or otherwise) as a deed simply, or as a conveyance, deed of exchange, vesting deed, trust instrument, settlement, mortgage, charge, transfer of mortgage, appointment, lease or otherwise according to the nature of the transaction intended to be effected.

58.   Provisions as to supplemental instruments

Any instrument (whether executed before or after the commencement of this Act) expressed to be supplemental to a previous instrument, shall, as far as may be, be read and have effect as if the supplemental instrument contained a full recital of the previous instrument, but this section does not operate to give any right to an abstract or production of any such previous instrument, and a purchaser may accept the same evidence that the previous instrument does not affect the title as if it had merely been mentioned in the supplemental instrument.

59.   Conditions and certain covenants not implied

(1)   An exchange or other conveyance of land made by deed after the first day of October, eighteen hundred and forty-five, does not imply any condition in law.

(2)   The word 'give' or 'grant' does not in a deed made after the date last aforesaid, imply any covenant in law, save where otherwise provided by statute.

60.   Abolition of technicalities in regard to conveyances and deeds

(1)   A conveyance of freehold land to any person without words of limitation, or any equivalent expression, shall pass to the grantee the fee simple or other the whole interest which the grantor had power to convey in such land, unless a contrary intention appears in the conveyance.

(2)   A conveyance of freehold land to a corporation sole by his corporate designation without the word 'successors' shall pass to the corporation the fee simple or other the whole interest which the grantor had power to convey in such land, unless a contrary intention appears in the conveyance.

(3)   In a voluntary conveyance a resulting trust for the grantor shall not be implied merely by reason that the property is not expressed to be conveyed for the use or benefit of the grantee.

(4)   The foregoing provisions of this section apply only to conveyances and deeds executed after the commencement of this Act:

Provided that in a deed executed after the thirty-first day of December, eighteen hundred and eighty-one, it is sufficient—

(a)   In the limitation of an estate in fee simple, to use the words 'in fee simple,' without the word 'heirs';

. . .

61.   Construction of expressions used in deeds and other instruments

In all deeds, contracts, wills, orders and other instruments executed, made or coming into operation after the commencement of this Act, unless the context otherwise requires—

(a)   'Month' means calendar month;

(b)   'Person' includes a corporation;

(c)   The singular includes the plural and vice versa;

(d)   The masculine includes the feminine and vice versa.

62.   General words implied in conveyances

(1)   A conveyance of land shall be deemed to include and shall by virtue of this Act operate to convey, with the land, all buildings, erections, fixtures, commons, hedges, ditches, fences, ways, waters, water-courses, liberties, privileges, easements, rights, and advantages whatsoever, appertaining or reputed to appertain to the land, or any part thereof, or, at the time of conveyance, demised, occupied, or enjoyed with, or reputed or known as part or parcel of or appurtenant to the land or any part thereof.

(2)   A conveyance of land, having houses or other buildings thereon, shall be deemed to include and shall by virtue of this Act operate to convey, with the land, houses, or other buildings, all outhouses, erections, fixtures, cellars, areas, courts, courtyards, cisterns, sewers, gutters, drains, ways, passages, lights, water-courses, liberties, privileges, easements, rights, and advantages whatsoever, appertaining or reputed to appertain to the land, houses, or other buildings conveyed, or any of them, or any part thereof, or, at the time of conveyance, demised, occupied, or enjoyed with, or reputed or known as part or parcel of or appurtenant to, the land, houses, or other buildings conveyed, or any of them, or any part thereof.

(3)   A conveyance of a manor shall be deemed to include and shall by virtue of this Act operate to convey, with the manor, all pastures, feedings, wastes, warrens, commons, mines, minerals, quarries, furzes, trees, woods, underwoods, coppices, and the ground and soil thereof, fishings, fisheries, fowlings, courts leet, courts baron, and other courts, view of frankpledge and all that to view of frankpledge doth belong, mills, mulctures, customs, tolls,

duties, reliefs, heriots, fines, sums of money, amerciaments, waifs, estrays, chief-rents, quitrents, rentscharge, rents seck, rents of assize, fee farm rents, services, royalties, jurisdictions, franchises, liberties, privileges, easements, profits, advantages, rights, emoluments, and hereditaments whatsoever, to the manor appertaining or reputed to appertain, or, at the time of conveyance, demised, occupied, or enjoyed with the same, or reputed or known as part, parcel, or member thereof.

For the purposes of this subsection the right to compensation for manorial incidents on the extinguishment thereof shall be deemed to be a right appertaining to the manor.

(4)   This section applies only if and as far as a contrary intention is not expressed in the conveyance, and has effect subject to the terms of the conveyance and to the provisions therein contained.

(5)   This section shall not be construed as giving to any person a better title to any property, right, or thing in this section mentioned than the title which the conveyance gives to him to the land or manor expressed to be conveyed, or as conveying to him any property, right, or thing in this section mentioned, further or otherwise than as the same could have been conveyed to him by the conveying parties.

(6)   This section applies to conveyances made after the thirty-first day of December, eighteen hundred and eighty-one.

63.   All estate clause implied

(1)   Every conveyance is effectual to pass all the estate, right, title, interest, claim, and demand which the conveying parties respectively have, in, to, or on the property conveyed, or expressed or intended so to be, or which they respectively have power to convey in, to, or on the same.

(2)   This section applies only if and as far as a contrary intention is not expressed in the conveyance, and has effect subject to the terms of the conveyance and to the provisions therein contained.

(3)   This section applies to conveyances made after the thirty-first day of December, eighteen hundred and eighty-one.

64.   Production and safe custody of documents

(1)   Where a person retains possession of documents, and gives to another an acknowledgment in writing of the right of that other to production of those documents, and to delivery of copies thereof (in this section called an acknowledgment), that acknowledgment shall have effect as in this section provided.

(2)   An acknowledgment shall bind the documents to which it relates in the possession or under the control of the person who retains them, and in the possession or under the control of every other person having possession or control thereof from time to time, but shall bind each individual possessor or person as long only as he has possession or control thereof; and every person so having possession or control from time to time shall be bound specifically to perform the obligations imposed under this section by an acknowledgment, unless prevented from so doing by fire or other inevitable accident.

(3)   The obligations imposed under this section by an acknowledgment are to be performed from time to time at the request in writing of the person to whom an acknowledgment is given, or of any person, not being a lessee at a rent, having or claiming any estate, interest, or right through or under that person, or otherwise becoming through or under that person interested in or affected by the terms of any document to which the acknowledgment relates.

(4)   The obligations imposed under this section by an acknowledgment are—

(i)   An obligation to produce the documents or any of them at all reasonable times for the purpose of inspection, and of comparison with abstracts or copies thereof, by the person entitled to request production or by any person by him authorised in writing; and

(ii)   An obligation to produce the documents or any of them at any trial, hearing, or examination in any court, or in the execution of any commission, or elsewhere in the United Kingdom, on any occasion on which production may properly be required, for proving or supporting the title or claim of the person entitled to request production, or for any other purpose relative to that title or claim; and

(iii) An obligation to deliver to the person entitled to request the same true copies or extracts, attested or unattested, of or from the documents or any of them.

(5) All costs and expenses of or incidental to the specific performance of any obligation imposed under this section by an acknowledgment shall be paid by the person requesting performance.

(6) An acknowledgment shall not confer any right to damages for loss or destruction of, or injury to, the documents to which it relates, from whatever cause arising.

(7) Any person claiming to be entitled to the benefit of an acknowledgment may apply to the court for an order directing the production of the documents to which it relates, or any of them, or the delivery of copies of or extracts from those documents or any of them to him, or some person on his behalf; and the court may, if it thinks fit, order production, or production and delivery, accordingly, and may give directions respecting the time, place, terms, and mode of production or delivery, and may make such order as it thinks fit respecting the costs of the application, or any other matter connected with the application.

(8) An acknowledgment shall by virtue of this Act satisfy any liability to give a covenant for production and delivery of copies of or extracts from documents.

(9) Where a person retains possession of documents and gives to another an undertaking in writing for safe custody thereof, that undertaking shall impose on the person giving it, and on every person having possession or control of the documents from time to time, but on each individual possessor or person as long only as he has possession or control thereof, an obligation to keep the documents safe, whole, uncancelled, and undefaced, unless prevented from so doing by fire or other inevitable accident.

(10) Any person claiming to be entitled to the benefit of such an undertaking may apply to the court to assess damages for any loss or destruction of, or injury to, the documents or any of them, and the court may, if it thinks fit, direct an inquiry respecting the amount of damages, and order payment thereof by the person liable, and may make such order as it thinks fit respecting the costs of the application, or any other matter connected with the application.

(11) An undertaking for safe custody of documents shall by virtue of this Act satisfy any liability to give a covenant for safe custody of documents.

(12) The rights conferred by an acknowledgment or an undertaking under this section shall be in addition to all such other rights relative to the production, or inspection, or the obtaining of copies of documents, as are not, by virtue of this Act, satisfied by the giving of the acknowledgment or undertaking, and shall have effect subject to the terms of the acknowledgment or undertaking, and to any provisions therein contained.

(13) This section applies only if and as far as a contrary intention is not expressed in the acknowledgment or undertaking.

(14) This section applies to an acknowledgment or undertaking given, or a liability respecting documents incurred, after the thirty-first day of December, eighteen hundred and eighty-one.

65.   Reservation of legal estates

(1) A reservation of a legal estate shall operate at law without any execution of the conveyance by the grantee of the legal estate out of which the reservation is made, or any regrant by him, so as to create the legal estate reserved, and so as to vest the same in possession in the person (whether being the grantor or not) for whose benefit the reservation is made.

(2) A conveyance of a legal estate expressed to be made subject to another legal estate not in existence immediately before the date of the conveyance, shall operate as a reservation, unless a contrary intention appears.

(3) This section applies only to reservations made after the commencement of this Act.

66.   Confirmation of past transactions

(1) A deed containing a declaration by the estate owner that his estate shall go and devolve in such a manner as may be requisite for confirming any interests intended to affect his estate

and capable under this Act of subsisting as legal estates which, at some prior date, were expressed to have been transferred or created, and any dealings therewith which would have been legal if those interests had been legally and validly transferred or created, shall, to the extent of the estate of the estate owner, but without prejudice to the restrictions imposed by this Act in the case of mortgages, operate to give legal effect to the interests so expressed to have been transferred or created and to the subsequent dealings aforesaid.

(2) The powers conferred by this section may be exercised by a tenant for life or statutory owner, trustee of land or a personal representative (being in each case an estate owner) as well as by an absolute owner, but if exercised by any person, other than an absolute owner, only with the leave of the court.

(3) This section applies only to deeds containing such a declaration as aforesaid if executed after the commencement of this Act.

(4) The county court has jurisdiction under this section where the land which is to be dealt with in the court does not exceed £30,000 in capital value . . . .

67. Receipt in deed sufficient

(1) A receipt for consideration money or securities in the body of a deed shall be a sufficient discharge for the same to the person paying or delivering the same, without any further receipt for the same being indorsed on the deed.

(2) This section applies to deeds executed after the thirty-first day of December, eighteen hundred and eighty-one.

68. Receipt in deed or indorsed evidence

(1) A receipt for consideration money or other consideration in the body of a deed or indorsed thereon shall, in favour of a subsequent purchaser, not having notice that the money or other consideration thereby acknowledged to be received was not in fact paid or given, wholly or in part, be sufficient evidence of the payment or giving of the whole amount thereof.

(2) This section applies to deeds executed after the thirty-first day of December, eighteen hundred and eighty-one.

69. Receipt in deed or indorsed authority for payment to solicitor

(1) Where a solicitor produces a deed, having in the body thereof or indorsed thereon a receipt for consideration money or other consideration, the deed being executed, or the indorsed receipt being signed, by the person entitled to give a receipt for that consideration, the deed shall be a sufficient authority to the person liable to pay or give the same for his paying or giving the same to the solicitor, without the solicitor producing any separate or other direction or authority in that behalf from the person who executed or signed the deed or receipt.

(2) This section applies whether the consideration was paid or given before or after the commencement of this Act.

70. Partial release of security from rentcharge

(1) A release from a rentcharge of part of the land charged therewith does not extinguish the whole rentcharge, but operates only to bar the right to recover any part of the rentcharge out of the land released, without prejudice to the rights of any persons interested in the land remaining unreleased, and not concurring in or confirming the release.

(2) This section applies to releases made after the twelfth day of August, eighteen hundred and fifty-nine.

71. Release of part of land affected from a judgment

(1) A release from a judgment (including any writ or order imposing a charge) or part of any land charged therewith does not affect the validity of the judgment as respects any land not specifically released.

(2) This section operates without prejudice to the rights of any persons interested in the property remaining unreleased and not concurring in or confirming the release.

(3) This section applies to releases made after the twelfth day of August, eighteen hundred and fifty-nine.

72.   **Conveyances by a person to himself, etc.**

(1)   In conveyances made after the twelfth day of August, eighteen hundred and fifty-nine, personal property, including chattels real, may be conveyed by a person to himself jointly with another person by the like means by which it might be conveyed by him to another person.

(2)   In conveyances made after the thirty-first day of December, eighteen hundred and eighty-one, freehold land, or a thing in action, may be conveyed by a person to himself jointly with another person, by the like means by which it might be conveyed by him to another person; and may, in like manner, be conveyed by a husband to his wife, and by a wife to her husband, alone or jointly with another person.

(3)   After the commencement of this Act a person may convey land to or vest land in himself.

(4)   Two or more persons (whether or not being trustees or personal representatives) may convey, and shall be deemed always to have been capable of conveying, any property vested in them to any one or more of themselves in like manner as they could have conveyed such property to a third party; provided that if the persons in whose favour the conveyance is made are, by reason of any fiduciary relationship or otherwise, precluded from validly carrying out the transaction, the conveyance shall be liable to be set aside.

74.   **Execution of instruments by or on behalf of corporations**

(1)   In favour of a purchaser an instrument shall be deemed to have been duly executed by a corporation aggregate if a seal purporting to be the corporation's seal purports to be affixed to the instrument in the presence of and attested by—

(a)   two members of the board of directors, council or other governing body of the corporation, or

(b)   one such member and the clerk, secretary or other permanent officer of the corporation or his deputy.

(1A) Subsection (1) of this section applies in the case of an instrument purporting to have been executed by a corporation aggregate in the name or on behalf of another person whether or not that person is also a corporation aggregate.

(1B) For the purposes of subsection (1) of this section, a seal purports to be affixed in the presence of and attested by an officer of the corporation, in the case of an officer which is not an individual, if it is affixed in the presence of and attested by an individual authorised by the officer to attest on its behalf.

(2)   The board of directors, council or other governing body of a corporation aggregate may, by resolution or otherwise, appoint an agent either generally or in any particular case, to execute on behalf of the corporation any agreement or other instrument which is not a deed in relation to any matter within the powers of the corporation.

(3)   Where a person is authorised under a power of attorney or under any statutory or other power to convey any interest in property in the name or on behalf of a corporation sole or aggregate, he may as attorney execute the conveyance by signing the name of the corporation in the presence of at least one witness who attests the signature, . . . and such execution shall take effect and be valid in like manner as if the corporation had executed the conveyance.

(4)   Where a corporation aggregate is authorised under a power of attorney or under any statutory or other power to convey any interest in property in the name or on behalf of any other person (including another corporation), an officer appointed for that purpose by the board of directors, council or other governing body of the corporation by resolution or otherwise, may execute the instrument by signing it in the name of such other person or, if the instrument is to be a deed, by so signing it in the presence of a witness who attests the signature; and where an instrument appears to be executed by an officer so appointed, then in favour of a purchaser the instrument shall be deemed to have been executed by an officer duly authorised.

(5)   The foregoing provisions of this section apply to transactions wherever effected, but only to deeds and instruments executed after the commencement of this Act, except that, in the case of powers or appointments of an agent or officer, they apply whether the power was

conferred or the appointment was made before or after the commencement of this Act or by this Act.

(6) Notwithstanding anything contained in this section, any mode of execution or attestation authorised by law or by practice or by the statute, charter, memorandum or articles, deed of settlement or other instrument constituting the corporation or regulating the affairs thereof, shall (in addition to the modes authorised by this section) be as effectual as if this section had not been passed.

74A. Execution of instrument as a deed

(1) An instrument is validly executed by a corporation aggregate as a deed for the purposes of section 1(2)(b) of the Law of Property (Miscellaneous Provisions) Act 1989, if and only if—

(a) it is duly executed by the corporation, and

(b) it is delivered as a deed.

(2) An instrument shall be presumed to be delivered for the purposes of subsection (1)(b) of this section upon its being executed, unless a contrary intention is proved.

75. Rights of purchaser as to execution

(1) On a sale, the purchaser shall not be entitled to require that the conveyance to him be executed in his presence, or in that of his solicitor, as such; but shall be entitled to have, at his own cost, the execution of the conveyance attested by some person appointed by him, who may, if he thinks fit, be his solicitor.

(2) This section applies to sales made after the thirty-first day of December, eighteen hundred and eighty-one.

Covenants

77. Implied covenants in conveyances subject to rents

(1) In addition to the covenants implied under Part I of the Law of Property (Miscellaneous Provisions) Act 1994, there shall in the several cases in this section mentioned, be deemed to be included and implied, a covenant to the effect in this section stated, by and with such persons as are hereinafter mentioned, that is to say:—

(A) In a conveyance for valuable consideration, other than a mortgage, of the entirety of the land affected by a rentcharge, a covenant by the grantee or joint and several covenants by the grantees, if more than one, with the conveying parties and with each of them, if more than one, in the terms set out in Part VII of the Second Schedule to this Act. Where a rentcharge has been apportioned in respect of any land, with the consent of the owner of the rentcharge, the covenants in this paragraph shall be implied in the conveyance of that land in like manner as if the apportioned rentcharge were the rentcharge referred to, and the document creating the rentcharge related solely to that land:

(B) In a conveyance for valuable consideration, other than a mortgage, of part of land affected by a rentcharge, subject to a part of that rentcharge which has been or is by that conveyance apportioned (but in either case without the consent of the owner of the rentcharge) in respect of the land conveyed:—

(i) A covenant by the grantee of the land or joint and several covenants by the grantees, if more than one, with the conveying parties and with each of them, if more than one, in the terms set out in paragraph (i) of Part VIII of the Second Schedule to this Act;

(ii) A covenant by a person who conveys or is expressed to convey as beneficial owner, or joint and several covenants by the persons who so convey or are expressed to so convey, if at the date of the conveyance any part of the land affected by such rentcharge is retained, with the grantees of the land and with each of them (if more than one) in the terms set out in paragraph (ii) of Part VIII of the Second Schedule to this Act:

(2) Where in a conveyance for valuable consideration, other than a mortgage, part of land affected by a rentcharge is, without the consent of the owner of the rentcharge, expressed to

be conveyed subject to or charged with the entire rent, paragraph (B)(i) of subsection (1) of this section shall apply as if, in paragraph (i) of Part VII of the Second Schedule to this Act—

(a)   any reference to the apportioned rent were to the entire rent; and

(b)   the words '(other than the covenant to pay the entire rent)' were omitted.

(2A) Where in a conveyance for valuable consideration, other than a mortgage, part of land affected by a rentcharge is, without the consent of the owner of the rentcharge, expressed to be conveyed discharged or exonerated from the entire rent, paragraph (B)(ii) of subsection (1) of this section shall apply as if, in paragraph (ii) of Part VIII of the Second Schedule to this Act—

(a)   any reference to the balance of the rent were to the entire rent; and

(b)   the words ', other than the covenant to pay the entire rent,' were omitted.

(3)   In this section 'conveyance' does not include a demise by way of lease at a rent.

(4)   Any covenant which would be implied under this section by reason of a person conveying or being expressed to convey as beneficial owner may, by express reference to this section, be implied, with or without variation, in a conveyance, whether or not for valuable consideration, by a person who conveys or is expressed to convey as settlor, or as trustee, or as mortgagee, or as personal representative of a deceased person, . . . or under an order of the court.

(5)   The benefit of a covenant implied as aforesaid shall be annexed and incident to, and shall go with, the estate or interest of the implied covenantee, and shall be capable of being enforced by every person in whom that estate or interest is, for the whole or any part thereof, from time to time vested.

(6)   A covenant implied as aforesaid may be varied or extended by deed, and, as so varied or extended, shall, as far as may be, operate in the like manner, and with all the like incidents, effects and consequences, as if such variations or extensions were directed in this section to be implied.

(7)   In particular any covenant implied under this section may be extended by providing that—

(a)   the land conveyed; or

(b)   the part of the land affected by the rentcharge which remains vested in the covenantor;

shall, as the case may require, stand charged with the payment of all money which may become payable under the implied covenant.

(8)   This section applies only to conveyances made after the commencement of this Act.

78.   Benefit of covenants relating to land

(1)   A covenant relating to any land of the covenantee shall be deemed to be made with the covenantee and his successors in title and the persons deriving title under him or them, and shall have effect as if such successors and other persons were expressed.

For the purposes of this subsection in connexion with covenants restrictive of the user of land 'successors in title' shall be deemed to include the owners and occupiers for the time being of the land of the covenantee intended to be benefited.

(2)   This section applies to covenants made after the commencement of this Act, but the repeal of section fifty-eight of the Conveyancing Act, 1881, does not affect the operation of covenants to which that section applied.

79.   Burden of covenants relating to land

(1)   A covenant relating to any land of a covenantor or capable of being bound by him, shall, unless a contrary intention is expressed, be deemed to be made by the covenantor on behalf of himself his successors in title and the persons deriving title under him or them, and, subject as aforesaid, shall have effect as if such successors and other persons were expressed.

This subsection extends to a covenant to do some act relating to the land, notwithstanding that the subject-matter may not be in existence when the covenant is made.

(2)   For the purposes of this section in connexion with covenants restrictive of the user of land 'successors in title' shall be deemed to include the owners and occupiers for the time being of such land.

(3)   This section applies only to covenants made after the commencement of this Act.

80.   Covenants binding land

(1)   A covenant and a bond and an obligation or contract made under seal after 31st December 1881 but before the coming into force of section 1 of the Law of Property (Miscellaneous Provisions) Act 1989 or executed as a deed in accordance with that section after its coming into force binds the real estate as well as the personal estate of the person making the same if and so far as a contrary intention is not expressed in the covenant, bond, obligation, or contract.

       This subsection extends to a covenant implied by virtue of this Act.

(2)   Every covenant running with the land, whether entered into before or after the commencement of this Act, shall take effect in accordance with any statutory enactment affecting the devolution of the land, and accordingly the benefit or burden of every such covenant shall vest in or bind the persons who by virtue of any such enactment or otherwise succeed to the title of the covenantee or the covenantor, as the case may be.

(3)   The benefit of a covenant relating to land entered into after the commencement of this Act may be made to run with the land without the use of any technical expression if the covenant is of such a nature that the benefit could have been made to run with the land before the commencement of this Act.

(4)   For the purposes of this section, a covenant runs with the land when the benefit or burden of it, whether at law or in equity, passes to the successors in title of the covenantee or the covenantor, as the case may be.

81.   Effect of covenant with two or more jointly

(1)   A covenant, and a contract under seal, and a bond or obligation under seal, made with two or more jointly, to pay money or to make a conveyance, or to do any other act, to them or for their benefit, shall be deemed to include, and shall, by virtue of this Act, imply, an obligation to do the act to, or for the benefit of, the survivor or survivors of them, and to, or for the benefit of, any other person to whom the right to sue on the covenant, contract, bond, or obligation devolves, and where made after the commencement of this Act shall be construed as being also made with each of them.

(2)   This section extends to a covenant implied by virtue of this Act.

(3)   This section applies only if and as far as a contrary intention is not expressed in the covenant, contract, bond, or obligation, and has effect subject to the covenant, contract, bond, or obligation, and to the provisions therein contained.

(4)   Except as otherwise expressly provided, this section applies to a covenant, contract, bond, or obligation made or implied after the thirty-first day of December, eighteen hundred and eighty-one.

(5)   In its application to instruments made after the coming into force of section 1 of the Law of Property (Miscellaneous Provisions) Act 1989 subsection (1) above shall have effect as if the words 'under seal, and a bond or obligation under seal,' there were substituted the words 'bond or obligation executed as a deed in accordance with section 1 of the Law of Property (Miscellaneous Provisions) Act 1989'.

82.   Covenants and agreements entered into by a person with himself and another or others

(1)   Any covenant, whether express or implied, or agreement entered into by a person with himself and one or more other persons shall be construed and be capable of being enforced in like manner as if the covenant or agreement had been entered into with the other person or persons alone.

(2)   This section applies to covenants or agreements entered into before or after the commencement of this Act, and to covenants implied by statute in the case of a person who

conveys or is expressed to convey to himself and one or more other persons, but without prejudice to any order of the court made before such commencement.

83. Construction of implied covenants

In the construction of a covenant or proviso, or other provision, implied in a deed or assent by virtue of this Act, words importing the singular or plural number, or the masculine gender, shall be read as also importing the plural or singular number, or as extending to females, as the case may require.

84. Power to discharge or modify restrictive covenants affecting land

(1)   the Lands Tribunal shall (without prejudice to any concurrent jurisdiction of the court) have power from time to time, on the application of any person interested in any freehold land affected by any restriction arising under covenant or otherwise as to the user thereof or the building thereon, by order wholly or partially to discharge or modify any such restriction . . . on being satisfied—

    (a)   that by reason of changes in the character of the property or the neighbourhood or other circumstances of the case which the Lands Tribunal may deem material, the restriction ought to be deemed obsolete, or

    (aa) that in a case falling within subsection (1A) below the continued existence thereof would impede some reasonable user of the land for public or private purposes . . . or, as the case may be, would unless modified so impede such user; or

    (b)   that the persons of full age and capacity for the time being or from time to time entitled to the benefit of the restriction, whether in respect of estates in fee simple or any lesser estates or interests in the property to which the benefit of the restriction is annexed, have agreed, either expressly or by implication, by their acts or omissions, to the same being discharged or modified; or

    (c)   that the proposed discharge or modification will not injure the persons entitled to the benefit of the restriction:

and an order discharging or modifying a restriction under this subsection may direct the applicant to pay to any person entitled to the benefit of the restriction such sum by way of consideration as the Tribunal may think it just to award under one, but not both, of the following heads, that is to say, either—

    (i)   a sum to make up for any loss or disadvantage suffered by that person in consequence of the discharge or modification; or

    (ii)   a sum to make up for any effect which the restriction had, at the time when it was imposed, in reducing the consideration then received for the land affected by it.

(1A) Subsection (1)(aa) above authorises the discharge or modification of a restriction by reference to its impeding some reasonable user of land in any case in which the Lands Tribunal is satisfied that the restriction, in impeding that user, either—

    (a)   does not secure to persons entitled to the benefit of it any practical benefits of substantial value or advantage to them; or

    (b)   is contrary to the public interest;

and that money will be an adequate compensation for the loss or disadvantage (if any) which any such person will suffer from the discharge or modification.

(1B) In determining whether a case is one falling within subsection (1A) above, and in determining whether (in any such case or otherwise) a restriction ought to be discharged or modified, the Lands Tribunal shall take into account the development plan and any declared or ascertainable pattern for the grant or refusal of planning permissions in the relevant areas, as well as the period at which and context in which the restriction was created or imposed and any other material circumstances.

(1C) It is hereby declared that the power conferred by this section to modify a restriction includes power to add such further provisions restricting the user of or the building on the land affected as appear to the Lands Tribunal to be reasonable in view of the relaxation of the existing provisions, and as may be accepted by the applicant; and the Lands Tribunal may accordingly refuse to modify a restriction without some such addition.

(2)   The court shall have power on the application of any person interested—

     (a)   To declare whether or not in any particular case any freehold land is or would in any given event be affected by a restriction imposed by any instrument; or

     (b)   To declare what, upon the true construction of any instrument purporting to impose a restriction, is the nature and extent of the restriction thereby imposed and whether the same is or would in any given event be enforceable and if so by whom.

Neither subsections (7) and (11) of this section nor, unless the contrary is expressed, any later enactment providing for this section not to apply to any restrictions shall affect the operation of this subsection or the operation for purposes of this subsection of any other provisions of this section.

(3)   The Lands Tribunal shall, before making any order under this section, direct such enquiries, if any, to be made of any government department or local authority, and such notices, if any, whether by way of advertisement or otherwise, to be given to such of the persons who appear to be entitled to the benefit of the restriction intended to be discharged, modified, or dealt with as, having regard to any enquiries notices or other proceedings previously made, given or taken, the Lands Tribunal may think fit.

(3A) On an application to the Lands Tribunal under this section the Lands Tribunal shall give any necessary directions as to the persons who are or are not to be admitted (as appearing to be entitled to the benefit of the restriction) to oppose the application, and no appeal shall lie against any such direction; but rules under the Lands Tribunal Act 1949 shall make provision whereby, in cases in which there arises on such an application (whether or not in connection with the admission of persons to oppose) any such question as is referred to in subsection (2)(a) or (b) of this section, the proceedings on the application can and, if the rules so provide, shall be suspended to enable the decision of the court to be obtained on that question by an application under that subsection, or by means of a case stated by the Lands Tribunal, or otherwise, as may be provided by those rules or by rules of court.

(4)   . . .

(5)   Any order made under this section shall be binding on all persons, whether ascertained or of full age or capacity or not, then entitled or thereafter capable of becoming entitled to the benefit of any restriction, which is thereby discharged, modified, or dealt with, and whether such persons are parties to the proceedings or have been served with notice or not . . .

(6)   An order may be made under this section notwithstanding that any instrument which is alleged to impose the restriction intended to be discharged, modified, or dealt with, may not have been produced to the court or the Lands Tribunal, and the court or the Lands Tribunal may act on such evidence of that instrument as it may think sufficient.

(7)   This section applies to restrictions whether subsisting at the commencement of this Act or imposed thereafter, but this section does not apply where the restriction was imposed on the occasion of a disposition made gratuitously or for a nominal consideration for public purposes.

(8)   This section applies whether the land affected by the restrictions is registered or not . . .

(9)   Where any proceedings by action or otherwise are taken to enforce a restrictive covenant, any person against whom the proceedings are taken, may in such proceedings apply to the court for an order giving leave to apply to the Lands Tribunal under this section, and staying the proceedings in the meantime.

(10) . . .

(11) This section does not apply to restrictions imposed by the Commissioners of Works under any statutory power for the protection of any Royal Park or Garden or to restrictions of a like character imposed upon the occasion of any enfranchisement effected before the commencement of this Act in any manor vested in His Majesty in right of the Crown or the Duchy on Lancaster, nor subject to subsection (11A) below to restrictions created or imposed—

     (a)   for Naval, Military or Air Force purposes,

(b) for civil aviation purposes under the powers of the Air Navigation Act, 1920 or of section 19 or 23 of the Civil Aviation Act 1949 or of sections 30 or 41 of the Civil Aviation Act 1982.

(11A) Subsection (11) of this section—

(a) shall exclude the application of this section to a restriction falling within subsection (11)(a), and not created or imposed in connection with the use of any land as an aerodrome, only so long as the restriction is enforceable by or on behalf of the Crown; and

(b) shall exclude the application of this section to a restriction falling within subsection (11)(b), or created or imposed in connection with the use of any land as an aerodrome, only so long as the restriction is enforceable by or on behalf of the Crown or any public or international authority.

(12) Where a term of more than forty years is created in land (whether before or after the commencement of this Act) this section shall, after the expiration of twenty-five years of the term, apply to restrictions affecting such leasehold land in like manner as it would have applied had the land been freehold:

Provided that this subsection shall not apply to mining leases.

PART III
MORTGAGES, RENTCHARGES, AND POWERS OF ATTORNEY

85.   Mode of mortgaging freeholds

(1) A mortgage of an estate in fee simple shall only be capable of being effected at law either by a demise for a term of years absolute, subject to a provision for cesser on redemption, or by a charge by deed expressed to be by way of legal mortgage:

Provided that a first mortgagee shall have the same right to the possession of documents as if his security included the fee simple.

(2) Any purported conveyance of an estate in fee simple by way of mortgage made after the commencement of this Act shall (to the extent of the estate of the mortgagor) operate as a demise of the land to the mortgagee for a term of years absolute, without impeachment for waste, but subject to cesser on redemption, in manner following, namely:—

(a) A first or only mortgagee shall take a term of three thousand years from the date of the mortgage:

(b) A second or subsequent mortgagee shall take a term (commencing from the date of the mortgage) one day longer than the term vested in the first or other mortgagee whose security ranks immediately before that of such second or subsequent mortgagee: and, in this subsection, any such purported conveyance as aforesaid includes an absolute conveyance with a deed of defeasance and any other assurance which, but for this subsection, would operate in effect to vest the fee simple in a mortgagee subject to redemption.

(3) Subsection (2) does not apply to registered land, but, subject to that, this section applies whether or not the land is registered land and whether or not the mortgage is expressed to be made by way of trust for sale or otherwise.

(4) Without prejudice to the provisions of this Act respecting legal and equitable powers, every power to mortgage or to lend money on mortgage of an estate in fee simple shall be construed as a power to mortgage the estate for a term of years absolute, without impeachment for waste, or by a charge by way of legal mortgage or to lend on such security.

86.   Mode of mortgaging leaseholds

(1) A mortgage of a term of years absolute shall only be capable of being effected at law either by a subdemise for a term of years absolute, less by one day at least than the term vested in the mortgagor, and subject to a provision for cesser on redemption, or by a charge by deed expressed to be by way of legal mortgage; and where a licence to subdemise by way of mortgage is required, such licence shall not be unreasonably refused:

Provided that a first mortgagee shall have the same right to the possession of documents as if his security had been effected by assignment.

(2) Any purported assignment of a term of years absolute by way of mortgage made after the commencement of this Act shall (to the extent of the estate of the mortgagor) operate as a subdemise of the leasehold land to the mortgagee for a term of years absolute, but subject to cesser on redemption, in manner following, namely:—

(a) The term to be taken by a first or only mortgagee shall be ten days less than the term expressed to be assigned:

(b) The term to be taken by a second or subsequent mortgagee shall be one day longer than the term vested in the first or other mortgagee whose security ranks immediately before that of the second or subsequent mortgagee, if the length of the last mentioned term permits, and in any case for a term less by one day at least than the term expressed to be assigned:

and, in this subsection, any such purported assignment as aforesaid includes an absolute assignment with a deed of defeasance and any other assurance which, but for this subsection, would operate in effect to vest the term of the mortgagor in a mortgagee subject to redemption.

(3) Subsection (2) does not apply to registered land, but, subject to that, this section applies whether or not the land is registered land and whether or not the mortgage is made by way of sub-mortgage of a term of years absolute, or is expressed to be by way of trust for sale or otherwise.

(4) Without prejudice to the provisions of this Act respecting legal and equitable powers, every power to mortgage for or to lend money on mortgage of a term of years absolute by way of assignment shall be construed as a power to mortgage the term by subdemise for a term of years absolute or by a charge by way of legal mortgage, or to lend on such security.

87. Charges by way of legal mortgage

(1) Where a legal mortgage of land is created by a charge by deed expressed to be by way of legal mortgage, the mortgagee shall have the same protection, powers and remedies (including the right to take proceedings to obtain possession from the occupiers and the persons in receipt of rents and profits, or any of them) as if—

(a) where the mortgage is a mortgage of an estate in fee simple, a mortgage term for three thousand years without impeachment of waste had been thereby created in favour of the mortgagee; and

(b) where the mortgage is a mortgage of a term of years absolute, a sub-term less by one day than the term vested in the mortgagor had been thereby created in favour of the mortgagee.

(2) Where an estate vested in a mortgagee immediately before the commencement of this Act has by virtue of this Act been converted into a term of years absolute or sub-term, the mortgagee may, by a declaration in writing to that effect signed by him, convert the mortgage into a charge by way of legal mortgage, and in that case the mortgage term shall be extinguished in the inheritance or in the head term as the case may be, and the mortgagee shall have the same protection, powers and remedies (including the right to take proceedings to obtain possession from the occupiers and the persons in receipt of rents and profits or any of them) as if the mortgage term or sub-term had remained subsisting.

The power conferred by this subsection may be exercised by a mortgagee notwithstanding that he is a trustee or personal representative.

(3) Such declaration shall not affect the priority of the mortgagee or his right to retain possession of documents, nor affect his title to or right over any fixtures or chattels personal comprised in the mortgage.

(4) Subsection (1) of this section shall not be taken to be affected by section 23(1)(a) of the Land Registration Act 2002 (under which owner's powers in relation to a registered estate do not include power to mortgage by demise or sub-demise).

88.   Realisation of freehold mortgages

(1)   Where an estate in fee simple has been mortgaged by the creation of a term of years absolute limited thereout or by a charge by way of legal mortgage and the mortgagee sells under his statutory or express power of sale—

   (a)   the conveyance by him shall operate to vest in the purchaser the fee simple in the land conveyed subject to any legal mortgage having priority to the mortgage in right of which the sale is made and to any money thereby secured, and thereupon;

   (b)   the mortgage term or the charge by way of legal mortgage and any subsequent mortgage term or charges shall merge or be extinguished as respects the land conveyed; and such conveyance may, as respects the fee simple, be made in the name of the estate owner in whom it is vested.

(2)   Where any such mortgagee obtains an order for foreclosure absolute, the order shall operate to vest the fee simple in him (subject to any legal mortgage having priority to the mortgage in right of which the foreclosure is obtained and to any money thereby secured), and thereupon the mortgage term, if any, shall thereby be merged in the fee simple, and any subsequent mortgage term or charge by way of legal mortgage bound by the order shall thereupon be extinguished.

(3)   Where any such mortgagee acquires a title under the Limitation Acts, he, or the persons deriving title under him, may enlarge the mortgage term into a fee simple under the statutory power for that purpose discharged from any legal mortgage affected by the title so acquired, or in the case of a chargee by way of legal mortgage may by deed declare that the fee simple is vested in him discharged as aforesaid, and the same shall vest accordingly.

(4)   Where the mortgage includes fixtures or chattels personal any statutory power of sale and any right to foreclose or take possession shall extend to the absolute or other interest therein affected by the charge.

(5)   In the case of a sub-mortgage by subdemise of a long term (less a nominal period) itself limited out of an estate in fee simple, the foregoing provisions of this section shall operate as if the derivative term, if any, created by the sub-mortgage had been limited out of the fee simple, and so as to enlarge the principal term and extinguish the derivative term created by the sub-mortgage as aforesaid, and to enable the sub-mortgagee to convey the fee simple or acquire it by foreclosure, enlargement, or otherwise as aforesaid.

(6)   This section applies to a mortgage whether created before or after the commencement of this Act, and to a mortgage term created by this Act, but does not operate to confer a better title to the fee simple than would have been acquired if the same had been conveyed by the mortgage (being a valid mortgage) and the restrictions imposed by this Act in regard to the effect and creation of mortgages were not in force, and all prior mortgages (if any) not being merely equitable charges had been created by demise or by charge by way of legal mortgage.

89.   Realisation of leasehold mortgages

(1)   Where a term of years absolute has been mortgaged by the creation of another term of years absolute limited thereout or by a charge by way of legal mortgage and the mortgagee sells under his statutory or express power of sale,—

   (a)   the conveyance by him shall operate to convey to the purchaser not only the mortgage term, if any, but also (unless expressly excepted with the leave of the court) the leasehold reversion affected by the mortgage, subject to any legal mortgage having priority to the mortgage in right of which the sale is made and to any money thereby secured, and thereupon

   (b)   the mortgage term, or the charge by way of legal mortgage and any subsequent mortgage term or charge, shall merge in such leasehold reversion or be extinguished unless excepted as aforesaid;

and such conveyance may, as respects the leasehold reversion, be made in the name of the estate owner in whom it is vested.

   Where a licence to assign is required on a sale by a mortgagee, such licence shall not be unreasonably refused.

(2)   Where any such mortgagee obtains an order for foreclosure absolute, the order shall, unless it otherwise provides, operate (without giving rise to a forfeiture for want of a licence to assign) to vest the leasehold reversion affected by the mortgage and any subsequent mortgage term in him, subject to any legal mortgage having priority to the mortgage in right of which the foreclosure is obtained and to any money thereby secured, and thereupon the mortgage term and any subsequent mortgage term or charge by way of legal mortgage bound by the order shall, subject to any express provision to the contrary contained in the order, merge in such leasehold reversion or be extinguished.

(3)   Where any such mortgagee acquires a title under the Limitation Acts, he, or the persons deriving title under him, may by deed declare that the leasehold reversion affected by the mortgage and any mortgage term affected by the title so acquired shall vest in him, free from any right of redemption which is barred, and the same shall (without giving rise to a forfeiture for want of a licence to assign) vest accordingly, and thereupon the mortgage term, if any, and any other mortgage term or charge by way of legal mortgage affected by the title so acquired shall, subject to any express provision to the contrary contained in the deed, merge in such leasehold reversion or be extinguished.

(4)   Where the mortgage includes fixtures or chattels personal, any statutory power of sale and any right to foreclose or take possession shall extend to the absolute or other interest therein affected by the charge.

(5)   In the case of a sub-mortgage by subdemise of a term (less a nominal period) itself limited out of a leasehold reversion, the foregoing provisions of this section shall operate as if the derivative term created by the sub-mortgage had been limited out of the leasehold reversion, and so as (subject as aforesaid) to merge the principal mortgage term therein as well as the derivative term created by the sub-mortgage and to enable the sub-mortgagee to convey the leasehold reversion or acquire it by foreclosure, vesting, or otherwise as aforesaid.

(6)   This section takes effect without prejudice to any incumbrance or trust affecting the leasehold reversion which has priority over the mortgage in right of which the sale, foreclosure, or title is made or acquired, and applies to a mortgage whether executed before or after the commencement of this Act, and to a mortgage term created by this Act, but does not apply where the mortgage term does not comprise the whole of the land included in the leasehold reversion unless the rent (if any) payable in respect of that reversion has been apportioned as respects the land affected, or the rent is of no money value or no rent is reserved, and unless the lessee's covenants and conditions (if any) have been apportioned, either expressly or by implication, as respects the land affected.

      In this subsection references to an apportionment include an equitable apportionment made without the consent of the lessor.

(7)   The county court has jurisdiction under this section where the amount owing in respect of the mortgage or charge at the commencement of the proceedings does not exceed £30,000.

90.   Realisation of equitable charges by the court

(1)   Where an order for sale is made by the court in reference to an equitable mortgage on land (not secured by a legal term of years absolute or by a charge by way of legal mortgage) the court may, in favour of a purchaser, make a vesting order conveying the land or may appoint a person to convey the land or create and vest in the mortgagee a legal term of years absolute to enable him to carry out the sale, as the case may require, in like manner as if the mortgage had been created by deed by way of legal mortgage pursuant to this Act, but without prejudice to any incumbrance having priority to the equitable mortgage unless the incumbrancer consents to the sale.

(2)   This section applies to equitable mortgages made or arising before or after the commencement of this Act, but not to a mortgage which has been overreached under the powers conferred by this Act or otherwise.

(3)   The county court has jurisdiction under this section where the amount owing in respect of the mortgage or charge at the commencement of the proceedings does not exceed £30,000.

91.   Sale of mortgaged property in action for redemption or foreclosure

(1)   Any person entitled to redeem mortgaged property may have a judgment or order for sale instead of for redemption in an action brought by him either for redemption alone, or for sale alone, or for sale or redemption in the alternative.

(2)   In any action, whether for foreclosure, or for redemption, or for sale, or for the raising and payment in any manner of mortgage money, the court, on the request of the mortgagee, or of any person interested either in the mortgage money or in the right of redemption, and, notwithstanding that—

(a)   any other person dissents; or

(b)   the mortgagee or any person so interested does not appear in the action;

and without allowing any time for redemption or for payment of any mortgage money, may direct a sale of the mortgaged property, on such terms as it thinks fit, including the deposit in court of a reasonable sum fixed by the court to meet the expenses of sale and to secure performance of the terms.

(3)   But, in an action brought by a person interested in the right of redemption and seeking a sale, the court may, on the application of any defendant, direct the plaintiff to give such security for costs as the court thinks fit, and may give the conduct of the sale to any defendant, and may give such directions as it thinks fit respecting the costs of the defendants or any of them.

(4)   In any case within this section the court may, if it thinks fit, direct a sale without previously determining the priorities of incumbrancers.

(5)   This section applies to actions brought either before or after the commencement of this Act.

(6)   In this section 'mortgaged property' includes the estate or interest which a mortgagee would have had power to convey if the statutory power of sale were applicable.

(7)   For the purposes of this section the court may, in favour of a purchaser, make a vesting order conveying the mortgaged property, or appoint a person to do so, subject or not to any incumbrance, as the court may think fit; or, in the case of an equitable mortgage, may create and vest a mortgage term in the mortgagee to enable him to carry out the sale as if the mortgage had been made by deed by way of legal mortgage.

(8)   The county court has jurisdiction under this section where the amount owing in respect of the mortgage or charge at the commencement of the proceedings does not exceed £30,000.

92.   Power to authorise land and minerals to be dealt with separately

(1)   Where a mortgagee's power of sale in regard to land has become exercisable but does not extend to the purposes mentioned in this section, the court may, on his application, authorise him and the persons deriving title under him to dispose—

(a)   of the land, with an exception or reservation of all or any mines and minerals, and with or without rights and powers of or incidental to the working, getting or carrying away of minerals; or

(b)   of all or any mines and minerals, with or without the said rights or powers separately from the land;

and thenceforth the powers so conferred shall have effect as if the same were contained in the mortgage.

(2) The county court has jurisdiction under this section where the amount owing in respect of the mortgage or charge at the commencement of the proceedings does not exceed £30,000.

93.   Restriction on consolidation of mortgages

(1)   A mortgagor seeking to redeem any one mortgage is entitled to do so without paying any money due under any separate mortgage made by him, or by any person through whom he claims, solely on property other than that comprised in the mortgage which he seeks to redeem.

This subsection applies only if and as far as a contrary intention is not expressed in the mortgage deeds or one of them.

(2)   This section does not apply where all the mortgages were made before the first day of January, eighteen hundred and eight-two.

(3)   Save as aforesaid, nothing in this Act, in reference to mortgages, affects any right of consolidation or renders inoperative a stipulation in relation to any mortgage made before or after the commencement of this Act reserving a right to consolidate.

94.   Tacking and further advances

(1)   After the commencement of this Act, a prior mortgagee shall have a right to make further advances to rank in priority to subsequent mortgages (whether legal or equitable)—

(a)   if an arrangement has been made to that effect with the subsequent mortgagees, or

(b)   if he had no notice of such subsequent mortgages at the time when the further advance was made by him; or

(c)   whether or not he had such notice as aforesaid, where the mortgage imposes an obligation on him to make such further advances.

This subsection applies whether or not the prior mortgage was made expressly for securing further advances.

(2)   In relation to the making of further advances after the commencement of this Act a mortgagee shall not be deemed to have notice of a mortgage merely by reason that it was registered as a land charge . . . if it was not so registered at the time when the original mortgage was created or when the last search (if any) by or on behalf of the mortgagee was made, whichever last happened.

This subsection only applies where the prior mortgage was made expressly for securing a current account or other further advances.

(3)   Save in regard to the making of further advances as aforesaid, the right to tack is hereby abolished:

Provided that nothing in this Act shall affect any priority acquired before the commencement of this Act by tacking, or in respect of further advances made without notice of a subsequent incumbrance or by arrangement with the subsequent incumbrancer.

(4)   This section applies to mortgages of land made before or after the commencement of this Act, but not to charges on registered land.

95.   Obligation to transfer instead of re-conveying, and as to right to take possession

(1)   Where a mortgagor in entitled to redeem, then subject to compliance with the terms on compliance with which he would be entitled to require a reconveyance or surrender, he shall be entitled to require the mortgagee, instead of re-conveying or surrendering, to assign the mortgage debt and convey the mortgaged property to any third person, as the mortgagor directs; and the mortgagee shall be bound to assign and convey accordingly.

(2)   The rights conferred by this section belong to and are capable of being enforced by each incumbrancer, or by the mortgagor, notwithstanding any intermediate incumbrance; but a requisition of an incumbrancer prevails over a requisition of the mortgagor, and, as between incumbrancers, a requisition of a prior incumbrancer prevails over a requisition of a subsequent incumbrancer.

(3)   The foregoing provisions of this section do not apply in the case of a mortgagee being or having been in possession.

(4)   Nothing in this Act affects prejudicially the right of a mortgagee of land whether or not his charge is secured by a legal term of years absolute to take possession of the land, but the taking of possession by the mortgagee does not convert any legal estate of the mortgagor into an equitable interest.

(5)   This section applies to mortgages made either before or after the commencement of this Act, and takes effect notwithstanding any stipulation to the contrary.

96.   Regulations respecting inspection, production and delivery of documents, and priorities

(1)   A mortgagor, as long as his right to redeem subsists, shall be entitled from time to time, at reasonable times, on his request, and at his own cost, and on payment of the mortgagee's costs and expenses in this behalf, to inspect and make copies or abstracts of or extracts from the documents of title relating to the mortgaged property in the custody or power of the mortgagee.

This section applies to mortgages made after the thirty-first day of December, eighteen hundred and eighty-one, and takes effect notwithstanding any stipulation to the contrary.

(2) A mortgagee, whose mortgage is surrendered or otherwise extinguished, shall not be liable on account of delivering documents of title in his possession to the person not having the best right thereto, unless he has notice of the right or claim of a person having a better right, whether by virtue of a right to require a surrender or reconveyance or otherwise.

In this sub-section notice does not include notice implied by reason of registration under the Land Charges Act, 1925, ...

97. Priorities as between puisne mortgages

Every mortgage affecting a legal estate in land made after the commencement of this Act, whether legal or equitable (not being a mortgage protected by the deposit of documents relating to the legal estate affected) shall rank according to its date of registration as a land charge pursuant to the Land Charges Act, 1925.

This section does not apply to mortgages or charges to which the Land Charges Act 1972 does not apply by virtue of section 14(3) of that Act (which excludes certain land charges created by instruments necessitating registration under the Land Registration Act 2002), or to mortgages or charges of registered land . . . .

98. Actions for possession by mortgagors

(1) A mortgagor for the time being entitled to the possession or receipt of the rents and profits of any land, as to which the mortgagee has not given notice of his intention to take possession or to enter into the receipt of the rents and profits thereof, may sue for such possession, or for the recovery of such rents or profits, or to prevent or recover damages in respect of any trespass or other wrong relative thereto, in his own name only, unless the cause of action arises upon a lease or other contract made by him jointly with any other person.

(2) This section does not prejudice the power of a mortgagor independently of this section to take proceedings in his own name only, either in right of any legal estate vested in him or otherwise.

(3) This section applies whether the mortgage was made before or after the commencement of this Act.

99. Leasing powers of mortgagor and mortgagee in possession

(1) A mortgagor of land while in possession shall, as against every incumbrancer, have power to make from time to time any such lease of the mortgaged land, or any part thereof, as is by this section authorised.

(2) A mortgagee of land while in possession shall, as against all prior incumbrancers, if any, and as against the mortgagor, have power to make from time to time any such lease as aforesaid.

(3) The leases which this section authorises are—
  (i) agricultural or occupation leases for any term not exceeding twenty-one years, or, in the case of a mortgage made after the commencement of this Act, fifty years; and
  (ii) building leases for any term not exceeding ninety-nine years, or, in the case of a mortgage made after the commencement of this Act, nine hundred and ninety-nine years.

(4) Every person making a lease under this section may execute and do all assurances and things necessary or proper in that behalf.

(5) Every such lease shall be made to take effect in possession not later than twelve months after its date.

(6) Every such lease shall reserve the best rent that can reasonably be obtained, regard being had to the circumstances of the case, but without any fine being taken.

(7) Every such lease shall contain a covenant by the lessee for payment of the rent, and condition of re-entry on the rent not being paid within a time therein specified not exceeding thirty days.

(8) A counterpart of every such lease shall be executed by the lessee and delivered to the lessor, of which execution and delivery the execution of the lease by the lessor shall, in favour of the lessee and all persons deriving title under him, be sufficient evidence.

(9) Every such building lease shall be made in consideration of the lessee, or some person by whose direction the lease is granted, having erected, or agreeing to erect within not more than five years from the date of the lease, buildings, new or additional, or having improved or repaired buildings, or agreeing to improve or repair buildings within that time, or having executed, or agreeing to execute within that time, on the land leased, an improvement for or in connexion with building purposes.

(10) In any such building lease a peppercorn rent, or a nominal or other rent less than the rent ultimately payable, may be made payable for the first five years, or any less part of the term.

(11) In case of a lease by the mortgagor, he shall, within one month after making the lease, deliver to the mortgagee, or, where there are more than one, to the mortgagee first in priority, a counterpart of the lease duly executed by the lessee, but the lessee shall not be concerned to see that this provision is complied with.

(12) A contract to make or accept a lease under this section may be enforced by or against every person on whom the lease if granted would be binding.

(13) Subject to subsection 13A below this section applies only if and as far as a contrary intention is not expressed by the mortgagor and mortgagee in the mortgage deed, or otherwise in writing, and has effect subject to the terms of the mortgage deed or of any such writing and to the provisions therein contained.

(13A) Subection 13 of this section—

(a) shall not enable the application of any provision of this section to be excluded or restricted in relation to any mortgage of agricultural land made after 1st March 1984 but before 1st September 1995; and

(b) shall not enable the power to grant a lease of any agricultural holding to which, by virtue of section 4 of the Agricultural Tenancies Act 1995, the Agricultural Holdings Act 1986 will apply, to be excluded or restricted in relation to any mortgage of agricultural land made on or after 1st September 1995.

(13B) In subsection (13A) of this section—

'agricultural holding' has the same meaning as in the Agricultural Holdings Act 1986; and 'agricultural land' has the same meaning as in the Agricultural Act 1947.

(14) The mortgagor and mortgagee may, by agreement in writing, whether or not contained in the mortgage deed, reserve to or confer on the mortgagor or the mortgagee, or both, any further or other powers of leasing or having reference to leasing; and any further or other powers so reserved or conferred shall be exercisable, as far as may be, as if they were conferred by this Act, and with all the like incidents, effects, and consequences:

Provided that the powers so reserved or conferred shall not prejudicially affect the rights of any mortgagee interested under any other mortgage subsisting at the date of the agreement, unless that mortgagee joins in or adopts the agreement.

(15) Nothing in this Act shall be construed to enable a mortgagor or mortgagee to make a lease for any longer term or on any other conditions than such as could have been granted or imposed by the mortgagor, with the concurrence of all the incumbrancers, if this Act and the enactments replaced by this section had not been passed:

Provided that, in the case of a mortgage of leasehold land, a lease granted under this section shall reserve a reversion of not less than one day.

(16) Subject as aforesaid, this section applies to any mortgage made after the thirty-first day of December, eighteen hundred and eighty-one, but the provisions thereof, or any of them, may, by agreement in writing made after that date between mortgagor and mortgagee, be applied to a mortgage made before that date, so nevertheless that any such agreement shall not prejudicially affect any right or interest of any mortgagee not joining in or adopting the agreement.

(17) The provisions of this section referring to a lease shall be construed to extend and apply, as far as circumstances admit, to any letting, and to an agreement, whether in writing or not, for leasing or letting.

(18) For the purposes of this section 'mortgagor' does not include an incumbrancer deriving title under the original mortgagor.

(19) The powers of leasing conferred by this section shall, after a receiver of the income of the mortgaged property or any part thereof has been appointed by a mortgagee under his statutory power, and so long as the receiver acts, be exercisable by such mortgagee instead of by the mortgagor, as respects any land affected by the receivership, in like manner as if such mortgagee were in possession of the land, and the mortgagee may, by writing, delegate any of such powers to the receiver.

100. Powers of mortgagor and mortgagee in possession to accept surrenders of leases

(1) For the purpose only of enabling a lease authorised under the last preceding section, or under any agreement made pursuant to that section, or by the mortgage deed (in this section referred to as an authorised lease) to be granted, a mortgagor of land while in possession shall, as against every incumbrancer, have, by virtue of this Act, power to accept from time to time a surrender of any lease of the mortgaged land or any part thereof comprised in the lease, with or without an exception of or in respect of all or any of the mines and minerals therein, and, on a surrender of the lease so far as it comprises part only of the land or mines and minerals leased, the rent may be apportioned.

(2) For the same purpose, a mortgagee of land while in possession shall, as against all prior or other incumbrancers, if any, and as against the mortgagor, have, by virtue of this Act, power to accept from time to time any such surrender as aforesaid.

(3) On a surrender of part only of the land or mines and minerals leased, the original lease may be varied, provided that the lease when varied would have been valid as an authorised lease if granted by the person accepting the surrender; and, on a surrender and the making of a new or other lease, whether for the same or for any extended or other term, and whether subject or not to the same or to any other covenants, provisions, or conditions, the value of the lessee's interest in the lease surrendered may, subject to the provisions of this section, be taken into account in the determination of the amount of the rent to be reserved, and of the nature of the covenants, provisions and conditions to be inserted in the new or other lease.

(4) Where any consideration for the surrender, other than an agreement to accept an authorised lease, is given by or on behalf of the lessee to or on behalf of the person accepting the surrender, nothing in this section authorises a surrender to a mortgagor without the consent of the incumbrancers, or authorises a surrender to a second or subsequent incumbrancer without the consent of every prior incumbrancer.

(5) No surrender shall, by virtue of this section, be rendered valid unless:—

  (a) An authorised lease is granted of the whole of the land or mines and minerals comprised in the surrender to take effect in possession immediately or within one month after the date of the surrender; and

  (b) The term certain or other interest granted by the new lease is not less in duration than the unexpired term or interest which would have been subsisting under the original lease if that lease had not been surrendered; and

  (c) Where the whole of the land mines and minerals originally leased has been surrendered, the rent reserved by the new lease is not less than the rent which would have been payable under the original lease if it had not been surrendered; or where part only of the land or mines and minerals has been surrendered, the aggregate rents respectively remaining payable or reserved under the original lease and new lease are not less than the rent which would have been payable under the original lease if no partial surrender had been accepted.

(6) A contract to make or accept a surrender under this section may be enforced by or against every person on whom the surrender, if completed, would be binding.

(7) This section applies only if and as far as a contrary intention is not expressed by the mortgagor and mortgagee in the mortgage deed, or otherwise in writing, and shall have

effect subject to the terms of the mortgage deed or of any such writing and to the provisions therein contained.

(8) This section applies to a mortgage made after the thirty-first day of December, nineteen hundred and eleven, but the provisions of this section, or any of them, may, by agreement in writing made after that date, between mortgagor and mortgagee, be applied to a mortgage made before that date, so nevertheless that any such agreement shall not prejudicially affect any right or interest of any mortgagee not joining in or adopting the agreement.

(9) The provisions of this section referring to a lease shall be construed to extend and apply, as far as circumstances admit, to any letting, and to an agreement, whether in writing or not, for leasing or letting.

(10) The mortgagor and mortgagee may, by agreement in writing, whether or not contained in the mortgage deed, reserve or confer on the mortgagor or mortgagee, or both, any further or other powers relating to the surrender of leases; and any further or other powers so conferred or reserved shall be exercisable, as far as may be, as if they were conferred by this Act, and with all the like incidents, effects and consequences:

Provided that the powers so reserved or conferred shall not prejudicially affect the rights of any mortgagee interested under any other mortgage subsisting at the date of the agreement, unless that mortgagee joins in or adopts the agreement.

(11) Nothing in this section operates to enable a mortgagor or mortgagee to accept a surrender which could not have been accepted by the mortgagor with the concurrence of all the incumbrancers if his Act and the enactments replaced by this section had not been passed.

(12) For the purposes of this section 'mortgagor' does not include an incumbrancer deriving title under the original mortgagor.

(13) The powers of accepting surrenders conferred by this section shall, after a receiver of the income of the mortgaged property or any part thereof has been appointed by the mortgagee, under the statutory power, and so long as the receiver acts, be exercisable by such mortgagee instead of by the mortgagor, as respects any land affected by the receivership, in like manner as if such mortgagee were in possession of the land; and the mortgagee may, by writing, delegate any of such powers to the receiver.

101.   Powers incident to estate or interest of mortgagee

(1) A mortgagee, where the mortgage is made by deed, shall, by virtue of this Act, have the following powers, to the like extent as if they had been in terms conferred by the mortgage deed, but not further (namely):

(i)   A power, when the mortgage money has become due, to sell, or to concur with any other person in selling, the mortgaged property, or any part thereof, either subject to prior charges or not, and either together or in lots, by public auction or by private contract, subject to such conditions respecting title, or evidence of title, or other matter, as the mortgagee thinks fit, with power to vary any contract for sale, and to buy in at an auction, or to rescind any contract for sale, and to re-sell, without being answerable for any loss occasioned thereby; and

(ii)   A power, at any time after the date of the mortgage deed, to insure and keep insured against loss or damage by fire any building, or any effects or property of an insurable nature, whether affixed to the freehold or not, being or forming part of the property which or an estate or interest wherein is mortgaged, and the premiums paid for any such insurance shall be a charge on the mortgaged property or estate or interest, in addition to the mortgage money, and with the same priority, and with interest at the same rate, as the mortgage money; and

(iii) A power, when the mortgage money has become due, to appoint a receiver of the income of the mortgaged property, or any part thereof; or, if the mortgaged property consists of an interest in income, or of a rentcharge or an annual or other periodical sum, a receiver of that property or any part thereof; and

(iv)   A power, while the mortgagee is in possession, to cut and sell timber and other trees ripe for cutting, and not planted or left standing for shelter or ornament, or to contract for any such cutting and sale, to be completed within any time not exceeding twelve months from the making of the contract.

(1A) Subsection (1)(i) is subject to section 21 of the Commonhold and Leasehold Reform Act 2002 (no disposition of part-units).

(2) Where the mortgage deed is executed after the thirty-first day of December, nineteen hundred and eleven, the power of sale aforesaid includes the following powers as incident thereto (namely):—

    (i) A power to impose or reserve or make binding, as far as the law permits, by covenant, condition, or otherwise, on the unsold part of the mortgaged property or any part thereof, or on the purchaser and any property sold, any restriction or reservation with respect to building on or other user of land, or with respect to mines and minerals, or for the purpose of the more beneficial working thereof, or with respect to any other thing:

    (ii) A power to sell the mortgaged property, or any part thereof, or all or any mines and minerals apart from the surface:—

        (a) With or without a grant or reservation of rights of way, rights of water, easements, rights, and privileges for or connected with building or other purposes in relation to the property remaining in mortgage or any part thereof, or to any property sold: and

        (b) With or without an exception or reservation of all or any of the mines and minerals in or under the mortgaged property, and with or without a grant or reservation of powers or working, wayleaves, or rights of way, rights of water and drainage and other powers, easements, rights, and privileges for or connected with mining purposes in relation to the property remaining unsold or any part thereof, or to any property sold: and

        (c) With or without covenants by the purchaser to expend money on the land sold.

(3) The provisions of this Act relating to the foregoing powers, comprised either in this section, or in any other section regulating the exercise of those powers, may be varied or extended by the mortgage deed, and, as so varied or extended, shall, as far as may be, operate in the like manner and with all the like incidents, effects, and consequences, as if such variations or extensions were contained in this Act.

(4) This section applies only if and as far as a contrary intention is not expressed in the mortgage deed, and has effect subject to the terms of the mortgage deed and to the provisions therein contained.

(5) Save as otherwise provided, this section applies where the mortgage deed is executed after the thirty-first day of December, eighteen hundred and eighty-one.

(6) The power of sale conferred by this section includes such power of selling the estate in fee simple or any leasehold reversion as is conferred by the provisions of this Act relating to the realisation of mortgages.

102. Provision as to mortgages of undivided shares in land

(1) A person who was before the commencement of this Act a mortgagee of an undivided share in land shall have the same power to sell his interest under the trust to which the land is subject, as, independently of this Act, he would have had in regard to the share in the land; and shall also have a right to require the trustees in whom the land is vested to account to him for the income attributable to that share or to appoint a receiver to receive the same from such trustees corresponding to the right which, independently of this Act, he would have had to take possession or to appoint a receiver of the rents and profits attributable to the same share.

(2) The powers conferred by this section are exercisable by the persons deriving title under such mortgagee.

103. Regulation of exercise of power of sale

A mortgagee shall not exercise the power of sale conferred by this Act unless and until—

(i)   Notice requiring payment of the mortgage money has been served on the mortgagor or one of two or more mortgagors, and default has been made in payment of the mortgage money, or of part thereof, for three months after such service; or

(ii)   Some interest under the mortgage is in arrear and unpaid for two months after becoming due; or

(iii) There has been a breach of some provision contained in the mortgage deed or in this Act, or in an enactment replaced by this Act, and on the part of the mortgagor, or of some person concurring in making the mortgage, to be observed or performed, other than and besides a covenant for payment of the mortgage money or interest thereon.

104.   Conveyance on sale

(1)   A mortgagee exercising the power of sale conferred by this Act shall have power, by deed, to convey the property sold, for such estate and interest therein as he is by this Act authorised to sell or convey or may be the subject of the mortgage, freed from all estates, interests, and rights to which the mortgage has priority, but subject to all estates, interests, and rights which have priority to the mortgage.

(2)   Where a conveyance is made in exercise of the power of sale conferred by this Act, or any enactment replaced by this Act, the title of the purchaser shall not be impeachable on the ground—

(a)   that no case had arisen to authorise the sale; or

(b)   that due notice was not given; or

(c)   where the mortgage is made after the commencement of this Act, that leave of the court, when so required, was not obtained; or

(d)   whether the mortgage was made before or after such commencement, that the power was otherwise improperly or irregularly exercised;

and a purchaser is not, either before or on conveyance, concerned to see or inquire whether a case has arisen to authorise the sale, or due notice has been given, or the power is otherwise properly and regularly exercised; but any person damnified by an unauthorised, or improper, or irregular exercise of the power shall have his remedy in damages against the person exercising the power.

(3)   A conveyance on sale by a mortgagee, made after the commencement of this Act, shall be deemed to have been made in exercise of the power of sale conferred by this Act unless a contrary intention appears.

105.   Application of proceeds of sale

The money which is received by the mortgagee, arising from the sale, after discharge of prior incumbrances to which the sale is not made subject, if any, or after payment into court under this Act of a sum to meet any prior incumbrance, shall be held by him in trust to be applied by him, first, in payment of all costs, charges, and expenses properly incurred by him as incident to the sale or any attempted sale, or otherwise; and secondly, in discharge of the mortgage money, interest, and costs, and other money, if any, due under the mortgage; and the residue of the money so received shall be paid to the person entitled to the mortgaged property, or authorised to give receipts for the proceeds of the sale thereof.

106.   Provisions as to exercise of power of sale

(1)   The power of sale conferred by this Act may be exercised by any person for the time being entitled to receive and give a discharge for the mortgage money.

(2)   The power of sale conferred by this Act does not affect the right of foreclosure.

(3)   The mortgagee shall not be answerable for any involuntary loss happening in or about the exercise or execution of the power of sale conferred by this Act, or of any trust connected therewith, or, where the mortgage is executed after the thirty-first day of December, nineteen hundred and eleven, of any power or provision contained in the mortgage deed.

(4)   At any time after the power of sale conferred by this Act has become exercisable the person entitled to exercise the power may demand and recover from any person, other than a person having in the mortgaged property an estate, interest, or right in priority to the mortgage, all

the deeds and documents relating to the property, or to the title thereto, which a purchaser under the power of sale would be entitled to demand and recover from him.

107. Mortgagee's receipts, discharges, etc.

(1) The receipt in writing of a mortgagee shall be a sufficient discharge for any money arising under the power of sale conferred by this Act, or for any money or securities comprised in his mortgage, or arising thereunder; and a person paying or transferring the same to the mortgagee shall not be concerned to inquire whether any money remains due under the mortgage.

(2) Money received by a mortgagee under his mortgage or from the proceeds of securities comprised in his mortgage shall be applied in like manner as in this Act directed respecting money received by him arising from a sale under the power of sale conferred by this Act, but with this variation, that the costs, charges, and expenses payable shall include the costs, charges, and expenses properly incurred of recovering and receiving the money or securities, and of conversion of securities into money, instead of those incident to sale.

108. Amount and application of insurance money

(1) The amount of an insurance effected by a mortgagee against loss or damage by fire under the power in that behalf conferred by this Act shall not exceed the amount specified in the mortgage deed, or, if no amount is therein specified, two third parts of the amount that would be required, in case of total destruction, to restore the property insured.

(2) An insurance shall not, under the power conferred by this Act, be effected by a mortgagee in any of the following cases (namely):
  (i) Where there is a declaration in the mortgage deed that no insurance is required:
  (ii) Where an insurance is kept up by or on behalf of the mortgagor in accordance with the mortgage deed:
  (iii) Where the mortgage deed contains no stipulation respecting insurance, and an insurance is kept up by or on behalf of the mortgagor with the consent of the mortgagee to the amount to which the mortgagee is by this Act authorised to insure.

(3) All money received on an insurance of mortgaged property against loss or damage by fire or otherwise effected under this Act, or any enactment replaced by this Act, or on an insurance for the maintenance of which the mortgagor is liable under the mortgage deed, shall, if the mortgagee so requires, be applied by the mortgagor in making good the loss or damage in respect of which the money is received.

(4) Without prejudice to any obligation to the contrary imposed by law, or by special contract, a mortgagee may require that all money received on an insurance of mortgaged property against loss or damage by fire or otherwise effected under this Act, or any enactment replaced by this Act, or on an insurance for the maintenance of which the mortgagor is liable under the mortgage deed, be applied in or towards the discharge of the mortgage money.

109. Appointment, powers, remuneration and duties of receiver

(1) A mortgagee entitled to appoint a receiver under the power in that behalf conferred by this Act shall not appoint a receiver until he has become entitled to exercise the power of sale conferred by this Act, but may then, by writing under his hand, appoint such person as he thinks fit to be receiver.

(2) A receiver appointed under the powers conferred by this Act, or any enactment replaced by this Act, shall be deemed to be the agent of the mortgagor; and the mortgagor shall be solely responsible for the receiver's acts or defaults unless the mortgage deed otherwise provides.

(3) The receiver shall have power to demand and recover all the income of which he is appointed receiver, by action, distress, or otherwise, in the name either of the mortgagor or of the mortgagee, to the full extent of the estate or interest which the mortgagor could dispose of, and to give effectual receipts accordingly for the same, and to exercise any powers which may have been delegated to him by the mortgagee pursuant to this Act.

(4) A person paying money to the receiver shall not be concerned to inquire whether any case has happened to authorise the receiver to act.

(5)   The receiver may be removed, and a new receiver may be appointed, from time to time by the mortgagee by writing under his hand.

(6)   The receiver shall be entitled to retain out of any money received by him, for his remuneration, and in satisfaction of all costs, charges, and expenses incurred by him as receiver, a commission at such rate, not exceeding five per centum on the gross amount of all money received, as is specified in his appointment, and if no rate is so specified, then at the rate of five per centum on that gross amount, or at such other rate as the court thinks fit to allow, on application made by him for that purpose.

(7)   The receiver shall, if so directed in writing by the mortgagee, insure to the extent, if any, to which the mortgagee might have insured and keep insured against loss or damage by fire, out of the money received by him, any building, effects, or property comprised in the mortgage, whether affixed to the freehold or not, being of an insurable nature.

(8)   Subject to the provisions of this Act as to the application of insurance money, the receiver shall apply all money received by him as follows, namely:

  (i)   In discharge of all rents, taxes, rates, and outgoings whatever affecting the mortgaged property; and

  (ii)   In keeping down all annual sums or other payments, and the interest on all principal sums, having priority to the mortgage in right whereof he is receiver; and

  (iii) In payment of his commission, and of the premiums on fire, life, or other insurances, if any, properly payable under the mortgage deed or under this Act, and the cost of executing necessary or proper repairs directed in writing by the mortgagee; and

  (iv)   In payment of the interest accruing due in respect of any principal money due under the mortgage; and

  (v)   In or towards discharge of the principal money if so directed in writing by the mortgagee;

and shall pay the residue, if any, of the money received by him to the person who, but for the possession of the receiver, would have been entitled to receive the income of which he is appointed receiver, or who is otherwise entitled to the mortgaged property.

110.   Effect of bankruptcy of the mortgagor on the power to sell or appoint a receiver

(1)   Where the statutory or express power for a mortgagee either to sell or to appoint a receiver is made exercisable by reason of the mortgagor . . . being adjudged a bankrupt, such power shall not be exercised only on account of the . . . adjudication, without the leave of the court.

(2)   This section applies only where the mortgage deed is executed after the commencement of this Act; . . . .

111.   Effect of advance on joint account

(1)   Where—

  (a)   in a mortgage, or an obligation for payment of money, or a transfer of a mortgage or of such an obligation, the sum, or any part of the sum, advanced or owing is expressed to be advanced by or owing to more persons than one out of money, or as money, belonging to them on a joint account; or

  (b)   a mortgage, or such an obligation, or such a transfer is made to more persons than one, jointly;

the mortgage money, or other money or money's worth, for the time being due to those persons on the mortgage or obligation, shall, as between them and the mortgagor or obligor, be deemed to be and remain money or money's worth belonging to those persons on a joint account; and the receipt in writing of the survivors or last survivor of them, or of the personal representative of the last survivor, shall be a complete discharge for all money or money's worth for the time being due, notwithstanding any notice to the payer of a severance of the joint account.

(2)   This section applies if and so far as a contrary intention is not expressed in the mortgage, obligation, or transfer, and has effect subject to the terms of the mortgage, obligation, or transfer, and to the provisions therein contained.

(3)   This section applies to any mortgage obligation or transfer made after the thirty-first day of December, eighteen hundred and eighty-one.

113.   Notice of trusts affecting mortgage debts

(1)   A person dealing in good faith with a mortgagee, or with the mortgagor if the mortgage has been discharged released or postponed as to the whole or any part of the mortgaged property, shall not be concerned with any trust at any time affecting the mortgage money or the income thereof, whether or not he has notice of the trust, and may assume unless the contrary is expressly stated in the instruments relating to the mortgage—

(a)   that the mortgagees (if more than one) are or were entitled to the mortgage money on a joint account; and

(b)   that the mortgagee has or had power to give valid receipts for the purchase money or mortgage money and the income thereof (including any arrears of interest) and to release or postpone the priority of the mortgage debt or any part thereof or to deal with the same or the mortgaged property or any part thereof;

without investigating the equitable title to the mortgage debt or the appointment or discharge of trustees in reference thereto.

(2)   This section applies to mortgages made before or after the commencement of this Act, but only as respects dealings effected after such commencement.

(3)   This section does not affect the liability of any person in whom the mortgage debt is vested for the purposes of any trust to give effect to that trust.

114.   Transfers of mortgages

(1)   A deed executed by a mortgagee purporting to transfer his mortgage or the benefit thereof shall, unless a contrary intention is therein expressed, and subject to any provisions therein contained, operate to transfer to the transferee—

(a)   the right to demand, sue for, recover, and give receipts for, the mortgage money or the unpaid part thereof, and the interest then due, if any, and thenceforth to become due thereon; and

(b)   the benefit of all securities for the same, and the benefit of and the right to sue on all covenants with the mortgagee, and the right to exercise all powers of the mortgagee; and

(c)   all the estate and interest in the mortgaged property then vested in the mortgagee subject to redemption or cesser, but as to such estate and interest subject to the right of redemption then subsisting.

(2)   In this section 'transferee' includes his personal representatives and assigns.

. . .

(4)   This section applies, whether the mortgage transferred was made before or after the commencement of this Act, but applies only to transfers made after the commencement of this Act.

(5)   This section does not extend to a transfer of a bill of sale of chattels by way of security.

115.   Reconveyances of mortgages by endorsed receipts

(1)   A receipt endorsed on, written at the foot of, or annexed to, a mortgage for all money thereby secured, which states the name of the person who pays the money and is executed by the chargee by way of legal mortgage or the person in whom the mortgaged property is vested and who is legally entitled to give a receipt for the mortgage money shall operate, without any reconveyance, surrender, or release—

(a)   Where a mortgage takes effect by demise or subdemise, as a surrender of the term, so as to determine the term or merge the same in the reversion immediately expectant thereon;

(b)   Where the mortgage does not take effect by demise or subdemise, as a reconveyance thereof to the extent of the interest which is the subject matter of the mortgage, to the person who immediately before the execution of the receipt was entitled to the equity of redemption;

and in either case, as a discharge of the mortgaged property from all principal money and interest secured by, and from all claims under the mortgage, but without prejudice to any term or other interest which is paramount to the estate or interest of the mortgagee or other person in whom the mortgaged property was vested.

(2) Provided that, where by the receipt the money appears to have been paid by a person who is not entitled to the immediate equity of redemption, the receipt shall operate as if the benefit of the mortgage had by deed been transferred to him; unless—

   (a) it is otherwise expressly provided; or

   (b) the mortgage is paid off out of capital money, or other money in the hands of a personal representative or trustee properly applicable for the discharge of the mortgage,

   and it is not expressly provided that the receipt is to operate as a transfer.

(3) Nothing in this section confers on a mortgagor a right to keep alive a mortgage paid off by him, so as to affect prejudicially any subsequent incumbrancer; and where there is no right to keep the mortgage alive, the receipt does not operate as a transfer.

(4) This section does not affect the right of any person to require a reassignment, surrender, release, or transfer to be executed in lieu of a receipt.

   . . .

(6) In a receipt given under this section the same covenants shall be implied as if the person who executes the receipt had by deed been expressed to convey the property as mortgagee, subject to any interest which is paramount to the mortgage.

(7) Where the mortgage consists of a mortgage and a further charge or of more than one deed, it shall be sufficient for the purposes of this section, if the receipt refers either to all the deeds whereby the mortgage money is secured or to the aggregate amount of the mortgage money thereby secured and for the time being owing, and is endorsed on, written at the foot of, or annexed to, one of the mortgage deeds.

(8) This section applies to the discharge of a charge by way of legal mortgage, and to the discharge of a mortgage, whether made by way of statutory mortgage or not, executed before or after the commencement of this Act, but only as respects discharges effected after such commencement.

(9) The provisions of this section relating to the operation of a receipt shall (in substitution for the like statutory provisions relating to receipts given by or on behalf of a building . . . society) apply to the discharge of a mortgage made to any such society, provided that the receipt is executed in the manner required by the statute relating to the society . . .

(10) This section does not apply to the discharge of a registered charge (within the meaning of the Land Registration Act 2002).

(11) In this section 'mortgaged property' means the property remaining subject to the mortgage at the date of the receipt.

116.　Cesser of mortgage terms

Without prejudice to the right of a tenant for life or other person having only a limited interest in the equity of redemption to require a mortgage to be kept alive by transfer or otherwise, a mortgage term shall, when the money secured by the mortgage has been discharged, become a satisfied term and shall cease.

Rentcharges

121.　Remedies for the recovery of annual sums charged on land

(1) Where a person is entitled to receive out of any land, or out of the income of any land, any annual sum, payable half-yearly or otherwise, whether charged on the land or on the income of the land, and whether by way of rentcharge of otherwise not being rent incident to a reversion, then, subject and without prejudice to all estates, interests, and rights having priority to the annual sum, the person entitled to receive the annual sum shall have such remedies for recovering and compelling payment thereof as are described in this section, as far as those remedies might have been conferred by the instrument under which the annual sum arises, but not further.

(2) If at any time the annual sum or any part thereof is unpaid for twenty-one days next after the time appointed for any payment in respect thereof, the person entitled to receive the annual sum may enter into and distrain on the land charged or any part thereof, and dispose according to law of any distress found, to the intent that thereby or otherwise the annual sum and all arrears thereof, and all costs and expenses occasioned by non-payment thereof, may be fully paid.

(3) If at any time the annual sum or any part thereof is unpaid for forty days next after the time appointed for any payment in respect thereof, then, although no legal demand has been made for payment thereof, the person entitled to receive the annual sum may enter into possession of and hold the land charged or any part thereof, and take the income thereof, until thereby or otherwise the annual sum and all arrears thereof due at the time of his entry, or afterwards becoming due during his continuance in possession, and all costs and expenses occasioned by nonpayment of the annual sum, are fully paid; and such possession when taken shall be without impeachment of waste.

(4) In the like case the person entitled to the annual sum, whether taking possession or not, may also by deed demise the land charged, or any part thereof, to a trustee for a term of years, with or without impeachment of waste, on trust, by all or any of the means hereinafter mentioned, or by any other reasonable means, to raise and pay the annual sum and all arrears thereof due or to become due, and all costs and expenses occasioned by nonpayment of the annual sum, or incurred in compelling or obtaining payment thereof, or otherwise relating thereto, including the costs of the preparation and execution of the deed of demise, and the costs of the execution of the trusts of that deed:

Provided that this subsection shall not authorise the creation of a legal term of years absolute after the commencement of this Act, save where the annual sum is a rentcharge held for a legal estate.

The surplus, if any, of the money raised, or of the income received, under the trusts of the deed shall be paid to the person for the time being entitled to the land therein comprised in reversion immediately expectant on the term thereby created.

The means by which such annual sum, arrears, costs, and expenses may be raised includes—

(a) the creation of a legal mortgage or a sale (effected by assignment or subdemise) of the term created in the land charged or any part thereof,

(b) the receipt of the income of the land comprised in the term.

(5) This section applies only if and as far as a contrary intention is not expressed in the instrument under which the annual sum arises, and has effect subject to the terms of that instrument and to the provisions therein contained.

(6) The rule of law relating to perpetuities does not apply to any powers or remedies conferred by this section . . .

(7) . . .

122. Creation of rentcharges charged on another rentcharge and remedies for recovery thereof

(1) A rentcharge or other annual sum (not being rent incident to a reversion) payable half yearly or otherwise may be granted, reserved, charged or created out of or on another rentcharge or annual sum (not being rent incident to a reversion) charged on or payable out of land or on or out of the income of land, in like manner as the same could have been made to issue out of land.

(2) If at any time the annual sum so created or any part thereof is unpaid for twenty-one days next after the time appointed for any payment in respect thereof, the person entitled to receive the annual sum shall (without prejudice to any prior interest or charge) have power to appoint a receiver of the annual sum charged or any part thereof, and the provisions of this Act relating to the appointment, powers, remuneration and duties of a receiver, shall apply in like manner as if such person were a mortgagee entitled to exercise the power of sale conferred by this Act, and the annual sum charged were the mortgaged property and the person entitled thereto were the mortgagor.

(3) The power to appoint a receiver conferred by this section shall (where the annual sum is charged on a rentcharge) take effect in substitution for the remedies conferred, in the case of annual sums charged on land, by the last preceding section, but subsection (6) of that section shall apply and have effect as if herein re-enacted and in terms made applicable to the powers conferred by this section.

(4) This section applies to annual sums expressed to be created before as well as after the commencement of this Act, and, but without prejudice to any order of the court made before the commencement of this Act, operates to confirm any annual sum which would have been validly created if this section had been in force.

PART IV

EQUITABLE INTERESTS AND THINGS IN ACTION

130. . . . Entailed interests in real and personal property

(1)–(3) . . .

(4) In default of and subject to the execution of a disentailing assurance or the exercise of the testamentary power conferred by this Act, an entailed interest (to the extent of the property affected) shall devolve as an equitable interest, from time to time, upon the persons who would have been successively entitled thereto as the heirs of the body (either generally or of a particular class) of the tenant in tail or other person, or as tenant by the curtesy, if the entailed interest had, before the commencement of this Act, been limited in respect of freehold land governed by the general law in force immediately before such commencement, and such law had remained unaffected.

(5) Where personal chattels are settled without reference to settled land on trusts creating entailed interests therein, the trustees, with the consent of the usufructuary for the time being if of full age, may sell the chattels or any of them, and the net proceeds of any such sale shall be held in trust for and shall go to the same persons successively, in the same manner and for the same interests, as the chattels sold would have been held and gone if they had not been sold, and the income of investments representing such proceeds of sale shall be applied accordingly.

(6) . . .

(7) In this Act where the context so admits 'entailed interest' includes an estate tail (now made to take effect as an equitable interest) created before the commencement of this Act.

131. Abolition of the rule in Shelley's case

Where by any instrument coming into operation after the commencement of this Act an interest in any property is expressed to be given to the heir or heirs or issue or any particular heir or any class of the heirs or issue of any person in words which, but for this section (and paragraph 5 of Schedule 1 of the Trusts of Land and Appointment of Trustees Act 1996) would, under the rule of law known as the Rule in Shelley's case, have operated to give to that person an interest in fee simple or an entailed interest, such words shall operate in equity as words of purchase and not of limitation, and shall be construed and have effect accordingly, and in the case of an interest in any property expressed to be given to an heir or heirs or any particular heir or class of heirs, the same person or persons shall take as would in the case of freehold land have answered that description under the general law in force before the commencement of this Act.

132. As to heirs taking by purchase

(1) A limitation of real or personal property in favour of the heir, either general or special, of a deceased person which, if limited in respect of freehold land before the commencement of this Act, would have conferred on the heir an estate in the land by purchase, shall operate to confer a corresponding equitable interest in the property on the person who would, if the general law in force immediately before such commencement had remained unaffected, have answered the description of the heir, either general or special, of the deceased in respect of his freehold land, either at the death of the deceased or at the time named in the limitation, as the case may require.

(2)   This section applies whether the deceased person dies before or after the commencement of this Act, but only applies to limitations or trusts created by an instrument coming into operation after such commencement.

134.   Restriction on executory limitations

(1)   Where there is a person entitled to—

(a)   an equitable interest in land for an estate in fee simple or for any less interest not being an entailed interest, or

(b)   any interest in other property, not being an entailed interest,

with an executory limitation over on default or failure of all or any of his issue, whether within or at any specified period or time or not, that executory limitation shall be or become void and incapable of taking effect, if and as soon as there is living any issue who has attained the age of eighteen years of the class on default or failure whereof the limitation over was to take effect.

(2)   This section applies where the executory limitation is contained in an instrument coming into operation after the thirty-first day of December, eighteen hundred and eighty-two, save that, as regards instruments coming into operation before the commencement of this Act, it only applies to limitations of land for an estate in fee, or for a term of years absolute or determinable on life, or for a term of life.

135.   Equitable waste

An equitable interest for life without impeachment of waste does not confer upon the tenant for life any right to commit waste of the description known as equitable waste, unless an intention to confer such right expressly appears by the instrument creating such equitable interest.

136.   Legal assignments of things in action

(1)   Any absolute assignment by writing under the hand of the assignor (not purporting to be by way of charge only) of any debt or other legal thing in action, of which express notice in writing has been given to the debtor, trustee or other person from whom the assignor would have been entitled to claim such debt or thing in action, is effectual in law (subject to equities having priority over the right of the assignee) to pass and transfer from the date of such notice—

(a)   the legal right to such debt or thing in action;

(b)   all legal and other remedies for the same; and

(c)   the power to give a good discharge for the same without the concurrence of the assignor:

Provided that, if the debtor, trustee or other person liable in respect of such debt or thing in action has notice—

(a)   that the assignment is disputed by the assignor or any person claiming under him; or

(b)   of any other opposing or conflicting claims to such debt or thing in action;

he may, if he thinks fit, either call upon the persons making claim thereto to interplead concerning the same, or pay the debt or other thing in action into court under the provisions of the Trustee Act, 1925.

(2)   This section does not affect the provisions of the Policies of Assurance Act, 1867.

(3)   The county court has jurisdiction (including power to receive payments of money or securities into court) under the proviso to subsection (1) of this section where the amount or value of the debt or thing in action does not exceed £30,000.

137.   Dealings with life interests, reversions and other equitable interests

(1)   The law applicable to dealings with equitable things in action which regulates the priority of competing interests therein, shall, as respects dealings with equitable interests in land, capital money, and securities representing capital money effected after the commencement of this Act, apply to and regulate the priority of competing interests therein.

This subsection applies whether or not the money or securities are in court.

(2)   (i)   In the case of a dealing with an equitable interest in settled land, capital money or securities representing capital money, the persons to be served with notice of the

dealing shall be the trustees of the settlement; and where the equitable interest is created by a derivative or subsidiary settlement, the persons to be served with notice shall be the trustees of that settlement.

(ii)   In the case of a dealing with an equitable interest in land subject to a trust of land, or the proceeds of the sale of such land, the persons to be served with notice shall be the trustees.

(iii)   In any other case the person to be served with notice of a dealing with an equitable interest in land shall be the estate owner of the land affected.

The persons on whom notice is served pursuant to this subsection shall be affected thereby in the same manner as if they had been trustees of personal property out of which the equitable interest was created or arose.

This subsection does not apply where the money or securities are in court.

(3)   A notice, otherwise than in writing, given to, or received by, a trustee after the commencement of this Act as respects any dealing with an equitable interest in real or personal property, shall not affect the priority of competing claims of purchasers in that equitable interest.

(4)   Where, as respects any dealing with an equitable interest in real or personal property—

(a)   the trustees are not persons to whom a valid notice of the dealing can be given; or

(b)   there are no trustees to whom a notice can be given; or

(c)   for any other reason a valid notice cannot be served, or cannot be served without unreasonable cost or delay;

a purchaser may at his own cost require that—

(i)   a memorandum of the dealing be endorsed, written on or permanently annexed to the instrument creating the trust;

(ii)   the instrument be produced to him by the person having the possession or custody thereof to prove that a sufficient memorandum has been placed thereon or annexed thereto.

Such memorandum shall, as respects priorities, operate in like manner as if notice in writing of the dealing had been given to trustees duly qualified to receive the notice at the time when the memorandum is placed on or annexed to the instrument creating the trust.

(5)   Where the property affected is settled land, the memorandum shall be placed on or annexed to the trust instrument and not the vesting instrument.

Where the property affected is land subject to a trust of land, the memorandum shall be placed on or annexed to the instrument whereby the equitable interest is created.

(6)   Where the trust is created by statute or by operation of law, or in any other case where there is no instrument whereby the trusts are declared, the instrument under which the equitable interest is acquired or which is evidence of the devolution thereof shall, for the purposes of this section, be deemed the instrument creating the trust.

In particular, where the trust arises by reason of an intestacy, the letters of administration or probate in force when the dealing was effected shall be deemed such instrument.

(7)   Nothing in this section affects any priority acquired before the commencement of this Act.

(8)   Where a notice in writing of a dealing with an equitable interest in real or personal property has been served on a trustee under this section, the trustees from time to time of the property affected shall be entitled to the custody of the notice, and the notice shall be delivered to them by any person who for the time being may have the custody thereof; and subject to the payment of costs, any person interested in the equitable interest may require production of the notice.

(9)   The liability of the estate owner of the legal estate affected to produce documents and furnish information to persons entitled to equitable interests therein shall correspond to the liability of a trustee for sale to produce documents and furnish information to persons entitled to equitable interests in the proceeds of sale of the land.

(10)   This section does not apply until a trust has been created, and in this section 'dealing' includes a disposition by operation of law.

138.   Power to nominate a trust corporation to receive notices

(1)   By any settlement or other instrument creating a trust, a trust corporation may be nominated to whom notices of dealings affecting real or personal property may be given, whether or not under the foregoing section, and in default of such nomination the trustees (if any) of the instrument, or the court on the application of any person interested, may make the nomination.

(2)   The person having the possession or custody of any instrument on which notices under that section may be endorsed shall cause the name of the trust corporation to whom notices may be given to be endorsed upon that instrument.

(3)   Notice given to any trust corporation whose name is so endorsed shall operate in the same way as a notice or endorsement under the foregoing section.

(4)   Where a trust corporation is acting for the purposes of this section a notice given to a trustee of the trust instrument of a dealing relating to the trust property shall forthwith be delivered or sent by post by the trustee to the trust corporation, and until received by the corporation shall not affect any priority.

(5)   A trust corporation shall not be nominated for the purposes of this section—

(a)   unless that corporation consents to act; or

(b)   where that corporation has any beneficial interest in or charge upon the trust property; or

(c)   where a trust corporation is acting as the trustee or one of the trustees of the instrument creating the trust.

(6)   Where a trust corporation acting for the purposes of this section becomes entitled to any beneficial interest in or charge upon the trust property, another trust corporation shall be nominated in its place and all documents relating to notices affecting the trust shall be delivered to the corporation so nominated.

(7)   A trust corporation acting for the purposes of this section shall be bound to keep a separate register of notices of dealings in respect of each equitable interest and shall enter therein—

(a)   the date of the notice;

(b)   the name of the person giving the notice;

(c)   short particulars of the equitable interest intended to be affected; and

(d)   short particulars of the effect of the dealing if mentioned in the notice.

(8)   The trust corporation may, before making any entry in the register, require the applicant to pay a fee not exceeding the prescribed fee.

(9)   Subject to the payment of a fee not exceeding the prescribed fee, the trust corporation shall permit any person who would, if the corporation had been the trustee of the trust instrument, have been entitled to inspect notices served on the trustee, to inspect and take copies of the register and any notices held by the corporation.

(10)   Subject to the payment by the applicant of a fee not exceeding the prescribed fee, the trust corporation shall reply to all inquiries respecting notices received by the corporation in like manner and in the same circumstances as if the corporation had been the trustee of the trust instrument.

(11)   In this section 'prescribed fee' means the fee prescribed by the Lord Chancellor, in cases where the Public Trustee acts as a trust corporation for the purposes of this section.

PART V
LEASES AND TENANCIES

139.   Effect of extinguishment of reversion

(1)   Where a reversion expectant on a lease of land is surrendered or merged, the estate or interest which as against the lessee for the time being confers the next vested right to the land, shall be deemed the reversion for the purpose of preserving the same incidents and obligations as would have affected the original reversion had there been no surrender or merger thereof.

(2)   This section applies to surrenders or mergers effected after the first day of October, eighteen hundred and forty-five.

140.   Apportionment of conditions on severance

(1)   Notwithstanding the severance by conveyance, surrender, or otherwise of the reversionary estate in any land comprised in a lease, and notwithstanding the avoidance or cesser in any other manner of the term granted by a lease as to part only of the land comprised therein, every condition or right of re-entry, and every other condition contained in the lease, shall be apportioned, and shall remain annexed to the severed parts of the reversionary estate as severed, and shall be in force with respect to the term whereon each severed part is reversionary, or the term in the part of the land as to which the term has not been surrendered, or has not been avoided or has not otherwise ceased, in like manner as if the land comprised in each severed part, or the land as to which the term remains subsisting, as the case may be, had alone originally been comprised in the lease.

(2)   In this section 'right of re-entry' includes a right to determine the lease by notice to quit or otherwise; but where the notice is served by a person entitled to a severed part of the reversion so that it extends to part only of the land demised, the lessee may within one month determine the lease in regard to the rest of the land by giving to the owner of the reversionary estate therein a counter notice expiring at the same time as the original notice.

(3)   This section applies to leases made before or after the commencement of this Act and whether the severance of the reversionary estate or the partial avoidance or cesser of the term was effected before or after such commencement:

Provided that, where the lease was made before the first day of January eighteen hundred and eighty-two nothing in this section shall affect the operation of a severance of the reversionary estate or partial avoidance or cesser of the term which was effected before the commencement of this Act.

141.   Rent and benefit of lessee's covenants to run with the reversion

(1)   Rent reserved by a lease, and the benefit of every covenant or provision therein contained, having reference to the subject-matter thereof, and on the lessee's part to be observed or performed, and every condition of re-entry and other condition therein contained, shall be annexed and incident to and shall go with the reversionary estate in the land, or in any part thereof, immediately expectant on the term granted by the lease, notwithstanding severance of that reversionary estate, and without prejudice to any liability affecting a covenantor or his estate.

(2)   Any such rent, covenant or provision shall be capable of being recovered, received, enforced, and taken advantage of, by the person from time to time entitled, subject to the term, to the income of the whole or any part, as the case may require, of the land leased.

(3)   Where that person becomes entitled by conveyance or otherwise, such rent, covenant or provision may be recovered, received, enforced or taken advantage of by him notwithstanding that he becomes so entitled after the condition of re-entry of forfeiture has become enforceable, but this subsection does not render enforceable any condition of re-entry or other condition waived or released before such person becomes entitled as aforesaid.

(4)   This section applies to leases made before or after the commencement of this Act, but does not affect the operation of—

(a)   any severance of the reversionary estate; or

(b)   any acquisition by conveyance or otherwise of the right to receive or enforce any rent covenant or provision;

effected before the commencement of this Act.

142.   Obligation of lessor's covenants to run with reversion

(1)   The obligation under a condition or of a covenant entered into by a lessor with reference to the subject-matter of the lease shall, if and as far as the lessor has power to bind the reversionary estate immediately expectant on the term granted by the lease, be annexed and incident to and shall go with that reversionary estate, or the several parts thereof, notwithstanding severance of that reversionary estate, and may be taken advantage of and enforced by the person in whom the term is from time to time vested by conveyance,

devolution in law, or otherwise; and, if and as far as the lessor has power to bind the person from time to time entitled to that reversionary estate, the obligation aforesaid may be taken advantage of and enforced against any person so entitled.

(2) This section applies to leases made before or after the commencement of this Act, whether the severance of the reversionary estate was effected before or after such commencement:

Provided that, where the lease was made before the first day of January eighteen hundred and eighty-two, nothing in this section shall affect the operation of any severance of the reversionary estate effected before such commencement.

This section takes effect without prejudice to any liability affecting a covenantor or his estate.

143. Effect of licences granted to lessees

(1) Where a licence is granted to a lessee to do any act, the licence, unless otherwise expressed, extends only—

(a) to the permission actually given; or

(b) to the specific breach of any provision or covenant referred to; or

(c) to any other matter thereby specifically authorised to be done; and the licence does not prevent any proceeding for any subsequent breach unless otherwise specified in the licence.

(2) Notwithstanding any such licence—

(a) All rights under covenants and powers of re-entry contained in the lease remain in full force and are available as against any subsequent breach of covenant, condition or other matter not specifically authorised or waived, in the same manner as if no licence had been granted; and

(b) The condition or right of entry remains in force in all respects as if the licence had not been granted, save in respect of the particular matter authorised to be done.

(3) Where in any lease there is a power or condition of re-entry on the lessee assigning, subletting or doing any other specified act without a licence, and a licence is granted—

(a) to any one or two or more lessees to do any act, or to deal with his equitable share or interest; or

(b) to any lessee, or to any one of two or more lessees to assign or underlet part only of the property, or to do any act in respect of part only of the property; the licence does not operate to extinguish the right of entry in case of any breach of covenant or condition by the co-lessees of the other shares or interests in the property, or by the lessee or lessees of the rest of the property (as the case may be) in respect of such shares or interests or remaining property, but the right of entry remains in force in respect of the shares, interests or property not the subject of the licence.

This subsection does not authorise the grant after the commencement of this Act of a licence to create an undivided share in a legal estate.

(4) This section applies to licences granted after the thirteenth day of August, eighteen hundred and fifty-nine.

144. No fine to be exacted for licence to assign

In all leases containing a covenant, condition, or agreement against assigning, underletting, or parting with the possession, or disposing of the land or property leased without licence or consent, such covenant, condition, or agreement shall, unless the lease contains an express provision to the contrary, be deemed to be subject to a proviso to the effect that no fine or sum of money in the nature of a fine shall be payable for or in respect of such licence or consent; but this proviso does not preclude the right to require the payment of a reasonable sum in respect of any legal or other expense incurred in relation to such licence or consent.

145. Lessee to give notice of ejectment to lessor

Every lessee to whom there is delivered any writ for the recovery of premises demised to or held by him, or to whose knowledge any such writ comes, shall forthwith give notice thereof to his lessor or his bailiff or receiver, and, if he fails so to do, he shall be liable to forfeit to the person of whom he holds the premises an amount equal to the value of three years' improved or rack rent of the premises, to be recovered by action in any court having jurisdiction in respect of claims for such an amount.

146. Restrictions on and relief against forfeiture of leases and underleases

(1) A right of re-entry or forfeiture under any proviso or stipulation in a lease for a breach of any covenant or condition in the lease shall not be enforceable, by action or otherwise, unless and until the lessor serves on the lessee a notice—

(a) specifying the particular breach complained of; and

(b) if the breach is capable of remedy, requiring the lessee to remedy the breach; and

(c) in any case, requiring the lessee to make compensation in money for the breach;

and the lessee fails, within a reasonable time thereafter, to remedy the breach, if it is capable of remedy, and to make reasonable compensation in money, to the satisfaction of the lessor, for the breach.

(2) Where a lessor is proceeding, by action or otherwise, to enforce such a right of re-entry or forfeiture, the lessee may, in the lessor's action, if any, or in any action brought by himself, apply to the court for relief; and the court may grant or refuse relief, as the court, having regard to the proceedings and conduct of the parties under the foregoing provisions of this section, and to all the other circumstances, thinks fit; and in case of relief may grant it on such terms, if any, as to costs, expenses, damages, compensation, penalty, or otherwise, including the granting of an injunction to restrain any like breach in the future, as the court, in the circumstances of each case, thinks fit.

(3) A lessor shall be entitled to recover as a debt due to him from a lessee, and in addition to damages (if any), all reasonable costs and expenses properly incurred by the lessor in the employment of a solicitor and surveyor or valuer, or otherwise, in reference to any breach giving rise to a right of re-entry or forfeiture which, at the request of the lessee, is waived by the lessor, or from which the lessee is relieved, under the provisions of this Act.

(4) Where a lessor is proceeding by action or otherwise to enforce a right of re-entry or forfeiture under any covenant, proviso, or stipulation in a lease, or for non-payment of rent, the court may, on application by any person claiming as under-lessee any estate or interest in the property comprised in the lease or any part thereof, either in the lessor's action (if any) or in any action brought by such person for that purpose, make an order vesting, for the whole term of the lease or any less term, the property comprised in the lease or any part thereof in any person entitled as under-lessee to any estate or interest in such property upon such conditions as to execution of any deed or other document, payment of rent, costs, expenses, damages, compensation, giving security, or otherwise, as the court in the circumstances of each case may think fit, but in no case shall any such under-lessee be entitled to require a lease to be granted to him for any longer than he had under his original sub-lease.

(5) For the purposes of this section—

(a) 'Lease' includes an original or derivative under-lease; also an agreement for a lease where the lessee has become entitled to have his lease granted; also a grant at a fee arm rent, or securing a rent by condition;

(b) 'Lessee' includes an original or derivative under-lessee, and the persons deriving title under a lessee; also a grantee under any such grant as aforesaid and the persons deriving title under him;

(c) 'Lessor' includes an original or derivative under-lessor, and the persons deriving title under a lessor; also a person making such grant as aforesaid and the persons deriving title under him;

(d) 'Under-lease' includes an agreement for an under-lease where the under-lessee has become entitled to have his under-lease granted;

(e) 'Under-lessee' includes any person deriving title under an under-lessee.

(6)   This section applies although the proviso or stipulation under which the right of re-entry or forfeiture accrues is inserted in the lease in pursuance of the directions of any Act of Parliament.

(7)   For the purposes of this section a lease limited to continue as long only as the lessee abstains from committing a breach of covenant shall be and take effect as a lease to continue for any longer term for which it could subsist, but determinable by a proviso for re-entry on such a breach.

(8)   This section does not extend—

(i)   To a covenant or condition against assigning, underletting, parting with the possession, or disposing of the land leased where the breach occurred before the commencement of this Act; or

(ii)   In the case of a mining lease, to a covenant or condition for allowing the lessor to have access to or inspect books, accounts, records, weighing machines or other things, or to enter or inspect the mine or the workings thereof.

(9)   This section does not apply to a condition for forfeiture on the bankruptcy of the lessee or on taking in execution of the lessee's interest if contained in a lease of—

(a)   Agricultural or pastoral land;

(b)   Mines or minerals;

(c)   A house used or intended to be used as a public-house or beershop;

(d)   A house let as a dwelling-house, with the use of any furniture, books, works of art, or other chattels not being in the nature of fixtures;

(e)   Any property with respect to which the personal qualifications of the tenant are of importance for the preservation of the value or character of the property, or on the ground of neighbourhood to the lessor, or to any person holding under him.

(10)   Where a condition of forfeiture on the bankruptcy of the lessee or on taking in execution of the lessee's interest is contained in any lease, other than a lease of any of the classes mentioned in the last sub-section, then—

(a)   if the lessee's interest is sold within one year from the bankruptcy or taking in execution, this section applies to the forfeiture condition aforesaid;

(b)   if the lessee's interest is not sold before the expiration of that year, this section only applies to the forfeiture condition aforesaid during the first year from the date of the bankruptcy or taking in execution.

(11)   This section does not, save as otherwise mentioned, affect the law relating to re-entry or forfeiture or relief in case of non-payment of rent.

(12)   This section has effect notwithstanding any stipulation to the contrary.

(13)   The county court has jurisdiction under this section . . . .

147.   Relief against notice to effect decorative repairs

(1)   After a notice is served on a lessee relating to the internal decorative repairs to a house or other building, he may apply to the court for relief, and if, having regard to all the circumstances of the case (including in particular the length of the lessee's term or interest remaining unexpired), the court is satisfied that the notice is unreasonable, it may, by order, wholly or partially relieve the lessee from liability for such repairs.

(2)   This section does not apply:—

(i)   where the liability arises under an express covenant or agreement to put the property in a decorative state of repair and the covenant or agreement has never been performed;

(ii)   to any matter necessary or proper—

(a)   for putting or keeping the property in a sanitary condition, or

(b)   for the maintenance or preservation of the structure;

(iii) to any statutory liability to keep a house in all respects reasonably fit for human habitation;

(iv) to any covenant or stipulation to yield up the house or other building in a specified state of repair at the end of the term.

(3)   In this section 'lease' includes an underlease and an agreement for a lease, and 'lessee' has a corresponding meaning and includes any person liable to effect the repairs.

(4)   This section applies whether the notice is served before or after the commencement of this Act, and has effect notwithstanding any stipulation to the contrary.

(5)   The county court has jurisdiction under this section . . . .

148.   Waiver of a covenant in a lease

(1)   Where any actual waiver by a lessor or the persons deriving title under him of the benefit of any covenant or condition in any lease is proved to have taken place in any particular instance, such waiver shall not be deemed to extend to any instance, or to any breach of covenant or condition save that to which such waiver specially relates, nor operate as a general waiver of the benefit of any such covenant or condition.

(2)   This section applies unless a contrary intention appears and extends to waivers effected after the twenty-third day of July, eighteen hundred and sixty.

149.   Abolition of interesse termini, and as to reversionary leases and leases for lives

(1)   The doctrine of interesse termini is hereby abolished.

(2)   As from the commencement of this Act all terms of years absolute shall, whether the interest is created before or after such commencement, be capable of taking effect at law or in equity, according to the estate interest or powers of the grantor, from the date fixed for commencement of the term, without actual entry.

(3)   A term, at a rent or granted in consideration of a fine, limited after the commencement of this Act to take effect more than twenty-one years from the date of the instrument purporting to create it, shall be void, and any contract made after such commencement to create such a term shall likewise be void; but this subsection does not apply to any term taking effect in equity under a settlement, or created out of an equitable interest under a settlement, or under an equitable power for mortgage, indemnity or other like purposes.

(4)   Nothing in subsections (1) and (2) of this section prejudicially affects the right of any person to recover any rent or to enforce or take advantage of any covenants or conditions, or, as respects terms or interests created before the commencement of this Act, operates to vary any statutory or other obligations imposed in respect of such terms or interests.

(5)   Nothing in this Act affects the rule of law that a legal term, whether or not being a mortgage term, may be created to take effect in reversion expectant on a longer term, which rule is hereby confirmed.

(6)   Any lease or underlease, at a rent, or in consideration of a fine, for life or lives or for any term of years determinable with life or lives, or on the marriage of the lessee or on the formation of a civil partnership between the lessee and another person, or any contract therefor, made before or after the commencement of this Act, or created by virtue of Part V. of the Law of Property Act, 1922, shall take effect as a lease, underlease or contract therefor, for a term of ninety years determinable after the death or marriage of, or the formation of a civil partnership by, the original lessee or the survivor of the original lessees, by at least one month's notice in writing given to determine the same on one of the quarter days applicable to the tenancy, either by the lessor or the persons deriving title under him, to the person entitled to the leasehold interest, or if no such person is in existence by affixing the same to the premises, or by the lessee or other persons in whom the leasehold interest is vested to the lessor or the persons deriving title under him:
      Provided that—

(a)   this subsection shall not apply to any term taking effect in equity under a settlement or created out of an equitable interest under a settlement for mortgage, indemnity, or other like purposes;

(b)   the person in whom the leasehold interest is vested by virtue of Part V of the Law of Property Act, 1922, shall, for the purposes of this subsection, be deemed an original lessee;

(c)   if the lease, underlease, or contract therefor is made determinable on the dropping of the lives of persons other than or besides the lessees, then the notice shall be capable of being served after the death of any person or of the survivor of any persons (whether or not including the lessees) on the cesser of whose life or lives the lease, underlease, or contract is made determinable, instead of after the death of the original lessee or of the survivor of the original lessees;

    (d)   if there are no quarter days specially applicable to the tenancy, notice may be given to determine the tenancy on one of the usual quarter days.

(7)   Subsection (8) applies where a lease, underlease or contract—

    (a)   relates to commonhold land, and

    (b)   would take effect by virtue of subsection (6) as a lease, underlease or contract of the kind mentioned in that subsection.

(8)   The lease, underlease or contract shall be treated as if it purported to be a lease, underlease or contract of the kind referred to in subsection 7(b) (and sections 17 and 18 of the Commonhold and Leasehold Reform Act 2002 (residential and non-residential leases) shall apply accordingly).

150. Surrender of a lease, without prejudice to underleases with a view to the grant of a new lease

(1)   A lease may be surrendered with a view to the acceptance of a new lease in place thereof, without a surrender of any under-lease derived thereout.

(2)   A new lease may be granted and accepted, in place of any lease so surrendered, without any such surrender of an under-lease as aforesaid, and the new lease operates as if all under-leases derived out of the surrendered lease had been surrendered before the surrender of that lease was effected.

(3)   The lessee under the new lease and any person deriving title under him is entitled to the same rights and remedies in respect of the rent reserved by and the covenants, agreements and conditions contained in any under-lease as if the original lease had not been surrendered but was or remained vested in him.

(4)   Each under-lessee and any person deriving title under him is entitled to hold and enjoy the land comprised in his under-lease (subject to the payment of any rent reserved by and to the observance of the covenants agreements and conditions contained in the under-lease) as if the lease out of which the under-lease was derived had not been surrendered.

(5)   The lessor granting the new lease and any person deriving title under him is entitled to the same remedies, by distress or entry in and upon the land comprised in any such under-lease for rent reserved by or for breach of any covenant, agreement or condition contained in the new lease (so far only as the rents reserved by or the covenants, agreements or conditions contained in the new lease do not exceed or impose greater burdens than those reserved by or contained in the original lease out of which the under-lease is derived) as he would have had—

    (a)   If the original lease had remained on foot; or

    (b)   If a new under-lease derived out of the new lease had been granted to the under—lessee or a person deriving title under him; as the case may require.

(6)   This section does not affect the powers of the court to give relief against forfeiture.

151. Provision as to attornments by tenants

(1)   Where land is subject to a lease—

    (a)   the conveyance of a reversion in the land expectant on the determination of the lease; or

    (b)   the creation or conveyance of a rentcharge to issue or issuing out of the land;

    shall be valid without any attornment of the lessee:

      Nothing in this subsection—

    (i)   affects the validity of any payment of rent by the lessee to the person making the conveyance or grant before notice of the conveyance or grant is given to him by the person entitled thereunder; or

    (ii)   renders the lessee liable for any breach of covenant to pay rent, on account of his failure to pay rent to the person entitled under the conveyance or grant before such notice is given to the lessee.

(2) An attornment by the lessee in respect of any land to a person claiming to be entitled to the interest in the land of the lessor, if made without the consent of the lessor, shall be void.

This subsection does not apply to an attornment—

(a) made pursuant to a judgment of a court of competent jurisdiction; or

(b) to a mortgagee, by a lessee holding under a lease from the mortgagor where the right of redemption is barred; or

(c) to any other person rightfully deriving title under the lessor.

152. Leases invalidated by reason of non-compliance with terms of powers under which they are granted

(1) Where in the intended exercise of any power of leasing, whether conferred by an Act of Parliament or any other instrument, a lease (in this section referred to as an invalid lease) is granted, which by reason of any failure to comply with the terms of the power is invalid, then—

(a) as against the person entitled after the determination of the interest of the grantor to the reversion; or

(b) as against any other person who, subject to any lease properly granted under the power, would have been entitled to the land comprised in the lease;

the lease, if it was made in good faith, and the lessee has entered, thereunder, shall take effect in equity as a contract for the grant, at the request of the lessee, of a valid lease under the power, of like effect as the invalid lease, subject to such variations as may be necessary in order to comply with the terms of the power:

Provided that a lessee under an invalid lease shall not, by virtue of any such implied contract, be entitled to obtain a variation of the lease if the other persons who would have been bound by the contract are willing and able to confirm the lease without variation.

(2) Where a lease granted in the intended exercise of such a power is invalid by reason of the grantor not having power to grant the lease at the date thereof, but the grantor's interest in the land comprised therein continues after the time when he might, in the exercise of the power, have properly granted a lease in the like terms, the lease shall take effect as a valid lease in like manner as if it had been granted at that time.

(3) Where during the continuance of the possession taken under an invalid lease the person for the time being entitled, subject to such possession, to the land comprised therein or to the rents and profits thereof, is able to confirm the lease without variation, the lessee, or other person who would have been bound by the lease had it been valid, shall, at the request of the person so able to confirm the lease, be bound to accept a confirmation thereof, and thereupon the lease shall have effect and be deemed to have had effect as a valid lease from the grant thereof.

Confirmation under this subsection may be by a memorandum in writing signed by or on behalf of the persons respectively confirming and accepting the confirmation of the lease.

(4) Where a receipt or a memorandum in writing confirming an invalid lease is, upon or before the acceptance of the rent thereunder, signed by or on behalf of the person accepting the rent, that acceptance shall, as against that person, be deemed to be a confirmation of the lease.

(5) The foregoing provisions of this section do not affect prejudicially—

(a) any right of action or other right or remedy to which, but for those provisions or any enactment replaced by those provisions, the lessee named in an invalid lease would or might have been entitled under any covenant on the part of the grantor for title or quiet enjoyment contained therein or implied thereby; or

(b) any right of re-entry or other right or remedy to which, but for those provisions or any enactment replaced thereby, the grantor or other person for the time being entitled to the reversion expectant on the termination of the lease, would or might have been entitled by reason of any breach of the covenants, conditions or provisions contained in the lease and binding on the lessee.

(6) Where a valid power of leasing is vested in or may be exercised by a person who grants a lease which, by reason of the determination of the interest of the grantor or otherwise,

cannot have effect and continuance according to the terms thereof independently of the power, the lease shall for the purposes of this section be deemed to have been granted in the intended exercise of the power although the power is not referred to in the lease.

(7) This section does not apply to a lease of land held on charitable, ecclesiastical or public trusts.

(8) This section takes effect without prejudice to the provision in this Act for the grant of leases in the name and on behalf of the estate owner of the land affected.

153. Enlargement of residue of long terms into fee simple estates

(1) Where a residue unexpired of not less than two hundred years of a term, which, as originally created, was for not less than three hundred years, is subsisting in land, whether being the whole land originally comprised in the term, or part only thereof,—

    (a) without any trust or right of redemption affecting the term in favour of the freeholder, or other person entitled in reversion expectant on the term; and

    (b) without any rent, or with merely a peppercorn rent or other rent having no money value, incident to the reversion, or having had a rent, not being merely a peppercorn rent or other rent having no money value, originally so incident, which subsequently has been released or has become barred by lapse of time, or has in any other way ceased to be payable;

the term may be enlarged into a fee simple in the manner, and subject to the restrictions in this section provided.

(2) This section applies to and includes every such term as aforesaid whenever created, whether or not having the freehold as the immediate reversion thereon; but does not apply to—

    (i) Any term liable to be determined by re-entry for condition broken; or

    (ii) Any term created by subdemise out of a superior term, itself incapable of being enlarged into fee simple.

(3) This section extends to mortgage terms, where the right of redemption is barred.

(4) A rent not exceeding the yearly sum of one pound which has not been collected or paid for a continuous period of twenty years or upwards shall, for the purposes of this section, be deemed to have ceased to be payable:

. . .

(5) Where a rent incident to a reversion expectant on a term to which this section applies is deemed to have ceased to be payable for the purposes aforesaid, no claim for such rent or for any arrears thereof shall be capable of being enforced.

(6) Each of the following persons, namely—

    (i) Any person beneficially entitled in right of the term, whether subject to any incumbrance or not, to possession of any land comprised in the term, and, in the case of a married woman without the concurrence of her husband, whether or not she is entitled for her separate use or as her separate property . . . ;

    (ii) Any person being in receipt of income as trustee, in right of the term, or having the term vested in him as a trustee of land, whether subject to any incumbrance or not;

    (iii) Any person in whom, as personal representative of any deceased person, the term is vested, whether subject to any incumbrance or not;

shall, so far as regards the land to which he is entitled, or in which he is interested in right of the term, in any such character as aforesaid, have power by deed to declare to the effect that, from and after the execution of the deed, the term shall be enlarged into a fee simple.

(7) Thereupon, by virtue of the deed and of this Act, the term shall become and be enlarged accordingly, and the person in whom the term was previously vested shall acquire and have in the land a fee simple instead of the term.

(8) The estate in fee simple so acquired by enlargement shall be subject to all the same trusts, powers, executory limitations over, rights, and equities, and to all the same covenants and provisions relating to user and enjoyment, and to all the same obligations of every kind, as the term would have been subject to if it had not been so enlarged.

(9) But where—

(a)   any land so held for the residue of a term has been settled in trust by reference to other land, being freehold land, so as to go along with that other land, or, in the case of settlements coming into operation before the commencement of this Act, so as to go along with that other land as far as the law permits; and

(b)   at the time of enlargement, the ultimate beneficial interest in the term, whether subject to any subsisting particular estate or not, has not become absolutely and indefeasibly vested in any person, free from charges or powers of charging created by a settlement;

the estate in fee simple acquired as aforesaid shall, without prejudice to any conveyance for value previously made by a person having a contingent or defeasible interest in the term, be liable to be, and shall be, conveyed by means of a subsidiary vesting instrument and settled in like manner as the other land, being freehold land, aforesaid, and until so conveyed and settled shall devolve beneficially as if it had been so conveyed and settled.

(10) The estate in fee simple so acquired shall, whether the term was originally created without impeachment of waste or not, include the fee simple in all mines and minerals which at the time of enlargement have not been severed in right or in fact, or have not been severed or reserved by an inclosure Act or award.

154.   Application of Part V to existing leases

This Part of this Act, except where otherwise expressly provided, applies to leases created before or after the commencement of this Act, and 'lease' includes an under-lease or other tenancy.

PART VI

POWERS

155.   Release of powers simply collateral

A person to whom any power, whether coupled with an interest or not, is given may by deed release, or contract not to exercise, the power.

156.   Disclaimer of power

(1)   A person to whom any power, whether coupled with an interest or not, is given may by deed disclaim the power, and, after disclaimer, shall not be capable of exercising or joining in the exercise of the power.

(2)   On such disclaimer, the power may be exercised by the other person or persons or the survivor or survivors of the other persons, to whom the power is given, unless the contrary is expressed in the instrument creating the power.

157.   Protection of purchasers claiming under certain void appointments

(1)   An instrument purporting to exercise a power of appointment over property, which, in default of and subject to any appointment, is held in trust for a class or number of persons of whom the appointee is one, shall not (save as hereinafter provided) be void on the ground of fraud on the power as against a purchaser in good faith:

Provided that, if the interest appointed exceeds, in amount or value, the interest in such property to which immediately before the execution of the instrument the appointee was presumptively entitled under the trust in default of appointment, having regard to any advances made in his favour and to any hotchpot provision, the protection afforded by this section to a purchaser shall not extend to such excess.

(2)   In this section 'a purchaser in good faith' means a person dealing with an appointee of the age of not less than twenty-five years for valuable consideration in money or money's worth, and without notice of the fraud, or of any circumstances from which, if reasonable inquiries had been made, the fraud might have been discovered.

(3)   Persons deriving title under any purchaser entitled to the benefit of this section shall be entitled to the like benefit.

(4)   This section applies only to dealings effected after the commencement of this Act.

158.   Validation of appointments where objects are excluded or take illusory shares

(1)   No appointment made in exercise of any power to appoint any property among two or more objects shall be invalid on the ground that—

(a)   an unsubstantial, illusory, or nominal share only is appointed to or left unappointed to devolve upon any one or more of the objects of the power; or

(b)   any object of the power is thereby altogether excluded;

but every such appointment shall be valid notwithstanding that any one or more of the objects is not thereby, or in default of appointment, to take any share in the property.

(2)   This section does not affect any provision in the instrument creating the power which declares the amount of any share from which any object of the power is not to be excluded.

(3)   This section applies to appointments made before or after the commencement of this Act.

159.   Execution of powers not testamentary

(1)   A deed executed in the presence of and attested by two or more witnesses (in the manner in which deeds are ordinarily executed and attested) is so far as respects the execution and attestation thereof, a valid execution of a power of appointment by deed or by any instrument in writing, not testamentary, notwithstanding that it is expressly required that a deed or instrument in writing, made in exercise of the power, is to be executed or attested with some additional or other form of execution or attestation or solemnity.

(2)   This section does not operate to defeat any direction in the instrument creating the power that—

(a)   the consent of any particular person is to be necessary to a valid execution;

(b)   in order to give validity to any appointment, any act is to be performed having no relation to the mode of executing and attesting the instrument.

(3)   This section does not prevent the donee of a power from executing it in accordance with the power by writing, or otherwise than by an instrument executed and attested as a deed; and where a power is so executed this section does not apply.

(4)   This section applies to appointments by deed made after the thirteenth day of August, eighteen hundred and fifty-nine.

160.   Application of Part VI to existing powers

This Part of this Act applies to powers created or arising either before or after the commencement of this Act.

PART VII
PERPETUITIES AND ACCUMULATIONS

Perpetuities

161.   Abolition of the double possibility rule

(1)   The rule of law prohibiting the limitation, after a life interest to an unborn person, of an interest in land to the unborn child or other issue of an unborn person is hereby abolished, but without prejudice to any other rule relating to perpetuities.

(2)   This section only applies to limitations or trusts created by an instrument coming into operation after the commencement of this Act.

162.   Restrictions on the perpetuity rule

(1)   For removing doubts, it is hereby declared that the rule of law relating to perpetuities does not apply and shall be deemed never to have applied—

(a) To any power to distrain on or to take possession of land or the income thereof given by way of indemnity against a rent, whether charged upon or payable in respect of any part of that land or not; or

(b)   To any rentcharge created only as an indemnity against another rentcharge, although the indemnity rentcharge may only arise or become payable on breach of a condition or stipulation; or

(c)   To any power, whether exercisable on breach of a condition or stipulation or not, to retain or withhold payment of any instalment of a rentcharge as an indemnity against another rentcharge; or

(d)   To any grant, exception, or reservation of any right of entry on, or user of, the surface of land or of any easements, rights, or privileges over or under land for the purpose of—

     (i)   winning, working, inspecting, measuring, converting, manufacturing, carrying away, and disposing of mines and minerals;

     (ii)   inspecting, grubbing up, felling and carrying away timber and other trees, and the tops and lops thereof;

     (iii)   executing repairs, alterations, or additions to any adjoining land, or the buildings and erections thereon;

     (iv)   constructing, laying down, altering, repairing, renewing, cleansing, and maintaining sewers, watercourses, cesspools, gutters, drains, water-pipes, gas-pipes, electric wires or cables or other like works.

(2)   This section applies to instruments coming into operation before or after the commencement of this Act.

Accumulations

164.   General restrictions on accumulation of income

(1)   No person may by any instrument or otherwise settle or dispose of any property in such manner that the income thereof shall, save as hereinafter mentioned, be wholly or partially accumulated for any longer period than one of the following, namely:—

(a)   the life of the grantor or settlor; or

(b)   a term of twenty-one years from the death of the grantor, settlor or testator; or

(c)   the duration of the minority or respective minorities of any person or persons living or en ventre sa mere at the death of the grantor, settlor or testator; or

(d)   the duration of the minority or respective minorities only of any person or persons who under the limitations of the instrument directing the accumulations would, for the time being, if of full age, be entitled to the income directed to be accumulated.

In every case where any accumulation is directed otherwise than as aforesaid, the direction shall (save as hereinafter mentioned) be void; and the income of the property directed to be accumulated shall, so long as the same is directed to be accumulated contrary to this section, go to and be received by the person or persons who would have been entitled thereto if such accumulation had not been directed.

(2)   This section does not extend to any provision—

     (i)   for payment of the debts of any grantor, settlor, testator or other person;

     (ii)   for raising portions for—

        (a)   any child, children or remoter issue of any grantor, settlor or testator; or

        (b)   any child, children or remoter issue of a person taking any interest under any settlement or other disposition directing the accumulations or to whom any interest is thereby limited;

     (iii)   respecting the accumulation of the produce of timber or wood;

and accordingly such provisions may be made as if no statutory restrictions on accumulation of income had been imposed.

(3)   The restrictions imposed by this section apply to instruments made on or after the twenty-eighth day of July, eighteen hundred, but in the case of wills only where the testator was living and of testamentary capacity after the end of one year from that date.

165.   Qualification of restrictions on accumulation

Where accumulations of surplus income are made during a minority under any statutory power or under the general law, the period for which such accumulations are made is not (whether the trust was created or the accumulations were made before or after the commencement of this Act) to be taken into account in determining the periods for which accumulations are permitted to be made by the last preceding section, and accordingly an express trust for accumulation for any other permitted period shall not be deemed to have been invalidated or become invalid, by reason of accumulations also having been made as aforesaid during such minority.

166. Restriction on accumulation for the purchase of land

(1) No person may settle or dispose of any property in such manner that the income thereof shall be wholly or partially accumulated for the purchase of land only, for any longer period than the duration of the minority or respective minorities of any person or persons who, under the limitations of the instrument directing the accumulation, would for the time being, if of full age, be entitled to the income so directed to be accumulated.

(2) This section does not, nor do the enactments which it replaces, apply to accumulations to be held as capital money for the purposes of the Settled Land Act, 1925, or the enactments replaced by that Act, whether or not the accumulations are primarily liable to be laid out in the purchase of land.

(3) This section applies to settlements and dispositions made after the twenty-seventh day of June eighteen hundred and ninety-two.

PART IX
VOIDABLE DISPOSITIONS

173. Voluntary disposition of land how far voidable as against purchasers

(1) Every voluntary disposition of land made with intent to defraud a subsequent purchaser is voidable at the instance of that purchaser.

(2) For the purposes of this section, no voluntary disposition, whenever made, shall be deemed to have been made with intent to defraud by reason only that a subsequent conveyance for valuable consideration was made, if such subsequent conveyance was made after the twenty-eighth day of June, eighteen hundred and ninety-three.

174. Acquisitions of reversions at an under value

(1) No acquisition made in good faith, without fraud or unfair dealing, of any reversionary interest in real or personal property, for money or money's worth, shall be liable to be opened or set aside merely on the ground of under value.

In this subsection 'reversionary interest' includes an expectancy or possibility.

(2) This section does not affect the jurisdiction of the court to set aside or modify unconscionable bargains.

PART X
WILLS

175. Contingent and future testamentary gifts to carry the intermediate income

(1) A contingent or future specific devise or bequest of property, whether real or personal, and a contingent residuary devise of freehold land, and a specific or residuary devise of freehold land to trustees upon trust for persons whose interests are contingent or executory shall, subject to the statutory provisions relating to accumulations, carry the intermediate income of that property from the death of the testator, except so far as such income, or any part thereof, may be otherwise expressly disposed of.

(2) This section applies only to wills coming into operation after the commencement of this Act.

176. Power for tenant in tail in possession to dispose of property by specific devise or bequest

(1) A tenant in tail of full age shall have power to dispose by will, by means of a devise or bequest referring specifically either to the property or to the instrument under which it was acquired or to entailed property generally—

(a) of all property of which he is tenant in tail in possession at his death; and

(b) of money (including the proceeds of property directed to be sold) subject to be invested in the purchase of property, of which if it had been so invested he would have been tenant in tail in possession at his death;

in like manner as if, after barring the entail, he had been tenant in fee-simple or absolute owner thereof for an equitable interest at his death, but, subject to and in default of any such disposition by will, such property shall devolve in the same manner as if this section had not been passed.

(2) This section applies to entailed interests authorised to be created by this Act as well as to estates tail created before the commencement of this Act, but does not extend to a tenant in tail who is by statute restrained from barring or defeating his estate tail, whether the land or property in respect whereof he is so restrained was purchased with money provided by Parliament in consideration of public services or not, or to a tenant in tail after possibility of issue extinct, and does not render any interest which is not disposed of by the will of the tenant in tail liable for his debts or other liabilities.

(3) In this section 'tenant in tail' includes an owner of a base fee in possession who has power to enlarge the base fee into a fee-simple without the concurrence of any other person.

(4) This section only applies to wills executed after the commencement of this Act, or confirmed or republished by codicil executed after such commencement.

PART XI
MISCELLANEOUS

184. Presumption of survivorship in regard to claims to property

In all cases where, after the commencement of this Act, two or more persons have died in circumstances rendering it uncertain which of them survived the other or others, such deaths shall (subject to any order of the court), for all purposes affecting the title to property, be presumed to have occurred in order of seniority, and accordingly the younger shall be deemed to have survived the elder.

185. Merger

There is no merger by operation of law only of any estate the beneficial interest in which would not be deemed to be merged or extinguished in equity.

186. Rights of preemption capable of release

All statutory and other rights of preemption affecting a legal estate shall be and be deemed always to have been capable of release, and unless released shall remain in force as equitable interests only.

187. Legal easements

(1) Where an easement, right or privilege for a legal estate is created, it shall enure for the benefit of the land to which it is intended to be annexed.

(2) Nothing in this Act affects the right of a person to acquire, hold or exercise an easement, right or privilege over or in relation to land for a legal estate in common with any other person, or the power of creating or conveying such an easement right or privilege.

188. Power to direct division of chattels

(1) Where any chattels belong to persons in undivided shares, the persons interested in a moiety or upwards may apply to the court for an order for division of the chattels or any of them, according to a valuation or otherwise, and the court may make such order and give any consequential directions as it thinks fit.

(2) . . .

189. Indemnities against rents

(1) A power of distress given by way of indemnity against a rent or any part thereof payable in respect of any land, or against the breach of any covenant or condition in relation to land, is not and shall not be deemed ever to have been a bill of sale within the meaning of the Bills of Sale Acts, 1878 and 1882, as amended by any subsequent enactment.

(2) The benefit of all covenants and powers given by way of indemnity against a rent or any part thereof payable in respect of land, or against the breach of any covenant or condition in relation to land, is and shall be deemed always to have been annexed to the land to which the indemnity is intended to relate, and may be enforced by the estate owner for the time being of the whole or any part of that land, notwithstanding that the benefit may not have been expressly apportioned or assigned to him or to any of his predecessors in title.

Redemption and Apportionment of Rents, etc.

190. Equitable apportionment of rents and remedies for non-payment or breach of covenant

(1) Where in a conveyance for valuable consideration, other than a mortgage, or part of land which is affected by a rentcharge, such rentcharge or a part thereof is, without the consent of the owner thereof, expressed to be—

(a) charged exclusively on the land conveyed or any part thereof in exoneration of the land retained or other land; or

(b) charged exclusively on the land retained or any part thereof in exoneration of the land conveyed or other land; or

(c) apportioned between the land conveyed or any part thereof, and the land retained by the grantor or any part thereof;

then, without prejudice to the rights of the owner of the rentcharge, such charge or apportionment shall be binding as between the grantor and the grantee under the conveyance and their respective successors in title.

(2) Where—

(a) any default is made in payment of the whole or part of a rentcharge by the person who, by reason of such charge or apportionment as aforesaid, is liable to pay the same; or

(b) any breach occurs of any of the covenants (other than in the case of an apportionment the covenant to pay the entire rentcharge) or conditions contained in the deed or other document creating the rentcharge, so far as the same relate to the land retained or conveyed, as the case may be;

the owner for the time being of any other land affected by the entire rentcharge who—

(i) pays or is required to pay the whole or part of the rentcharge which ought to have been paid by the defaulter aforesaid; or

(ii) incurs any costs, damages or expenses by reason of the breach of covenant or condition aforesaid,

may enter into and distrain on the land in respect of which the default or breach is made or occurs, or any part of that land, and dispose according to law of any distress found, and may also take possession of the income of the same land until, by means of such distress and receipt of income or otherwise the whole or part of the rentcharge (charged or apportioned as aforesaid) so unpaid and all costs, damages and expenses incurred by reason of the non-payment thereof or of the breach of the said covenants and conditions, are fully paid or satisfied.

(3) Where in a conveyance for valuable consideration, other than a mortgage, of part of land comprised in a lease, for the residue of the term or interest created by the lease, the rent reserved by such lease or a part thereof is, without the consent of the lessor, expressed to be—

(a) charged exclusively on the land conveyed or any part thereof in exoneration of the land retained by the assignor or other land; or

(b) charged exclusively on the land retained by the assignor or any part thereof in exoneration of the land conveyed or other land; or

(c) apportioned between the land conveyed or any part thereof and the land retained by the assignor or any part thereof;

then, without prejudice to the rights of the lessor, such charge or apportionment shall be binding as between the assignor and the assignee under the conveyance and their respective successors in title.

(4) Where—

(a) any default is made in payment of the whole or part of a rent by the person who, by reason of such charge or apportionment as aforesaid, is liable to pay the same; or

(b) any breach occurs of any of the lessee's covenants (other than in the case of an apportionment the covenant to pay the entire rent) or conditions contained in the lease, so far as the same relate to the land retained or conveyed, as the case may be; the lessee for the time being of any other land comprised in the lease, in whom, as respects that land, the residue of the term or interest created by the lease is vested, who—

(i)   pays or is required to pay the whole or part of the rent which ought to have been paid by the defaulter aforesaid; or

(ii)   incurs any costs, damages or expenses by reason of the breach of covenant or condition aforesaid;

may enter into and distrain on the land comprised in the lease in respect of which the default or breach is made or occurs, or any part of that land, and dispose according to law of any distress found, and may also take possession of the income of the same land until (so long as the term or interest created by the lease is subsisting) by means of such distress and receipt of income or otherwise, the whole or part of the rent (charged or apportioned as aforesaid) so unpaid and all costs, damages and expenses incurred by reason of the non-payment thereof or of the breach of the said covenants and conditions, are fully paid or satisfied.

(5)   The remedies conferred by this section take effect so far only as they might have been conferred by the conveyance whereby the rent or any part thereof is expressed to be charged or apportioned as aforesaid, but a trustee, personal representative, mortgagee or other person in a fiduciary position has, and shall be deemed always to have had, power to confer the same or like remedies.

(6)   This section applies only if and so far as a contrary intention is not expressed in the conveyance whereby the rent or any part thereof is expressed to be charged or apportioned as aforesaid, and takes effect subject to the terms of that conveyance and to the provisions therein contained.

(7)   The remedies conferred by this section apply only where the conveyance whereby the rent or any part thereof is expressed to be charged or apportioned is made after the commencement of this Act, and do not apply where the rent is charged exclusively as aforesaid or legally apportioned with the consent of the owner or lessor.

(8)   The rule of law relating to perpetuities does not affect the powers or remedies conferred by this section or any like powers or remedies expressly conferred, before or after the commencement of this Act, by an instrument.

Commons and Waste Lands

193.   Rights of the public over commons and waste lands

(1)   Members of the public shall, subject as hereinafter provided, have rights of access for air and exercise to any land which is a metropolitan common within the meaning of the Metropolitan Commons Acts, 1866 to 1898, or manorial waste, or a common which is wholly or partly situated within an area which immediately before 1st April 1974 was a borough or urban district, and to any land which at the commencement of this Act is subject to rights of common and to which this section may from time to time be applied in manner hereinafter provided:

Provided that—

(a)   such rights of access shall be subject to any Act, scheme, or provisional order for the regulation of the land, and to any byelaw, regulation or order made thereunder or under any other statutory authority; and

(b)   the Minister shall, on the application of any person entitled as lord of the manor or otherwise to the soil of the land, or entitled to any commonable rights affecting the land, impose such limitations on and conditions as to the exercise of the rights of access or as to the extent of the land to be affected as, in the opinion of the Minister, are necessary or desirable for preventing any estate, right or interest of a profitable or beneficial nature in, over, or affecting the land from being injuriously affected, for conserving flora, fauna or geological or physiographical features of the land, or for protecting any object of historical interest and, where any such limitations or conditions are so imposed, the rights of access shall be subject thereto; and

  (c) such rights of access shall not include any right to draw or drive upon the land a carriage, cart, caravan, truck, or other vehicle, or to camp or light any fire thereon; and

  (d) the rights of access shall cease to apply—

    (i) to any land over which the commonable rights are extinguished under any statutory provision;

    (ii) to any land over which the commonable rights are otherwise extinguished if the council of the county or county borough in which the land is situated by resolution assent to its exclusion from the operation of this section, and the resolution is approved by the Minister.

. . .

194. Restrictions on inclosure of commons

(1) The erection of any building or fence, or the construction of any other work, whereby access to land to which this section applies is prevented or impeded, shall not be lawful unless the consent of the Minister thereto is obtained, and in giving or withholding his consent the Minister shall have regard to the same considerations and shall, if necessary, hold the same inquiries as are directed by the Commons Act, 1876, to be taken into consideration and held by the Minister before forming an opinion whether an application under the Inclosure Acts, 1845 to 1882, shall be acceded to or not.

(2) Where any building or fence is erected, or any other work constructed without such consent as is required by this section, the county court within whose jurisdiction the land is situated, shall, on an application being made by the council of any county or county borough . . . or district concerned, or by the lord of the manor or any other person interested in the common, have power to make an order for the removal of the work, and the restoration of the land to the condition in which it was before the work was erected or constructed, but any such order shall be subject to the like appeal as an order made under section thirty of the Commons Act, 1876.

(3) This section applies to any land which at the commencement of this Act is subject to rights of common:

  Provided that this section shall cease to apply—

  (a) to any land over which the rights of common are extinguished under any statutory provision

  (b) to any land over which the rights of common are otherwise extinguished, if the council of the county . . . or metropolitan district in which the land is situated by resolution assent to its exclusion from the operation of this section and the resolution is approved by the Minister.

(4) This section does not apply to any building or fence erected or work constructed if specially authorised by Act of Parliament, or in pursuance of an Act of Parliament or Order having the force of an Act, or if lawfully erected or constructed in connexion with the taking or working of minerals in or under any land to which the section is otherwise applicable, or to any electronic communications apparatus installed for the purposes of an electronic communications code network.

Judgments, etc. affecting Land

195. Equitable charges in right of judgment debt, etc.

(1)–(3) . . .

(4) A recognisance, on behalf of the Crown or otherwise, whether entered into before or after the commencement of this Act, and an inquisition finding a debt due to the Crown, and any obligation or speciality made to or in favour of the Crown, whatever may have been its date, shall not operate as a charge on any interest in land, or on the unpaid purchase money for any land, unless or until a writ or order, for the purpose of enforcing it, is registered in the register of writs and orders at the Land Registry.

(5) . . .

196.   Regulations respecting notices

(1)   Any notice required or authorised to be served or given by this Act shall be in writing.

(2)   Any notice required or authorised by this Act to be served on a lessee or mortgagor shall be sufficient, although only addressed to the lessee or mortgagor by that designation, without his name, or generally to the persons interested, without any name, and notwithstanding that any person to be affected by the notice is absent, under disability, unborn, or unascertained.

(3)   Any notice required or authorised by this Act to be served shall be sufficiently served if it is left at the last-known place of abode or business in the United Kingdom of the lessee, lessor, mortgagee, mortgagor, or other person to be served, or, in case of a notice required or authorised to be served on a lessee or mortgagor, is affixed or left for him on the land or any house or building comprised in the lease or mortgage, or, in case of a mining lease, is left for the lessee at the office or counting-house of the mine.

(4)   Any notice required or authorised by this Act to be served shall also be sufficiently served, if it is sent by post in a registered letter addressed to the lessee, lessor, mortgagee, mortgagor, or other person to be served, by name, at the aforesaid place of abode or business, office, or counting-house, and if that letter is not returned by the postal operator (within the meaning of the Postal Services Act 2000) concerned undelivered; and that service shall be deemed to be made at the time at which the registered letter would in the ordinary course by delivered.

(5)   The provisions of the section shall extend to notices required to be served by any instrument affecting property executed or coming into operation after the commencement of this Act unless a contrary intention appears.

(6)   This section does not apply to notices served in proceedings in the court.

198.   Registration under the Land Charges Act, 1925, to be notice

(1)   The registration of any instrument or matter in any register kept under the Land Charges Act 1972 or any local land charges register, shall be deemed to constitute actual notice of such instrument or matter, and of the fact of such registration, to all persons and for all purposes connected with the land affected, as from the date of registration or other prescribed date and so long as the registration continues in force.

(2)   This section operates without prejudice to the provisions of this Act respecting the making of further advances by a mortgagee, and applies only to instruments and matters required or authorised to be registered in any such register.

199.   Restrictions on constructive notice

(1)   A purchaser shall not be prejudicially affected by notice of—

   (i)   any instrument or matter capable of registration under the provisions of the Land Charges Act, 1925, or any enactment which it replaces, which is void or not enforceable as against him under that Act or enactment, by reason of the non-registration thereof;

   (ii)   any other instrument or matter or any fact or thing unless—

      (a)   it is within his own knowledge, or would have come to his knowledge if such inquiries and inspections had been made as ought reasonably to have been made by him; or

      (b)   in the same transaction with respect to which a question of notice to the purchaser arises, it has come to the knowledge of his counsel, as such, or of his solicitor or other agent, as such, or would have come to the knowledge of his solicitor or other agent, as such, if such inquiries and inspections had been made as ought reasonably to have been made by the solicitor or other agent.

(2)   Paragraph (ii) of the last subsection shall not exempt a purchaser from any liability under, or any obligation to perform or observe, any covenant, condition, provision, or restriction contained in any instrument under which his title is derived, mediately or immediately; and such liability or obligation may be enforced in the same manner and to the same extent as if that paragraph had not been enacted.

(3)	A purchaser shall not by reason of anything in this section be affected by notice in any case where he would not have been so affected if this section had not been enacted.

(4)	This section applies to purchases made either before or after the commencement of this Act.

**200.	Notice of restrictive covenants and easements**

(1)	Where land having a common title with other land is disposed of to a purchaser (other than a lessee or a mortgagee) who does not hold or obtain possession of the documents forming the common title, such purchaser, notwithstanding any stipulation to the contrary, may require that a memorandum giving notice of any provision contained in the disposition to him restrictive of user of, or giving rights over, any other land comprised in the common title, shall, where practicable, be written or indorsed on, or, where impracticable, be permanently annexed to some one document selected by the purchaser but retained in the possession or power of the person who makes the disposition, and being or forming part of the common title.

(2)	The title of any person omitting to require an indorsement to be made or a memorandum to be annexed shall not, by reason only of this enactment, be prejudiced or affected by the omission.

(3)	This section does not apply to dispositions of registered land.

(4)	Nothing in this section affects the obligation to register a land charge in respect of—

(a)	any restrictive covenant or agreement affecting freehold land; or

(b)	any estate contract; or

(c)	any equitable easement, liberty or privilege.

PART XII
CONSTRUCTION, JURISDICTION, AND GENERAL PROVISIONS

**201.	Provisions of Act to apply to incorporeal hereditaments**

(1)	The provisions of this Act relating to freehold land apply to manors, reputed manors, lordships, advowsons, . . . perpetual rentcharges, and other incorporeal hereditaments, subject only to the qualifications necessarily arising by reason of the inherent nature of the hereditament affected.

(2)	This Act does not affect the special restrictions imposed on dealing with advowsons by the Benefices Act, 1898, or any other statute or measure, nor affect the limitation of, or authorise any disposition to be made of, a title or dignity of honour which in its nature is inalienable.

(3)	. . .

**202.	Provisions as to enfranchisement of copyholds, etc.**

For giving effect to this Act, the enfranchisement of copyhold land, and the conversion into long terms of perpetually renewable leaseholds, and of leases for lives and of leases for years terminable with life or lives or on marriage, effected by the Law of Property Act, 1922, as amended by any subsequent enactment, shall be deemed to have been effected immediately before the commencement of this Act.

**205.	General definitions**

(1)	In this Act unless the context otherwise requires, the following expressions have the meanings hereby assigned to them respectively, that is to say:—

(i)	'Bankruptcy' includes liquidation by arrangement; also in relation to a corporation means the winding up thereof;

(ii)	'Conveyance' includes a mortgage, charge, lease, assent, vesting declaration, vesting instrument, disclaimer, release and every other assurance of property or of an interest therein by any instrument, except a will; 'convey' has a corresponding meaning; and 'disposition' includes a conveyance and also a devise, bequest, or an appointment of property contained in a will; and 'dispose of' has a corresponding meaning;

(iii)	'Building purposes' include the erecting and improving of, and the adding to, and the repairing of buildings; and a 'building lease' is a lease for building purposes or purposes connected therewith;

(iiiA). . . .

(iv) 'Death duty' means estate duty . . . and every other duty leviable or payable on a death;

(v) 'Estate owner' means the owner of a legal estate, but an infant is not capable of being an estate owner;

(vi) 'Gazette' means the London Gazette;

(vii) 'Incumbrance' includes a legal or equitable mortgage and a trust for securing money, and a lien, and a charge of a portion, annuity, or other capital or annual sum; and 'incumbrancer' has a meaning corresponding with that of incumbrance, and includes every person entitled to the benefit of an incumbrance, or to require payment or discharge thereof;

(viii) 'Instrument' does not include a statute, unless the statute creates a settlement;

(ix) 'Land' includes land of any tenure, and mines and minerals, whether or not held apart from the surface, buildings or parts of buildings (whether the division is horizontal, vertical or made in any other way) and other corporeal hereditaments, also a manor, an advowson, and a rent and other incorporeal hereditaments, and an easement, right, privilege, or benefit in, over, or derived from land; . . . and 'mines and minerals' include any strata or seam of minerals or substances in or under any land, and powers of working and getting the same . . .; and 'manor' includes a lordship, and reputed manor or lordship; and 'hereditament' means any real property which on an intestacy occurring before the commencement of this Act might have devolved upon an heir;

(x) 'Legal estates' mean the estates, interests and charges, in or over land (subsisting or created at law) which are by this Act authorised to subsist or to be created as legal estates; 'equitable interests' means all the other interests and charges in or over land . . .; an equitable interest 'capable of subsisting as a legal estate' means such as could validly subsist or be created as a legal estate under this Act;

(xi) 'Legal powers' include the powers vested in a chargee by way of legal mortgage or in an estate owner under which a legal estate can be transferred or created; and 'equitable powers' mean all the powers in or over land under which equitable interests or powers only can be transferred or created;

(xii) 'Limitation Acts' mean the Real Property Limitation Acts, 1833, 1837 and 1874, and 'limitation' includes a trust;

(xiii) 'Mental disorder' has the meaning assigned to it by section one of the Mental Health Act, 1983, and 'receiver', in relation to a person suffering from mental disorder, means a receiver appointed for that person under Part VIII of the Mental Health Act 1959 or Part VII of the said Act of 1983;

(xiv) A 'mining lease' means a lease for mining purposes, that is, the searching for, winning, working, getting, making merchantable, carrying away, or disposing of mines and minerals, or purposes connected therewith, and includes a grant or licence for mining purposes;

(xv) . . .

(xvi) 'Mortgage' includes any charge or lien on any property for securing money or money's worth; 'legal mortgage' means a mortgage by demise or subdemise or a charge by way of legal mortgage and 'legal mortgagee' has a corresponding meaning; 'mortgage money' means money or money's worth secured by a mortgage; 'mortgagor' includes any person from time to time deriving title under the original mortgagor or entitled to redeem a mortgage according to his estate interest or right in the mortgaged property; 'mortgagee' includes a chargee by way of legal mortgage and any person from time to time deriving title under the original mortgagee; and 'mortgagee in possession' is, for the purposes of this Act, a mortgagee who, in right of the mortgage, has entered into and is in possession of the mortgaged property; and 'right of redemption' includes an option to repurchase only if the option in effect creates a right of redemption;

(xvii) 'Notice' includes constructive notice;

(xviii)'Personal representative' means the executor, original or by representation, or administrator for the time being of a deceased person, and as regards any liability for the payment of death duties includes any person who takes possession of or intermeddles with the property of a deceased person without the authority of the personal representatives or the court;

(xix) 'Possession' includes receipt of rents and profits or the right to receive the same, if any; and 'income' includes rents and profits;

(xx) 'Property' includes any thing in action, and any interest in real or personal property;

(xxi) 'Purchaser' means a purchaser in good faith for valuable consideration and includes a lessee, mortgagee or other person who for valuable consideration acquires an interest in property except that in Part I of this Act and elsewhere where so expressly provided 'purchaser' only means a person who acquires an interest in or charge on property for money or money's worth; and in reference to a legal estate includes a chargee by way of legal mortgage; and where the context so requires 'purchaser' includes an intending purchaser; 'purchase' has a meaning corresponding with that of 'purchaser'; and 'valuable consideration' includes marriage, and formation of a civil partnership, but does not include a nominal consideration in money;

(xxii)'Registered land' has the same meaning as in the Land Registration Act 2002 . . .

(xxiii)'Rent' includes a rent service or a rentcharge, or other rent, toll, duty, royalty, or annual or periodical payment in money or money's worth, reserved or issuing out of or charged upon land, but does not include mortgage interest; 'rentcharge' includes a fee farm rent; 'fine' includes a premium or foregift and any payment, consideration, or benefit in the nature of a fine, premium or foregift; 'lessor' includes an underlessor and a person deriving title under a lessor or underlessor; and 'lessee' includes an underlessee and a person deriving title under a lessee or underlessee, and 'lease' includes an underlease or other tenancy;

(xxiv)'Sale' includes an extinguishment of manorial incidents, but in other respects means a sale properly so called;

(xxv)'Securities' include stocks, funds and shares;

(xxvi)'Tenant for life,' 'statutory owner,' 'settled land,' 'settlement,' 'vesting deed,' 'subsidiary vesting deed,' 'vesting order,' 'vesting instrument,' 'trust instrument,' 'capital money,' and 'trustees of the settlement' have the same meanings as in the Settled Land Act, 1925;

(xxvii)'Term of years absolute' means a term of years (taking effect either in possession or in reversion whether or not at a rent) with or without impeachment for waste, subject or not to another legal estate, and either certain or liable to determination by notice, re-entry, operation of law, or by a provision for cesser on redemption, or in any other event (other than the dropping of a life, or the determination of a determinable life interest); but does not include any term of years determinable with life or lives or with the cesser of a determinable life interest, nor, if created after the commencement of this Act, a term of years which is not expressed to take effect in possession within twenty-one years after the creation thereof where required by this Act to take effect within that period; and in this definition the expression 'term of years' includes a term for less than a year, or for a year or years and a fraction of a year or from year to year;

(xxviii)'Trust Corporation' means the Public Trustee or a corporation either appointed by the court in any particular case to be a trustee or entitled by rules made under subsection (3) of section four of the Public Trustee Act, 1906, to act as custodian trustee;

(xxix)'Trust for sale,' in relation to land, means an immediate . . . trust for sale, whether or not exercisable at the request or with the consent of any person . . . ; 'trustees for sale' mean the persons (including a personal representative) holding land on trust for sale . . . ;

(xxx)'United Kingdom' means Great Britain and Northern Ireland;

(xxxi)'Will' includes codicil.

(1A) Any reference in this Act to money being paid into court shall be construed as referring to the money being paid into the Supreme Court or any other court that has jurisdiction, and any reference in this Act to the court, in a context referring to the investment or application of money paid into court, shall be construed, in the case of money paid into the Supreme Court, as referring to the High Court, and in the case of money paid into another court, as referring to that other court.

(2) Where an equitable interest in or power over property arises by statute or operation of law, references to the creation of an interest or power include references to any interest or power so arising.

(3) References to registration under the Land Charges Act, 1925, apply to any registration made under any other statute which is by the Land Charges Act, 1925, to have effect as if the registration had been made under that Act.

207. Repeals as respects England and Wales

... without prejudice to the provisions of section thirty-eight of the Interpretation Act, 1889:—

(a) Nothing in this repeal shall affect the validity or legality of any dealing in property or other transaction completed before the commencement of this Act, or any title or right acquired or appointment made before such commencement, but, subject as aforesaid, this Act shall, except where otherwise expressly provided, apply to and in respect of instruments whether made or coming into operation before or after such commencement:

(b) Nothing in this repeal shall affect any rules, orders, or other instruments made under any enactment so repealed, but all such rules, orders and instruments shall continue in force as if made under the corresponding enactment in this Act:

(c) References in any document to any enactment repealed by this Act shall be construed as references to this Act or to the corresponding enactment in this Act.

208. Application to the Crown

(1) Nothing in this Act shall be construed as rendering any property of the Crown subject to distress, or liable to be taken or disposed of by means of any distress.

(2) This Act shall not in any manner (save as otherwise expressly provided and except so far as it relates to undivided shares, joint ownership, leases for lives or leases for years terminable with life or marriage) affect or alter the descent, devolution or tenure or the nature of the estates and interests of or in any land for the time being vested in His Majesty either in right of the Crown or of the Duchy of Lancaster or of or in any land for the time being belonging to the Duchy of Cornwall and held in right or in respect of the said Duchy, but so nevertheless that, after the commencement of this Act, no estates, interests or charges in or over any such lands as aforesaid shall be conveyed or created, except such estates, interests or charges as are capable under this Act of subsisting or of being conveyed or created.

(3) Subject as aforesaid the provisions of this Act bind the Crown.

SCHEDULES

Section 39

FIRST SCHEDULE
TRANSITIONAL PROVISIONS

PART I
CONVERSION OF CERTAIN EXISTING LEGAL ESTATES INTO EQUITABLE INTERESTS

All estates, interests and charges in or over land, including fees determinable whether by limitation or condition, which immediately before the commencement of this Act were estates, interests or charges, subsisting at law, or capable of taking effect as such, but which by virtue of Part I. of this Act are not capable of taking effect as legal estates, shall as from the commencement of this Act be converted into equitable interests, and shall not fail by reason of being so converted into equitable interests either in the land or in the proceeds of sale thereof, nor shall the priority of any such estate, charge or interest over other equitable interests be affected.

PART II
VESTING OF LEGAL ESTATES

1. Where the purposes of a term of years, created or limited out of leasehold land, are satisfied at the commencement of this Act, that term shall merge in the reversion expectant thereon and shall cease accordingly; but where the term was vested in the owner of the reversion, the merger and cesser shall take effect without prejudice to any protection which would have been afforded to the owner for the time being of that reversion had the term remained subsisting.

    Where the purposes are satisifed only as respects part of the land comprised in a term, this provision has effect as if a separate term had been created in regard to that part of the land.

2. Where immediately after the commencement of this Act any owner of a legal estate is entitled, subject or not to the payment of the costs of tracing the title and of conveyance, to require any other legal estate in the same land to be surrendered, released or conveyed to him so as to merge or be extinguished, the last-mentioned estate shall by virtue of this Part of this Schedule be extinguished, but without prejudice to any protection which would have been afforded to him had that estate remained subsisting.

3. Where immediately after the commencement of this Act any person is entitled, subject or not to the payment of the costs of tracing the title and of conveyance, to require any legal estate (not vested in trustees for sale) to be conveyed to or otherwise vested in him, such legal estate shall, by virtue of this Part of this Schedule, vest in manner hereinafter provided.

    The divesting of a legal estate by virtue of this paragraph shall not, where the person from whom the estate is so divested was a trustee, operate to prevent the legal estate being conveyed, or a legal estate being created, by him in favour of a purchaser for money or money's worth, if the purchaser has no notice of the trust and if the documents of title relating to the estate divested are produced by the trustee or by persons deriving title under him.

    This paragraph shall (without prejudice to any claim, in respect of fines, fees, and other customary payments) apply to a person who, under a surrender or any disposition having the effect of a surrender, or under a covenant to surrender or otherwise, was, immediately before the commencement of this Act, entitled to require a legal customary estate of inheritance to be vested in him, or who, immediately after such commencement becomes entitled to enfranchised land.

4. Any person who, immediately after the commencement of this Act, is entitled to an equitable interest capable of subsisting as a legal estate which has priority over any legal estate in the same land, shall be deemed to be entitled for the foregoing purposes to require a legal estate to be vested in him for an interest of a like nature not exceeding in extent or duration the equitable interest:

    Provided that this paragraph shall not—

    (a) apply where the equitable interest is capable of being overreached by virtue of a subsisting trust for sale or a settlement;

    (b) operate to prevent such person from acquiring any other legal estate under this Part of this Schedule to which he may be entitled.

5. For the purposes of this Part of this Schedule, a tenant for life, statutory owner or personal representative, shall be deemed to be entitled to require to be vested in him any legal estate in settled land (whether or not vested in the Crown) which he is, by the Settled Land Act, 1925, given power to convey.

6. Under the provisions of this Part of this Schedule, the legal estate affected (namely, any estate which a person is entitled to require to be vested in him as aforesaid) shall vest as follows:—

    (a) Where at the commencement of this Act land is subject to a mortgage (not being an equitable charge unsecured by any estate), the legal estate affected shall vest in accordance with the provisions relating to mortgages contained in this Schedule;

    (b) Where the land is at the commencement or by virtue of this Act or any Act coming into operation at the same time subject or is by virtue of any statute made subject to a trust for sale, the legal estate affected shall vest in the trustees for sale (including personal representatives holding land on trust for sale) but subject to any mortgage term subsisting or created by this Act;

(c) Where at the commencement of this Act or by virtue of any statute coming into operation at the same time the land is settled land, the legal estate affected shall vest in the tenant for life or statutory owner entitled under the Settled Land Act, 1925, to require a vesting deed to be executed in his favour, or in the personal representative, if any, in whom the land may be vested or the Public Trustee, as the case may require but subject to any mortgage term subsisting or created by this Act;

(d) In any case to which the foregoing sub-paragraphs do not apply the legal estate affected shall vest in the person of full age who, immediately after the commencement of this Act, is entitled (subject or not to the payment of costs and any customary payments) to require the legal estate to be vested in him, but subject to any mortgage term subsisting or created by this Act.

7. Nothing in this Part of this Schedule shall operate—

(a) To vest in a mortgagee of a term of years absolute any nominal leasehold reversion which is held in trust for him subject to redemption; or

(b) To vest in a mortgagee any legal estate except a term of years absolute; or

(c) To vest in a person entitled to a leasehold interest, as respects such interest, any legal estate except a term of years absolute; or

(d) To vest in a person entitled to a rentcharge (either perpetual or held for a term of years absolute) as respects such rentcharge, any legal estate except a legal estate in the rentcharge; or

(e) To vest in a person entitled to an easement, right or privilege with reference thereto, any legal estate except a legal estate in the easement, right or privilege; or

(f) To vest any legal estate in a person for an undivided share, or

(g) To vest any legal estate in an infant; or

(h) To affect prejudicially the priority of any mortgage or other incumbrance or interest subsisting at the commencement of this Act; or

(i) To render invalid any limitation or trust which would have been capable of taking effect as an equitable limitation or trust; or

(j) To vest in a purchaser or his personal representatives any legal estate which he has contracted to acquire and in regard to which a contract, including an agreement to create a legal mortgage, is pending at the commencement of this Act, although the consideration may have been paid or satisfied and the title accepted, or to render unnecessary the conveyance of such estate; or

(k) To vest in the managing trustees or committee of management of a charity any legal estate vested in the Official Trustee of Charity Lands; or

(l) To vest in any person any legal estate which failed to pass to him by reason of his omission to be registered as proprietor under the Land Transfer Acts, 1875 and 1897, until brought into operation by virtue of the Land Registration Act, 1925.

(m) To vest in any person any legal estate affected by any rent covenants or conditions if, before any proceedings are commenced in respect of the rent covenants or conditions, and before any conveyance of the legal estate or dealing therewith inter vivos is effected, he or his personal representatives disclaim it in writing signed by him or them.

8. Any legal estate acquired by virtue of this Part of this Schedule shall be held upon the trusts and subject to the powers, provisions, rents, covenants, conditions, rights of redemption (as respects terms of years absolute) and other rights, burdens and obligations, if any, upon or subject to which the estate acquired ought to be held.

9. No stamp duty shall become payable by reason only of any vesting surrender or release effected by this Schedule.

PART III
PROVISIONS AS TO LEGAL ESTATE VESTED IN INFANT

1. Where immediately before the commencement of this Act a legal estate in land is vested in one or more infants beneficially, or where immediately after the commencement of this Act a legal estate in land would by virtue of this Act have become vested in one or more infants beneficially if he or

they had been of full age, the legal estate shall vest in the manner provided by the Settled Land Act, 1925.

2. Where immediately before the commencement of this Act a legal estate in land is vested in an infant jointly with one or more other persons of full age beneficially, the legal estate shall by virtue of this Act vest in that other person or those other persons on the statutory trusts, but not so as to sever any joint tenancy in the net proceeds of sale or in the rents and profits until sale:

Provided that, if by virtue of this paragraph the legal estate becomes vested in one person as trustee, then, if no other person is able and willing to do so, the parents or parent, testamentary or other guardian of the infant, if respectively able and willing to act, (in the order named) may, and at the request of any person interested shall (subject to the costs being provided for) by writing appoint an additional trustee and thereupon by virtue of this Act the legal estate shall vest in the additional trustee and existing trustee as joint tenants.

3. Where, immediately before the commencement of this Act, a legal estate in land is vested solely in an infant as a personal representative, or a trustee of a settlement, or on trust for sale or on any other trust, or by way of mortgage, or where immediately after the commencement of this Act a legal estate in land would by virtue of any provision of this Act or otherwise have been so vested if the infant were of full age, the legal estate and the mortgage debt (if any) and interest thereon shall, by virtue of this Act, vest in the Public Trustee, pending the appointment of trustees as hereinafter provided—

(a) as to the land, upon the trusts, and subject to the equities affecting the same (but in the case of a mortgage estate for a term of years absolute in accordance with this Act); and

(b) as to the mortgage debt and interest, upon such trusts as may be requisite for giving effect to the rights (if any) of the infant or other persons beneficially interested therein:

Provided that—

(i) The Public Trustee shall not be entitled to act in the trust, or charge any fee, or be liable in any manner, unless and until requested in writing to act by or on behalf of the persons interested in the land or the income thereof, or in the mortgage debt or interest thereon (as the case may be), which request may be made on behalf of the infant by his parents or parent, or testamentary or other guardian (in the order named), and those persons may, in the order aforesaid (if no other person is able and willing to do so) appoint new trustees in the place of the Public Trustee, and thereupon by virtue of this Act the land or term and mortgage money shall vest in the trustees so appointed upon the trusts and subject to the equities aforesaid: Provided that the Public Trustee may, before he accepts the trust, but subject to the payment of his costs, convey to a person of full age who becomes entitled;

(ii) After the Public Trustee has been so requested to act, and has accepted the trust, no trustee shall (except by an order of the court) be appointed in his place without his consent;

(iii) Any person interested in the land or the income thereof, or in the mortgage debt or in the interest thereon (as the case may be), may, at any time during the minority, apply to the court for the appointment of trustees of the trust, and the court may make such order as it thinks fit, and if thereby new trustees are appointed the legal estate (but in the case of a mortgage estate only for a term of years absolute as aforesaid) and the mortgage debt (if any) and interest shall, by virtue of this Act, vest in the trustees as joint tenants upon the trusts and subject to the equities aforesaid;

(iv) Neither a purchaser of the land nor a transferee for money or money's worth of the mortgage shall be concerned in any way with the trusts affecting the legal estate or the mortgage debt and interest thereon;

(v) The vesting in the Public Trustee of a legal estate or a mortgage debt by virtue of this Part of this Schedule shall not affect any directions previously given as to the payment of income or of interest on any mortgage money, but such instructions may, until he accepts the trust, continue to be acted on as if no such vesting had been effected.

3A. The county court has jurisdiction under proviso (iii) to paragraph 3 of this Part where the land which is to be dealt with in the court does not exceed £30,000 in capital value . . . .

4. Where, immediately before the commencement of this Act, a legal estate in land is vested in two or more persons jointly as personal representatives, trustees, or mortgagees, and anyone of them

is an infant, or where immediately after the commencement of this Act a legal estate in land would, by virtue of this Act, or otherwise have been so vested if the infant were of full age, the legal estate in the land with the mortgage debt (if any) and the interest thereon shall, by virtue of this Act, vest in the other person or persons of full age—

(a)   as to the legal estate, upon the trusts and subject to the equities affecting the same (but in the case of a mortgage estate only for a term of years absolute as aforesaid); and

(b)   as to the mortgage debt and interest, upon such trusts as may be requisite for giving effect to the rights (if any) of the infant or other persons beneficially interested therein;

but neither a purchaser of the land nor a transferee for money or money's worth of the mortgage shall be concerned in any way with the trusts affecting the legal estate or the mortgage debt and interest thereon:

Provided that, if, by virtue of this paragraph, the legal estate and mortgage debt, if any, become vested in a sole trustee, then, if no other person is able and willing to do so, the parents or parent, testamentary or other guardian of the infant (in the order named) may, and at the request of any person interested shall, (subject to the costs being provided for) by writing appoint a new trustee in place of the infant, and thereupon by virtue of this Act the legal estate and mortgage money shall vest in the new and continuing trustees upon the trusts and subject to the equities aforesaid.

5.   This Part of this Schedule does not affect the estate or powers of an administrator durante minore aetate, nor, where there is a tenant for life or statutory owner of settled land, operate to vest the legal estate therein in the Public Trustee.

PART IV

PROVISIONS SUBJECTING LAND HELD IN UNDIVIDED SHARES TO A TRUST FOR SALE

1.   Where, immediately before the commencement of this Act, land is held at law or in equity in undivided shares vested in possession, the following provisions shall have effect:—

(1)   If the entirety of the land is vested in trustees or personal representatives (whether subject or not to incumbrances affecting the entirety or an undivided share) in trust for persons entitled in undivided shares, then—

(a)   if the land is subject to incumbrances affecting undivided shares or to incumbrances affecting the entirety which under this Act or otherwise are not secured by legal terms of years absolute, the entirety of the land shall vest free from such incumbrances in such trustees or personal representatives and be held by them upon the statutory trusts; and

(b)   in any other case, the land shall be held by such trustees or personal representatives upon the statutory trusts;

subject in the case of personal representatives, to their rights and powers for the purposes of administration.

(2)   If the entirety of the land (not being settled land) is vested absolutely and beneficially in not more than four persons of full age entitled thereto in undivided shares free from incumbrances affecting undivided shares, but subject or not to incumbrances affecting the entirety, it shall, by virtue of this Act, vest in them as joint tenants upon the statutory trusts.

(3)   If the entirety of the land is settled land (whether subject or not to incumbrances affecting the entirety or an undivided share) held under one and the same settlement, it shall, by virtue of this Act, vest, free from incumbrances affecting undivided shares, and from incumbrances affecting the entirety, which under this Act or otherwise are not secured by a legal mortgage, and free from any interests, powers, and charges subsisting under the settlement, which have priority to the interests of the persons entitled to the undivided shares, in the trustees (if any) of the settlement as joint tenants upon the statutory trusts.

Provided that if there are no such trustees, then—

(i)   pending their appointment, the land shall, by virtue of this Act, vest (free as aforesaid) in the Public Trustee upon the statutory trusts;

(ii)   the Public Trustee shall not be entitled to act in the trust, or charge any fee, or be liable in any manner, unless and until requested in writing to act by or on behalf of persons interested in more than an undivided half of the land or the income thereof;

(iii) after the Public Trustee has been so requested to act, and has accepted the trust, no trustee shall (except by an order of the Court) be appointed in the place of the Public Trustee without his consent;

(iv) if, before the Public Trustee has accepted the trust, trustees of the settlement are appointed, the land shall, by virtue of this Act, vest (free as aforesaid) in them as joint tenants upon the statutory trusts;

(v) if, before the Public Trustee has accepted the trust, the persons having power to appoint new trustees are unable or unwilling to make an appointment, or if the tenant for life having power to apply to the court for the appointment of trustees of the settlement neglects to make the application for at least three months after being requested by any person interested in writing so to do, or if the tenants for life of the undivided shares are unable to agree, any person interested under the settlement may apply to the court for the appointment of such trustees.

(3A) The county court has jurisdiction under proviso (v) to sub-paragraph (3) of this paragraph where the land to be dealt with in the court does not exceed £30,000 in capital value . . . .

(4) In any case to which the foregoing provisions of this Part of this Schedule do not apply, the entirety of the land shall vest (free as aforesaid) in the Public Trustee upon the statutory trusts:

Provided that—

(i) The Public Trustee shall not be entitled to act in the trust, or charge any fee, or be liable in any manner, unless and until requested in writing to act by or on behalf of the persons interested in more than an undivided half of the land or the income thereof;

(ii) After the Public Trustee had been so requested to act, and has accepted the trust, no trustee shall (except by an order of the court) be appointed in the place of the Public Trustee without his consent;

(iii) Subject as aforesaid, any persons interested in more than an undivided half of the land or the income thereof may appoint new trustees in the place of the Public Trustee with the consent of any incumbrances of undivided shares (but so that a purchaser shall not be concerned to see whether any such consent has been given) and thereupon the land shall by virtue of this Act vest in the persons so appointed (free as aforesaid) upon the statutory trusts; or such persons may (without such consent as aforesaid), at any time, whether or not the Public Trustee has accepted the trust, apply to the court for the appointment of trustees of the land, and the court may make such order as it thinks fit, and if thereby trustees of the land are appointed, the same shall by virtue of this Act, vest (free as aforesaid) in the trustees as joint tenants upon the statutory trusts;

(iv) If the persons interested in more than an undivided half of the land or the income thereof do not either request the Public Trustee to act, or (whether he refuses to act or has not been requested to act) apply to the court for the appointment of trustees in his place, within three months from the time when they have been requested in writing by any person interested so to do, then and in any such case, any person interested may apply to the court for the appointment of trustees in the place of the Public Trustee, and the court may make such order as it thinks fit, and if thereby trustees of the land are appointed the same shall by virtue of this Act, vest (free as aforesaid) in the trustees upon the statutory trusts.

(4A) The county court has jurisdiction under provisos (iii) and (iv) to sub-paragraph (4) of this paragraph where the land which is to be dealt with in the court does not exceed £30,000 in capital value . . . .

(5) The vesting in the Public Trustee of land by virtue of this Part of this Schedule shall not affect any directions previously given as to the payment of income or of interest on any mortgage money, but such instructions may, until he accepts the trust, continue to be acted on as if no such vesting had been effected.

(6) The court or the Public Trustee may act on evidence given by affidavit or by statutory declaration as respects the undivided shares without investigating the title to the land.

(7)   Where all the undivided shares in the land are vested in the same mortgagees for securing the same mortgage money and the rights of redemption affecting the land are the same as might have been subsisting if the entirety had been mortgaged by an owner before the undivided shares were created, the land shall, by virtue of this Act, vest in the mortgagees as joint tenants for a legal term of years absolute (in accordance with this Act) subject to cesser on redemption by the trustees for sale in whom the right of redemption is vested by this Act, and for the purposes of this Part of this Schedule the mortgage shall be deemed an incumbrance affecting the entirety.

(8)   This Part of this Schedule does not (except where otherwise expressly provided) prejudice incumbrancers whose incumbrances affect the entirety of the land at the commencement of this Act, but (if the nature of the incumbrance admits) the land shall vest in them for legal terms of years absolute in accordance with this Act but not so as to affect subsisting priorities.

(9)   The trust for sale and powers of management vested in persons who hold the entirety of the land on trust for sale shall, save as hereinafter mentioned, not be exercisable without the consent of any incumbrancer, being of full age, affected whose incumbrance is divested by this Part of this Schedule, but a purchaser shall not be concerned to see or inquire whether any such consent has been given, nor, where the incumbrancer is not in possession, shall any such consent be required if, independently of this Part of this Schedule or any enactment replaced thereby the transaction would have been binding on him, had the same been effected by the mortgagor.

(10) This Part of this Schedule does not apply to land in respect of which a subsisting contract for sale (whether made under an order in a partition action or by or on behalf of all the tenants in common or coparceners) is in force at the commencement of this Act if the contract is completed in due course (in which case title may be made in like manner as if this Act, and any enactment thereby replaced, had not been passed), nor to the land in respect of which a partition action is pending at such commencement if an order for a partition or sale is subsequently made in such action within eighteen months from the commencement of this Act.

(11) The repeal of the enactments relating to partition shall operate without prejudice to any proceedings thereunder commenced before the commencement of this Act, and to the jurisdiction of the court to make any orders in reference thereto, and subject to the following provisions, namely:—

    (i)   In any such proceedings, and at any stage thereof, any person or persons interested individually or collectively in one half or upwards of the land to which the proceedings relate, may apply to the court for an order staying such proceedings;

    (ii)   The court may upon such application make an order staying the proceedings as regards the whole or any part, not being an undivided share, of the land;

    (iii) As from the date of such order the said enactments shall cease to apply to the land affected by the order and the provisions of this Part of this Schedule shall apply thereto;

    (iv) The court may by such order appoint trustees of the land and the same shall by virtue of this Act vest (free as aforesaid) in the trustees as joint tenants upon the statutory trusts;

    (v)   The court may order that the costs of the proceedings and of the application shall be raised by the trustees, by legal mortgage of the land or any part thereof, and paid either wholly or partially into court or to the trustees;

    (vi) The court may act on such evidence as appears to be sufficient, without investigating the title to the land.

(12) In this Part of this Schedule 'incumbrance' does not include a legal rentcharge affecting the entirety, land tax, tithe rentcharge, or any similar charge on the land not created by an instrument.

2.   Where undivided shares in land, created before the commencement of this Act, fall into possession after such commencement, and the land is not settled land when the shares fall into

possession, the personal representatives (subject to their rights and powers for purposes of administration) or other estate owners in whom the entirety of the land is vested shall, by an assent or a conveyance, give effect to the foregoing provisions of this Part of this Schedule in like manner as if the shares had fallen into possession immediately before the commencement of this Act, and in the meantime the land shall be held on the statutory trusts.

3.   This Part of this Schedule shall not save as hereinafter mentioned apply to party structures and open spaces within the meaning of the next succeeding Part of this Schedule.

4.   Where, immediately before the commencement of this Act, there are two or more tenants for life of full age entitled under the same settlement in undivided shares, and, after the cesser of all their interests in the income of the settled land, the entirety of the land is limited so as to devolve together (not in undivided shares), their interests shall, but without prejudice to any beneficial interest, be converted into a joint tenancy, and the joint tenants and the survivor of them shall, until the said cesser occurs, constitute the tenant for life for the purposes of the Settled Land Act, 1925, and this Act.

PART V
PROVISIONS AS TO PARTY STRUCTURES AND OPEN SPACES

1.   Where, immediately before the commencement of this Act, a party wall or other party structure is held in undivided shares, the ownership thereof shall be deemed to be severed vertically as between the respective owners, and the owner of each part shall have such rights to support and of user over the rest of the structure as may be requisite for conferring rights corresponding to those subsisting at the commencement of this Act.

2.   Where, immediately before the commencement of this Act, an open space of land (with or without any building used in common for the purposes of any adjoining land) is held in undivided shares, in right whereof each owner has rights of access and user over the open space, the ownership thereof shall vest in the Public Trustee on the statutory trusts which shall be executed only with the leave of the court, and, subject to any order of the court to the contrary, each person who would have been a tenant in common shall, until the open space is conveyed to a purchaser, have rights of access and user over the open space corresponding to those which would have subsisted if the tenancy in common had remained subsisting.

3.   Any person interested may apply to the court for an order declaring the rights and interests under this Part of this Schedule, of the persons interested in any such party structure or open space, or generally may apply in relation to the provisions of this Part of this Schedule, and the court may make such order as it thinks fit.

PART VI

. . .

PART VII
CONVERSION OF EXISTING FREEHOLD MORTGAGES INTO MORTGAGES BY DEMISE

1.   All land, which immediately before the commencement of this Act, was vested in a first or only mortgagee for an estate in fee simple in possession, whether legal or equitable, shall, from and after the commencement of this Act, vest in the first or only mortgagee for a term of three thousand years from such commencement, without impeachment of waste, but subject to a provision for cesser corresponding to the right of redemption which, at such commencement, was subsisting with respect to the fee simple.

2.   All land, which immediately before the commencement of this Act, was vested in a second or subsequent mortgagee for an estate in fee simple in possession, whether legal or equitable, shall, from and after the commencement of this Act, vest in the second or subsequent mortgagee for a term one day longer than the term vested in the first or other mortgagee whose security ranks immediately before that of such second or subsequent mortgagee, without impeachment of waste, but subject to the term or terms vested in such first or other prior mortgagee and subject to a provision for cesser corresponding to the right of redemption which, at such commencement, was subsisting with respect to the fee simple.

3. The estate in fee simple which, immediately before the commencement of this Act, was vested in any such mortgagee shall, from and after such commencement, vest in the mortgagor or tenant for life, statutory owner, trustee for sale, personal representative, or other person of full age who, if all money owing on the security of the mortgage and all other mortgages or charges (if any) had been discharged at the commencement of this Act, would have been entitled to have the fee simple conveyed to him, but subject to any mortgage term created by this Part of this Schedule or otherwise and to the money secured by any such mortgage or charge.

4. If a sub-mortgage by conveyance of the fee simple is subsisting immediately before the commencement of this Act, the principal mortgagee shall take the principal term created by paragraphs 1 or 2 of this Part of this Schedule (as the case may require) and the sub-mortgagee shall take a derivative term less by one day than the term so created, without impeachment of waste, subject to a provision for cesser corresponding to the right of redemption subsisting under the sub-mortgage.

5. This Part of this Schedule applies to land enfranchised by statute as well as to land which was freehold before the commencement of this Act, and (save where expressly excepted) whether or not the land is registered under the Land Registration Act, 1925, or the mortgage is made by way of trust for sale or otherwise.

6. A mortgage affecting a legal estate made before the commencement of this Act which is not protected, either by a deposit of documents of title relating to the legal estate or by registration as a land charge, shall not, as against a purchaser in good faith without notice thereof, obtain any benefit by reason of being converted into a legal mortgage by this Schedule, but shall, in favour of such purchaser, be deemed to remain an equitable interest.

    This paragraph does not apply to mortgages or charges registered or protected under the Land Registration Act, 1925, or to mortgages or charges registered in a local deeds register.

7. Nothing in this Part of this Schedule shall affect priorities or the right of any mortgagee to retain possession of documents, nor affect his title to or rights over any fixtures or chattels personal comprised in the mortgage.

8. This Part of this Schedule does not apply unless a right of redemption is subsisting immediately before the commencement of this Act.

PART VIII
CONVERSION OF EXISTING LEASEHOLD MORTGAGES INTO MORTGAGES BY SUBDEMISE

1. All leasehold land, which immediately before the commencement of this Act, was vested in a first or only mortgagee by way of assignment of a term of years absolute shall, from and after the commencement of this Act, vest in the first or only mortgagee for a term equal to the term assigned by the mortgage, less the last ten days thereof, but subject to a provision for cesser corresponding to the right of redemption which at such commencement was subsisting with respect to the term assigned.

2. All leasehold land, which immediately before the commencement of this Act, was vested in a second or subsequent mortgagee by way of assignment of a term of years absolute (whether legal or equitable) shall, from and after the commencement of this Act, vest in the second or subsequent mortgagee for a term one day longer than the term vested in the first or other mortgagee whose security ranks immediately before that of such second or subsequent mortgagee if the length of the last-mentioned term permits, and in any case for a term less by one day at least than the term assigned by the mortgage, but subject to the term or terms vested in such first or other prior mortgagee, and subject to a provision for cesser corresponding to the right of redemption which, at the commencement of this Act, was subsisting with respect to the term assigned by the mortgage.

3. The term of years absolute which was assigned by any such mortgage shall from and after the commencement of this Act, vest in the mortgagor or tenant for life, statutory owner, trustee for sale, personal representative, or other person of full age who, if all the money owing on the security of the mortgage and all other mortgages or charges, if any, had been discharged at the commencement of this Act, would have been entitled to have the term assigned or surrendered to him, but subject to any derivative mortgage term created by this Part of this Schedule or otherwise and to the money secured by any such mortgage or charge.

4.   If a sub-mortgage by assignment of a term is subsisting immediately before the commencement of this Act, the principal mortgagee shall take the principal derivative term created by paragraphs 1 or 2 of this Part of this Schedule or the derivative term created by his mortgage (as the case may require), and the sub-mortgagee shall take a derivative term less by one day than the term so vested in the principal mortgagee, subject to a provision for cesser corresponding to the right of redemption subsisting under the sub-mortgage.

5.   A mortgage affecting a legal estate made before the commencement of this Act which is not protected, either by a deposit of documents of title relating to the legal estate or by registration as a land charge shall not, as against a purchaser in good faith without notice thereof, obtain any benefit by reason of being converted into a legal mortgage by this Schedule, but shall, in favour of such purchaser, be deemed to remain an equitable interest.

   This paragraph does not apply to mortgages or charges registered or protected under the Land Registration Act, 1925, or to mortgages or charges registered in a local deeds register.

   6.   This Part of this Schedule applies to perpetually renewable leaseholds, and to leaseholds for lives, which are by statute converted into long terms, with the following variations, namely:—

      (a)   The term to be taken by a first or only mortgagee shall be ten days less than the term created by such statute:

      (b)   The term to be taken by a second or subsequent mortgagee shall be one day longer than the term vested in the first or other mortgagee whose security ranks immediately before that of the second or subsequent mortgagee, if the length of the last-mentioned term permits, and in any case for a term less by one day at least than the term created by such statute:

      (c)   The term created by such statute shall, from and after the commencement of this Act, vest in the mortgagor or tenant for life, statutory owner, trustee for sale, personal representative, or other person of full age, who if all the money owing on the security of the mortgage and all other mortgages or charges, if any, had been discharged at the commencement of this Act, would have been entitled to have the term assigned or surrendered to him, but subject to any derivative mortgage term created by this Part of this Schedule or otherwise and to the money secured by any such mortgage or charge.

7.   This Part of this Schedule applies (save where expressly excepted) whether or not the leasehold land is registered under the Land Registration Act, 1925, or the mortgage is made by way of trust for sale or otherwise.

8.   Nothing in this Part of this Schedule shall affect priorities or the right of any mortgagee to retain possession of documents, nor affect his title to or rights over any fixtures or chattels personal comprised in the mortgage, but this Part of this Schedule does not apply unless a right of redemption is subsisting at the commencement of this Act.

LAND REGISTRATION ACT 1925
(1925, c. 21)

[Repealed]

Note. References to the Land Charges Act 1925 should be read as references to the Land Charges Act 1972; the Companies (Consolidation) Act 1908 is now the Companies Act 1985.

PRELIMINARY

2.   What estates may be registered

   (1)   After the commencement of this Act, estates capable of subsisting as legal estates shall be the only interests in land in respect of which a proprietor can be registered and all other interests in registered land (except overriding interests and interests entered on the register at or before such commencement) shall take effect in equity as minor interests, but all interests (except undivided shares in land) entered on the register at such commencement which are not legal estates shall be capable of being dealt with under this Act:

      Provided that, on the occasion of the first dealing with any such interest, the register shall be rectified in such manner as may be provided by rules made to secure that the entries therein shall be similar to those which would have been made if the title to the land had been registered after the commencement of this Act.

(2)   Subject as aforesaid, and save as otherwise expressly provided by this Act, this Act applies to land registered under any enactment replaced by this Act in like manner as it applies to land registered under this Act.

3.   Interpretation

In this Act unless the context otherwise requires, the following expressions have the meanings hereby assigned to them respectively, that is to say:—

(i)   'Charge by way of legal mortgage' means a mortgage created by charge under which, by virtue of the Law of Property Act 1925, the mortgagee is to be treated as an estate owner in like manner as if a mortgage term by demise or subdemise were vested in him, and 'legal mortgage' has the same meaning as in that Act;

(ii)   'the court' means the High Court or, where county courts have jurisdiction by virtue of rules made under section 138(1) of this Act, the county court;

(iii)   . . .

(iv)   'Estate owner' means the owner of a legal estate, but an infant is not capable of being an estate owner;

(v)   'Gazette' means the London Gazette;

(vi)   'Income' includes rents and profits;

(vii) 'Instrument' does not include a statute, unless the statute creates a settlement;

(viii) 'Land' includes land of any tenure (including land, subject or not to manorial incidents, enfranchised under Part V of the Law of Property Act 1922), and mines and minerals, whether or not held with the surface, buildings or parts of buildings (whether the division is horizontal, vertical or made in any other way) and other corporeal hereditaments; also a manor . . . and a rent and other incorporeal hereditaments, and an easement, right, privilege, or benefit in, over, or derived from land; . . . and 'hereditaments' mean real property which on an intestacy might, before the commencement of this Act, have devolved on an heir;

(ix)   'Land charge' means a land charge of any class described in section 2 of the Land Charges Act 1972 or a local land charge;

(x)   'Lease' includes an under-lease and any tenancy or agreement for a lease, under-lease or tenancy;

(xi)   'Legal estates' mean the estates interests and charges in or over land subsisting or created at law which are by the Law of Property Act 1925, authorised to subsist or to be created at law; and 'Equitable interests' mean all the other interests and charges in or over land . . . ; an equitable interest 'capable of subsisting at law' means such as could validly subsist at law if clothed with the legal estate;

(xii) 'Limitation Acts' mean the Real Property Limitation Acts 1833, 1837 and 1874, and any Acts amending those Acts;

(xiii) 'Manorial incidents' have the same meaning as in Part V of the Law of Property Act 1922;

(xiv) 'Mines and minerals' include any strata or seam of minerals or substances in or under any land, and powers of working and getting the same . . . ;

(xv)   'Minor interests' mean the interests not capable of being disposed of or created by registered dispositions and capable of being overridden (whether or not a purchaser has notice thereof) by the proprietors unless protected as provided by this Act, and all rights and interests which are not registered or protected on the register and are not overriding interests, and include—

(a)   in the case of land subject to a trust of land, all interests and powers which are under the Law of Property Act 1925, capable of being overridden by the trustees, whether or not such interests and powers are so protected; and

(b)   in the case of settled land, all interests and powers which are under the settled Land Act 1925, and the Law of Property Act 1925, or either of them, capable of being overridden by the tenant for fife or statutory owner, whether or not such interests and powers are so protected as aforesaid;

(xvi) 'Overriding interests' mean all the incumbrances, interests, rights, and powers not entered on the register but subject to which registered dispositions are by this Act to take effect, and in regard to land registered at the commencement of this Act include the matters which are by any enactment repealed by this Act declared not to be incumbrances;

(xvii) 'Personal representative' means the executor, original or by representation, or administrator for the time being of a deceased person, and as regards any liability for the payment of death duties includes any person who takes possession of or intermeddles with the property of a deceased person without the authority of the personal representatives for the purposes of any settled land, it means, in relation to that land, those representatives;

(xviii) 'Possession' includes receipt of rents and profits or the right to receive the same, if any;

(xviiia) 'PPP lease', has the same meaning as in chapter VII of Part IV of the Greater London Authority Act 1999 (public-private partnership agreements);

(xix) 'Prescribed' means prescribed by general rules made in pursuance of this Act;

(xx) 'Proprietor' means the registered proprietor for the time being of an estate in land or of a charge

(xxi) 'Purchaser' means a purchaser in good faith for valuable consideration and includes a lessee, mortgagee, or other person who for valuable consideration acquires any interest in land or in any charge on land;

(xxii) 'Registered dispositions' mean dispositions which take effect under the powers conferred on the proprietor by way of transfer, charge, lease or otherwise and to which (when required to be registered) special effect or priority is given by this Act on registration—

(xxiii) 'Registered estate,' in reference to land, means the legal estate, or other registered interest, if any, as respects which a person is for the time being registered as proprietor, but does not include a registered charge and a 'registered charge' includes a mortgage or incumbrance registered as a charge under this Act;

(xxiv) 'Registered land' means land or any estate or interest in land the title to which is registered under this Act or any enactment replaced by this Act, and includes any easement, right, privilege, or benefit which is appurtenant or appendant thereto, and any mines and minerals within or under the same and held therewith;

(xxv) 'Rent' includes a rent service or a rent-charge, or other rent, toll, duty, royalty, or annual or periodical payment, in money or money's worth, issuing out of or charged upon land, but does not include mortgage interest;

(xxvi) 'Settled land' 'settlement' 'tenant for life' 'statutory owner' 'trustees of the settlement' 'capital money' . . . 'trust corporation' 'trust instrument' 'vesting deed' 'vesting order' 'vesting assent' and 'vesting instrument' have the same meaning as in the Settled Land Act 1925;

(xxvii) A 'term of years absolute' means a term of years, whether at a rent or not, taking effect either in possession or in reversion, with or without impeachment for waste, subject or not to another legal estate and either certain or liable to determination by notice, re-entry, operation of law, or by a provision for cesser on redemption, or in any other event (other than the dropping of a life, or the determination of a determinable life interest), but does not include any term of years determinable with life or lives or with the cesser of a determinable life interest, nor, if created after the commencement of this Act, a term of years which is not expressed to take effect in possession within twenty-one years after the creation thereof where required by the Law of Property Act 1925, to take effect within that period; and in this definition the expression 'term of years' includes a term for less than a year, or for a year or years and a fraction of a year or from year to year . . . ;

(xxx) 'United Kingdom' means Great Britain and Northern Ireland;

(xxxi) 'Valuable consideration' includes marriage, but does not include a nominal consideration in money;

(xxxii) 'Will' includes codicil.

20. Effect of registration of dispositions of freeholds

(1) In the case of a freehold estate registered with an absolute title, a disposition of the registered land or of a legal estate therein, including a lease thereof, for valuable

consideration shall, when registered, confer on the transferee or grantee an estate in fee simple or the term of years absolute or other legal estate expressed to be created in the land dealt with, together with all rights, privileges, and appurtenances belonging or appurtenant thereto, including (subject to any entry to the contrary in the register) the appropriate rights and interests which would, under the Law of Property Act 1925, have been transferred if the land had not been registered, subject—

(a)   to the incumbrances and other entries, if any, appearing on the register and any charge for inheritance tax subject to which the disposition takes effect under section 73 of this Act; and

(b)   unless the contrary is expressed on the register, to the overriding interests, if any, affecting the estate transferred or created,

but free from all other estates and interests whatsoever, including estates and interests of His Majesty, and the disposition shall operate in like manner as if the registered transferor or grantor were (subject to any entry to the contrary in the register) entitled to the registered land in fee simple in possession for his own benefit.

(2)   In the case of a freehold estate registered with a qualified title a disposition of the registered land or of a legal estate therein, including a lease thereof, for valuable consideration shall, when registered, have the same effect as it would have had if the land had been registered with an absolute title, save that such disposition shall not affect or prejudice the enforcement of any right or interest appearing by the register to be excepted.

(3)   In the case of a freehold estate registered with a possessory title, a disposition of the registered land or of a legal estate therein, including a lease thereof, for valuable consideration shall not affect or prejudice the enforcement of any right or interest adverse to or in derogation of the title of the first registered proprietor, and subsisting or capable of arising at the time of the registration of such proprietor; but, save as aforesaid, shall when registered have the same effect as it would have had if the land had been registered with an absolute title.

(4)   Where any such disposition is made without valuable consideration, it shall, so far as the transferee or grantee is concerned, be subject to any minor interests subject to which the transferor or grantor held the same, but, save as aforesaid, shall, when registered, in all respects, and in particular as respects any registered dealings on the part of the transferee or grantee, have the same effect as if the disposition had been made for valuable consideration.

Dispositions of Leasehold Land

21.   Powers of disposition of registered leaseholds

(1)   Where the registered land is a leasehold interest the proprietor may, in the prescribed manner, transfer the registered estate in the land or any part thereof, and, subject to any entry in the register to the contrary may in the prescribed manner—

(a)   transfer all or any of the leasehold mines and minerals apart from the surface; or the surface without all or any of the leasehold mines and minerals;

(b)   grant (to the extent of the registered estate) any annuity or rentcharge in possession, easement, right or privilege in, over, or derived from the registered land or any part thereof, in any form which sufficiently refers, in the prescribed manner, to the registered lease, and to the dominant tenement, whether being registered land or not;

(c)   transfer the registered land or any part thereof subject to a reservation to any person of any such annuity, rentcharge, easement, right, or privilege;

(d)   grant (subject or not to the reservation of an easement, right or privilege) an underlease of the registered land, or any part thereof, or of all or any mines and minerals apart from the surface, or of the surface without all or any of the mines and minerals, or of an easement, right or privilege, in or over the registered land or any part thereof, for any term of years absolute of less duration than the registered estate and for any purpose (but where by way of mortgage, subject to the provisions of this Act and of the Law of Property Act 1925 relating thereto), and in any form which sufficiently refers in the prescribed manner to the registered land, and in the case of an easement right, or privilege, to the dominant tenement, whether being registered land or not.

(2)   A disposition of registered leasehold land may be made subject to a rent legally apportioned in the prescribed manner, or to a rent not so apportioned.

(3)   An underlease for a term, not exceeding twenty-one years, to take effect in possession or within one year from the date thereof . . . may be granted and shall take effect under this section, notwithstanding that a caution, notice of deposit of a certificate, restriction, or inhibition (other than a bankruptcy inhibition) may be subsisting, but, subject to the interests intended to be protected by any such caution, notice, restriction or inhibition.

(4)   The foregoing powers of disposition shall (subject to the express provisions of this Act and the Law of Property Act 1925, relating to mortgages) apply to dispositions by the registered proprietor by way of charge or mortgage, but no estate, other than a legal estate, shall be capable of being disposed of or created under this section.

(5)   In this Act 'transfer' or 'disposition' when referring to registered leasehold land includes any disposition authorised as aforesaid, and 'transferee' has a corresponding meaning.

22.   Registration of dispositions of leaseholds

(1)   A transfer of the registered estate in the land or part thereof shall be completed by the registrar entering on the register the transferee as proprietor of the estate transferred, but until such entry is made the transferor shall be deemed to remain the proprietor of the registered estate; and where part only of the land is transferred, notice thereof shall also be noted on the register.

(2)   All interests transferred or created by dispositions by the registered proprietor other than the transfer of his registered estate in the land or in part thereof shall (subject to the provisions relating to mortgages) be completed by registration in the same manner and with the same effect as provided by this Act with respect to transfers of the registered estate, and notice thereof shall also be noted on the register in accordance with this Act:

    Provided that nothing in this subsection—

    (a)   shall authorise the registration of an underlease originally granted for a term not exceeding twenty-one years, or of an underlease which is a PPP lease or require the entry of a notice of such an underlease . . . ; or

    (b)   shall authorise the registration of a mortgage term where there is a subsisting right of redemption, or

    (c)   shall render necessary the registration of any easement, right, or privilege except as appurtenant to registered land, or the entry of notice thereof except as against the registered title of the servient land.

    Every such disposition shall, when registered, take effect as a registered disposition, and an underlease made by the registered proprietor which is not required to be registered or noted on the register shall nevertheless take effect as if it were a registered disposition immediately on being granted.

(3)   The general words implied in conveyances under the Law of Property Act 1925, shall apply, so far as applicable thereto, to transfers of a registered leasehold estate.

23.   Effect of registration of dispositions of leaseholds

(1)   In the case of a leasehold estate registered with an absolute title, a disposition (including a subdemise thereof) for valuable consideration shall, when registered, be deemed to vest in the transferee or underlessee the estate transferred or created to the extent of the registered estate, or for the term created by the subdemise, as the case may require, with all implied or expressed rights, privileges, and appurtenances attached to the estate transferred or created, including (subject to any entry to the contrary on the register) the appropriate rights and interests which would under the Law of Property Act 1925, have been transferred if the land had not been registered, but subject as follows—

    (a)   To all implied and express covenants, obligations, and liabilities incident to the estate transferred or created; and

     (b)   To the incumbrances and other entries (if any) appearing on the register and any charge for inheritance tax subject to which the disposition takes effect under section 73 of this Act; and

     (c)   Unless the contrary is expressed on the register, to the overriding interests, if any, affecting the estate transferred or created,

but free from all other estates and interests whatsoever, including estates and interests of His Majesty; and the transfer or subdemise shall operate in like manner as if the registered transferor or sublessor were (subject to any entry to the contrary on the register) absolutely entitled to the registered lease for his own benefit.

(2)   In the case of a leasehold estate registered with a good leasehold title, a disposition (including a subdemise thereof) for valuable consideration shall, when registered, have the same effect as it would have had if the land had been registered with an absolute title, save that it shall not affect or prejudice the enforcement of any right or interest affecting or in derogation of the title of the lessor to grant the lease.

(3)   In the case of a leasehold estate registered with a qualified title, a disposition (including a subdemise thereof) for valuable consideration shall, when registered, have the same effect as it would have had if the land had been registered with an absolute title, save that such disposition shall not affect or prejudice the enforcement of any right or interest (whether in respect of the lessor's title or otherwise) appearing by the register to be excepted.

(4)   In the case of a leasehold estate registered with a possessory title, a disposition (including a subdemise thereof) for valuable consideration shall not affect or prejudice the enforcement of any right or interest (whether in respect of the lessor's title or otherwise) adverse to or in derogation of the title of the first registered proprietor, and subsisting or capable of arising at the time of the registration of such proprietor, but save as aforesaid shall, when registered, have the same effect as it would have had if the land had been registered with an absolute title.

(5)   Where any such disposition is made without valuable consideration it shall, so far as the transferee or underlessee is concerned, be subject to any minor interests subject to which the transferor or sublessor held the same; but, save as aforesaid, shall, when registered, in all respects, and in particular as respects any registered dealings on the part of the transferee or underlessee, have the same effect as if the disposition had been made for valuable consideration.

PART IV
NOTICES, CAUTIONS, INHIBITIONS AND RESTRICTIONS

Notices

48.   **Registration of notice of lease**

(1)   Any lessee or other person entitled to or interested in a lease of registered land, where the term granted is not an overriding interest, may apply to the registrar to register notice of such lease in the prescribed manner, and when so registered, every proprietor and the persons deriving title under him shall be deemed to be affected with notice of such lease, as being an incumbrance on the registered land in respect of which the notice is entered:

     Provided that a proprietor of a charge or incumbrance registered or protected on the register prior to the registration of such notice shall not be deemed to be so affected by the notice unless such proprietor is, by reason of the lease having been made under a statutory or other power or by reason of his concurrence or otherwise, bound by the terms of the lease.

(2)   In order to register notice of a lease, if the proprietor of the registered land affected does not concur in registration thereof, the applicant shall obtain an order of the court authorising the registration of notice of the lease, and shall deliver the order to the registrar, accompanied with the original lease or a copy thereof, and thereupon the registrar shall make a note in the register identifying the lease or copy so deposited, and the lease or copy so deposited shall be deemed to be the instrument of which notice is given; but if the proprietor concurs in the notice being registered, notice may be entered in such manner as may be agreed upon:

Provided that, where the lease is binding on the proprietor of the land, neither the concurrence of such proprietor nor an order of the court shall be required.

49.   Rules to provide for notices of other rights, interests and claims

(1)   The provisions of the last foregoing section shall be extended by the rule so as to apply to the registration of notices of or of claims in respect of—

(a)   The grant or reservation of any annuity or rentcharge in possesion, either perpetual or for a term of years absolute:

(b)   The severance of any mines or minerals from the surface, except where the mines and minerals servered are expressly included in the registration:

(c)   Land charges until the land charge is registered as a registered charge:

(d)   The right of any person interested in land subject to a trust of land or in land subject to a settlement to require that (unless a trust corporation is acting as trustee) there shall be at least two trustees of the trust or settlement:

(e)   The rights of any widow in respect of dower or under the Intestates' Estates Act 1890, and any right to free bench or other like right saved by any statute coming into force concurrently with this Act (which rights shall take effect in equity as minor interests):

(f)   Creditors' notices and any other right, interest, or claim which it may be deemed expedient to protect by notice instead of by caution, inhibition, or restriction.

(g)   charging orders (within the meaning of the Charging Orders Act 1979 or the Criminal Justice Act 1988 or the Drug Trafficking Offences Act 1994) or regulations under paragraph 11 of Schedule 4 to the Local Government Finance Act 1988, or regulations under paragraph 11 of Schedule 4 of the Local Government Finance Act 1992 which in the case of unregistered land may be protected by registration under the Land Charges Act 1972 and which, notwithstanding section 59 of this Act, it may be deemed expedient to protect by notice instead of by caution.

(h)   Acquisition orders (within the meaning of Part III of the Landlord and Tenant Act 1987) which in the case of unregistered land may be protected by registration under the Land Charges Act 1972 and which, notwithstanding section 59 of this Act, it may be deemed expedient to protect by notice instead of by caution.

(j)   Access orders under the Access to Neighbouring Land Act 1992 which, notwithstanding section 59 of this Act, it may be deemed expedient to protect by notice instead of by caution.

(k)   Orders made under section 26(1) or 50(1) of the Leasehold Reform, Housing and Urban Development Act 1993 which in the case of unregistered land may be protected by registration under the Land Charges Act 1972 and which, notwithstanding section 59 of this Act, it may be deemed expedient to protect by notice instead of by caution.

(2)   A notice shall not be registered in respect of any estate, right, or interest which (independently of this Act) is capable of being overridden by the proprietor under a trust of land or the powers of the Settled Land Act 1925, or any other statute, or of a settlement, and of being protected by a restriction in the prescribed manner:

Provided that notice of such an estate right or interest may be lodged pending the appointment of trustees of land, or trustees of or a settlement, and if so lodged, shall be cancelled if and when the appointment is made and the proper restriction (if any) is entered.

(3)   A notice when registered in respect of a right, interest, or claim shall not affect prejudicially—

(a)   The powers of disposition of the personal representative of the deceased under whose will or by the operation of whose intestacy the right, interest, or claim arose; or

(b)   The powers of disposition (independently of this Act) of a proprietor holding the registered land subject to a trust of land.

50.   Notices of restrictive covenants

(1)   Any person entitled to the benefit of a restrictive covenant or agreement (not being a covenant or agreement made between a lessor and lessee) with respect to the building on or other user of registered land may apply to the registrar to enter notice thereof on the register,

and where practicable the notice shall be by reference to the instrument, if any, which contains the covenant or agreement, and a copy or abstract of such instrument shall be filed at the registry; and where any such covenant or agreement appears to exist at the time of first registration, notice thereof shall be entered on the register. In the case of registered land the notice aforesaid shall take the place of registration as a land charge.

(2) When such a notice is entered the proprietor of the land and the persons deriving title under him (except incumbrancers or other persons who at the time when the notice is entered may not be bound by the covenant or agreement) shall be deemed to be affected with notice of the covenant or agreement as being an incumbrance on the land.

(3) Where the covenant or agreement is discharged modified or dealt with by an order under the Law of Property Act 1925, or otherwise, or the court refuses to grant an injunction for enforcing the same, the entry shall either be cancelled or reference made to the order or other instrument and a copy of the order, judgment or instrument shall be filed at the registry.

(4) The notice shall, when practicable, refer to the land, whether registered or not, for the benefit of which the restriction was made.

51.   Notice of manorial incidents

Where land is affected by manorial incidents, the registrar may enter a note of that fact on the register, and may cancel such note when extinguishment of the manorial incidents has been proved to his satisfaction.

52.   Effect of notices

(1) A disposition by the proprietor shall take effect subject to all estates, rights and claims which are protected by way of notice on the register at the date of the registration or entry of notice of the disposition, but only if and so far as such estates, rights, and claims may be valid and are not (independently of this Act) overridden by the disposition.

(2) Where notice of a claim is entered on the register, such entry shall operate by way of notice only, and shall not operate to render the claim valid whether made adversely to or for the benefit of the registered land or charge.

Cautions

53.   Cautions against first registration

(1) Any person having or claiming such an interest in land not already registered as entities him to object to any disposition thereof being made without his consent, may lodge a caution with the registrar to the effect that the cautioner is entitled to notice in the prescribed form, and to be served in the prescribed manner, of any application that may be made for the registration of an interest in the land affecting the right of the cautioner.

(2) The caution shall be supported by an affidavit or declaration in the prescribed form, stating the nature of the interest of the cautioner, the land and estate therein to be affected by such caution, and such other matters as may be prescribed.

(3) After a caution has been lodged in respect of any estate, which has not already been registered, registration shall not be made of such estate until notice has been served on the cautioner to appear and oppose, if he thinks fit, such registration, and the prescribed time has elapsed since the date of the service of such notice, or the cautioner has entered an appearance, whichever may first happen.

54.   Cautions against dealings

(1) Any person interested under any unregistered instrument, or interested as a judgment creditor, or otherwise howsoever, in any land or charge registered in the name of any other person, may lodge a caution with the registrar to the effect that no dealing with such land or charge on the part of the proprietor is to be registered until notice has been served upon the cautioner:

Provided that a person whose estate, right, interest, or claim has been registered or protected by a notice or restriction shall not be entitled (except with the consent of the registrar) to lodge a caution in respect of such estate, right, interest, or claim . . .

(2) A caution lodged under this section shall be supported by such evidence as may be prescribed.

55. Effect of cautions against dealings

(1) After any such caution against dealings has been lodged in respect of any registered land or charge, the registrar shall not, without the consent of the cautioner, register any dealing or make any entry on the register for protecting the rights acquired under a deposit of a land or charge certificate or other dealing by the proprietor with such land or charge until he has served notice on the cautioner, warning him that his caution will cease to have any effect after the expiration of the prescribed number of days next following the date at which such notice is served; and after the expiration of such time as aforesaid the caution shall cease unless an order to the contrary is made by the registrar, and upon the caution so ceasing the registered land or charge may be dealt with in the same manner as if no caution had been lodged.

(2) If before the expiration of the said period the cautioner, or some person on his behalf, appears before the registrar, and where so required by the registrar gives sufficient security to indemnify every party against any damage that may be sustained by reason of any dealing with the registered land or charge, or the making of any such entry as aforesaid, being delayed, the registrar may thereupon, if he thinks fit to do so, delay registering any dealing with the land or charge or making any such entry for such period as he thinks just.

56. General provisions as to cautions

(1) Any person aggrieved by any act done by the registrar in relation to a caution under this Act may appeal to the court in the prescribed manner.

(2) A caution lodged in pursuance of this Act shall not prejudice the claim or title of any person and shall have no effect whatever except as in this Act mentioned.

(3) If any person lodges a caution with the registrar without reasonable cause, he shall be liable to make to any person who may have sustained damage by the lodging of the caution such compensation as may be just, and such compensation shall be recoverable as a debt by the person who has sustained damage from the person who lodged the caution.

(4) The personal representative of a deceased cautioner may consent or object to registration or a dealing in the same manner as the cautioner.

Inhibitions

57. Power for court or registrar to inhibit registered dealings

(1) The court, or, subject to an appeal to the court, the registrar, upon the application of any person interested, made in the prescribed manner, in relation to any registered land or charge, may, after directing such inquiries (if any) to be made and notices to be given and hearing such persons as the court or registrar thinks expedient, issue an order or make an entry inhibiting for a time, or until the occurrence of an event to be named in such order or entry, or generally until further order or entry, the registration or entry of any dealing with any registered land or registered charge.

(2) The court or registrar may make or refuse to make any such order or entry, and annex thereto any terms or conditions the court or registrar may think fit, and discharge such order or cancel such entry when granted, with or without costs, and generally act in the premises in such manner as the justice of the case requires.

(3) Any person aggrieved by any act done by the registrar in pursuance of this section may appeal to the court in the prescribed manner.

(4) The court or the registrar may, in lieu of an inhibition, order a notice or restriction to be placed on the register.

Restrictions

58. Power to place restrictions on register

(1) Where the proprietor of any registered land or charge desires to place restrictions on transferring or charging the land or on disposing of or dealing with the land or charge in any

manner in which he is by this Act authorised to dispose of or deal with it, or on the deposit by way of security of any certificate, the proprietor may apply to the registrar to make an entry in the register that no transaction to which the application relates shall be effected, unless the following things, or such of them as the proprietor may determine, are done—

(a)   unless notice of any application for the transaction is transmitted by post to such address as he may specify to the registrar,

(b)   unless the consent of some person or persons, to be named by the proprietor, is given to the transaction;

(c)   unless some other matter or thing is done as may be required by the applicant and approved by the registrar:

Provided that no restriction under this section shall extend or apply to dispositions of or dealings with minor interests.

(2)   The registrar shall thereupon, if satisfied of the right of the applicant to give the directions, enter the requisite restriction on the register, and no transaction to which the restriction relates shall be effected except in conformity therewith; but it shall not be the duty of the registrar to enter any such restriction, except upon such terms as to payment of fees and otherwise as may be prescribed, or to enter any restriction that the registrar may deem unreasonable or calculated to cause inconvenience.

(3)   In the case of joint proprietors the restriction may be to the effect that when the number of proprietors is reduced below a certain specified number no disposition shall be registered except under an order of the court, or of the registrar after inquiry into title, subject to appeal to the court, and, subject to general rules, such an entry under this subsection as may be prescribed shall be obligatory unless it is shown to the registrar's satisfaction that the joint proprietors are entitled for their own benefit, or can give valid receipts for capital money, or that one of them is a trust corporation.

(4)   Any such restrictions, except such as are in this section declared to be obligatory, may at any time be withdrawn or modified at the instance of all the persons for the time being appearing by the register to be interested in such directions, and shall also be liable to be set aside by an order of the court.

(5)   Rules may be made to enable applications to be made for the entry of restrictions by persons other than the proprietor.

Protection of Various Interests

59.   Writs, orders, deeds of arrangement, pending actions, etc.

(1)   A writ, order, deed of arrangement, pending action, or other interest which in the case of unregistered land may be protected by registration under the Land Charges Act 1925, shall, where the land affected or the charge securing the debt affected is registered, be protected only by lodging a creditor's notice, a bankruptcy inhibition or a caution against dealings with the land or charge.

(2)   Registration of a land charge (other than a local land charge) shall, where the land affected is registered, be effected only by registering under this Act a notice caution or other prescribed entry:

Provided that before a land charge including a local land charge affecting registered land (being a charge to secure money) is realised, it shall be registered and take effect as a registered charge under this Act in the prescribed manner, without prejudice to the priority conferred by the land charge.

(3)   . . .

(4)   When a land charge protected by notice has been discharged as to all or any part of the land comprised therein, the notices relating thereto and to all devolutions of and dealings therewith shall be vacated as to the registered land affected by the discharge.

(5)   The foregoing provisions of this section shall apply only to writs and orders, deeds of arrangement, pending actions and land charges which if the land were unregistered would for purposes of protection be required to be registered or re-registered after the

commencement of this Act under the Land Charges Act 1925; and for the purposes of this section a land charge does not include a puisne mortgage . . .

(6)   Subject to the provisions of this Act relating to fraud and to the title of a trustee in bankruptcy, a purchaser acquiring title under a registered disposition, shall not be concerned with any pending action, writ, order, deed of arrangment, or other document, matter, or claim (not being an overriding interest or a charge for inheritance tax subject to which the disposition takes effect under section 73 of this Act) which is not protected by a caution or other entry on the register, whether he has or has not notice thereof, express, implied, or constructive.

(7)   In this section references to registration under the Land Charges Act 1925, apply to any registration made under any other statute which, in the case of unregistered land, is by the Land Charges Act 1925, to have effect as if the registration had been made under that Act.

60.   Notice of incumbrances registered under the Companies Act

(1)   Where a company, registered under the Companies (Consolidation) Act 1908, is registered as a proprietor of any estate or charge already registered, the registrar shall not be concerned with any mortgage, charge, debenture, debenture stock, trust deed for securing the same, or other incumbrance created or issued by the company, whether or not registered under that Act, unless the same is registered or protected by caution or otherwise under this Act.

(2)   No indemnity shall be payable under this Act by reason of a purchaser acquiring any interest under a registered disposition from the company free from any such incumbrance.

61.   Protection of creditors prior to registration of trustee in bankruptcy

(1)   The registrar shall as soon as practicable after registration of a petition in bankruptcy as a pending action under the Land Charges Act 1925, register a notice (in this Act called a creditors' notice) against the title of any proprietor of any registered land or charge which appears to be affected, and such notice shall protect the rights of all creditors, and unless cancelled by the registrar in the prescribed manner such notice shall remain in force until a bankruptcy inhibition is registered or the trustee in bankruptcy is registered as proprietor.

      No fee shall be charged for the registration of the notice.

(2)   . . .

(3)   The registrar shall, as soon as practicable after registration of a bankruptcy order under the Land Charges Act 1925, enter an inhibition (in this Act called a bankruptcy inhibition) against the title of any proprietor of any registered land or charge which appear to be affected.

      No fee shall be charged for the registration of the inhibition.

(4)   From and after the entry of a bankruptcy inhibition (but without prejudice to dealings with or in right of interests of charges having priority over the estate or charge of the bankrupt proprietor), no dealing affecting the registered land or charge of the proprietor, other than the registration of the trustee in bankruptcy, shall be entered on the register until the inhibition is vacated as to the whole or part of the land or charge dealt with.

(5)   If and when a proprietor of any registered land or charge is adjudged bankrupt, his registered estate or interest, if belonging, to him beneficially, and whether acquired before or after the date of adjudication, shall vest in the trustee in bankruptcy in accordance with the statutory provisions relating to bankruptcy for the time being in force.

(6)   Where under a disposition to a purchaser in good faith for money or money's worth such purchaser is registered as proprietor of an estate or a charge, then notwithstanding that the person making the disposition is adjudged bankrupt, the title of his trustee in bankruptcy acquired after the commencement of this Act shall, as from the date of such disposition, be void as against such purchaser unless at the date of such disposition, either a creditor's notice or a bankruptcy inhibition has been registered, but a purchaser who, at the date of the execution of the registered disposition, has notice of the bankruptcy petition or the adjudication, shall not be deemed to take in good faith.

      Nothing in this section shall impose on a purchaser a liability to make any search under the Land Charges Act 1925.

(7)   Where the estate or assets of a bankrupt proprietor suffer loss by reason of the omission of the registrar to register a creditor's notice or bankruptcy inhibition, as required by this section, or on account of the execution or registration of a disposition after a petition is registered as a pending action or after a bankruptcy order is registered and before the registration of a creditors' notice or bankruptcy inhibition, the trustee in a bankruptcy shall be entitled to indemnity as a person suffering loss by reason of an error or omission in the register.

(8)   If neither a creditors' notice nor a bankruptcy inhibition is registered against a bankrupt proprietor, nothing in this section shall prejudicially affect a registered disposition of any registered land or charge acquired by the bankrupt after adjudication . . .

(9)   If and when a bankruptcy inhibition is wholly or partly vacated, for any cause other than by reason of the registration of the trustee in bankruptcy, any registered estate If and when a bankruptcy inhibition is wholly or partially vacated, for any cause or interest vested in the trustee in bankruptcy shall, as respects the registered land or charge to which the vacation extends, be divested and the same shall vest in the proprietor in whom it would have been vested if there had been no adjudication in bankruptcy.

(10) . . .

PART VI
GENERAL PROVISIONS AS TO REGISTRATION AND THE EFFECT THEREOF

70.   Liability of registered land to overriding interests

(1)   All registered land shall, unless under the provisions of this Act the contrary is expressed on the register, be deemed to be subject to such of the following overriding interests as may be for the time being subsisting in reference thereto, and such interests shall not be treated as incumbrances within the meaning of this Act, (that is to say):—

(a)   Rights of common, drainage rights, customary rights (until extinguished), public rights, profits a prendre, rights of sheepwalk, rights of way, watercourses, rights of water, and other easements not being equitable easements required to be protected by notice on the register;

(b)   Liability to repair highways by reason of tenure, quit-rents, crown rents, heriots and other rents and charges (until extinguished) having their origin in tenure;

(c)   Liability to repair the chancel of any church;

(d)   Liability in respect of embankments, and sea and river walls;

(e)   . . . payments in lieu of tithe, and charges or annuities payable for the redemption of tithe rentcharges;

(f)   Subject to the provisions of this Act, rights acquired or in course of being acquired under the Limitation Acts;

(g)   The rights of every person in actual occupation of the land or in receipt of the rents and profits thereof, save where enquiry is made of such person and the rights are not disclosed;

(h)   In the case of a possessory, qualified, or good leasehold title, all estates, rights, interests, and powers excepted from the effect of registration;

(i)   Rights under local land charges unless and until registered or protected on the register in the prescribed manner;

(j)   Rights of fishing and sporting, seignorial and manorial rights of all descriptions (until extinguished), and franchises;

(k)   Leases granted for a term not exceeding twenty-one years;

(kk) PPP leases;

(l)   In respect of land registered before the commencement of this Act, rights to mines and minerals, and rights of entry, search, and user, and other rights and reservations incidental to or required for the purpose of giving full effect to the enjoyment of rights to mines and minerals or of property in mines or minerals, being rights which, where the title was first registered before the first day of January, eighteen hundred and ninety-eight, were created before that date, and where the title was first registered after the thirty-first day of December, eighteen hundred and ninety-seven, were created before the date of first registration;

(m) any interest or right which is an overriding interest by virtue of paragraph 1(1) of Schedule 9 of the Coal Industry Act 1994.

Provided that, where it is proved to the satisfaction of the registrar that any land registered or about to be registered is exempt from land tax, or tithe rentcharge or payments in lieu of tithe, or from charges or annuities payable for the redemption of tithe rentcharge, the registrar may notify the fact on the register in the prescribed manner.

(2) Where at the time of first registration any easement, right, privilege, or benefit created by an instrument and appearing on the title adversely affects the land, the registrar shall enter a note thereof on the register.

(3) Where the existence of any overriding interest mentioned in this section is proved to the satisfaction of the registrar or admitted, he may (subject to any prescribed exceptions) enter notice of the same or of a claim thereto on the register, but no claim to an easement, right, or privilege not created by an instrument shall be noted against the title to the servient land if the proprietor of such land (after the prescribed notice is given to him) shows sufficient cause to the contrary.

(3A) Neither subsection (2) nor subsection (3) of this section shall apply in the case of a PPP lease.

(4) Neither subsection (2) nor subsection (3) of this section shall apply in the case of any such interest or right as is mentioned in subsection (1)(m) of this subsection.

75.   Acquisition of title by possession

(1) The Limitation Acts shall apply to registered land in the same manner and to the same extent as those Acts apply to land not registered, except that where, if the land were not registered, the estate of the person registered as proprietor would be extinguished, such estate shall not be extinguished but shall be deemed to be held by the proprietor for the time being in trust for the person who, by virtue of the said Acts, has acquired title against any proprietor, but without prejudice to the estates and interests of any other person interested in the land whose estate or interest is not extinguished by those Acts.

(2) Any person claiming to have acquired a title under the Limitation Acts to a registered estate in the land may apply to be registered as proprietor thereof.

(3) The registrar shall, on being satisfied as to the applicant's title, enter the applicant as proprietor either with absolute, good leasehold, qualified, or possessory title, as the case may require, but without prejudice to any estate or interest protected by any entry on the register which may not have been extinguished under the Limitation Acts, and such registration shall, subject as aforesaid, have the same effect as the registration of a first proprietor; but the proprietor or the applicant or any other person interested may apply to the court for the determination of any question arising under this section.

(4) . . .

(5) Rules may be made for applying (subject to any necessary modifications) the provisions of this section to cases where an easement, right or privilege has been acquired by prescription.

PART VII
RECTIFICATION OF REGISTER AND INDEMNITY

82.   Rectification of the register

(1) The register may be rectified pursuant to an order of the court or by the registrar, subject to an appeal to the court, in any of the following cases, but subject to the provisions of this section:—

(a) Subject to any express provisions of this Act to the contrary, where a court of competent jurisdiction has decided that any person is entitled to any estate right or interest in or to any registered land or charge, and as a consequence of such decision such court is of opinion that a rectification of the register is required, and makes an order to that effect;

(b)   Subject to any express provision of this Act to the contrary, where the court, on the application in the prescribed manner of any person who is aggrieved by any entry made in, or by the omission of any entry from, the register, or by any default being made, or unnecessary delay taking place, in the making of any entry in the register, makes an order for the rectification of the register;

(c)   In any case and at any time with the consent of all persons interested;

(d)   Where the court or the registrar is satisfied that any entry in the register has been obtained by fraud;

(e)   Where two or more persons are, by mistake, registered as proprietors of the same registered estate or of the same charge;

(f)   Where a mortgagee has been registered as proprietor of the land instead of as proprietor of a charge and a right of redemption is subsisting;

(g)   Where a legal estate has been registered in the name of a person who if the land had not been registered would not have been the estate owner; and

(h)   In any other case where, by reason of any error or omission in the register, or by reason of any entry made under a mistake, it may be deemed just to rectify the register.

(2)   The register may be rectified under this section, notwithstanding that the rectification may affect any estates, rights, charges, or interests acquired or protected by registration, or by any entry on the register, or otherwise.

(3)   The register shall not be rectified, except for the purpose of giving effect to an overriding interest or an order of the court, so as to affect the title of the proprietor who is in possession—

(a)   unless the proprietor has caused or substantially contributed to the error or omission by fraud or lack of proper care; or

(b)   . . .

(c)   unless for any other reason, in any particular case, it is considered that it would be unjust not to rectify the register against him.

(4)   Where a person is in possession of registered land in right of a minor interest, he shall, for the purpose of this section, be deemed to be in possession as agent for the proprietor.

(5)   The registrar shall obey the order of any competent court in relation to any registered land on being served with the order or an official copy thereof.

(6)   On every rectification of the register the land certificate and any charge certificate which may be affected shall be produced to the registrar unless an order to the contrary is made by him.

83.   Indemnity for errors or omissions in the register

(1)   Where the register is rectified under this Act, then, subject to the provisions of this Act—

(a)   any person suffering loss by reason of the rectification shall be entitled to be indemnified; and

(b)   if, notwithstanding the rectification, the person in whose favour the register is rectified suffers loss by reason of an error or omission in the register in respect of which it is so rectified, he also shall be entitled to be indemnified.

(2)   Where an error or omission has occurred in the register, but the register is not rectified, any person suffering loss by reason of the error or omission shall, subject to the provisions of this Act, be entitled to be indemnified.

(3)   Where any person suffers loss by reason of the loss or destruction of any document lodged at the registry for inspection or safe custody or by reason of an error in any official search, he shall be entitled to be indemnified under this Act.

(4)   Subject to the following provisions of this section, a proprietor of any registered land or charge claiming in good faith under a forged disposition shall, where the register is rectified, be deemed to have suffered loss by reason of such rectification and shall be entitled to be indemnified under this Act.

(5)   No indemnity shall be payable under this Act—

(a)   on account of any loss suffered by a claimant wholly or partly as a result of his own fraud or wholly as a result of his own lack of proper care;

    (b)   on account of any mines or minerals, or the existence of any right to work or get mines or minerals, unless it is noted on the register that the mines or minerals are included in the title; or

    (c)   on account of any costs or expenses (of whatever nature) incurred without the consent of the registrar, unless—

        (i)   by reason of urgency it was not practicable to apply for the registrar's consent before they were incurred, and

        (ii)   the registrar subsequently approves them for the purposes of this paragraph.

(6)   Where any loss suffered by a claimant is suffered partly as a result of his own lack of proper care, any indemnity payable to him shall be reduced to such extent as is just and equitable having regard to his share in the responsibility for the loss.

(7)   For the purposes of subsections (5)(a) and (6) above, any fraud or lack of proper care on the part of a person from whom the claimant derives title (otherwise than under a disposition for valuable consideration which is registered or protected on the register) shall be treated as if it were fraud or lack of proper care on the part of the claimant (and the reference in subsection (6) to the claimant's share in the responsibility for the loss shall be construed accordingly).

(8)   Where an indemnity is paid in respect of the loss of an estate or interest in or charge on land, the amount so paid shall not exceed—

    (a)   where the register is not rectified, the value of the estate, interest charge at the time when the error or omission which caused the loss was made;

    (b)   where the register is rectified, the value (if there had been no rectification) of the estate, interest or charge, immediately before the time of rectification.

(9)   Subject to subsection (5)(c) above, as restricted by section 2(2) of the Land Registration and Land Charges Act 1971—

    (a)   an indemnity under any provision of this Act shall include such amount, if any, as may be reasonable in respect of any costs or expenses properly incurred by the claimant in relation to the matter; and

    (b)   a claimant for an indemnity under any such provision shall be entitled to an indemnity thereunder of such amount, if any, as may be reasonable in respect of any such costs or expenses, notwithstanding that no other indemnity money is payable thereunder.

(10)   Where indemnity is paid to a claimant in respect of any loss, the registrar, on behalf of the Crown, shall be entitled—

    (a)   to recover the amount paid from any person who caused or substantially contributed to the loss by his fraud; or

    (b)   for the purpose of recovering the amount paid, to enforce—

        (i)   any right of action (of whatever nature and however arising) which the claimant would have been entitled to enforce had the indemnity not been paid, and

        (ii)   where the register has been rectified, any right of action (of whatever nature and however arising) which the person in whose favour the register has been rectified would have been entitled to enforce had it not been rectified.

(11)   Subsection (10) above does not prejudice any other rights of recovery which by virtue of any enactment are exercisable by the registrar where he has made a payment of indemnity.

(12)   A liability to pay indemnity under this Act shall be deemed to be a simple contract debt; and for the purposes of the Limitation Act 1980, the cause of action shall be deemed to arise at the time when the claimant knows, or but for his own default might have known, of the existence of his claim.

(13)   This section applies to the Crown in like manner as it applies to a private person.

PART IX

UNREGISTERED DEALINGS WITH REGISTERED LAND

Powers of dealing with Registered Land off the Register

101.   Dispositions off register creating 'minor interests'

(1)   Any person, whether being the proprietor or not, having a sufficient interest or power in or over registered land, may dispose of or deal with the same, and create any interests or rights therein which are permissible in like manner and by the like modes of assurance in all respects as if the land were not registered, but subject as provided by this section.

(2)   All interests and rights disposed of or created under subsection (1) of this section (whether by the proprietor or any other person) shall, subject to the provisions of this section, take effect as minor interests, and be capable of being overridden by registered dispositions for valuable consideration.

(3)   Minor interests shall, subject to the express exceptions contained in this section, take effect only in equity, but may be protected by entry on the register of such notices, cautions, inhibitions and restrictions as are provided for by this Act or rules.

(4)   A minor interest in registered land subsisting or capable of taking effect at the commencement of this Act, shall not fail or become invalid by reason of the same being converted into an equitable interest; but after such commencement a minor interest in registered land shall only be capable of being validly created in any case in which an equivalent equitable interest could have been validly created if the land had not been registered.

(5)   Where after the commencement of this Act, the proprietor of the registered estate which is settled, disposes of or deals with his beneficial interest in possession in favour of a purchaser, and accordingly the minor interest disposed of or created would, but for the restrictions imposed by the Law of Property Act 1925, and this section, on the creation of legal estates, have been a legal estate, the purchaser (subject as provided by the next following section in regard to priorities) may exercise all such rights and remedies as he might have exercised had the minor interest been a legal estate, and the reversion (if any) on any leases or tenancies derived out of the registered estate had been vested in him.

(6)   A minor interest created under this section does not operate to prevent a registered estate passing to the personal representative of a deceased proprietor, or to the survivor or survivors of two or more joint proprietors, nor does this section affect the right of any person entitled to an overriding interest, or having any power to dispose of or create an overriding interest, to dispose of or create the same.

102.   Priorities as between minor interests

(1)   If a minor interest subsisting or capable of taking effect at the commencement of this Act, would, if the Law of Property Acts 1922 and 1925, and this Act had not been passed have taken effect as a legal estate, then (subject and without prejudice to the estate and powers of the proprietor whose estate is affected) the conversion thereof into an equitable interest shall not affect its priority over other minor interests.

(2)–(3). . .

103.   Obligation to give effect on the register to certain minor interests

(1)   Where by the operation of any statute or statutory or other power, or by virtue of any vesting order of any court or other competent authority, or an order appointing a person to convey, or of a vesting declaration (express or implied) or of an appointment or other assurance, a minor interest in the registered land is disposed of or created which would, if registered, be capable of taking effect as a legal estate or charge by way of legal mortgage, then—

   (i)   if the estate owner would, had the land not been registered, have been bound to give effect thereto by conveying or creating a legal estate or charge by way of legal mortgage, the proprietor shall, subject to proper provision being made for payment of costs, be bound to give legal effect to the transaction by a registered disposition:

(ii)　if the proprietor is unable or refuses to make the requisite disposition or cannot be found, or if for any other reason a disposition by him cannot be obtained within a reasonable time, or if, had the land not been registered, no conveyance by the estate owner would have been required to give legal effect to the transaction, the registrar shall give effect thereto in the prescribed manner in like manner and with the like consequences as if the transaction had been carried out by a registered disposition:

Provided that—

(a)　So long as the proprietor has power under the Settled Land Act 1925, or any other statute conferring special powers on a tenant for life or statutory owner, or under the settlement, to override the minor interest so disposed of or created, no estate or charge shall be registered which would prejudicially affect any such powers:

(b)　So long as the proprietor holds the land subject to a trust of land, no estate or charge shall be registered in respect of an interest which, under the Law of Property Act 1925, or otherwise ought to remain liable to be overridden on a sale of the land by the trustees:

(c)　Nothing in this subsection shall impose on a proprietor an obligation to make a disposition unless the person requiring the disposition to be made has a right in equity to call for the same:

(d)　Nothing in this subsection shall prejudicially affect the rights of a personal representative in relation to the administration of the estate of the deceased.

(2)　On every alteration in the register made pursuant to this section the land certificate and any charge certificate which may be affected shall be produced to the registrar unless an order to the contrary is made by him.

PART XI
COMPULSORY REGISTRATION

123.　Compulsory registration: dispositions to which requirement to register applies

(1)　The requirement of compulsory registration applies in relation to the following dispositions of unregistered land—

(a)　any qualifying conveyance of the freehold estate;

(b)　any qualifying grant of a term of years absolute of more than 21 years from the date of the grant;

(c)　any qualifying assignment of a term of years absolute which on the date of the assignment has more than 21 years to run; and

(d)　any disposition effected by an assent (including a vesting assent) or by a vesting deed which is a disposition of—

(i)　the freehold estate, or

(ii)　a term of years absolute on which the date of the disposition has more than 21 years to run.

(2)　The requirement of compulsory registration also applies in relation to any disposition by the estate owner of unregistered land which is a legal mortgage of—

(a)　the freehold estate, or

(b)　a term of years absolute which on the date of the mortgage has more than 21 years to run,

where, on its creation, the mortgage takes effect as a mortgage to be protected by the deposit of documents relating to that estate or term of years, and ranks in priority ahead of all other mortgages (if any) then affecting that estates or term of years.

(3)　Without prejudice to the power to make an order under subsection (4) below, nothing in this section or section 123A of this Act has the effect of requiring the registration of title to—

(a)　an incorporeal hereditament;

(b)　mines and minerals apart from the surface; or

(c)　corporeal hereditaments which are part of a manor and included in the sale of a manor as such.

(4)　The Lord Chancellor may by order—

(a)   amend this section so as to add to the dispositions in relation to which the requirement of compulsory registration applies any such disposition of, or otherwise affecting, a legal estate in unregistered land as is specified in the order; and

(b)   make such consequential amendments of any provision of, or having effect under, any Act as he thinks appropriate.

(5)   Any order under subsection (4) above shall be made by statutory instrument subject to annulment in pursuance of a resolution of either House of Parliament.

(6)   For the purposes of this section—

(a)   a conveyance, grant or assignment is a 'qualifying' conveyance, grant or assignment if it is made—

(i)   for valuable or other consideration,

(ii)   by way of gift, or

(iii) in pursuance of an order of any court;

(b)   a conveyance, grant or assignment of property with a negative value is to be regarded (without prejudice to the generality of paragraph (a)(i) above) as made for valuable or other consideration;

(c)   'assignment' does not include an assignment or surrender of a lease to the owner of the immediate reversion where the term is to merge in that reversion; and

(d)   'term of years' does not include a PPP lease.

123A. Compulsory registration: effect of requirement to register

(1)   This section applies to any disposition which, by virtue of any provision of section 123 of this Act, is one in relation to which the requirement of compulsory registration applies.

(2)   Where any such disposition is effected, then—

(a)   if it is a disposition falling within section 123(1), the person who under the disposition is entitled to the legal estate transferred or created by it, or

(b)   if it is a disposition falling within section 123(2), the estate owner of the legal estate charged by the mortgage, or

(c)   (in either case) that person's successor in title or assign,

must before the end of the applicable period apply to the registrar to be registered (or alternatively, where he is not a person in a fiduciary position, to have any nominee registered) as the first proprietor of that estate.

(3)   In this section 'the applicable period' means in the first instance the period of two months beginning with the date of the disposition, but—

(a)   the registrar may, if satisfied on the application of any interested person that there is good reason for doing so, make an order extending or further extending that period; and

(b)   if he does so 'the applicable period' means that period as for the time being extended under this subsection.

(4)   Pending compliance with subsection (2) above the disposition shall operate to transfer or grant a legal estate, or (as the case may be) create a legal mortgage, in accordance with its terms.

(5)   If subsection (2) above is not complied with, the disposition shall at the end of the applicable period become void as regards any such transfer, grant or creation of a legal estate; and—

(a)   if it is a disposition purporting to transfer a legal estate, the title to that estate shall thereupon revert to the transferor who shall hold that estate on a bare trust for the transferee;

(b)   if it is a disposition purporting to grant a legal estate or create a legal mortgage, the disposition shall thereupon take effect as if it were a contract to grant or create that estate or mortgage made for valuable consideration (whether or not it was so made or satisfies any of the formal requirements of such a contract).

(6)   If an order extending the applicable period under subsection (3) above is made at a time when the disposition has become void in accordance with subsection (5) above, then as from the making of the order—

(a)   subsection (5) shall cease to apply to the disposition, and

(b)   subsection (4) above shall apply to it instead,

and similarly in the case of any further order so made.

(7)   If any disposition is subsequently effected by way of replacement for a disposition which has become void in accordance with subsection (5) above, the requirement of compulsory registration shall apply in relation to it under section 123 in the same way as it applied in relation to the void disposition, and the provisions of this section shall have effect accordingly.

(8)   Except to the extent to which the parties to any such replacement disposition agree otherwise, the transferee or grantee (as the case may be) shall—

(a)   bear all the proper costs of and incidental to the disposition, and

(b)   indemnify the transferor or grantor (as the case may be) in respect of any other liability reasonably incurred by him in consequence of the failure to comply with subsection (2) above.

(9)   Where any such replacement disposition is a mortgage falling within section 123(2) of this Act, subsection (8) above shall apply as if the reference to the grantee were a reference to the mortgagor and the reference to the grantor were a reference to the mortgagee.

(10) Rules under this Act may make provision—

(a)   applying to provisions of this Act to any dealings which take place between—

(i)   the date of any disposition to which this section applies, and

(ii)   the date of the application for first registration,

as if the dealings had taken place after the date of the registration, and for the registration to be effective as of the date of the application.

(b)   enabling the mortgagee under any mortgage falling within section 123(2) of this Act to require the legal estate charged by the mortgage to be registered whether or not the mortgagor consents.

RECREATIONAL CHARITIES ACT 1958
(1958, c. 17)

1.   General provision as to recreational and similar trusts, etc.

(1)   Subject to the provisions of this Act, it shall be and be deemed always to have been charitable to provide, or assist in the provision of, facilities for recreation or other leisure-time occupation, if the facilities are provided in the interests of social welfare:

Provided that nothing in this section shall be taken to derogate from the principle that a trust or institution to be charitable must be for the public benefit.

(2)   The requirement of the foregoing subsection that the facilities are provided in the interests of social welfare shall not be treated as satisfied unless—

(a)   the facilities are provided with the object of improving the conditions of life for the persons for whom the facilities are primarily intended; and

(b)   either—

(i)   those persons have need of such facilities as aforesaid by reason of their youth, age, infirmity or disablement, poverty or social and economic circumstances; or

(ii)   the facilities are to be available to the members or female members of the public at large.

(3)   Subject to the said requirement, subsection (1) of this section applies in particular to the provision of facilities at village halls, community centres and women's institutes, and to the provision and maintenance of grounds and buildings to be used for purposes of recreation or leisure-time occupation, and extends to the provision of facilities for those purposes by the organising of any activity.

2.   Miners' welfare trust

(1)   Where trusts declared before the seventeenth day of December, nineteen hundred and fifty-seven, required or purported to require property to be held for the purpose of activities

which are social welfare activities within the meaning of the Miners' Welfare Act 1952 and at that date the whole or part of the property held on those trusts or of any property held with that property represented an application of moneys standing to the credit of the miners' welfare fund or moneys provided by the Coal Industry Social Welfare Organisation, those trusts shall be treated as if they were and always had been charitable.

(2) For the purposes of this section property held on the same trusts as other property shall be deemed to be held with it, though vested in different trustees.

3. Savings and other provisions as to past transactions

(1) Nothing in this Act shall be taken to restrict the purposes which are to be regarded as charitable independently of this Act.

. . .

RIGHTS OF LIGHT ACT 1959
(1959, c. 56)

Note. References to the Land Charges Act 1925 should be read as references to the Land Charges Act 1972.

2. Registration of notice in lieu of obstruction of access of light

(1) For the purpose of preventing the access and use of light from being taken to be enjoyed without interruption, any person who is an owner of land (in this and the next following section referred to as 'the servient land') over which light passes to a dwelling-house, workshop or other building (in this and the next following section referred to as 'the dominant building') may apply to the local authority in whose area the dominant building is situated for the registration of a notice under this section.

(2) An application for the registration of a notice under this section shall be in the prescribed form and shall—

   (a) identify the servient land and the dominant building in the prescribed manner, and

   (b) state that the registration of a notice in pursuance of the application is intended to be equivalent to the obstruction of the access of light to the dominant building across the servient land which would be caused by the erection, in such position on the servient land as may be specified in the application, of an opaque structure of such dimensions (including, if the application so states, unlimited height) as may be so specified.

(3) Any such application shall be accompanied by one or other of the following certificates issued by the Lands Tribunal, that is to say,—

   (a) a certificate certifying that adequate notice of the proposed application has been given to all persons who, in the circumstances existing at the time when the certificate is issued, appear to the Lands Tribunal to be persons likely to be affected by the registration of a notice in pursuance of the application;

   (b) a certificate certifying that, in the opinion of the Lands Tribunal, the case is one of exceptional urgency, and that accordingly a notice should be registered forthwith as a temporary notice for such period as may be specified in the certificate.

(4) Where application is duly made to a local authority for the registration of a notice under this section, it shall be the duty of that authority to register the notice in the appropriate local land charges register, and—

   (a) any notice so registered under this section shall be a local land charge; but

   (b) section 5(1) and (2) and section 10 of the Local Land Charges Act 1975 shall not apply in relation thereto.

. . .

3. Effect of registered notice and proceedings relating thereto

(1) Where, in pursuance of an application made in accordance with the last preceding section, a notice is registered thereunder, then, for the purpose of determining whether any person is entitled (by virtue of the Prescription Act, 1832, or otherwise) to a right to the access of light to the dominant building across the servient land, the access of light to that building across

that land shall be treated as obstructed to the same extent, and with the like consequences, as if an opaque structure, of the dimensions specified in the application,—

    (a)   had, on the date of registration of the notice, been erected in the position on the servient land specified in the application, and had been so erected by the person who made the application, and

    (b)   had remained in that position during the period for which the notice has effect and had been removed at the end of that period.

(2)   For the purposes of this section a notice registered under the last preceding section shall be taken to have effect until either—

    (a)   the registration is cancelled, or

    (b)   the period of one year beginning with the date of registration of the notice expires, or

    (c)   in the case of a notice registered in pursuance of an application accompanied by a certificate issued under paragraph (b) of subsection (3) of the last preceding section, the period specified in the certificate expires without such a further certificate as is mentioned in paragraph (c) of subsection (5) of that section having before the end of that period been lodged with the local authority,

and shall cease to have effect on the occurrence of any one of those events.

(3)   Subject to the following provisions of this section, any person who, if such a structure as is mentioned in subsection (1) of this section had been erected as therein mentioned, would have had a right of action in any court in respect of that structure, on the grounds that he was entitled to a right to the access of light to the dominant building across the servient land, and that the said right was infringed by that structure, shall have the like right of action in that court in respect of the registration of a notice under the last preceding section:

    Provided that an action shall not be begun by virtue of this subsection after the notice in question has ceased to have effect.

(4)   Where, at any time during the period for which a notice registered under the last preceding section has effect, the circumstances are such that, if the access of light to the dominant building had been enjoyed continuously from a date one year earlier than the date on which the enjoyment thereof in fact began, a person would have had a right of action in any court by virtue of the last preceding subsection in respect of the registration of the notice, that person shall have the like right of action in that court by virtue of this subsection in respect of the registration of the notice.

(5)   The remedies available to the plaintiff in an action brought by virtue of subsection (3) or subsection (4) of this section (apart from any order as to costs) shall be such declaration as the court may consider appropriate in the circumstances, and an order directing the registration of the notice to be cancelled or varied, as the court may determine.

(6)   For the purposes of section four of the Prescription Act, 1832 (under which a period of enjoyment of any of the rights to which that Act applies is not to be treated as interrupted except by a matter submitted to or acquiesced in for one year after notice thereof)—

    (a)   as from the date of registration of a notice under the last preceding section, all persons interested in the dominant building or any part thereof shall be deemed to have notice of the registration thereof and of the person on whose application it was registered;

    (b)   until such time as an action is brought by virtue of subsection (3) or subsection (4) of this section in respect of the registration of a notice under the last preceding section, all persons interested in the dominant building or any part thereof shall be deemed to acquiesce in the obstruction which, in accordance with subsection (1) of this section, is to be treated as resulting from the registration of the notice;

    (c)   as from the date on which such an action is brought, no person shall be treated as submitting to or acquiescing in that obstruction.

Provided that if, in any such action, the court decides against the claim of the plaintiff, the court may direct that the preceding provisions of this subsection shall apply in relation to the notice as if that action had not been brought.

7.   Interpretation

(1)   In this Act, except in so far as the context otherwise requires, the following expressions have the meanings hereby assigned to them respectively, that is to say:—

'action' includes a counterclaim, and any reference to the plaintiff in an action shall be construed accordingly;

'local authority', in relation to land in a district or London Borough, means the council of the borough or district, and, in relation to land in the City of London, means the Common Council of the City;

'owner', in relation to any land, means a person who is the estate owner in respect of the fee simple thereof, or is entitled to a tenancy thereof (within the meaning of the Landlord and Tenant Act, 1954) for a term of years certain of which, at the time in question, not less than seven years remain unexpired, or is a mortgagee in possession (within the meaning of the Law of Property Act, 1925) where the interest mortgaged is either the fee simple of the land or such a tenancy thereof;

'prescribed' means prescribed by rules made by virtue of subsection (6) of section fifteen of the Land Charges Act, 1925; as applied by section five of this Act.

(2)   References in this Act to any enactment shall, except where the context otherwise requires, be construed as references to that enactment as amended by or under any other enactment.

PERPETUITIES AND ACCUMULATIONS ACT 1964
(1964, c. 55)

Perpetuities

1.   Power to specify perpetuity period

(1)   Subject to section 9(2) of this Act and subsection (2) below, where the instrument by which any disposition is made so provides, the perpetuity period applicable to the disposition under the rule against perpetuities, instead of being of any other duration, shall be of a duration equal to such number of years not exceeding eighty as is specified in that behalf in the instrument.

(2)   Subsection (1) above shall not have effect where the disposition is made in exercise of a special power of appointment, but where a period is specified under that subsection in the instrument creating such a power the period shall apply in relation to any disposition under the power as it applies in relation to the power itself.

2.   Presumptions and evidence as to future parenthood

(1)   Where in any proceedings there arises on the rule against perpetuities a question which turns on the ability of a person to have a child at some future time, then—

(a)   subject to paragraph (b) below, it shall be presumed that a male can have a child at the age of fourteen years or over, but not under that age, and that a female can have a child at the age of twelve years or over, but not under that age or over the age of fifty-five years; but

(b)   in the case of a living person evidence may be given to show that he or she will or will not be able to have a child at the time in question.

(2)   Where any such question is decided by treating a person as unable to have a child at a particular time, and he or she does so, the High Court may make such order as it thinks fit for placing the persons interested in the property comprised in the disposition, so far as may be just, in the position they would have held if the question had not been so decided.

(3)   Subject to subsection (2) above, where any such question is decided in relation to a disposition by treating a person as able or unable to have a child at a particular time, then he or she shall be so treated for the purpose of any question which may arise on the rule against perpetuities in relation to the same disposition in any subsequent proceedings.

(4)   In the foregoing provisions of this section references to having a child are references to begetting or giving birth to a child, but those provisions (except subsection (1)(b) shall apply

in relation to the possibility that a person will at any time have a child by adoption, legitimation or other means as they apply to his or her ability at that time to beget or give birth to a child.

3.   Uncertainty as to remoteness

(1)   Where, apart from the provisions of this section and section 4 and 5 of this Act, a disposition would be void on the ground that the interest disposed of might not become vested until too remote a time, the disposition shall be treated, until such time (if any) as it becomes established that the vesting must occur, if at all, after the end of the perpetuity period, as if the disposition were not subject to the rule against perpetuities; and its becoming so established shall not affect the validity of anything previously done in relation to the interest disposed of by way of advancement, application of intermediate income or otherwise.

(2)   Where, apart from the said provisions, a disposition consisting of the conferring of a general power of appointment would be void on the ground that the power might not become exercisable until too remote a time, the disposition shall be treated, until such time (if any) as it becomes established that the power will not be exercisable within the perpetuity period, as if the disposition were not subject to the rule against perpetuities.

(3)   Where, apart from the said provisions, a disposition consisting of the conferring of any power, option or other right would be void on the ground that the right might be exercised at too remote a time, the disposition shall be treated as regards any exercise of the right within the perpetuity period as if it were not subject to the rule against perpetuities and, subject to the said provisions, shall be treated as void for remoteness only if, and so far as, the right is not fully exercised within that period.

(4)   Where this section applies to a disposition and the duration of the perpetuity period is not determined by virtue of section 1 or 9(2) of this Act, it shall be determined as follows:—

(a)   where any persons failing within subsection (5) below are individuals in being and ascertainable at the commencement of the perpetuity period the duration of the period shall be determined by reference to their lives and no others, but so that the lives of any description of persons falling within paragraph (b) or (c) of that subsection shall be disregarded if the number of persons of that description is such as to render it impracticable to ascertain the date of death of the survivor;

(b)   where there are no lives under paragraph (a) above the period shall be twenty-one years.

(5)   The said persons are as follows:—

(a)   the person by whom the disposition was made;

(b)   a person to whom or in whose favour the disposition was made, that is to say—

(i)   in the case of a disposition to a class of persons, any member or potential member of the class;

(ii)   in the case of an individual disposition to a person taking only on certain conditions being satisfied, any person as to whom some of the conditions are satisfied and the remainder may in time be satisfied;

(iii)   in the case of a special power of appointment exercisable in favour of members of a class, any member or potential member of the class;

(iv)   in the case of a special power of appointment exercisable in favour of one person only, that person or, where the object of the power is ascertainable only on certain conditions being satisfied, any person as to whom some of the conditions are satisfied and the remainder may in time be satisfied;

(v)   in the case of any power, option or other right, the person on whom the right is conferred;

(c)   a person having a child or grandchild within sub-paragraphs (i) to (iv) of paragraph (b) above, or any of those children or grandchildren, if subsequently born, would by virtue of his or her descent fall within those sub-paragraphs;

(d)   any person on the failure or determination of whose prior interest the disposition is limited to take effect.

4.   Reduction of age and exclusion of class members to avoid remoteness

(1)   Where a disposition is limited by reference to the attainment by any person or persons of a specified age exceeding twenty-one years, and it is apparent at the time the disposition is made or becomes apparent at a subsequent time—

(a)   that the disposition would, apart from this section, be void for remoteness, but

(b)   that it would not be so void if the specified age had been twenty-one years,

the disposition shall be treated for all purposes as if, instead of being limited by reference to the age in fact specified, it had been limited by reference to the age nearest to that age which would, if specified instead, have prevented the disposition from being so void.

(2)   Where in the case of any disposition different ages exceeding twenty-one years are specified in relation to different persons—

(a)   the reference in paragraph (b) of subsection (1) above to the specified age shall be construed as a reference to all the specified ages, and

(b)   that subsection shall operate to reduce each such age so far as is necessary to save the disposition from being void for remoteness.

(3)   Where the inclusion of any persons, being potential members of a class of unborn persons who at birth would become members or potential members of the class, prevents the foregoing provisions of this section from operating to save a disposition from being void for remoteness, those persons shall thenceforth be deemed for all the purposes of the disposition to be excluded from the class, and the said provisions shall thereupon have effect accordingly.

(4)   Where, in the case of a disposition to which subsection (3) above does not apply, it is apparent at the time the disposition is made or becomes apparent at a subsequent time that, apart from this subsection, the inclusion of any persons, being potential members of a class or unborn persons who at birth would become members or potential members of the class, would cause the disposition to be treated as void for remoteness, those persons shall, unless their exclusion would exhaust the class, thenceforth be deemed for all the purposes of the disposition to be excluded from the class.

(5)   Where this section has effect in relation to a disposition to which section 3 above applies, the operation of this section shall not affect the validity of anything previously done in relation to the interest disposed of by way of advancement, application or intermediate income or otherwise.

(6)   . . .

(7)   For the avoidance of doubt it is hereby declared that a question arising under section 3 of this Act or subsection (1)(a) above of whether a disposition would be void apart from this section is to be determined as if subsection (6) above had been a separate section of this Act.

5.   Condition relating to death of surviving spouse

Where a disposition is limited by reference to the time of death of the survivor of a person in being at the commencement of the perpetuity period and any spouse of that person, and that time has not arrived at the end of the perpetuity period, the disposition shall be treated for all purposes, where to do so would save it from being void for remoteness, as if it had been limited by reference to the time immediately before the end of that period.

6.   Saving and acceleration of expectant interests

A disposition shall not be treated as void for remoteness by reason only that the interest disposed of is ulterior to and dependant upon an interest under a disposition which is so void, and the vesting of an interest shall not be prevented from being accelerated on the failure of a prior interest by reason only that the failure arises because of remoteness.

7.   Powers of appointment

For the purposes of the rule against perpetuities, a power of appointment shall be treated as a special power unless—

(a)   in the instrument creating the power it is expressed to be exercisable by one person only, and

(b)   it could, at all times during its currency when that person is of full age and capacity, be exercised by him so as immediately to transfer to himself the whole of the interest governed by the power without the consent of any other person or compliance with any other condition, not being a formal condition relating only to the mode of exercise of the power: Provided that for the purpose of determining whether a disposition made under a power of appointment exercisable by will only is void for remoteness, the power shall be treated as a general power where it would have fallen to be so treated if exercisable by deed.

8. Administrative powers of trustees

(1) The rule against perpetuities shall not operate to invalidate a power conferred on trustees or other persons to sell, lease, exchange or otherwise dispose of any property for full consideration, or to do any other act in the administration (as opposed to the distribution) of any property, and shall not prevent the payment to trustees or other persons or reasonable remuneration for their services.

(2) Subsection (1) above shall apply for the purpose of enabling a power to be exercised at any time after the commencement of this Act notwithstanding that the power is conferred by an instrument which took effect before that commencement.

9. Options relating to land

(1) The rule against perpetuities shall not apply to a disposition consisting of the conferring of an option to acquire for valuable consideration an interest reversionary (whether directly or indirectly) on the term of a lease if—

(a) the option is exercisable only by the lessee or his successors in title, and

(b) it ceases to be exercisable at or before the expiration of one year following the determination of the lease.

This subsection shall apply in relation to an agreement for a lease as it applies in relation to a lease, and 'lessee' shall be construed accordingly.

(2) In the case of a disposition consisting of the conferring of an option to acquire for valuable consideration any interest in land, the perpetuity period under the rule against perpetuities shall be twenty-one years, and section 1 of this Act shall not apply:

provided that this subsection shall not apply to a right of preemption conferred on a public or local authority in respect of land used or to be used for religious purposes where the right becomes exercisable only if the land ceases to be used for such purposes.

10. Avoidance of contractual and other rights in cases of remoteness

Where a disposition inter vivos would fall to be treated as void for remoteness if the rights and duties thereunder were capable of transmission to persons other than the original parties and had been so transmitted, it shall be treated as void as between the person by whom it was made and the person to whom or in whose favour it was made or any successor of his, and no remedy shall lie in contract or otherwise for giving effect to it or making restitution for its lack of effect.

11. Rights for enforcement of rentcharges 1925 c. 20

(1) The rule against perpetuities shall not apply to any powers or remedies for recovering or compelling the payment of an annual sum to which section 121 or 122 of the Law of Property Act 1925 applies, or otherwise becoming exercisable or enforceable on the breach of any condition or other requirement relating to that sum.

. . .

12. Possibilities of reverter, conditions subsequent, exceptions and reservations

(1) In the case of—

(a) a possibility of reverter on the determination of a determinable fee simple, or

(b) a possibility of a resulting trust on the determination of any other determinable interest in property,

the rule against perpetuities shall apply in relation to the provision causing the interest to be determinable as it would apply if that provision were expressed in the form of a condition subsequent giving rise, on breach thereof, to a right of re-entry or an equivalent right in the case of property other than land, and where the provision falls to be treated as void for remoteness the determinable interest shall become an absolute interest.

(2) Where a disposition is subject to any such provision, or to any such condition subsequent, or to any exception or reservation, the disposition shall be treated for the purposes of this Act as including a separate disposition of any rights arising by virtue of the provision, condition subsequent, exception or reservation.

Accumulations

13.   Amendment of s. 164 of Law of Property Act 1925

(1) The periods for which accumulations of income under a settlement or other disposition are permitted by section 164 of the Law of Property Act 1925 shall include—

(a)   a term of twenty-one years from the date of the making of the disposition, and

(b)   the duration of the minority or respective minorities of any person or persons in being at that date.

(2) It is hereby declared that the restrictions imposed by the said section 164 apply in relation to a power to accumulate income whether or not there is a duty to exercise that power, and that they apply whether or not the power to accumulate extends to income produced by the investment of income previously accumulated.

14.   Right to stop accumulations

Section 2 above shall apply to any question as to the right of beneficiaries to put an end to accumulations of income under any disposition as it applies to questions arising on the rule against perpetuities.

Supplemental

15.   Short title, interpretation and extent

(1) This Act may be cited as the Perpetuities and Accumulations Act 1964.

(2) In this Act—

'disposition' includes the conferring of a power of appointment and any other disposition of an interest in or right over property, and references to the interest disposed of shall be construed accordingly;

'in being' means living or en ventre sa mere;

'power of appointment' includes any discretionary power to transfer a beneficial interest in property without the furnishing of valuable consideration;

'will' includes a codicil;

and for the purposes of this Act a disposition contained in a will shall be deemed to be made at the death of the testator.

(3) For the purposes of this Act a person shall be treated as a member of a class if in his case all the conditions identifying a member of the class are satisfied, and shall be treated as a potential member if in his case some only of those conditions are satisfied but there is a possibility that the remainder will in time be satisfied.

(4) Nothing in this Act shall affect the operation of the rule of law rendering void for remoteness certain dispositions under which property is limited to be applied for purposes other than the benefit of any person or class of persons in cases where the property may be so applied after the end of the perpetuity period.

(5) The foregoing sections of this Act shall apply (except as provided in section 8(2) above) only in relation to instruments taking effect after the commencement of this Act, and in the case of an instrument made in the exercise of a special power of appointment shall apply only where the instrument creating the power takes effect after that commencement:

Provided that section 7 above shall apply in all cases for construing the foregoing reference to a special power of appointment.

(6) This Act shall apply in relation to a disposition made otherwise than by an instrument as if the disposition had been contained in an instrument taking effect when the disposition was made.

(7) This Act binds the Crown.

. . .

LAW OF PROPERTY (JOINT TENANTS) ACT 1964
(1964, c. 63)

1.   Assumptions on sale of land by survivor of joint tenants

(1)   For the purposes of section 36(2) of the Law of Property Act 1925, as amended by section 7 of and the Schedule to the Law of Property (Amendment) Act 1926, the survivor of two or more joint tenants shall, in favour of a purchaser of the legal estate, be deemed to be solely and beneficially interested if . . . the conveyance includes a statement that he is so interested.

Provided that the foregoing provisions of this subsection shall not apply if, at any time before the date of the conveyance by the survivor—

(a)   a memorandum of severance (that is to say a note or memorandum signed by the joint tenants or one of them and recording that the joint tenancy was severed in equity on a date therein specified) had been endorsed on or annexed to the conveyance by virtue of which the legal estate was vested in the joint tenants; or

(b)   a bankruptcy order made against any of the joint tenants, or a petition for such an order, had been registered under the Land Charges Act 1925, being an order or petition of which the purchaser has notice, by virtue of the registration, on the date of the conveyance by the survivor.

(2)   The foregoing provisions of this section shall apply with the necessary modifications in relation to a conveyance by the personal representatives of the survivor of joint tenants as they apply in relation to a conveyance by such a survivor.

2.   Retrospective and transitional provisions

Section 1 of this Act shall be deemed to have come into force on 1st January 1926, and for the purposes of that section in its application to a conveyance executed before the passing of this Act a statement signed by the vendor or by his personal representatives that he was solely and beneficially interested shall be treated as if it had been included in the conveyance.

3.   Exclusion of registered land

This Act shall not apply to registered land.

WILLS ACT 1968
(1968, c. 28)

1.   Restriction of operation of Wills Act 1837, s. 15

(1)   For the purposes of section 15 of the Wills Act 1837 (avoidance of gifts to attesting witnesses and their spouses) the attestation of a will by a person to whom or to whose spouse there is given or made any such disposition as is described in that section shall be disregarded if the will is duly executed without his attestation and without that of any other such person.

(2)   This section applies to the will of any person dying after the passing of this Act, whether executed before or after the passing of this Act.

LAW OF PROPERTY ACT 1969
(1969, c. 59)

Note. References to the Land Charges Act 1925 should be read as references to the Land Charges Act 1972.

PART III

AMENDMENT OF LAW RELATING TO DISPOSITIONS OF ESTATES AND INTERESTS IN LAND AND TO LAND CHARGES

23. Reduction of statutory period of title

Section 44(1) of the Law of Property Act 1925 (under which the period of commencement of title which may be required under a contract expressing no contrary intention is thirty years except in certain cases) shall have effect, in its application to contracts made after the commencement of this Act, as if it specified fifteen years instead of thirty years as the period of commencement of title which may be so required.

24. Contracts for purchase of land affected by land charge, etc.

(1) Where under a contract for the sale or other disposition of any estate or interest in land the title to which is not registered under the Land Registration Act 1925 or any enactment replaced by it any question arises whether the purchaser had knowledge, at the time of entering into the contract, of a registered land charge, that question shall be determined by reference to his actual knowledge and without regard to the provisions of section 198 of the Law of Property Act 1925 (under which registration under the Land Charges Act 1925 or any enactment replaced by it is deemed to constitute actual notice).

(2) Where any estate or interest with which such a contract is concerned is affected by a registered land charge and the purchaser, at the time of entering into the contract, had not received notice and did not otherwise actually know that the estate or interest was affected by the charge, any provision of the contract shall be void so far as it purports to exclude the operation of subsection (1) above or to exclude or restrict any right or remedy that might otherwise be exercisable by the purchaser on the ground that the estate or interest is affected by the charge.

(3) In this section—

'purchaser' includes a lessee, mortgagee or other person acquiring or intending to acquire an estate or interest in land; and

'registered land charge' means any instrument or matter registered, otherwise than in a register of local land charges, under the Land Charges Act 1925 or any Act replaced by it.

(4) For the purposes of this section any knowledge acquired in the course of a transaction by a person who is acting therein as counsel, or as solicitor or other agent, for another shall be treated as the knowledge of that other.

(5) This section does not apply to contracts made before the commencement of this Act.

25. Compensation in certain cases for loss due to undisclosed land charges

(1) Where a purchaser of any estate or interest in land under a disposition to which this section applies has suffered loss by reason that the estate or interest is affected by a registered land charge, then if—

(a) the date of completion was after the commencement of this Act; and

(b) on that date the purchaser had no actual knowledge of the charge, and

(c) the charge was registered against the name of an owner of an estate in the land who was not as owner of any such estate a party to any transaction, or concerned in any event, comprised in the relevant title;

the purchaser shall be entitled to compensation for the loss.

(2) For the purposes of subsection (1)(b) above, the question whether any person had actual knowledge of a charge shall be determined without regard to the provisions of section 198 of the Law of Property Act 1925 (under which registration under the Land Charges Act 1925 or any enactment replaced by it is deemed to constitute actual notice).

(3)   Where a transaction comprised in the relevant title was effected or evidenced by a document which expressly provided that it should take effect subject to an interest or obligation capable of registration in any of the relevant registers, the transaction which created that interest or obligation shall be treated for the purposes of subsection (1)(c) above as comprised in the relevant title.

(4)   Any compensation for loss under this section shall be paid by the Chief Land Registrar, and where the purchaser of the estate or interest in question has incurred expenditure for the purpose—

(a)   of securing that the estate or interest is no longer affected by the registered land charge or is so affected to a less extent; or

(b)   of obtaining compensation under this section;

the amount of the compensation shall include the amount of the expenditure (so far as it would not otherwise fall to be treated as compensation for loss) reasonably incurred by the purchaser for that purpose.

(5)   In the case of an action to recover compensation under this section, the cause of action shall be deemed for the purposes of the Limitation Act 1980 to accrue at the time when the registered land charge affecting the estate or interest in question comes to the notice of the purchaser.

. . .

(9)   This section applies to the following dispositions, that is to say—

(a)   any sale or exchange and, subject to the following provisions of this subsection, any mortgage of an estate or interest in land;

(b)   any grant of a lease for a term of years derived out of a leasehold interest;

(c)   any compulsory purchase, by whatever procedure, of land; and

(d)   any conveyance of a fee simple in land under Part I of the Leasehold Reform Act 1967;

but does not apply to the grant of a term of years derived out of the freehold or the mortgage of such a term by the lessee; and references in this section to a purchaser shall be construed accordingly.

(10)   In this section—

'date of completion', in relation to land which vests in the Land Commission or another acquiring authority by virtue of a general vesting declaration under the Land Commission Act 1967 or the Town and County Planning Act 1968, means the date on which it so vests;

'mortgage' includes any charge;

'registered land charge' means any instrument or matter registered, otherwise than in a register of local land charges, under the Land Charges Act 1925 or any Act replaced by it, except that—

(a)   in relation to an assignment of a lease or underlease or a mortgage by an assignee under such an assignment, it does not include any instrument or matter affecting the title to the freehold or to any relevant leasehold reversion; and

(b)   in relation to the grant of an underlease or the mortgage by the underlessee of the term of years created by an underlease, it does not include any instrument or matter affecting the title to the freehold or to any leasehold reversion superior to the leasehold interest out of which the term of years is derived—

'relevant registers' means the registers kept under section 1 of the Land Charges Act 1925;

'relevant title' means—

(a)   in relation to a disposition made under a contract, the title which the purchaser was, apart from any acceptance by him (by agreement or otherwise) of a shorter or an imperfect title, entitled to require; or

(b)   in relation to any other disposition, the title which he would have been entitled to require if the disposition had been made under a contract to which section 44(1) of the Law of Property Act 1925 applied and that contract had been made on the date of completion.

(11)   For the purposes of this section any knowledge acquired in the course of a transaction by a person who is acting therein as counsel, or as solicitor or other agent, for another shall be treated as the knowledge of that other.

ADMINISTRATION OF JUSTICE ACT 1970
(1970, c. 31)

PART IV

36. Additional powers of court in action by mortgagee for possession of dwelling-house

(1) Where the mortgagee under a mortgage of land which consists of or includes a dwelling-house brings an action in which he claims possession of the mortgaged property, not being an action for foreclosure in which a claim for possession of the mortgaged property is also made, the court may exercise any of the powers conferred on it by subsection (2) below if it appears to the court that in the event of its exercising the power the mortgagor is likely to be able within a reasonable period to pay any sums due under the mortgage or to remedy a default consisting of a breach of any other obligation arising under or by virtue of the mortgage.

(2) The court—
  (a) may adjourn the proceedings, or
  (b) on giving judgment, or making an order, for delivery of possession of the mortgaged property, or at any time before the execution of such judgment or order, may—
      (i)   stay or suspend execution of the judgment or order, or
      (ii) postpone the date for delivery of possession,
  for such period or periods as the court thinks reasonable.

(3) Any such adjournment, stay, suspension or postponement as is referred to in subsection (2) above may be made subject to such conditions with regard to payment by the mortgagor of any sum secured by the mortgage or the remedying of any default as the court thinks fit.

(4) The court may from time to time vary or revoke any condition imposed by virtue of this section.

. . .

38A. This Part of this Act shall not apply to a mortgage securing an agreement which is a regulated agreement within the meaning of the Consumer Credit Act 1974.

39. Interpretation of Part IV

(1) In this Part of this Act—
  'dwelling house' includes any building or part thereof which is used as a dwelling;
  'mortgage' includes a charge and 'mortgagor' and 'mortgagee' shall be construed accordingly;
  'mortgagor' and 'mortgagee' includes any person deriving title under the original mortgagor or mortgagee.

(2) The fact that part of the premises comprised in a dwelling-house is used as a shop or office or for business, trade or professional purposes shall not prevent the dwelling-house from being a dwelling-house for the purposes of this Part of this Act.

MATRIMONIAL PROCEEDINGS AND PROPERTY ACT 1970
(1970, c. 45)

Provisions relating to property of married persons

37. Contributions by spouse in money or money's worth to the improvement of property

It is hereby declared that where a husband or wife contributes in money or money's worth to the improvement of real or personal property in which or in the proceeds of sale of which either or both of them has or have a beneficial interest, the husband or wife so contributing shall, if the contribution is of a substantial nature and subject to any agreement between them to the contrary express or implied, be treated as having then acquired by virtue of his or her contribution a share or an enlarged share, as the case may be, in that beneficial interest of such an extent as may have been then agreed or, in default of such agreement, as may seem in all the circumstances just to any court before which the question of the existence or extent of the beneficial interest of the husband or wife arises (whether in proceedings between them or in any other proceedings).

POWERS OF ATTORNEY ACT 1971
(1971 c. 27)

5.   Protection of donee and third persons where power of attorney is revoked

(1)   A donee of a power of attorney who acts in pursuance of the power at a time when it has been revoked shall not, by reason of the revocation, incur any liability (either to the donor or to any other person) if at that time he did not know that the power had been revoked.

(2)   Where a power of attorney has been revoked and a person, without knowledge of the revocation, deals with the donee of the power, the transaction between them shall, in favour of that person, be as valid as if the power had then been in existence.

(3)   Where the power is expressed in the instrument creating it to be irrevocable and to be given by way of security then, unless the person dealing with the donee knows that it was not in fact given by way of security, he shall be entitled to assume that the power is incapable of revocation except by the donor acting with the consent of the donee and shall accordingly be treated for the purposes of subsection (2) of this section as having knowledge of the revocation only if he knows that it has been revoked in that manner.

(4)   Where the interest of a purchaser depends on whether a transaction between the donee of a power of attorney and another person was valid by virtue of subsection (2) of this section, it shall be conclusively presumed in favour of the purchaser that that person did not at the material time know of the revocation of the power if—

(a)   the transaction between that person and the donee was completed within twelve months of the date on which the power came into operation; or

(b)   that person makes a statutory declaration, before or within three months after the completion of the purchase, that he did not at the material time know of the revocation of the power.

(5)   Without prejudice to subsection (3) of this section, for the purposes of this section knowledge of the revocation of a power of attorney includes knowledge of the occurrence of any event (such as the death of the donor) which has the effect of revoking the power.

(6)   In this section 'purchaser' and 'purchase' have the meanings specified in section 205(1) of the Law of Property Act 1925.

(7)   This section applies whenever the power of attorney was created but only to acts and transactions after the commencement of this Act.

6.   Additional protection for transferees under stock exchange transactions

(1)   Without prejudice to section 5 of this Act, where—

(a)   the donee of a power of attorney executes, as transferor, an instrument transferring registered securities; and

(b)   the instrument is executed for the purposes of a stock exchange transaction,

it shall be conclusively presumed in favour of the transferee that the power had not been revoked at the date of the instrument if a statutory declaration to that effect is made by the donee of the power on or within three months after that date.

(2)   In this section 'registered securities' and 'stock exchange transaction' have the same meanings as in the Stock Transfer Act 1963.

7.   Execution of instruments etc. by donee of power of attorney

(1)   The donee of a power of attorney may, if he thinks fit—

(a)   execute any instrument with his own signature and, where sealing is required, with his own seal, and

(b)   do any other thing in his own name,

by the authority of the donor of the power; and any instrument executed or thing done in that manner shall, subject to subsection (1A) of this section, be as effective as if executed by the donee in any manner which would constitute due execution of that instrument by the donor or, as the case may be, as if done by the donee in the name of the donor.

(1A) Where an instrument is executed by the donee as a deed, it shall be effective as if executed by the donee in a manner which would constitute due execution of it as a deed by the donor only if it is executed in accordance with section 1(3)(a) of the Law of Property (Miscellaneous Provisions) Act 1989.

(2) For the avoidance of doubt it is hereby declared that an instrument to which subsection (3) ... of section 74 of the Law of Property Act 1925 applies may be executed either as provided in that subsection or as provided in this section.

(3) ...

(4) This section applies whenever the power of attorney was created.

LAND CHARGES ACT 1972
(1972, c. 61)

Preliminary

1.   The registers and the index

(1) The registrar shall continue to keep at the registry in the prescribed manner the following registers, namely—

(a)   a register of land charges;

(b)   a register of pending actions;

(c)   a register of writs and orders affecting land;

(d)   a register of deeds of arrangement affecting land;

(e)   a register of annuities,

and shall also continue to keep there an index whereby all entries made in any of those registers can readily be traced.

(2) Every application to register shall be in the prescribed form and shall contain the prescribed particulars.

(3) Where any charge or other matter is registrable in more than one of the registers kept under this Act it shall be sufficient if it is registered in one register, and if it is so registered the person entitled to the benefit of it shall not be prejudicially affected by the provision of this Act as to the effect of non-registration in any other such register.

(3A) Where any charge or other matter is registrable in a register kept under this Act and was also, before the commencement of the Local Land Charges Act 1975, registrable in a local land charges register, then, if before the commencement of the said Act it was registered in the appropriate local land charges register it shall be treated for the purposes of the provisions of this Act as to the effect of non-registration as if it had been registered in the appropriate register under this Act, and any certificate setting out the result of an official search of the appropriate local land charges register shall, in relation to it, have effect as if it were a certificate setting out the result of an official search under this Act.

(4) Schedule 1 to this Act shall have effect in relation to the register of annuities.

(5) An office copy of an entry in any register kept under this section shall be admissible in evidence in all proceedings and between all parties to the same extent as the original would be admissible.

(6) Subject to the provisions of this Act, registration may be vacated pursuant to an order of the court.

(6A) The county court has jurisdiction under subsection (6) above—

(a)   in the case of a land charge of Class C(i), C(ii) or D(i) if the amount does not exceed £30,000;

(b)   in the case of a land charge of Class C(iii), if it is for a specified capital sum of money, not exceeding £30,000 or, where it is not for a specified capital sum, if the land affected does not exceed the county court limit in capital value or in net annual value for rating;

    (c)   in the case of a land charge of Class A, Class B, Class C(iv), Class D(ii), Class D(iii) or Class E, if the land affected does not exceed £30,000;

    (d)   in the case of a land charge of Class F, if the land affected by it is the subject of an order made by the court under section 1 of the Matrimonial Homes Act 1983 or section 33 of the Family Law Act 1996 or an application for an order under either of those sections relating to that land has been made to the court.

    (e)   in a case where an application under section 23 of the Deeds of Arrangement Act 1914 could be entertained by the court.

(6B) . . .

(7)   In this section 'index' includes any device or combination of devices serving the purpose of an index.

Registration in register of land charges

2.   The register of land charges

(1)   If a charge on or obligation affecting land falls into one of the classes described in this section, it may be registered in the register of land charges as a land charge of that class.

(2)   A Class A land charge is—

    (a)   a rent or annuity or principal money payable by instalments or otherwise, with or without interest, which is not a charge created by deed but is a charge upon land (other than a rate) created pursuant to the application of some person under the provisions of any Act of Parliament, for securing to any person either the money spent by him or the costs, charges and expenses incurred by him under such Act, or the money advanced by him for repaying the money spent or the costs, charges and expenses incurred by another person under the authority of an Act of Parliament; or

    (b)   a rent or annuity or principal money payable as mentioned in paragraph (a) above which is not a charge created by deed but is a charge upon land (other than a rate) created pursuant to the application of some person under any of the enactments mentioned in Schedule 2 to this Act.

(3)   A Class B land charge is a charge on land (not being a local land charge . . .) of any of the kinds described in paragraph (a) of subsection (2) above, created otherwise than pursuant to the application of any person.

(4)   A Class C land charge is any of the following, (not being a local land charge), namely—

    (i)   a puisne mortgage;

    (ii)   a limited owner's charge;

    (iii)   a general equitable charge;

    (iv)   an estate contract;

and for this purpose—

    (i)   a puisne mortgage is a legal mortgage which is not protected by a deposit of documents relating to the legal estate affected;

    (ii)   a limited owner's charge is an equitable charge acquired by a tenant for life or statutory owner under the Inheritance Tax Act 1984 or under any other statute by reason of the discharge by him of any inheritance tax or other liabilities and to which special priority is given by the statute;

    (iii)   a general equitable charge is any equitable charge which—

        (a)   is not secured by a deposit of documents relating to the legal estate affected; and

        (b)   does not arise or affect an interest arising under a trust of land or a settlement; and

        (c)   is not a charge given by way of indemnity against rents equitably apportioned or charged exclusively on land in exoneration of other land and against the breach or non-observance of covenants or conditions; and

        (d)   is not included in any other class of land charge;

(iv) an estate contract is a contract by an estate owner or by a person entitled at the date of the contract to have a legal estate conveyed to him to convey or create a legal estate, including a contract conferring either expressly or by statutory implication a valid option to purchase, a right of preemption or any other like right.

(5) A Class D land charge is any of the following, (not being a local land charge), namely—

    (i) an Inland Revenue charge;

    (ii) a restrictive covenant;

    (iii) an equitable easement;

and for this purpose—

    (i) an Inland Revenue charge is a charge on land, being a charge acquired by the Board under the Inheritance Tax Act 1984;

    (ii) a restrictive covenant is a covenant or agreement (other than a covenant or agreement between a lessor and a lessee) restrictive of the user of land and entered into on or after 1st January 1926,

    (iii) an equitable easement is an easement, right or privilege over or affecting land created or arising on or after 1st January 1926, and being merely an equitable interest.

(6) A Class E land charge is an annuity created before 1st January 1926 and not registered in the register of annuities.

(7) A Class F land charge is a charge affecting any land by virtue of the Part IV of the Family Law Act 1996.

(8) A charge or obligation created before 1st January 1926 can only be registered as a Class B land charge or a Class C land charge if it is acquired under a conveyance made on or after that date.

(9) . . .

3. Registration of land charges

(1) A land charge shall be registered in the name of the estate owner whose estate is intended to be affected.

(1A) Where a person has died and a land charge created before his death would apart from his death have been registered in his name, it shall be so registered notwithstanding his death.

(2) A land charge registered before lst January 1926 under any enactment replaced by the Land Charges Act 1925 in the name of a person other than the estate owner may remain so registered until it is registered in the name of the estate owner in the prescribed manner.

(3) A puisne mortgage created before 1st January 1926 may be registered as a land charge before any transfer of the mortgage is made.

(4) The expenses incurred by the person entitled to the charge in registering a land charge of Class A, Class B or Class C (other than an estate contract) or by the Board in registering an Inland Revenue charge shall be deemed to form part of the land charge, and shall be recoverable accordingly on the day for payment of any part of the land charge next after such expenses arc incurred.

(5) Where a land charge is not created by an instrument, short particulars of the effect of the charge shall be furnished with the application to register the charge.

(6) An application to register an Inland Revenue charge shall state the tax in respect of which the charge is claimed and, so far as possible, shall define the land affected, and such particulars shall be entered or referred to in the register.

(7) In the case of a land charge for securing money created by a company before 1st January 1970 or so created at any time as a floating charge, registration under Part XII, or Chapter III of Part XXIII, of the Companies Act 1985 (or corresponding earlier enactments) shall be sufficient in place of registration under this Act, and shall have effect as if the land charge had been registered under this Act.

(8) The corresponding earlier enactments referred to in subsection (7) above are section 93 of the Companies (Consolidation) Act 1908, section 79 of the Companies Act 1929 and sections 395 to 398 of the Companies Act 1985 as originally enacted.

4. Effect of land charges and protection of purchasers

(1) A land charge of Class A (other than a land improvement charge registered after 31st December 1969) or of Class B shall, when registered, take effect as if it had been created by a deed of charge by way of legal mortgage, but without prejudice to the priority of the charge.

(2) A land charge of Class A created after 31st December 1888 shall be void as against a purchaser of the land charged with it or of any interest in such land, unless the land charge is registered in the register of land charges before the completion of the purchase.

(3) After the expiration of one year from the first conveyance occurring on or after 1st January 1889 of a land charge of Class A created before that date the person entitled to the land charge shall not be able to recover the land charge or any part of it as against a purchaser of the land charged with it or of any interest in the land, unless the land charge is registered in the register of land charges before the completion of the purchase.

(4) If a land improvement charge was registered as a land charge of Class A before 1st January 1970, any body corporate which, but for the charge, would have power to advance money on the security of the estate or interest affected by it shall have that power notwithstanding the charge.

(5) A land charge of Class B and a land charge of Class C (other than an estate contract) created or arising on or after 1st January 1926 shall be void as against a purchaser of the land charged with it, or of any interest in such land, unless the land charge is registered in the appropriate register before the completion of the purchase.

(6) An estate contract and a land charge of Class D created or entered into on or after 1st January 1926 shall be void as against a purchaser for money or money's worth (or in the case of an Inland Revenue charge, a purchaser within the meaning of the Inheritance Tax Act 1984) of a legal estate in the land charged with it, unless the land charge is registered in the appropriate register before the completion of the purchase.

(7) After the expiration of one year from the first conveyance occurring on or after 1st January 1926 of a land charge of Class B or Class C created before that date the person entitled to the land charge shall not be able to enforce or recover the land charge or any part of it as against a purchaser of the land charged with it, or of any interest in the land, unless the land charge is registered in the appropriate register before the completion of the purchase.

(8) A land charge of Class F shall be void as against a purchaser of the land charged with it, or of any interest in such land, unless the land charge is registered in the appropriate register before the completion of the purchase.

Registration in registers of pending actions, writs and orders and deeds of arrangement

5. The register of pending actions

(1) There may be registered in the register of pending actions—
   (a) a pending land action;
   (b) a petition in bankruptcy filed on or after 1st January 1926.

(2) Subject to general rules under section 16 of this Act, every application for registration under this section shall contain particulars of the title of the proceedings and the name, address and description of the estate owner or other person whose estate or interest is intended to be affected.

(3) An application for registration shall also state—
   (a) if it relates to a pending land action, the court in which and the day on which the action was commenced; and
   (b) if it relates to a petition in bankruptcy, the court in which and the day on which the petition was filed.

(4) The registrar shall forthwith enter the particulars in the register, in the name of the estate owner or other person whose estate or interest is intended to be affected.

(4A) Where a person has died and a pending land action would apart from his death have been registered in his name, it shall be so registered notwithstanding his death.

(5) An application to register a petition in bankruptcy against a firm shall state the names and addresses of the partners, and the registration shall be effected against each partner as well as against the firm.

(6) No fee shall be charged for the registration of a petition in bankruptcy if the application for registration is made by the registrar of the court in which the petition is filed.

(7) A pending land action shall not bind a purchaser without express notice of it unless it is for the time being registered under this section.

(8) A petition in bankruptcy shall not bind a purchaser of a legal estate in good faith, for money or money's worth, . . . unless it is for the time being registered under this section.

(9) . . .

(10) The court, if it thinks fit, may, upon the determination of the proceedings, or during the pendency of the proceedings if satisfied that they are not prosecuted in good faith, make an order vacating a registration under this section, and direct the party on whose behalf it was made to pay all or any of the costs and expenses occasioned by the registration and by its vacation.

(11) The county court has jurisdiction under subsection (10) of this section where the action was brought or the petition in bankruptcy was filed by the court.

6. The register of writs and orders affecting land

(1) There may be registered in the register of writs and orders affecting land—

    (a) any writ or order affecting land issued or made by any court for the purpose of enforcing a judgment or recognisance—

    (b) any order appointing a receiver or sequestrator of land;

    (c) any bankruptcy order whether or not the bankrupt's estate is known to include land

    (c) any receiving order in bankruptcy made on or after 1st January 1926, whether or not it is known to affect land.

    (d) any access order under the Access to Neighbouring Land Act 1992.

(1A) No writ or order affecting an interest under a trust of land may be registered under subsection (1) above.

(2) Every entry made pursuant to this section shall be made in the name of the estate owner or other person whose land, if any, is affected by the writ or order registered.

(2A) Where a person has died and any such writ or order as is mentioned in subsection (1)(a) or (b) above would apart from his death have been registered in his name, it shall be so registered notwithstanding his death.

(3) No fee shall be charged for the registration of a receiving order in bankruptcy if the application for registration is made by an official receiver.

(4) Except as provided by subsection (5) below and by section 37(5) of the Supreme Court Act 1981 and section 107(3) of the County Courts Act 1984 (which make special provision as to receiving orders in respect of land of judgment debtors) every such writ and order as is mentioned in subsection (1) above, and every delivery in execution or other proceeding taken pursuant to any such writ or order, or in obedience to any such writ or order, shall be void as against a purchaser of the land unless the writ or order is for the time being registered under this section.

(5) Subject to subsection (6) below, the title of a trustee in bankruptcy shall be void as against a purchaser of a legal estate in good faith for money or money's worth unless the bankruptcy order is for the time being registered under this section.

(6) Where a petition in bankruptcy has been registered under section 5 above, the title of the trustee in bankruptcy shall be void as against a purchaser of a legal estate in good faith for money or money's worth . . . claiming under a conveyance made after the date of registration, unless at the date of the conveyance either the registration of the petition is in force or a receiving order on the petition is registered under this section.

7.   The register of deeds of arrangement affecting land

(1)   A deed of arrangement affecting land may be registered in the register of deeds of arrangement affecting land, in the name of the debtor, on the application of a trustee of the deed or a creditor assenting to or taking the benefit of the deed.

(2)   Every deed of arrangement shall be void as against a purchaser of any land comprised in it or affected by it unless it is for the time being registered under this section.

8.   Expiry and renewal of registrations

A registration under section 5, section 6 or section 7 of this Act shall cease to have effect at the end of the period of five years from the date on which it is made, but may be renewed from time to time and, if so renewed, shall have effect for five years from the date of renewal.

Searches and official searches

9.   Searches

(1)   Any person may search in any register kept under this Act on paying the prescribed fee.

(2)   Without prejudice to subsection (1) above, the registrar may provide facilities for enabling persons entitled to search in any such register to see photographic or other images or copies of any portion of the register which they may wish to examine.

10.   Official searches

(1)   Where any person requires search to be made at the registry for entries of any matters or documents, entries of which are required or allowed to be made in the registry by this Act, he may make a requisition in that behalf to the registrar, which may be either—

(a)   a written requisition delivered at or sent by post to the registry, or

(b)   a requisition communicated by teleprinter, telephone or other means in such manner as may be prescribed in relation to the means in question, in which case it shall be treated as made to the registrar if, but only if, he accepts it;

and the registrar shall not accept a requisition made in accordance with paragraph (b) above unless it is made by a person maintaining a credit account at the registry, and may at his discretion refuse to accept it notwithstanding that it is made by such a person.

(2)   The prescribed fee shall be payable in respect of every requisition made under this section; and that fee—

(a)   in the case of a requisition made in accordance with subsection (1)(a) above, shall be paid in such manner as may be prescribed for the purposes of this paragraph unless the requisition is made by a person maintaining a credit account at the registry and the fee is debited to that account;

(b)   in the case of a requisition made in accordance with subsection (1)(b) above, shall be debited to the credit account of the person by whom the requisition is made.

(3)   Where a requisition is made under subsection (1) above and the fee payable in respect of it is paid or debited in accordance with subsection (2) above, the registrar shall thereupon make the search required and—

(a)   shall issue a certificate setting out the result of the search; and

(b)   without prejudice to paragraph (a) above, may take such other steps as he considers appropriate to communicate that result to the person by whom the requisition was made.

(4)   In favour of a purchaser or an intending purchaser, as against persons interested under or in respect of matters or documents entries of which are required or allowed as aforesaid, the certificate, according to its tenor, shall be conclusive, affirmatively or negatively, as the case may be.

(5)   If any officer, clerk or person employed in the registry commits, or is party or privy to, any act of fraud or collusion, or is wilfully negligent, in the making of or otherwise in relation to any certificate under this section, he shall be guilty of an offence and shall be liable on conviction on indictment to imprisonment for a term not exceeding two years, or on summary conviction to imprisonment for a term not exceeding three months or to a fine not exceeding the prescribed sum, or to both such imprisonment and fine.

(6)   Without prejudice to subsection (5) above, no officer, clerk or person employed in the registry shall, in the absence of fraud on his part, be liable for any loss which may be suffered—

(a)   by reason of any discrepancy between—

(i)   the particulars which are shown in a certificate under this section as being the particulars in respect of which the search for entries was made, and

(ii)   the particulars in respect of which a search for entries was required by the person who made the requisition; or

(b)   by reason of any communication of the result of a search under this section made otherwise than by issuing a certificate under this section.

Miscellaneous and supplementary

11.   Date of effective registration and priority notices

(1)   Any person intending to make an application for the registration of any contemplated charge, instrument or other matter in pursuance of this Act or any rule made under this Act may give a priority notice in the prescribed form at least the relevant number of days before the registration is to take effect.

(2)   Where a notice is given under subsection (1) above, it shall be entered in the register to which the intended application when made will relate.

(3)   If the application is presented within the relevant number of days thereafter and refers in the prescribed manner to the notice, the registration shall take effect as if the registration had been made at the time when the charge, instrument or matter was created, entered into, made or arose, and the date at which the registration so takes effect shall be deemed to be the date of registration.

(4)   Where—

(a)   any two charges, instruments or matters are contemporaneous; and

(b)   one of them (whether or not protected by a priority notice) is subject to or dependent on the other; and

(c)   the latter is protected by a priority notice,

the subsequent or dependent charge, instrument or matter shall be deemed to have been created, entered into or made, or to have arisen, after the registration of the other.

(5)   Where a purchaser has obtained a certificate under section 10 above, any entry which is made in the register after the date of the certificate and before the completion of the purchase, and is not made pursuant to a priority notice entered on the register on or before the date of the certificate, shall not affect the purchaser if the purchase is completed before the expiration of the relevant number of days after the date of the certificate.

(6)   The relevant number of days is—

(a)   for the purposes of subsection (1) and (5) above, fifteen;

(b)   for the purposes of subsection (3) above, thirty,

or such other number as may be prescribed; but in reckoning the relevant number of days for any of the purposes of this section any days when the registry is not open to the public shall be excluded.

12.   Protection of solicitors, trustees, etc.

A solicitor, or a trustee, personal representative, agent or other person in a fiduciary position, shall not be answerable—

(a)   in respect of any loss occasioned by reliance on an office copy of an entry in any register kept under this Act;

(b)   for any loss that may arise from error in a certificate under section 10 above obtained by him.

13.   Saving for overreaching powers

(1)   The registration of any charge, annuity or other interest under this Act shall not prevent the charge, annuity or interest being overreached under any other Act, except where otherwise provided by that other Act.

(2)   The registration as a land charge of a puisne mortgage or charge shall not operate to prevent that mortgage or charge being overreached in favour of a prior mortgagee or a person deriving title under him where, by reason of a sale or foreclosure, or otherwise, the right of the puisne mortgagee or subsequent chargee to redeem is barred.

14.   Exclusion of matters affecting registered land or created by instruments necessitating registration of land

(1)   This Act shall not apply to instruments or matters required to be registered or re-registered on or after 1st January 1926, if and so far as they affect registered land, and can be protected under the Land Registration Act 2002.

(2)   Nothing in this Act imposes on the registrar any obligation to ascertain whether or not an instrument or matter affects registered land.

(3)   Where an instrument executed on or after 27th July 1971 conveys, grants or assigns an estate in land and creates a land charge affecting that estate, this Act shall not apply to the land charge, so far as it affects that estate, if under section 7 of the Land Registration Act 2002 (effect of failure to comply with requirement of registration) the instrument will, unless the necessary application for registration under that Act is made within the time allowed by or under section 6 of that Act, become void so far as respects the conveyance, grant or assignment of that estate.

17.   Interpretation

(1)   In this Act, unless the context otherwise requires:—

'annuity' means a rentcharge or an annuity for a life or lives or for any term of years or greater estate determinable on a life or on lives and created after 25th April 1855 and before 1st January 1926, but does not include an annuity created by a marriage settlement or will;

'the Board' means the Commissioners of Inland Revenue;

'conveyance' includes a mortgage, charge, lease, assent, vesting declaration, vesting instrument, release and every other assurance of property, or of an interest in property, by any instrument except a will, and 'convey' has a corresponding meaning;

'court' means the High Court, or the county court in a case where that court has jurisdiction;

'deed of arrangement' has the same meaning as in the Deeds of Arrangement Act 1914;

'estate owner', 'legal estate', 'equitable interest', . . . , 'charge by way of legal mortgage', and 'will' have the same meanings as in the Law of Property Act 1925;

'judgment' includes any order or decree having the effect of a judgment;

'land' includes land of any tenure and mines and minerals, whether or not severed from the surface, buildings or parts of buildings (whether the division is horizontal, vertical or made in any other way) and other corporeal hereditaments, also a manor, an advowson and a rent and other incorporeal hereditaments, and an easement, right, privilege or benefit in, over or derived from land, but not an undivided share in land, and 'hereditament' means real property which, on an intestacy occurring before 1st January 1926, might have devolved on an heir;

'land improvement charge' means any charge under the Improvement of Land Act 1864 or under any special improvement Act within the meaning of the Improvement of Land Act 1899;

'pending land action' means any action or proceeding pending in court relating to land or any interest in or charge on land;

'prescribed' means prescribed by rules made pursuant to this Act;

'purchaser' means any person (including a mortgagee or lessee) who, for valuable consideration, takes any interest in land or in a charge on land, and 'purchase' has a corresponding meaning;

'registrar' means the Chief Land Registrar, 'registry' means Her Majesty's Land Registry, and 'registered land' has the same meaning as in the Land Registration Act 2002;

'tenant for life', 'statutory owner', 'vesting instrument' and 'settlement' have the same meanings as in the Settled Land Act 1925.

. . .

(3)   Any reference in this Act to any enactment is a reference to it as amended by or under any other enactment, including this Act.

ADMINISTRATION OF JUSTICE ACT 1973
(1973, c. 15)

8.   **Extension of powers by court in action by mortgagee of dwelling-house**

(1)   Where by a mortgage of land which consists of or includes a dwelling-house, or by any agreement between the mortgagee under such a mortgage and the mortgagor, the mortgagor is entitled or is to be permitted to pay the principal sum secured by instalments or otherwise to defer payment of it in whole or in part, but provision is also made for earlier payment in the event of any default by the mortgagor or of a demand by the mortgagee or otherwise, then for purposes of section 36 of the Administration of Justice Act 1970 (under which a court has power to delay giving a mortgagee possession of the mortgaged property so as to allow the mortgagor a reasonable time to pay any sums due under the mortgage) a court may treat as due under the mortgage on account of the principal sum secured and of interest on it only such amounts as the mortgagor would have expected to be required to pay if there had been no such provision for earlier payment.

(2)   A court shall not exercise by virtue of subsection (1) above the powers conferred by section 36 of the Administration of Justice Act 1970 unless it appears to the court not only that the mortgagor is likely to be able within a reasonable period to pay any amounts regarded (in accordance with subsection (1) above) as due on account of the principal sum secured, together with the interest on those amounts, but also that he is likely to be able by the end of that period to pay any further amounts that he would have expected to be required to pay by then on account of that sum and of interest on it if there had been no such provision as is referred to in subsection (1) above for earlier payment.

(3)   Where subsection (1) above would apply to an action in which a mortgagee only claimed possession of the mortgaged property, and the mortgagee brings an action for foreclosure (with or without also claiming possession of the property), then section 36 of the Administration of Justice Act 1970 together with subsections (1) and (2) above shall apply as they would apply if it were an action in which the mortgagee only claimed possession of the mortgaged property, except that—

(a)   section 36(2)(b) shall apply only in relation to any claim for possession; and

(b)   section 36(5) shall not apply.

(4)   For purposes of this section the expressions 'dwelling-house', 'mortgage', mortgagee' and 'mortgagor' shall be construed in the same way as for the purposes of Part IV of the Administration of Justice Act 1970.

. . .

INHERITANCE (PROVISION FOR FAMILY AND DEPENDANTS) ACT 1975
(1975, c. 63)

1.   **Application for financial provision from deceased's estate**

(1)   Where after the commencement of this Act a person dies domiciled in England and Wales and is survived by any of the following persons:—

(a)   the spouse or civil partner of the deceased;

(b)   a former spouse or former civil partner of the deceased, but not one who has formed a subsequent marriage or civil partnership;

(ba) any person (not being a person included in paragraph (a) or (b) above) to whom subsection (1A) or (1B) below applies

(c)   a child of the deceased;

      (d)   any person (not being a child of the deceased) who, in the case of any marriage or civil partnership to which the deceased was at any time a party, was treated by the deceased as a child of the family in relation to that marriage or civil partnership;

      (e)   any person (not being a person included in the foregoing paragraphs of this subsection) who immediately before the death of the deceased was being maintained, either wholly or partly, by the deceased;

that person may apply to the court for an order under section 2 of this Act on the ground that the disposition of the deceased's estate effected by his will or the law relating to intestacy, or the combination of his will and that law, is not such as to make reasonable financial provision for the applicant.

(1A) This section applies to a person if the deceased died on or after 1st January 1996 and, during the whole of the period of two years ending immediately before the date when the deceased died, the person was living—

      (a)   in the same household as the deceased, and

      (b)   as the husband or wife of the deceased.

(1B) This subsection applies to a person if for the whole of the period of two years ending immediately before the date when the deceased died the person was living

      (a)   in the same household as the deceased, and

      (b)   as the civil partner of the deceased.

(2)   In this Act 'reasonable financial provision'—

      (a)   in the case of an application made by virtue of subsection (1)(a) above by the husband or wife of the deceased (except where at the date of death, a separation order under the Family Law Act 1996 was in force in relation to the marriage and the separation was continuing), means such financial provision as it would be reasonable in all the circumstances of the case for a husband or wife to receive, whether or not that provision is required for his or her maintenance;

      (aa) in the case of an application made by virtue of subsection (1)(a) above by the civil partner of the deceased (except where, at the date of death, a separation order under Chapter 2 of Part 2 of the Civil Partnership Act 2004 was in force in relation to the civil partnership and the separation was continuing), means such financial provision as it would be reasonable in all the circumstances of the case for a civil partner to receive, whether or not that provision is required for his or her maintenance;

      (b)   in the case of any other application made by virtue of subsection (1) above, means such financial provision as it would be reasonable in all the circumstances of the case for the applicant to receive for his maintenance.

(3)   For the purposes of subsection (1)(e) above, a person shall be treated as being maintained by the deceased, either wholly or partly, as the case may be, if the deceased, otherwise than for full valuable consideration, was making a substantial contribution in money or money's worth towards the reasonable needs of that person.

2.   Powers of court to make orders

(1)   Subject to the provisions of this Act, where an application is made for an order under this section, the court may, if it is satisfied that the disposition of the deceased's estate effected by his will or the law relating to intestacy, or the combination of his will and that law, is not such as to make reasonable financial provision for the applicant, make any one or more of the following orders:—

      (a)   an order for the making to the applicant out of the net estate of the deceased of such periodical payments and for such term as may be specified in the order;

      (b)   an order for the payment to the applicant out of that estate of a lump sum of such amount as may be so specified;

      (c)   an order for the transfer to the applicant of such property comprised in that estate as may be so specified;

      (d)   an order for the settlement for the benefit of the applicant of such property comprised in that estate as may be so specified;

(e)   an order for the acquisition out of property comprised in that estate of such property as may be so specified and for the transfer of the property so acquired to the applicant or for the settlement thereof for his benefit;

(f)   an order varying any ante-nuptial or post-nuptial settlement (including such a settlement made by will) made on the parties to a marriage to which the deceased was one of the parties, the variation being for the benefit of the surviving party to that marriage, or any child of that marriage, or any person who was treated by the deceased as a child of the family in relation to that marriage;

(g)   an order varying any settlement made
        (i)   during the subsistence of a civil partnership formed by the deceased, or
        (ii)   in anticipation of the formation of a civil partnership by the deceased,
        on the civil partners (including such a settlement made by will), the variation being for the benefit of the surviving civil partner, or any child of both the civil partners, or any person who was treated by the deceased as a child of the family in relation to that civil partnership.

(2)   An order under subsection (1)(a) above providing for the making out of the net estate of the deceased of periodical payments may provide for—
        (a)   payments of such amount as may be specified in the order,
        (b)   payments equal to the whole of the income of the net estate or of such portion thereof as may be so specified,
        (c)   payments equal to the whole of the income of such part of the net estate as the court may direct to be set aside or appropriated for the making out of the income thereof of payments under this section,
        or may provide for the amount of the payments or any of them to be determined in any other way the court thinks fit.

(3)   Where an order under subsection (1)(a) above provides for the making of payments of an amount specified in the order, the order may direct that such part of the net estate as may be so specified shall be set aside or appropriated for the making out of the income thereof of those payments; but no larger part of the net estate shall be so set aside or appropriated than is sufficient, at the date of the order, to produce by the income thereof the amount required for the making of those payments.

(4)   An order under this section may contain such consequential and supplemental provisions as the court thinks necessary or expedient for the purpose of giving effect to the order or for the purpose of securing that the order operates fairly as between one beneficiary of the estate of the deceased and another and may, in particular, but without prejudice to the generality of this subsection—
        (a)   order any person who holds any property which forms part of the net estate of the deceased to make such payment or transfer such property as may be specified in the order;
        (b)   vary the disposition of the deceased's estate effected by the will or the law relating to intestacy, or by both the will and the law relating to intestacy, in such manner as the court thinks fair and reasonable having regard to the provisions of the order and all the circumstances of the case;
        (c)   confer on the trustees of any property which is the subject of an order under this section such powers as appear to the court to be necessary or expedient.

3.   Matters to which court is to have regard in exercising powers under s. 2

(1)   Where an application is made for an order under section 2 of this Act, the court shall, in determining whether the disposition of the deceased's estate effected by his will or the law relating to intestacy, or the combination of his will and that law, is such as to make reasonable financial provision for the applicant and, if the court considers that reasonable financial provision has not been made, in determining whether and in what manner it shall exercise its powers under that section, have regard to the following matters, that is to say—
        (a)   the financial resources and financial needs which the applicant has or is likely to have in the foreseeable future;

(b)   the financial resources and financial needs which any other applicant for an order under section 2 of this Act has or is likely to have in the foreseeable future;

(c)   the financial resources and financial needs which any beneficiary of the estate of the deceased has or is likely to have in the foreseeable future;

(d)   any obligations and responsibilities which the deceased had towards any applicant for an order under the said section 2 or towards any beneficiary of the estate of the deceased;

(e)   the size and nature of the net estate of the deceased;

(f)   any physical or mental disability of any applicant for an order under the said section 2 or any beneficiary of the estate of the deceased;

(g)   any other matter, including the conduct of the applicant or any other person, which in the circumstances of the case the court may consider relevant.

(2)   This section applies, without prejudice to the generality of paragraph (g) of subsection (1) above, where an application for an order under section 2 of this Act is made by virtue of section 1(1)(a) or (b) of this Act. The court shall, in addition to the matters specifically mentioned in paragraphs (a) to (f) of that subsection, have regard to—

(a)   the age of the applicant and the duration of the marriage or civil partnership;

(b)   the contribution made by the applicant to the welfare of the family of the deceased, including any contribution made by looking after the home or caring for the family.

In the case of an application by the wife or husband of the deceased, the court shall also, unless at the date of death a decree of judicial separation was in force and the separation was continuing, have regard to the provision which the applicant might reasonably have expected to receive if on the day on which the deceased died the marriage, instead of being terminated by death, had been terminated by a divorce order. In the case of an application by the civil partner of the deceased, the court shall also, unless at the date of the death a separation order under Chapter 2 of Part 2 of the Civil Partnership Act 2004 was in force and the separation was continuing, have regard to the provision which the applicant might reasonably have expected to receive if on the day on which the deceased died the civil partnership, instead of being terminated by death, had been terminated by a dissolution order.

(2A)   Without prejudice to the generality of paragraph (g) of subsection (1) above, where an application for an order under section 2 of this Act is made by virtue of section 1(1)(ba) of this Act, the court shall, in that subsection have regard to—

(a)   the age of the applicant and the length of the period during which the applicant lived as the husband or wife or civil partner of the deceased and in the same household as the deceased;

(b)   the contribution made by the applicant to the welfare of the family of the deceased, including any contribution made by looking after the home or caring for the family.

(3)   Without prejudice to the generality of paragraph (g) of subsection (1) above, where an application for an order under section 2 of this Act is made by virtue of section 1(1)(c) or 1(1)(d) of this Act, the court shall, in addition to the matters specifically mentioned in paragraphs (a) to (f) of that subsection, have regard to the manner in which the applicant was being or in which he might expect to be educated or trained, and where the application is made by virtue of section 1(1)(d) the court shall also have regard—

(a)   to whether the deceased had assumed any responsibility for the applicant's maintenance and, if so, to the extent to which and the basis upon which the deceased assumed that responsibility and to the length of time for which the deceased discharged that responsibility;

(b)   to whether in assuming and discharging that responsibility the deceased did so knowing that the applicant was not his own child;

(c)   to the liability of any other person to maintain the applicant.

(4)   Without prejudice to the generality of paragraph (g) of subsection (1) above, where an application for an order under section 2 of this Act is made by virtue of section 1(1)(e) of this Act, the court shall, in addition to the matters specifically mentioned in paragraphs (a)

to (f) of that subsection, have regard to the extent to which and the basis upon which the deceased assumed responsibility for the maintenance of the applicant and to the length of time for which the deceased discharged that responsibility.

(5) In considering the matters to which the court is required to have regard under this section, the court shall take into account the facts as known to the court at the date of the hearing.

(6) In considering the financial resources of any person for the purposes of this section the court shall take into account his earning capacity and in considering the financial needs of any person for the purposes of this section the court shall take into account his financial obligations and responsibilities.

Powers of court in relation to transactions intended to defeat applications for financial provision

10.   Dispositions intended to defeat applications for financial provisions

(1) Where an application is made to the court for an order under section 2 of this Act, the applicant may, in the proceedings on that application, apply to the court for an order under subsection (2) below.

(2) Where on an application under subsection (1) above the court is satisfied—

(a) that, less than six years before the date of the death of the deceased, the deceased with the intention of defeating an application for financial provision under this Act made a disposition, and

(b) that full valuable consideration for that disposition was not given by the person to whom or for the benefit of whom the disposition was made (in this section referred to as the donee') or by any other person, and

(c) that the exercise of the powers conferred by this section would facilitate the making of financial provision for the applicant under this Act, then, subject to the provisions of this section and of sections 12 and 13 of this Act, the court may order the donee (whether or not at the date of the order he holds any interest in the property disposed of to him or for his benefit by the deceased) to provide, for the purpose of the making of that financial provision, such sum of money or other property as may be specified in the order.

(3) Where an order is made under subsection (2) above as respects any disposition made by the deceased which consisted of the payment of money to or for the benefit of the donee, the amount of any sum of money or the value of any property ordered to be provided under that subsection shall not exceed the amount of the payment made by the deceased after deducting therefrom any inheritance tax borne by the donee in respect of that payment.

(4) Where an order is made under subsection (2) above as respects any disposition made by the deceased which consisted of the transfer of property (other than a sum of money) to or for the benefit of the donee, the amount of any sum of money or the value of any property ordered to be provided under that subsection shall not exceed the value at the date of the death of the deceased of the property disposed of by him to or for the benefit of the donee (or if that property has been disposed of by the person to whom it was transferred by the deceased, the value at the date of that disposal thereof) after deducting therefrom any inheritance tax borne by the donee in respect of the transfer of that property by the deceased.

(5) Where an application (in this subsection referred to as 'the original application') is made for an order under subsection (2) above in relation to any disposition, then, if on an application under this subsection by the donee or by any applicant for an order under section 2 of this Act the court is satisfied—

(a) that, less than six years before the date of the death of the deceased, the deceased with the intention of defeating an application for financial provision under this Act made a disposition other than the disposition which is the subject of the original application, and

(b) that full valuable consideration for that other disposition was not given by the person to whom or for the benefit of whom that other disposition was made or by any other person, the court may exercise in relation to the person to whom or for the benefit of whom that other disposition was made the powers which the court would have had under subsection (2) above if the original application had been made in respect of that other disposition and the court had been satisfied as to the matters set out in paragraphs (a), (b) and (c) of that subsection; and where any application is made under this subsection, any reference in this section (except in subsection (2)(b)) to the donee shall include a reference to the person to whom or for the benefit of whom that other disposition was made.

(6)   In determining whether and in what manner to exercise its powers under this section, the court shall have regard to the circumstances in which any disposition was made and any valuable consideration which was given therefor, the relationship, if any, of the donee to the deceased, the conduct and financial resources of the donee and all the other circumstances of the case.

(7)   In this section 'disposition' does not include—

(a)   any provision in a will, any such nomination as is mentioned in section 8(1) of this Act or any donatio mortis causa, or

(b)   any appointment of property made, otherwise than by will, in the exercise of a special power of appointment,

but, subject to these exceptions, includes any payment of money (including the payment of a premium under a policy of assurance) and any conveyance, assurance, appointment or gift of property of any description, whether made by an instrument or otherwise.

(8)   The provisions of this section do not apply to any disposition made before the commencement of this Act.

11.   Contracts to leave property by will

(1)   Where an application is made to a court for an order under section 2 of this Act, the applicant may, in the proceedings on that application, apply to the court for an order under this section.

(2)   Where on an application under subsection (1) above the court is satisfied—

(a)   that the deceased made a contract by which he agreed to leave by his will a sum of money or other property to any person or by which he agreed that a sum of money or other property would be paid or transferred to any person out of his estate, and

(b)   that the deceased made that contract with the intention of defeating an application for financial provision under this Act, and

(c)   that when the contract was made full valuable consideration for that contract was not given or promised by the person with whom or for the benefit of whom the contract was made (in this section referred to as 'the donee') or by any other person, and

(d)   that the exercise of the powers conferred by this section would facilitate the making of financial provision for the applicant under this Act,

then, subject to the provisions of this section and of sections 12 and 13 of this Act, the court may make any one or more of the following orders, that is to say—

(i)   if any money has been paid or any other property has been transferred to or for the benefit of the donee in accordance with the contract, an order directing the donee to provide, for the purpose of the making of that financial provision, such sum of money or other property as may be specified in the order;

(ii)   if the money or all the money has not been paid or the property or all the property has not been transferred in accordance with the contract, an order directing the personal representatives not to make any payment or transfer any property, or not to make any further payment or transfer any further property, as the case may be, in accordance therewith or directing the personal representatives only to make such payment or transfer such property as may be specified in the order.

(3)   Notwithstanding anything in subsection (2) above, the court may exercise its powers thereunder in relation to any contract made by the deceased only to the extent that the court considers that the amount of any sum of money paid or to be paid or the value of any property transferred or to be transferred in accordance with the contract exceeds the value of

any valuable consideration given or to be given for that contract, and for this purpose the court shall have regard to the value of property at the date of the hearing.

(4)   In determining whether and in what manner to exercise its powers under this section, the court shall have regard to the circumstances in which the contract was made, the relationship, if any, of the donee to the deceased, the conduct and financial resources of the donee and all the other circumstances of the case.

(5)   Where an order has been made under subsection (2) above in relation to any contract, the rights of any person to enforce that contract or to recover damages or to obtain other relief for the breach thereof shall be subject to any adjustment made by the court under section 12(3) of this Act and shall survive to such extent only as is consistent with giving effect to the terms of that order.

(6)   The provisions of this section do not apply to a contract made before the commencement of this Act.

12.   Provisions supplementary to ss. 10 and 11

(1)   Where the exercise of any of the powers conferred by section 10 or 11 of this Act is conditional on the court being satisfied that a disposition or contract was made by a deceased person with the intention of defeating an application for financial provision under this Act, that condition shall be fulfilled if the court is of the opinion that, on a balance of probabilities, the intention of the deceased (though not necessarily his sole intention) in making the disposition or contract was to prevent an order for financial provision being made under this Act or to reduce the amount of the provision which might otherwise be granted by an order thereunder.

(2)   Where an application is made under section 11 of this Act with respect to any contract made by the deceased and no valuable consideration was given or promised by any person for that contract then, notwithstanding anything in subsection (1) above, it shall be presumed, unless the contrary is shown, that the deceased made that contract with the intention of defeating an application for financial provision under this Act.

(3)   Where the court makes an order under section 10 or 11 of this Act it may give such consequential directions as it thinks fit (including directions requiring the making of any payment or the transfer of any property) for giving effect to the order or for securing a fair adjustment of the rights of the persons affected thereby.

(4)   Any power conferred on the court by the said section 10 or 11 to order the donee, in relation to any disposition or contract, to provide any sum of money or other property shall be exercisable in like manner in relation to the personal representative of the donee, and

(a)   any reference in section 10(4) to the disposal of property by the donee shall include a reference to disposal by the personal representative of the donee, and

(b)   any reference in section 10(5) to an application by the donee under that subsection shall include a reference to an application by the personal representative of a donee;

but the court shall not have power under the said section 10 or 11 to make an order in respect of any property forming part of the estate of the donee which has been distributed by the personal representative; and the personal representative shall not be liable for having distributed any such property before he has notice of the making of an application under the said section 10 or 11 on the ground that he ought to have taken into account the possibility that such an application would be made.

13.   Provisions as to trustees in relation to ss. 10 and 11

(1)   Where an application is made for—

(a)   an order under section 10 of this Act in respect of a disposition made by the deceased to any person as a trustee, or

(b)   an order under section 11 of this Act in respect of any payment made or property transferred, in accordance with a contract made by the deceased, to any person as a trustee,

the powers of the court under the said section 10 or 11 to order that trustee to provide a sum of money or other property shall be subject to the following limitation (in addition, in a case of an application under section 10, to any provision regarding the deduction of inheritance tax) namely, that the amount of any sum of money or the value of any property ordered to be provided—

(i)   in the case of an application in respect of a disposition which consisted of the payment of money or an application in respect of the payment of money in accordance with a contract, shall not exceed the aggregate of so much of that money as is at the date of the order in the hands of the trustee and the value at that date of any property which represents that money or is derived therefrom and is at that date in the hands of the trustee;

(ii)   in the case of an application in respect of a disposition which consisted of the transfer of property (other than a sum of money) or an application in respect of the transfer of property (other than a sum of money) in accordance with a contract, shall not exceed the aggregate of the value at the date of the order of so much of that property as is at that date in the hands of the trustee and the value at that date of any property which represents the first-mentioned property or is derived therefrom and is at that date in the hands of the trustee.

(2)   Where any such application is made in respect of a disposition made to any person as a trustee or in respect of any payment made or property transferred in pursuance of a contract to any person as a trustee, the trustee shall not be liable for having distributed any money or other property on the ground that he ought to have taken into account the possibility that such an application would be made.

(3)   Where any such application is made in respect of a disposition made to any person as a trustee or in respect of any payment made or property transferred in accordance with a contract to any person as a trustee, any reference in the said section 10 or 11 to the donee shall be construed as including a reference to the trustee or trustees for the time being of the trust in question and any reference in subsection (1) or (2) above to a trustee shall be construed in the same way.

Special provisions relating to cases of divorce, separation etc.

14.   Provision as to cases where no financial relief was granted in divorce proceedings etc.

(1)   Where, within twelve months from the date on which a divorce order or separation order has been made under the Family Law Act 1996 in relation to a marriage or a decree of nullity of marriage has been made absolute, a party to the marriage dies and—

(a)   an application for a financial provision order under section 22A or 23 of the Matrimonial Causes Act 1973 or a property adjustment order under section 23A or 24 of that Act has not been made by the other party to that marriage, or

(b)   such an application has been made but the proceedings thereon have not been determined at the time of the death of the deceased,

then, if an application for an order under section 2 of this Act is made by that other party, the court shall, notwithstanding anything in section 1 or section 3 of this Act, have power, if it thinks it just to do so, to treat that party for the purposes of that application as if, as the case may be, the divorce order or separation order had not been made or the decree of nullity had not been made absolute.

(2)   This section shall not apply in relation to a separation order unless at the date of the death of the deceased the order was in force and the separation was continuing.

14A.   Provision as to cases where no financial relief was granted in proceedings for the dissolution etc. of a civil partnership

(1)   Subsection (2) below applies where

(a)   a dissolution order, nullity order, separation order or presumption of death order has been made under Chapter 2 of Part 2 of the Civil Partnership Act 2004 in relation to a civil partnership,

(b)   one of the civil partners dies within twelve months from the date on which the order is made, and

(c) either
      (i)   an application for a financial provision order under Part 1 of Schedule 5 to that Act or a property adjustment order under Part 2 of that Schedule has not been made by the other civil partner, or
      (ii) such an application has been made but the proceedings on the application have not been determined at the time of the death of the deceased.

(2)   If an application for an order under section 2 of this Act is made by the surviving civil partner, the court shall, notwithstanding anything in section 1 or section 3 of this Act, have power, if it thinks it just to do so, to treat the surviving civil partner as if the order mentioned in subsection (1)(a) above had not been made.

(3)   This section shall not apply in relation to a separation order unless at the date of the death of the deceased the separation order was in force and the separation was continuing.

15. Restriction imposed in divorce proceedings etc. on application under this Act

(1)   At any time when the court—
    (a) has jurisdiction under section 23A or 24 of the Matrimonial Causes Act 1973 to make a property adjustment order in relation to a marriage; or
    (b) would have such jurisdiction if either the jurisdiction had not already been exercised or an application for such an order were made with the leave of the court,
the court, if it considers it just to do so, may, on the application of either party to the marriage order that either party to the marriage shall not on the death of the applicant be entitled to apply for an order under section 2 of this Act.
    In this subsection 'the court' means the High Court or, where a county court has jurisdiction by virtue of Part V of the Matrimonial and Family Proceedings Act 1984, a county court.

(2)   An order made under subsection (1) above with respect to any party to a marriage has effect in accordance with subsection (3) below at any time—
    (a) after the marriage has been dissolved;
    (b) after a degree of nullity has been made absolute in relation to the marriage; and
    (c) while a separation order under the Family Law Act 1996 is in force in relation to the marriage and the separation is continuing.

(3)   If at any time when an order made under subsection (1) above with respect to any party to a marriage has effect the other party to the marriage dies, the court shall not entertain any application made by the surviving party to the marriage for an order under section 2 of this Act.

15ZA. Restriction imposed in proceedings for the dissolution etc. of a civil partnership on application under this Act

(1)   On making a dissolution order, nullity order, separation order or presumption of death order under Chapter 2 of Part 2 of the Civil Partnership Act 2004, or at any time after making such an order, the court, if it considers it just to do so, may, on the application of either of the civil partners, order that the other civil partner shall not on the death of the applicant be entitled to apply for an order under section 2 of this Act.

(2)   In subsection (1) above 'the court' means the High Court or, where a county court has jurisdiction by virtue of Part 5 of the Matrimonial and Family Proceedings Act 1984, a county court.

(3)   In the case of a dissolution order, nullity order or presumption of death order ('the main order') an order may be made under subsection (1) above before (as well as after) the main order is made final, but if made before the main order is made final it shall not take effect unless the main order is made final.

(4)   Where an order under subsection (1) above made in connection with a dissolution order, nullity order or presumption of death order has come into force with respect to a civil partner, then, on the death of the other civil partner, the court shall not entertain any application for an order under section 2 of this Act made by the surviving civil partner.

(5)   Where an order under subsection (1) above made in connection with a separation order has come into force with respect to a civil partner, then, if the other civil partner dies while the separation order is in force and the separation is continuing, the court shall not entertain any application for an order under section 2 of this Act made by the surviving civil partner.

15A.   Restriction imposed in proceedings under the Matrimonial and Family Proceedings Act 1984 on application under this Act

(1)   On making an order under section 17 of the Matrimonial and Family Proceedings Act 1984 (orders for financial provision and property adjustment following overseas divorces etc.) the court, if it considers it just to do so, may, on the application of either party to the marriage order that the other party to the marriage shall not on the death of the applicant be entitled to apply for an order under section 2 of this Act.

In this subsection 'the court' means the High Court or, where a county court has jurisdiction by virtue of Part V of the Matrimonial and Family Proceedings Act 1984, a county court.

(2)   Where an order under subsection (1) above has been made with respect to a party to a marriage which has been dissolved or annulled then, on the death of the other party to that marriage, the court shall not entertain an application under section 2 of this Act by the first-mentioned party.

(3)   Where an order under subsection (1) above has been made with respect to a party to a marriage the parties to which have been legally separated, then, if the other party to the marriage dies while the legal separation is in force, the court shall not entertain an application under section 2 of this Act made by the first-mentioned party.

15B.   Restriction imposed in proceedings under Schedule 7 to the Civil Partnership Act 2004 on application under this Act

(1)   On making an order under paragraph 9 of Schedule 7 to the Civil Partnership Act 2004 (orders for financial provision, property adjustment and pension-sharing following overseas dissolution etc. of civil partnership) the court, if it considers it just to do so, may, on the application of either of the civil partners, order that the other civil partner shall not on the death of the applicant be entitled to apply for an order under section 2 of this Act.

(2)   In subsection (1) above 'the court' means the High Court or, where a county court has jurisdiction by virtue of Part 5 of the Matrimonial and Family Proceedings Act 1984, a county court.

(3)   Where an order under subsection (1) above has been made with respect to one of the civil partners in a case where a civil partnership has been dissolved or annulled, then, on the death of the other civil partner, the court shall not entertain an application under section 2 of this Act made by the surviving civil partner.

(4)   Where an order under subsection (1) above has been made with respect to one of the civil partners in a case where civil partners have been legally separated, then, if the other civil partner dies while the legal separation is in force, the court shall not entertain an application under section 2 of this Act made by the surviving civil partner.

16.   Variation and discharge of secured periodical payments orders made under Matrimonial Causes Act 1973

(1)   Where an application for an order under section 2 of this Act is made to the court by any person who was at the time of the death of the deceased entitled to payments from the deceased under a secured periodical payments order made under the Matrimonial Causes Act 1973 or Schedule 5 to the Civil Partnership Act 2004, then, in the proceedings on that application, the court shall have power, if an application is made under this section by that person or by the personal representative of the deceased, to vary or discharge that periodical payments order or to revive the operation of any provision thereof which has been suspended under section 31 of that Act of 1973 or Part 11 of that Schedule.

(2)   In exercising the powers conferred by this section the court shall have regard to all the circumstances of the case, including any order which the court proposes to make under

section 2 or section 5 of this Act and any change (whether resulting from the death of the deceased or otherwise) in any of the matters to which the court was required to have regard when making the secured periodical payments order.

(3) The power exercisable by the court under this section in relation to an order shall be exercisable also in relation to any instrument executed in pursuance of the order.

17.   Variation and revocation of maintenance agreements

(1) Where an application for an order under section 2 of this Act is made to the court by any person who was at the time of the death of the deceased entitled to payments from the deceased under a maintenance agreement which provided for the continuation of payments under the agreement after the death of the deceased, then, in the proceedings on that application, the court shall have power, if an application is made under this section by that person or by the personal representative of the deceased, to vary or revoke that agreement.

(2) In exercising the powers conferred by this section the court shall have regard to all the circumstances of the case, including any order which the court proposes to make under section 2 or section 5 of this Act and any change (whether resulting from the death of the deceased or otherwise) in any of the circumstances in the light of which the agreement was made.

(3) If a maintenance agreement is varied by the court under this section the like consequences shall ensue as if the variation had been made immediately before the death of the deceased by agreement between the parties and for valuable consideration.

(4) In this section 'maintenance agreement', in relation to a deceased person, means any agreement made, whether in writing or not and whether before or after the commencement of this Act, by the deceased with any person with whom he formed a marriage or civil partnership, being an agreement which contained provisions governing the rights and liabilities towards one another when living separately of the parties to that marriage or of the civil partners (whether or not the marriage or civil partnership has been dissolved or annulled) in respect of the making or securing of payments or the disposition or use of any property, including such rights and liabilities with respect to the maintenance or education of any child, whether or not a child of the deceased or a person who was treated by the deceased as a child of the family in relation to that marriage or civil partnership.

18.   Availability of court's powers under this Act in applications under ss. 31 and 36 of the Matrimonial Causes Act 1973

(1) Where—

   (a) a person against whom a secured periodical payments order was made under the Matrimonial Causes Act 1973 has died and an application is made under section 31(6) of that Act for the variation or discharge of that order or for the revival of the operation of any provision thereof which has been suspended, or

   (b) a party to a maintenance agreement within the meaning of section 34 of that Act has died, the agreement being one which provides for the continuation of payments thereunder after the death of one of the parties, and an application is made under section 36(1) of that Act for the alteration of the agreement under section 35 thereof,

   the court shall have power to direct that the application made under the said section 31(6) or 36(1) shall be deemed to have been accompanied by an application for an order under section 2 of this Act.

(2) Where the court gives a direction under subsection (1) above it shall have power, in the proceedings on the application under the said section 31(6) or 36(1), to make any order which the court would have had power to make under the provisions of this Act if the application under the said section 31(6) or 36(1), as the case may be, had been made jointly with an application for an order under the said section 2; and the court shall have power to give such consequential directions as may be necessary for enabling the court to exercise any of the powers available to the court under this Act in the case of an application for an order under section 2.

(3) Where an order made under section 15(1) of this Act is in force with respect to a party to a marriage, the court shall not give a direction under subsection (1) above with respect to any application made under the said section 31(6) or 36(1) by that party on the death of the other party.

18A. Availability of court's powers under this Act in applications under paragraphs 60 and 73 of Schedule 5 to the Civil Partnership Act 2004

(1) Where
  (a) a person against whom a secured periodical payments order was made under Schedule 5 to the Civil Partnership Act 2004 has died and an application is made under paragraph 60 of that Schedule for the variation or discharge of that order or for the revival of the operation of any suspended provision of the order, or
  (b) a party to a maintenance agreement within the meaning of Part 13 of that Schedule has died, the agreement being one which provides for the continuation of payments under the agreement after the death of one of the parties, and an application is made under paragraph 73 of that Schedule for the alteration of the agreement under paragraph 69 of that Schedule,

the court shall have power to direct that the application made under paragraph 60 or 73 of that Schedule shall be deemed to have been accompanied by an application for an order under section 2 of this Act.

(2) Where the court gives a direction under subsection (1) above it shall have power, in the proceedings on the application under paragraph 60 or 73 of that Schedule, to make any order which the court would have had power to make under the provisions of this Act if the application under that paragraph had been made jointly with an application for an order under section 2 of this Act; and the court shall have power to give such consequential directions as may be necessary for enabling the court to exercise any of the powers available to the court under this Act in the case of an application for an order under section 2.

(3) Where an order made under section 15ZA(1) of this Act is in force with respect to a civil partner, the court shall not give a direction under subsection (1) above with respect to any application made under paragraph 60 or 73 of that Schedule by that civil partner on the death of the other civil partner.

Miscellaneous and supplementary provisions

25. Interpretation

(1) In this Act—
  'beneficiary', in relation to the estate of a deceased person, means—
  (a) a person who under the will of the deceased or under the law relating to intestacy is beneficially interested in the estate or would be so interested if an order had not been made under this Act, and
  (b) a person who has received any sum of money or other property which by virtue of section 8(1) or 8(2) of this Act is treated as part of the net estate of the deceased or would have received that sum or other property if an order had not been made under this Act;
  'child' includes an illegitimate child and a child en ventre sa mere at the death of the deceased;
  'the court' means unless the context otherwise requires the High Court, or where a county court has jurisdiction by virtue of section 22 of this Act, a county court;
  'former civil partner' means a person whose civil partnership with the deceased was during the lifetime of the deceased either
  (a) dissolved or annulled by an order made under the law of any part of the British Islands, or
  (b) dissolved or annulled in any country or territory outside the British Islands by a dissolution or annulment which is entitled to be recognised as valid by the law of England and Wales;

'former wife' or 'former spouse' means a person whose marriage with the deceased was during the lifetime of the deceased either—

(a)   dissolved or annulled by an order or decree of divorce or a decree of nullity of marriage granted under the law of any part of the British Islands; or

(b)   dissolved or annulled in any country or territory outside the British Islands by a divorce or annulment which is entitled to be recognised as valid by the law of England and Wales;

'net estate', in relation to a deceased person, means—

(a)   all property of which the deceased had power to dispose by his will (otherwise than by virtue of a special power of appointment) less the amount of his funeral, testamentary and administration expenses, debts and liabilities, including any inheritance tax payable out of his estate on his death;

(b)   any property in respect of which the deceased held a general power of appointment (not being a power exercisable by will) which has not been exercised,

(c)   any sum of money or other property which is treated for the purposes of this Act as part of the net estate of the deceased by virtue of section 8(1) or (2) of this Act;

(d)   any property which is treated for the purposes of this Act as part of the net estate of the deceased by virtue of an order made under section 9 of the Act;

(e)   any sum of money or other property which is, by reason of a disposition or contract made by the deceased, ordered under section 10 or 11 of this Act to be provided for the purpose of the making of financial provision under this Act;

'property' includes any chose in action;

'reasonable financial provision' has the meaning assigned to it by section 1 of this Act;

'valuable consideration' does not include a marriage or a promise of marriage;

'will' includes codicil.

(2)   For the purposes of paragraph (a) of the definition of 'net estate' in subsection (1) above a person who is not of full age and capacity shall be treated as having power to dispose by will of all property of which he would have had power to dispose by will if he had been of full age and capacity.

(3)   Any reference in this Act to provision out of the net estate of a deceased person includes a reference to provision extending to the whole of that estate.

(4)   For the purposes of this Act any reference to a spouse, wife or husband shall be treated as including a reference to a person who in good faith entered into a void marriage with the deceased unless either—

(a)   the marriage of the deceased and that person was dissolved or annulled during the lifetime of the deceased and the dissolution or annulment is recognised by the law of England and Wales, or

(b)   that person has during the lifetime of the deceased formed a subsequent marriage or civil partnership.

(4A) For the purposes of this Act any reference to a civil partner shall be treated as including a reference to a person who in good faith formed a void civil partnership with the deceased unless either

(a)   the civil partnership between the deceased and that person was dissolved or annulled during the lifetime of the deceased and the dissolution or annulment is recognised by the law of England and Wales, or

(b)   that person has during the lifetime of the deceased formed a subsequent civil partnership or marriage.

(5)   Any reference in this Act to the formation of, or to a person who has formed, a subsequent marriage or civil partnership includes (as the case may be) a reference to the formation of, or to a person who has formed, a marriage or civil partnership which is by law void or voidable.

(5A) The formation of a marriage or civil partnership shall be treated for the purposes of this Act as the formation of a subsequent marriage or civil partnership, in relation to either of the spouses or civil partners, notwithstanding that the previous marriage or civil partnership of that spouse or civil partner was void or voidable.

(6) Any reference in this Act to an order or decree made under the Matrimonial Causes Act 1973 or under any section of that Act shall be construed as including a reference to an order or decree which is deemed to have been made under that Act or under that section thereof, as the case may be.

(6A) Any reference in this Act to an order made under, or under any provision of, the Civil Partnership Act 2004 shall be construed as including a reference to anything which is deemed to be an order made (as the case may be) under that Act or provision.

(7) Any reference in this Act to any enactment is a reference to that enactment as amended by or under any subsequent enactment.

LOCAL LAND CHARGES ACT 1975
(1975, c. 76)

Definition of local land charges

1. Local land charges

(1) A charge or other matter affecting land is a local land charge if it falls within any of the following descriptions and is not one of the matters set out in section 2 below:—

(a) any charge acquired either before of after the commencement of this Act by a local authority or National Park authority, water authority, sewerage undertaker or new town development corporation under the Public Health Acts 1936 and 1937, . . . the Public Health Act 1961 or the Highways Act 1980 (or any Act repealed by that Act) or the Building Act 1984 or any similar charge acquired by a local authority or National Park authority under any other Act, whether passed before or after this Act, being a charge that is binding on successive owners of the land affected;

(b) any prohibition of or restriction on the use of land—
   (i) imposed by a local authority or National Park authority on or after 1st January 1926 (including any prohibition or restriction embodied in any condition attached to a consent, approval or licence granted by a local authority on or after that date), or
   (ii) enforceable by a local authority or National Park Authority under any covenant or agreement made with them on or after that date,
   being a prohibition or restriction binding on successive owners of the land affected;

(c) any prohibition of or restriction on the use of land—
   (i) imposed by a Minister of the Crown or government department on or after the date of the commencement of this Act (including any prohibition or restriction embodied in any condition attached to a consent, approval or licence granted by such a Minister or department on or after that date), or
   (ii) enforceable by such a Minister or department under any covenant or agreement made with him or them on or after that date,
   being a prohibition or restriction binding on successive owners of the land affected,

(d) any positive obligation affecting land enforceable by a Minister of the Crown, government department or local authority or National Park authority under any covenant or agreement made with him or them on or after the date of the commencement of this Act and binding on successive owners of the land affected;

(e) any charge or other matter which is expressly made a local land charge by any statutory provision not contained in this section.

(2) For the purposes of subsection (1)(a) above, any sum which is recoverable from successive owners or occupiers of the land in respect of which the sum is recoverable shall be treated as a charge, whether the sum is expressed to be a charge on the land or not.

. . .

2.   Matters which are not local land charges

The following matters are not local land charges:—

(a)   a prohibition or restriction enforceable under a covenant or agreement made between a lessor and a lessee;

(b)   a positive obligation enforceable under a covenant or agreement made between a lessor and a lessee;

(c)   a prohibition or restriction enforceable by a Minister of the Crown, government department or local authority or National Park authority under any covenant or agreement, being a prohibition or restriction binding on successive owners of the land affected by reason of the fact that the covenant or agreement is made for the benefit of land of the Minister, government department or local authority or National Park authority;

(d)   a prohibition or restriction embodied in any bye-laws;

(e)   a condition or limitation subject to which planning permission was granted at any time before the commencement of this Act or was or is (at any time) deemed to be granted under any statutory provision relating to town and country planning, whether by a Minister of the Crown, government department or local authority or National Park authority;

(f)   a prohibition or restriction embodied in a scheme under the Town and Country Planning Act 1932 or any enactment repealed by that Act;

(g)   a prohibition or restriction enforceable under a forestry dedication covenant entered into pursuant to section 5 of the Forestry Act 1967;

(h)   a prohibition or restriction affecting the whole of any of the following areas:—

(i)   England, Wales or England and Wales;

(ii)   England, or England and Wales, with the exception of, or any part of, Greater London;

(iii)   Greater London.

7.   Effect of registering certain financial charges

A local land charge falling within section 1(1)(a) above shall, when registered, take effect as if it had been created by a deed of charge by way of legal mortgage within the meaning of the Law of Property Act 1925, but without prejudice to the priority of the charge.

Searches

8.   Personal searches

(1)   Any person may search in any local land charges register on paying the prescribed fee.

. . .

LIMITATION ACT 1980
(1980, c. 58)

Actions to recover land and rent

15.   Time limit for actions to recover land

(1)   No action shall be brought by any person to recover any land after the expiration of twelve years from the date on which the right of action accrued to him or, if it first accrued to some person through whom he claims, to that person.

(2)   Subject to the following provisions of this section, where—

(a)   the estate or interest claimed was an estate or interest in reversion or remainder or any other future estate or interest and the right of action to recover the land accrued on the date on which the estate or interest fell into possession by the determination of the preceding estate or interest; and

(b)   the person entitled to the preceding estate or interest (not being a term of years absolute) was not in possession of the land on that date;

no action shall be brought by the person entitled to the succeeding estate or interest after the expiration of twelve years from the date on which the right of action accrued to the person entitled to the preceding estate or interest or six years from the date on which the right of action accrued to the person entitled to the succeeding estate or interest, whichever period last expires.

(3)   Subsection (2) above shall not apply to any estate or interest which falls into possession on the determination of an entailed interest and which might have been barred by the person entitled to the entailed interest.

(4)   No person shall bring an action to recover any estate or interest in land under an assurance taking effect after the right of action to recover the land had accrued to the person by whom the assurance was made or some person through whom he claimed or some person entitled to a preceding estate or interest, unless the action is brought within the period during which the person by whom the assurance was made could have brought such an action.

(5)   Where any person is entitled to any estate or interest in land in possession and, while so entitled, is also entitled to any future estate or interest in that land, and his right to recover the estate or interest in possession is barred under this Act, no action shall be brought by that person, or by any person claiming through him, in respect of the future estate or interest, unless in the meantime possession of the land has been recovered by a person entitled to an intermediate estate or interest.

(6)   Part I of Schedule 1 to this Act contains provisions for determining the date of accrual of rights of action to recover land in the cases there mentioned.

(7)   Part II of that Schedule contains provisions modifying the provisions of this section in their application to actions brought by, or by a person claiming through, the Crown or any spiritual or eleemosynary corporation sole.

16.   Time limit for redemption actions

When a mortgagee of land has been in possession of any of the mortgaged land for a period of twelve years, no action to redeem the land of which the mortgagee has been so in possession shall be brought after the end of that period by the mortgagor or any person claiming through him.

17.   Extinction of title to land after expiration of time limit

Subject to—

(a)   section 18 of this Act, and

(b)   . . .

at the expiration of the period prescribed by this Act for any person to bring an action to recover land (including a redemption action) the title of that person to the land shall be extinguished.

18.   Settled land and land held on trust

(1)   Subject to section 21(1) and (2) of this Act, the provisions of this Act shall apply to equitable interests in land . . . , as they apply to legal estates.

Accordingly a right of action to recover the land shall, for the purposes of this Act but not otherwise, be treated as accruing to a person entitled in possession to such an equitable interest in the like manner and circumstances, and on the same date, as it would accrue if his interest were a legal estate in the land (and any relevant provision of Part I of Schedule 1 to this Act shall apply in any such case accordingly).

(2)   Where the period prescribed by this Act has expired for the bringing of an action to recover land by a tenant for life or a statutory owner of settled land—

(a)   his legal estate shall not be extinguished if and so long as the right of action to recover the land of any person entitled to a beneficial interest in the land either has not accrued or has not been barred by this Act; and

(b)   the legal estate shall accordingly remain vested in the tenant for life or statutory owner and shall devolve in accordance with the Settled Land Act 1925;

but if and when every such right of action has been barred by this Act, his legal estate shall be extinguished.

(3)   Where any land is held upon trust . . . and the period prescribed by this Act has expired for the bringing of an action to recover the land by the trustees, the estate of the trustees shall not be extinguished if and so long as the right of action to recover the land of any person entitled to a beneficial interest in the land . . . either has not accrued or has not been barred

by this Act; but if and when every such right of action has been so barred the estate of the trustees shall be extinguished.

(4) Where—

    (a)   any settled land is vested in a statutory owner; or

    (b)   any land is held upon trust . . . ;

an action to recover the land may be brought by the statutory owner or trustees on behalf of any person entitled to a beneficial interest in possession in the land . . . whose right of action has not been barred by this Act, notwithstanding that the right of action of the statutory owner or trustees would apart from this provision have been barred by this Act.

19.   **Time limit for actions to recover rent**

No action shall be brought, or distress made, to recover arrears of rent, or damages in respect of arrears of rent, after the expiration of six years from the date on which the arrears became due.

Commonhold

19A   **Actions for breach of commonhold duty**

An action in respect of a right or duty of a kind referred to in section 37(1) of the Commonhold and Leasehold Reform Act 2002 (enforcement) shall not be brought after the expiration of six years from the date on which the cause of action accrued.

Actions to recover money secured by a mortgage or charge or to recover proceeds of the sale of land

20.   **Time limit for actions to recover money secured by a mortgage or charge or to recover proceeds of the sale of land**

(1)   No action shall be brought to recover—

    (a)   any principal sum of money secured by a mortgage or other charge on property (whether real or personal); or

    (b)   proceeds of the sale of land;

after the expiration of twelve years from the date on which the right to receive the money accrued.

(2)   No foreclosure action in respect of mortgaged personal property shall be brought after the expiration of twelve years from the date on which the right to foreclose accrued.

But if the mortgagee was in possession of the mortgaged property after that date, the right to foreclose on the property which was in his possession shall not be treated as having accrued for the purposes of this subsection until the date on which his possession discontinued.

(3)   The right to receive any principal sum of money secured by a mortgage or other charge and the right to foreclose on the property subject to the mortgage or charge shall not be treated as accruing so long as that property comprises any future interest or any life insurance policy which has not matured or been determined.

(4)   Nothing in this section shall apply to a foreclosure action in respect of mortgaged land, but the provisions of this Act relating to actions to recover land shall apply to such an action.

(5)   Subject to subsections (6) and (7) below, no action to recover arrears of interest payable in respect of any sum of money secured by a mortgage or other charge or payable in respect of proceeds of the sale of land, or to recover damages in respect of such arrears shall be brought after the expiration of six years from the date on which the interest became due.

(6)   Where—

    (a)   a prior mortgagee or other incumbrancer has been in possession of the property charged; and

    (b)   an action is brought within one year of the discontinuance of that possession by the subsequent incumbrancer;

the subsequent incumbrancer may recover by that action all the arrears of interest which fell due during the period of possession by the prior incumbrancer or damages in respect of those arrears, notwithstanding that the period exceeded six years.

(7)   Where—

(a)   the property subject to the mortgage or charge comprises any future interest or fife insurance policy; and

(b)   it is a term of the mortgage or charge that arrears of interest shall be treated as part of the principal sum of money secured by the mortgage or charge; interest shall not be treated as becoming due before the right to recover the principal sum of money has accrued or is treated as having accrued.

Actions in respect of trust property or the personal estate of deceased persons

21.   Time limit for actions in respect of trust property

(1)   No period of limitation prescribed by this Act shall apply to an action by a beneficiary under a trust, being an action—

    (a)   in respect of any fraud or fraudulent breach of trust to which the trustee was a party or privy; or

    (b)   to recover from the trustee trust property or the proceeds of trust property in the possession of the trustee, or previously received by the trustee and converted to his use.

(2)   Where a trustee who is also a beneficiary under the trust receives or retains trust property or its proceeds as his share on a distribution of trust property under the trust, his liability in any action brought by virtue of subsection (1)(b) above to recover that property or its proceeds after the expiration of the period of limitation prescribed by this Act for bringing an action to recover trust property shall be limited to the excess over his proper share.

    This subsection only applies if the trustee acted honestly and reasonably in making the distribution.

(3)   Subject to the preceding provisions of this section, an action by a beneficiary to recover trust property or in respect of any breach of trust, not being an action for which a period of limitation is prescribed by any other provision of this Act, shall not be brought after the expiration of six years from the date on which the right of action accrued.

    For the purposes of this subsection, the right of action shall not be treated as having accrued to any beneficiary entitled to a future interest in the trust property until the interest fell into possession.

(4)   No beneficiary as against whom there would be a good defence under this Act shall derive any greater or other benefit from a judgment or order obtained by any other beneficiary that he could have obtained if he had brought the action and this Act had been pleaded in defence.

22.   Time limit for actions claiming personal estate of a deceased person

Subject to section 21(1) and (2) of this Act—

(a)   no action in respect of any claim to the personal estate of a deceased person or to any share or interest in any such estate (whether under a will or on intestacy) shall be brought after the expiration of twelve years from the date on which the right to receive the share or interest accrued; and

(b)   no action to recover arrears of interest in respect of any legacy, or damages in respect of such arrears, shall be brought after the expiration of six years from the date on which the interest became due.

Actions for an account

23.   Time limit in respect of actions for an account

An action for an account shall not be brought after the expiration of any time limit under this Act which is applicable to the claim which is the basis of the duty to account.

26.   Administration to date back to death

For the purposes of the provisions of this Act relating to actions for the recovery of land . . . an administrator of the estate of a deceased person shall be treated as claiming as if there had been no interval of time between the death of the deceased person and the grant of the letters of administration.

27. Cure of defective disentailing assurance

(1) This section applies where—

  (a) a person entitled in remainder to an entailed interest in any land makes an assurance of his interest which fails to bar the issue in tail or the estates and interests taking effect on the determination of the entailed interest, or fails to bar those estates and interests only; and

  (b) any person takes possession of the land by virtue of the assurance.

(2) If the person taking possession of the land by virtue of the assurance, or any other person whatsoever (other than a person entitled to possession by virtue of the settlement) is in possession of the land for a period of twelve years from the commencement of the time when the assurance could have operated as an effective bar, the assurance shall thereupon operate, and be treated as having always operated, to bar the issue in tail and the estates and interests taking effect on the determination of the entailed interest.

(3) The reference in subsection (2) above to the time when the assurance could have operated as an effective bar is a reference to the time at which the assurance, as it had then been executed by the person entitled to the entailed interest, would have operated, without the consent of any other person, to bar the issue in tail and the estates and interests taking effect on the determination of the entailed interest.

27A Actions for recovery of property obtained through unlawful conduct

(1) None of the time limits given in the preceding provisions of this Act applies to any proceedings under Chapter 2 of Part 5 of the Proceeds of Crime Act 2002 (civil recovery of proceeds of unlawful conduct).

(2) Proceedings under that Chapter for a recovery order in respect of any recoverable property shall not be brought after the expiration of the period of twelve years from the date on which the Director's cause of action accrued.

(3) Proceedings under that Chapter are brought when—

  (a) a claim form is issued, or

  (b) an application is made for an interim receiving order,

  whichever is the earlier.

(4) The Director's cause of action accrues in respect of any recoverable property—

  (a) in the case of proceedings for a recovery order in respect of property obtained through unlawful conduct, when the property is so obtained,

  (b) in the case of proceedings for a recovery order in respect of any other recoverable property, when the property obtained through unlawful conduct which it represents is so obtained.

(5) If—

  (a) a person would (but for the preceding provisions of this Act) have a cause of action in respect of the conversion of a chattel, and

  (b) proceedings are started under that Chapter for a recovery order in respect of the chattel, section 3(2) of this Act does not prevent his asserting on an application under section 281 of that Act that the property belongs to him, or the court making a declaration in his favour under that section.

(6) If the court makes such a declaration, his title to the chattel is to be treated as not having been extinguished by section 3(2) of this Act.

(7) Expressions used in this section and Part 5 of that Act have the same meaning in this section as in that Part.

PART II

EXTENSION OR EXCLUSION OF ORDINARY TIME LIMITS

Disability

28. Extension of limitation period in case of disability

(1) Subject to the following provisions of this section, if on the date when any right of action accrued for which a period of limitation is prescribed by this Act, the person to whom it

accrued was under a disability, the action may be brought at any time before the expiration of six years from the date when he ceased to be under a disability or died (whichever first occurred) notwithstanding that the period of limitation has expired.

(2)   This section shall not affect any case where the right of action first accrued to some person (not under a disability) through whom the person under a disability claims.

(3)   When a right of action which has accrued to a person under a disability accrues, on the death of that person while still under a disability, to another person under a disability, no further extension of time shall be allowed by reason of the disability of the second person.

(4)   No action to recover land or money charged on land shall be brought by virtue of this section by any person after the expiration of thirty years from the date on which the right of action accrued to that person or some person through whom he claims.

Acknowledgment and part payment

29.   Fresh accrual of action on acknowledgment or part payment

(1)   Subsections (2) and (3) below apply where any right of action (including a foreclosure action) to recover land . . . or any right of a mortgagee of personal property to bring a foreclosure action in respect of the property has accrued.

(2)   If the person in possession of the land, benefice or personal property in question acknowledges the title of the person to whom the right of action has accrued—

(a)   the right shall be treated as having accrued on and not before the date of the acknowledgment; and

(b)   in the case of a right of action to recover land which has accrued to a person entitled to an estate or interest taking effect on the determination of an entailed interest against whom time is running under section 27 of this Act, section 27 shall thereupon cease to apply to the land.

(3)   In the case of a foreclosure or other action by a mortgagee, if the person in possession of the land, benefice or personal property in question or the person liable for the mortgage debt makes any payment in respect of the debt (whether of principal or interest) the right shall be treated as having accrued on and not before the date of the payment.

(4)   Where a mortgagee is by virtue of the mortgage in possession of any mortgaged land and either—

(a)   receives any sum in respect of the principal or interest of the mortgage debt; or

(b)   acknowledges the title of the mortgagor, or his equity of redemption;

an action to redeem the land in his possession may be brought at any time before the expiration of twelve years from the date of the payment or acknowledgment.

(5)   Subject to subsection (6) below, where any right of action has accrued to recover—

(a)   any debt or other liquidated pecuniary claim; or

(b)   any claim to the personal estate of a deceased person or to any share or interest in any such estate;

and the person liable or accountable for the claim acknowledges the claim or makes any payment in respect of it the right shall be treated as having accrued on and not before the date of the acknowledgment or payment.

(6)   A payment of a part of the rent or interest due at any time shall not extend the period for claiming the remainder then due, but any payment of interest shall be treated as a payment in respect of the principal debt.

(7)   Subject to subsection (6) above, a current period of limitation may be repeatedly extended under this section by further acknowledgments or payments, but a right of action, once barred by this Act, shall not be revived by any subsequent acknowledgment or payment.

30.   Formal provisions as to acknowledgments and part payments

(1)   To be effective for the purposes of section 29 of this Act, an acknowledgment must be in writing and signed by the person making it.

(2)   For the purposes of section 29, any acknowledgment or payment—

(a)   may be sent by the agent of the person by whom it is required to be made under that section; and

     (b)   shall be made to the person, or to an agent of the person, whose title or claim is being acknowledged or, as the case may be, in respect of whose claim the payment is being made.

31.   Effect of acknowledgment or part payment on persons other than the maker or recipient

(1)   An acknowledgment of the title to any land, benefice, or mortgaged personalty by any person in possession of it shall bind all other persons in possession during the ensuing period of limitation.

(2)   A payment in respect of a mortgage debt by the mortgagor or any other person liable for the debt, or by any person in possession of the mortgaged property, shall, so far as any right of the mortgagee to foreclose or otherwise to recover the property is concerned, bind all other persons in possession of the mortgaged property during the ensuing period of limitation.

(3)   Where two or more mortgagees are by virtue of the mortgage in possession of the mortgaged land, an acknowledgment of the mortgagor's title or of his equity of redemption by one of the mortgagees shall only bind him and his successors and shall not bind any other mortgagee or his successors.

(4)   Where in a case within subsection (3) above the mortgagee by whom the acknowledgment is given is entitled to a part of the mortgaged land and not to any ascertained part of the mortgage debt the mortgagor shall be entitled to redeem that part of the land on payment, with interest, of the part of the mortgage debt which bears the same proportion to the whole of the debt as the value of the part of the land bears to the whole of the mortgaged land.

(5)   Where there are two or more mortgagors, and the title or equity of redemption of one of the mortgagors is acknowledged as mentioned above in this section, the acknowledgment shall be treated as having been made to all the mortgagors.

(6)   An acknowledgment of any debt or other liquidated pecuniary claim shall bind the acknowledgor and his successors but not any other person.

(7)   A payment made in respect of any debt or other liquidated pecuniary claim shall bind all persons liable in respect of the debt or claim.

(8)   An acknowledgment by one of several personal representatives of any claim to the personal estate of the deceased person or to any share or interest in any such estate, or a payment by one of several personal representatives in respect of any such claim, shall bind the estate of the deceased person.

(9)   In this section 'successor', in relation to any mortgagee or person liable in respect of any debt or claim, means his personal representatives and any other person on whom the rights under the mortgage or, as the case may be, the liability in respect of the debt or claim devolve (whether on death or bankruptcy or the disposition of property or the determination of a limited estate or interest in settled property or otherwise).

Fraud, concealment and mistake

32.   Postponement of limitation period in casc of fraud, concealment or mistake

(1)   Subject to subsection (3) . . . below, where in the case of any action for which a period of limitation is prescribed by this Act, either—

     (a)   the action is based upon the fraud of the defendant; or

     (b)   any fact relevant to the plaintiff s right of action has been deliberately concealed from him by the defendant; or

     (c)   the action is for relief from the consequences of a mistake;

the period of limitation shall not begin to run until the plaintiff has discovered the fraud, concealment or mistake (as the case may be) or could with reasonable diligence have discovered it.

     References in this subsection to the defendant include references to the defendant's agent and to any person through whom the defendant claims and his agent.

(2)   For the purposes of subsection (1) above, deliberate commission of a breach of duty in circumstances in which it is unlikely to be discovered for some time amounts to deliberate concealment of the facts involved in that breach of duty.

(3)   Nothing in this section shall enable any action—
    (a)   to recover, or recover the value of, any property; or
    (b)   to enforce any charge against, or set aside any transaction affecting, any property;
    to be brought against the purchaser of the property or any person claiming through him in any case where the property has been purchased for valuable consideration by an innocent third party since the fraud or concealment or (as the case may be) the transaction in which the mistake was made took place.

(4)   A purchaser is an innocent third party for the purposes of this section—
    (a)   in the case of fraud or concealment of any fact relevant to the plaintiff's right of action, if he was not a party to the fraud or (as the case may be) to the concealment of that fact and did not at the time of the purchase know or have reason to believe that the fraud or concealment had taken place; and
    (b)   in the case of mistake, if he did not at that time of the purchase know or have reason to believe that the mistake had been made.

38.   Interpretation

(1)   In this Act, unless the context otherwise requires—
'action' includes any proceeding in a court of law, including an ecclesiastical court;
'land' includes corporeal hereditaments, tithes and rentcharges and any legal or equitable estate or interest therein . . . , but except as provided above in this definition does not include any incorporeal hereditament;
'personal estate' and 'personal property' do not include chattels real; 'rent' includes a rentcharge and a rentservice;
'rentcharge' means any annuity or periodical sum of money charged upon or payable out of land, except a rent service or interest on a mortgage on land;
'settled land', 'statutory owner' and 'tenant for life' have the same meanings respectively as in the Settled Land Act 1925;
'trust' and 'trustee' have the same meanings respectively as in the Trustee Act 1925; and
. . .

(2)   For the purposes of this Act a person shall be treated as under a disability while he is an infant, or of unsound mind.

(3)   For the purposes of subsection (2) above a person is of unsound mind if he is a person who, by reason of mental disorder is incapable of managing and administering his property and affairs; and in this section 'mental disorder' has the same meaning as in the Mental Health Act 1983.

(4)   Without prejudice to the generality of subsection (3) above, a person shall be conclusively presumed for the purposes of subsection (2) above to be of unsound mind—
    (a)   while he is liable to be detained or subject to guardianship under the Mental Health Act 1983 (otherwise than by virtue of section 35 or 89) or
    (b)   while he is receiving treatment for mental disorder as an in-patient in any hospital within the meaning of the Mental Health Act 1983 or independent hospital or care home within the meaning of the Care Standards Act 2000 without being liable to be detained under the said Act of 1983 (otherwise than by virtue of section 35 or 89), being treatment which follows without any interval a period during which he was liable to be detained or subject to guardianship under the Mental Health Act 1959, or the said Act of 1983 (otherwise than by virtue of section 35 or 89) or by virtue of any enactment repealed or excluded by the Mental Health Act 1959.

(5)   Subject to subsection (6) below, a person shall be treated as claiming through another person if he became entitled by, through, under, or by the act of that other person to the right claimed, and any person whose estate or interest might have been barred by a person entitled to an entailed interest in possession shall be treated as claiming through the person so entitled.

(6)   A person becoming entitled to any estate or interest by virtue of a special power of appointment shall not be treated as claiming through the appointor.

(7)   References in this Act to a right of action to recover land shall include references to a right to enter into possession of the land or, in the case of rentcharges and tithes, to distrain for arrears of rent or tithe, and references to the bringing of such an action shall include references to the making of such an entry or distress.

(8)   References in this Act to the possession of land shall, in the case of tithes and rentcharges, be construed as references to the receipt of the tithe or rent, and references to the date of dispossession or discontinuance of possession of land shall, in the case of rentcharges, be construed as references to the date of the last receipt of rent.

(9)   References in Part II of this Act to a right of action shall include references to—

(a)   a cause of action;

(b)   a right to receive money secured by a mortgage or charge on any property,

(c)   a right to recover proceeds of the sale of land; and

(d)   a right to receive a share of interest in the personal estate of a deceased person.

SCHEDULES

Section 15(6), (7)

SCHEDULE I
PROVISIONS WITH RESPECT TO ACTIONS TO RECOVER LAND

PART I
ACCRUAL OF RIGHTS OF ACTION TO RECOVER LAND

Accrual of right of action in case of present interests in land

1.   Where the person bringing an action to recover land, or some person through whom he claims, has been in possession of the land, and has while entitled to the land been dispossessed or discontinued his possession, the right of action shall be treated as having accrued on the date of the dispossession or discontinuance.

2.   Where any person brings an action to recover any land of a deceased person (whether under a will or on intestacy) and the deceased person—

(a)   was on the date of his death in possession of the land or, in the case of a rent charge created by will or taking effect upon his death, in possession of the land charged; and

(b)   was the last person entitled to the land to be in possession of it;

the right of action shall be treated as having accrued on the date of his death.

3.   Where any person brings an action to recover land, being an estate or interest in possession assured otherwise than by will to him, or to some person through whom he claims, and—

(a)   the person making the assurance was on the date when the assurance took effect in possession of the land or, in the case of a rentcharge created by the assurance, in possession of the land charged; and

(b)   no person has been in possession of the land by virtue of the assurance; the right of action shall be treated as having accrued on the date when the assurance took effect.

Accrual of right of action in case of future interests

4.   The right of action to recover any land shall, in a case where—

(a)   the estate or interest claimed was an estate or interest in reversion or remainder or any other future estate or interest, and

(b)   no person has taken possession of the land by virtue of the estate or interest claimed;

be treated as having accrued on the date on which the estate or interest fell into possession by the determination of the preceding estate or interest.

5.   (1)   Subject to sub-paragraph (2) below, a tenancy from year to year or other period, without a lease in writing, shall for the purposes of this Act be treated as being determined at the expiration of the first year or other period; and accordingly the right of action of the person entitled to the land subject to the tenancy shall be treated as having accrued at the date on which in accordance with this sub-paragraph the tenancy is determined.

(2)   Where any rent has subsequently been received in respect of the tenancy, the right of action shall be treated as having accrued on the date of the last receipt of rent.

6.   (1)   Where—

(a)   any person is in possession of land by virtue of a lease in writing by which a rent of not less than ten pounds a year is reserved; and

(b)   the rent is received by some person wrongfully claiming to be entitled to the land in reversion immediately expectant on the determination of the lease; and

(c)   no rent is subsequently received by the person rightfully so entitled; the right of action to recover the land of the person rightfully so entitled shall be treated as having accrued on the date when the rent was first received by the person wrongfully claiming to be so entitled and not on the date of the determination of the lease.

(2)   Sub-paragraph (1) above shall not apply to any lease granted by the Crown.

Accrual of right of action in case of forfeiture or breach of condition

7.   (1)   Subject to sub-paragraph (2) below, a right of action to recover land by virtue of a forfeiture or breach of condition shall be treated as having accrued on the date on which the forfeiture was incurred or the condition broken.

(2)   If any such right has accrued to a person entitled to an estate or interest in reversion or remainder and the land was not recovered by virtue of that right, the right of action to recover the land shall not be treated as having accrued to that person until his estate or interest fell into possession, as if no such forfeiture or breach of condition had occurred.

Right of action not to accrue or continue unless there is adverse possession

8.   (1)   No right of action to recover land shall be treated as accruing unless the land is in the possession of some person in whose favour the period of limitation can run (referred to below in this paragraph as 'adverse possession'); and where under the preceding provisions of this Schedule any such right of action is treated as accruing on a certain date and no person is in adverse possession on that date, the right of action shall not be treated as accruing unless and until adverse possession is taken of the land.

(2)   Where a right of action to recover land has accrued and after its accrual, before the right is barred, the land ceases to be in adverse possession, the right of action shall no longer be treated as having accrued and no fresh right of action shall be treated as accruing unless and until the land is again taken into adverse possession.

(3)   For the purposes of this paragraph—

(a)   possession of any land subject to a rentcharge by a person (other than the person entitled to the rentcharge) who does not pay the rent shall be treated as adverse possession of the rentcharge; and

(b)   receipt of rent under a lease by a person wrongfully claiming to be entitled to the land in reversion immediately expectant on the determination of the lease shall be treated as adverse possession of the land.

(4)   For the purpose of determining whether a person occupying any land is in adverse possession of the land it shall not be assumed by implication of law that his occupation is by permission of the person entitled to the land merely by virtue of the fact that his occupation is not inconsistent with the latter's present or future enjoyment of the land.

This provision shall not be taken as prejudicing a finding to the effect that a person's occupation of any land is by implied permission of the person entitled to the land in any case where such a finding is justified on the actual facts of the case.

Possession of beneficiary not adverse to others interested in settled land or land subject to a trust of land

9.   Where any settled land or any land subject to a trust of land is in the possession of a person entitled to a beneficial interest in the land . . . (not being a person solely or absolutely entitled to the land or the proceeds), no right of action to recover the land shall be treated for the purposes of this Act as accruing during that possession to any person in whom the land is vested as tenant for life, statutory owner or trustee, or to any other person entitled to a beneficial interest in the land

. . . .

FORFEITURE ACT 1982
(1982, c. 34)

1.   The 'forfeiture rule'

(1)   In this Act, the 'forfeiture rule' means the rule of public policy which in certain circumstances precludes a person who has unlawfully killed another from acquiring a benefit in consequence of the killing.

(2)   References in this Act to a person who has unlawfully killed another include a reference to a person who has unlawfully aided, abetted, counselled or procured the death of that other and references in this Act to unlawful killing shall be interpreted accordingly.

2.   Power to modify the rule

(1)   Where a court determines that the forfeiture rule has precluded a person (in this section referred to as 'the offender') who has unlawfully killed another from acquiring any interest in property mentioned in subsection (4) below, the court may make an order under this section modifying the effect of that rule.

(2)   The court shall not make an order under this section modifying the effect of the forfeiture rule in any case unless it is satisfied that, having regard to the conduct of the offender and of the deceased and to such other circumstances as appear to the court to be material, the justice of the case requires the effect of the rule to be so modified in that case.

(3)   In any case where a person stands convicted of an offence of which unlawful killing is an element, the court shall not make an order under this section modifying the effect of the forfeiture rule in that case unless proceedings for the purpose are brought before the expiry of the period of three months beginning with his conviction.

(4)   The interests in property referred to in subsection (1) above are—

(a)   any beneficial interest in property which (apart from the forfeiture rule) the offender would have acquired—

(i)   under the deceased's will . . . or the law relating to intestacy or by way of ius relicti, ius relictae or legitim;

(ii)   on the nomination of the deceased in accordance with the provisions of any enactment,

(iii) as a donatio mortis causa made by the deceased;

(iv) under a special destination (whether relating to heritable or moveable property); or

(b)   any beneficial interest in property which (apart from the forfeiture rule) the offender would have acquired in consequence of the death of the deceased, being property which, before the death, was held on trust for any person.

(5)   An order under this section may modify the effect of the forfeiture rule in respect of any interest in property to which the determination referred to in subsection (1) above relates and may do so in either or both of the following ways, that is—

(a)   where there is more than one such interest, by excluding the application of the rule in respect of any (but not all) of those interests; and

(b)   in the case of any such interest in property, by excluding the application of the rule in respect of part of the property.

(6)   On the making of an order under this section, the forfeiture rule shall have effect for all purposes (including purposes relating to anything done before the order is made) subject to the modifications made by the order.

(7)   The court shall not make an order under this section modifying the effect of the forfeiture rule in respect of any interest in property which, in consequence of the rule, has been acquired before the coming into force of this section by a person other than the offender or a person claiming through him.

(8)   In this section—

'property' includes any chose in action or incorporeal moveable property; and

'will' includes codicil.

3. **Application for financial provision not affected by the rule**

(1)   The forfeiture rule shall not be taken to preclude any person from making any application under a provision mentioned in subsection (2) below or the making of any order on the application.

(2)   The provisions referred to in subsection (1) above are—

(a)   any provision of the Inheritance (Provision for Family and Dependants) Act 1975;

(b)   sections 31(6) and 36(1) of the Matrimonial Causes Act 1973 (variation by court in England and Wales of periodical payments orders and maintenance agreements in respect of marriages);

(c)   paragraphs 60(2) and 73(2) of Schedule 5 to the Civil Partnership Act 2004 (variation by court in England and Wales of periodical payments orders and maintenance agreements in respect of civil partnerships); and

(d)   section 13(4) of the Family Law (Scotland) Act 1985 (variation etc. of periodical allowances in respect of marriages and civil partnerships).

5. **Exclusion of murderers**

Nothing in this Act or in any order made under section 2 or referred to in section 3(1) of this Act . . . shall affect the application of the forfeiture rule in the case of a person who stands convicted of murder.

INSOLVENCY ACT 1986
(1986, c. 45)

CHAPTER V
EFFECT OF BANKRUPTCY ON CERTAIN RIGHTS, TRANSACTIONS, ETC.

Rights under trusts of land

335A. **Rights under trusts of land**

(1)   Any application by a trustee of a bankrupt's estate under section 14 of the Trusts of Land and Appointment of Trustees Act 1996 (powers of court in relation to trusts of land) for an order under that section for the sale of land shall be made to the court having jurisdiction in relation to the bankruptcy.

(2)   On such an application the court shall make such order as it thinks just and reasonable having regard to—

(a)   the interests of the bankrupt's creditors;

(b)   where the application is made in respect of land which includes a dwelling house which is or has been the home of the bankrupt or the bankrupt's spouse or civil partner or former spouse or former civil partner—

(i)   the conduct of the spouse, civil partner, former spouse or former civil partner, so far as contributing to the bankruptcy,

(ii)   the needs and financial resources of the spouse or former spouse, and

(iii)   the needs of any children; and

(c)   all the circumstances of the case other than the needs of the bankrupt.

(3)   Where such an application is made after the end of the period of one year beginning with the first vesting under Chapter IV of this Part of the bankrupt's estate in a trustee, the court shall assume, unless the circumstances of the case are exceptional, that the interests of the bankrupt's creditors outweigh all other considerations.

(4)   The powers conferred on the court by this section are exercisable on an application whether it is made before or after the commencement of this section.

Rights of occupation

336. **Rights of occupation etc. of bankrupt's spouse**

(1)   Nothing occurring in the initial period of the bankruptcy (that is to say, the period beginning with the day of the presentation of the petition for the bankruptcy order and ending with the

vesting of the bankrupt's estate in a trustee) is to be taken as having given rise to any home rights under Part IV of the Family Law Act 1996 in relation to a dwelling house comprised in the bankrupt's estate.

(2)   Where a spouse's or civil partner's home rights under the Act of 1996 are a charge on the estate or interest of the other spouse or civil partner, or of trustees for the other spouse or civil partner, and the other spouse or civil partner is adjudged bankrupt—

    (a)   the charge continues to subsist notwithstanding the bankruptcy and, subject to the provisions of that Act, binds the trustee of the bankrupt's estate and persons deriving title under that trustee, and

    (b)   any application for an order under section 33 of that Act shall be made to the court having jurisdiction in relation to the bankruptcy.

(3)   . . .

(4)   On such an application as is mentioned in subsection (2) . . . the court shall make such order under section 33 of the Act of 1996 . . . as it thinks just and reasonable having regard to—

    (a)   the interests of the bankrupt's creditors,

    (b)   the conduct of the spouse or former spouse, so far as contributing to the bankruptcy,

    (c)   the needs and financial resources of the spouse or former spouse,

    (d)   the needs of any children, and

    (e)   all the circumstances of the case other than the needs of the bankrupt.

(5)   Where such an application is made after the end of the period of one year beginning with the first vesting under Chapter IV of this Part of the bankrupt's estate in a trustee, the court shall assume, unless the circumstances of the case are exceptional, that the interests of the bankrupt's creditors outweigh all other considerations.

337.   Rights of occupation of bankrupt

(1)   This section applies where—

    (a)   a person who is entitled to occupy a dwelling house by virtue of a beneficial estate or interest is adjudged bankrupt, and

    (b)   any persons under the age of 18 with whom that person had at some time occupied that dwelling house had their home with that person at the time when the bankruptcy petition was presented and at the commencement of the bankruptcy.

(2)   Whether or not the bankrupt's spouse or civil partner (if any) has home rights under Part IV of the Family Law Act 1996—

    (a)   the bankrupt has the following rights as against the trustee of his estate—

        (i)   if in occupation, a right not to be evicted or excluded from the dwelling house or any part of it, except with the leave of the court,

        (ii)   if not in occupation, a right with the leave of the court to enter into and occupy the dwelling house, and

    (b)   the bankrupt's rights are a charge, having the like priority as an equitable interest created immediately before the commencement of the bankruptcy, on so much of his estate or interest in the dwelling house as vests in the trustee.

(3)   The Act of 1996 has effect, with the necessary modifications, as if—

    (a)   the rights conferred by paragraph (a) of subsection (2) were home rights under that Act,

    (b)   any application for such leave as is mentioned in that paragraph were an application for an order under section 33 of that Act, and

    (c)   any charge under paragraph (b) of that subsection on the estate or interest of the trustee were a charge under that Act on the estate or interest of a spouse or civil partner.

(4)   Any application for leave such as is mentioned in subsection (2)(a) or otherwise by virtue of this section for an order under section 33 of the Act of 1996 shall be made to the court having jurisdiction in relation to the bankruptcy.

(5)   On such an application the court shall make such order under section 33 of the Act of 1996 as it thinks just and reasonable having regard to the interests of the creditors, to the bankrupt's financial resources, to the needs of the children and to all the circumstances of the case other than the needs of the bankrupt.

(6)   Where such an application is made after the end of the period of one year beginning with the first vesting . . . of the bankrupt's estate in a trustee, the court shall asume, unless the circumstances of the case are exceptional, that the interests of the bankrupt's creditors outweight all other considerations.

338.   Payments in respect of premises occupied by bankrupt

Where any premises comprised in a bankrupt's estate are occupied by him (whether by virtue of the preceding section or otherwise) on condition that he makes payments towards satisfying any liability arising under a mortgage of the premises or otherwise towards the outgoings of the premises, the bankrupt does not, by virtue of those payments, acquire any interest in the premises.

Adjustment of prior transactions, etc.

339.   Transactions at an undervalue

(1)   Subject as follows in this section and sections 341 and 342, where an individual is adjudged bankrupt and he has at a relevant time (defined in section 341) entered into a transaction with any person at an undervalue, the trustee of the bankrupt's estate may apply to the court for an order under this section.

(2)   The court shall, on such an application, make such order as it thinks fit for restoring the position to what it would have been if that individual had not entered into that transaction.

(3)   For the purposes of this section and sections 341 and 342, an individual enters into a transaction with a person at an undervalue if—

(a)   he makes a gift to that person or he otherwise enters into a transaction with that person on terms that provide for him to receive no consideration,

(b)   he enters into a transaction with that person in consideration of marriage or the formation of a civil partnership, or

(c)   he enters into a transaction with that person for a consideration the value of which, in money or money's worth, is significantly less than the value, in money or money's worth, of the consideration provided by the individual.

340.   Preferences

(1)   Subject as follows in this and the next two sections, where an individual is adjudged bankrupt and he has at a relevant time (defined in section 341) given a preference to any person, the trustee of the bankrupt's estate may apply to the court for an order under this section.

(2)   The court shall, on such an application, make such order as it thinks fit for restoring the position to what it would have been if that individual had not given that preference.

(3)   For the purposes of this and the next two sections, an individual gives a preference to a person if—

(a)   that person is one of the individual's creditors or a surety or guarantor for any of his debts or other liabilities, and

(b)   the individual does anything or suffers anything to be done which (in either case) has the effect of putting that person into a position which, in the event of the individual's bankruptcy, will be better than the position he would have been in if that thing had not been done.

(4)   The court shall not make an order under this section in respect of a preference given to any person unless the individual who gave the preference was influenced in deciding to give it by a desire to produce in relation to that person the effect mentioned in subsection (3)(b) above.

(5)   An individual who has given a preference to a person who, at the time the preference was given, was an associate of his (otherwise than by reason only of being his employee) is presumed, unless the contrary is shown, to have been influenced in deciding to give it by such a desire as is mentioned in subsection (4).

(6)   The fact that something has been done in pursuance of the order of a court does not, without more, prevent the doing or suffering of that thing from constituting the giving of a preference.

341.   'Relevant time' under ss. 339, 340

(1)   Subject as follows, the time at which an individual enters into a transaction at an undervalue or gives a preference is a relevant time if the transaction is entered into or the preference given—

   (a)   in the case of a transaction at an undervalue, at a time in the period of 5 years ending with the day of the presentation of the bankruptcy petition on which the individual is adjudged bankrupt,

   (b)   in the case of a preference which is not a transaction at an undervalue and is given to a person who is an associate of the individual (otherwise than by reason only of being his employee), at a time in the period of 2 years ending with that day, and

   (c)   in any other case of a preference which is not a transaction at an undervalue, at a time in the period of 6 months ending with that day.

(2)   Where an individual enters into a transaction at an undervalue or gives a preference at a time mentioned in paragraph (a), (b) or (c) of subsection (1) (not being, in the case of a transaction at an undervalue, a time less than 2 years before the end of the period mentioned in paragraph (a)), that time is not a relevant time for the purposes of sections 339 and 340 unless the individual—

   (a)   is insolvent at that time, or

   (b)   becomes insolvent in consequence of the transaction or preference;

   but the requirements of this subsection are presumed to be satisfied, unless the contrary is shown, in relation to any transaction at an undervalue which is entered into by an individual with a person who is an associate of his (otherwise than by reason only of being his employee).

(3)   For the purposes of subsection (2), an individual is insolvent if—

   (a)   he is unable to pay his debts as they fall due, or

   (b)   the value of his assets is less than the amount of his liabilities, taking into account his contingent and prospective liabilities.

(4)–(5). . .

342.   Orders under ss. 339, 340

(1)   Without prejudice to the generality of section 339(2) or 340(2), an order under either of those sections with respect to a transaction or preference entered into or given by an individual who is subsequently adjudged bankrupt may (subject as follows)—

   (a)   require any property transferred as part of the transaction, or in connection with the giving of the preference, to be vested in the trustee of the bankrupt's estate as part of that estate;

   (b)   require any property to be so vested if it represents in any person's hands the application either of the proceeds of sale of property so transferred or of money so transferred;

   (c)   release or discharge (in whole or in part) any security given by the individual;

   (d)   require any person to pay, in respect of benefits received by him from the individual, such sums to the trustee of his estate as the court may direct,

   (e)   provide for any surety or guarantor whose obligations to any person were released or discharged (in whole or in part) under the transaction or by the giving of the preference to be under such new or revived obligations to that person as the court thinks appropriate;

   (f)   provide for security to be provided for the discharge of any obligation imposed by or arising under the order, for such an obligation to be charged on any property and for the security or charge to have the same priority as a security or charge released or discharged (in whole or in part) under the transaction or by the giving of the preference; and

   (g)   provide for the extent to which any person whose property is vested by the order in the trustee of the bankrupt's estate, or on whom obligations are imposed by the order, is to be able to prove in the bankruptcy for debts or other liabilities which arose from, or were released or discharged (in whole or in part) under or by, the transaction or the giving of the preference.

(2)   An order under section 339 or 340 may affect the property of, or impose any obligation on, any person whether or not he is the person with whom the individual in question entered into the transaction or, as the case may be, the person to whom the preference was given; but such an order—

(a)   shall not prejudice any interest in property which was acquired from a person other than that individual and was acquired in good faith and for value, or prejudice any interest deriving from such an interest, and

(b)   shall not require a person who received a benefit from the transaction or preference in good faith and for value to pay a sum to the trustee of the bankrupt's estate, except where he was a party to the transaction or the payment is to be in respect of a preference given to that person at a time when he was a creditor of that individual.

(2A)   Where a person has acquired an interest in property from a person other than the individual in question, or has received a benefit from the transaction or preference, and at the time of that acquisition a receipt—

(a)   he had notice of the relevant surrounding circumstances and of the relevant proceedings, or

(b)   he was an associate of, or was connected with, either the individual in question or the person with whom that individual gave the preference,

then, unless the contrary is shown, it shall be presumed for the purposes of paragraph (a) or (as the case may be) paragraph (b) of subsection (2) that the interest was acquired or the benefit was received otherwise than in good faith.

(3)   Any sums required to be paid to the trustee in accordance with an order under section 339 or 340 shall be comprised in the bankrupt's estate.

(4)   For the purposes of subsection (2A)(a), the relevant surrounding circumstances are (as the case may require)—

(a)   the fact that the individual in question entered into the transaction at an undervalue; or

(b)   the circumstances which amounted to the giving of the preference by the individual in question.

(5)   For the purposes of subsection (2A)(a), a person has notice of the relevant proceedings if he has notice—

(a)   of the fact that the petition on which the individual in question is adjudged bankrupt has been presented; or

(b)   of the fact that the individual in question has been adjudged bankrupt.

. . .

PART XVI
PROVISIONS AGAINST DEBT AVOIDANCE (ENGLAND AND WALES ONLY)

423.   Transactions defrauding creditors

(1)   This section relates to transactions entered into at an undervalue, and a person enters into such a transaction with another person if—

(a)   he makes a gift to the other person or he otherwise enters into a transaction with the other on terms that provide for him to receive no consideration;

(b)   he enters into a transaction with the other in consideration of marriage or the formation of a civil partnership; or

(c)   he enters into a transaction with the other for a consideration the value of which, in money or money's worth, is significantly less than the value, in money or money's worth, of the consideration provided by himself.

(2)   Where a person has entered into such a transaction, the court may, if satisfied under the next subsection, make such order as it thinks fit for—

(a)   restoring the position to what it would have been if the transaction had not been entered into, and

(b)   protecting the interests of persons who are victims of the transaction.

(3)   In the case of a person entering into such a transaction, an order shall only be made if the court is satisfied that it was entered into by him for the purpose—

  (a)   of putting assets beyond the reach of a person who is making, or may at some time make, a claim against him, or

  (b)   of otherwise prejudicing the interests of such a person in relation to the claim which he is making or may make.

(4)   In this section 'the court' means the High Court or—

  (a)   if the person entering into the transaction is an individual, any other court which would have jurisdiction in relation to a bankruptcy petition relating to him;

  (b)   if that person is a body capable of being wound up . . . any other court having jurisdiction to wind it up.

(5)   In relation to a transaction at an undervalue, references here and below to a victim of the transaction are to a person who is, or is capable of being, prejudiced by it; and in the following two sections the person entering into the transaction is referred to as 'the debtor'.

424.   Those who may apply for an order under s. 423

(1)   An application for an order under section 423 shall not be made in relation to a transaction except—

  (a)   in a case where the debtor has been adjudged bankrupt or is a body corporate which is being wound up or in relation to which an administration order is in force, by the official receiver, by the trustee of the bankrupt's estate or the liquidator or administrator of the body corporate or (with the leave of the court) by a victim of the transaction;

  (b)   in a case where a victim of the transaction is bound by a voluntary arrangement approved under Part I or Part VIII of this Act, by the supervisor of the voluntary arrangement or by any person who (whether or not so bound) is such a victim; or

  (c)   in any other case, by a victim of the transaction.

(2)   An application made under any of the paragraphs of subsection (1) is to be treated as made on behalf of every victim of the transaction.

425.   Provision which may be made by order under s. 423

(1)   Without prejudice to the generality of section 423, an order made under that section with respect to a transaction may (subject as follows)—

  (a)   require any property transferred as part of the transaction to be vested in any person, either absolutely or for the benefit of all the persons on whose behalf the application for the order is treated as made;

  (b)   require any property to be so vested if it represents, in any person's hands, the application either of the proceeds of sale of property so transferred or of money so tranferred;

  (c)   release or discharge (in whole or in part) any security given by the debtor;

  (d)   require any person to pay to any other person in respect of benefits received from the debtor such sums as the court may direct;

  (e)   provide for any surety or guarantor whose obligations to any person were released or discharged (in whole or in part) under the transaction to be under such new or revived obligations as the court thinks appropriate;

  (f)   provide for security to be provided for the discharge of any obligation imposed by or arising under the order, for such an obligation to be charged on any property and for such security or charge to have the same priority as a security or charge released or discharged (in whole are in part) under the transaction.

(2)   An order under section 423 may affect the property of, or impose any obligation on, any person whether or not he is the person with whom the debtor entered into the transaction; but such an order—

  (a)   shall not prejudice any interest in property which was acquired from a person other than the debtor and was acquired in good faith, for value and without notice of the relevant circumstances, or prejudice any interest deriving from such an interest, and

(b) shall not require a person who received a benefit from the transaction in good faith, for value and without notice of the relevant circumstances to pay any sum unless he was a party to the transaction.

(3) For the purposes of this section the relevant circumstances in relation to a transaction are the circumstances by virtue of which an order under section 423 may be made in respect of the transaction.

(4) In this section 'security' means any mortgage, charge, lien or other security.

LAW OF PROPERTY (MISCELLANEOUS PROVISIONS) ACT 1989
(1989, c. 34)

1. Deeds and their execution

(1) Any rule of law which—
  (a) restricts the substances on which a deed may be written;
  (b) requires a seal for the valid execution of an instrument as a deed by an individual; or
  (c) requires authority by one person to another to deliver an instrument as a deed on his behalf to be given by deed,
  is abolished.

(2) An instrument shall not be a deed unless—
  (a) it makes it clear on its face that it is intended to be a deed by the person making it or, as the case may be, by the parties to it (whether describing itself as a deed or expressing itself to be executed or signed as a deed or otherwise); and
  (b) it is validly executed as a deed—
    (i)   by that person or a person authorised to execute it in the name or on behalf of that person, or
    (ii) by one or more of those parties or a person authorised to execute it in the name or on behalf of one or more of those parties.

(2A) For the purposes of subsection (2)(a) above, an instrument shall not be taken to make it clear on its face that it is intended to be a deed merely because it is executed under seal.

(3) An instrument is validly executed as a deed by an individual if, and only if—
  (a) it is signed—
    (i)   by him in the presence of a witness who attests the signature; or
    (ii) at his direction and in his presence and the presence of two witnesses who each attest the signature; and
  (b) it is delivered as a deed . . ..

(4) In subsection (2) and (3) above 'sign', in relation to an instrument, includes—
  (a) an individual signing the name of the person or party on whose behalf he executes the instrument; and
  (b) making one's mark on the instrument,
  and 'signature' is to be construed accordingly.

(4A) Subsection (3) above applies in the case of an instrument executed by an individual in the name or on behalf of another person whether or not that person is also an individual.

(5) Where a solicitor, duly certified notary public or licensed conveyancer, or an agent or employee of a solicitor, duly certified notary public or licensed conveyancer, in the course of or in connection with a transaction . . ., purports to deliver an instrument as a deed on behalf of a party to the instrument, it shall be conclusively presumed in favour of a purchaser that he is authorised so to deliver the instrument.

(6) In subsection (5) above—
  . . . 'purchaser' has the same meaning as in the Law of Property Act 1925;
  'duly certified notary public' has the same meaning as it has in the Solicitors Act 1974 by virtue of section 87 of that Act; . . .

(7) Where an instrument under seal that constitutes a deed is required for the purposes of an Act passed before this section comes into force, this section shall have effect as to signing,

sealing or delivery of an instrument by an individual in place of any provision of that Act as to signing, sealing or delivery.

. . .

(10) The references in this section to the execution of a deed by an individual do not include execution by a corporation sole and the reference in subsection (7) above to signing, sealing or delivery by an individual does not include signing, sealing or delivery by such a corporation.

(11) Nothing in this section applies in relation to instruments delivered as deeds before this section comes into force.

2. Contracts for sale etc. of land to be made by signed writing

(1) A contract for the sale or other disposition of an interest in land can only be made in writing and only by incorporating all the terms which the parties have expressly agreed in one document or, where contracts are exchanged, in each.

(2) The terms may be incorporated in a document either by being set out in it or by reference to some other document.

(3) The document incorporating the terms or, where contracts are exchanged, one of the documents incorporating them (but not necessarily the same one) must be signed by or on behalf of each party to the contract.

(4) Where a contract for the sale or other disposition of an interest in land satisfies the conditions of this section by reason only of the rectification of one or more documents in pursuance of an order of a court, the contract shall come into being, or be deemed to have come into being, at such time as may be specified in the order.

(5) This section does not apply in relation to—
    (a) a contract to grant such a lease as is mentioned in section 54(2) of the Law of Property Act 1926 (short leases);
    (b) a contract made in the course of a public auction; or
    (c) a contract regulated under the Financial Services and Markets Act 2000, other than a regulated mortgage contract;
and nothing in this section affects the creation or operation of resulting, implied or constructive trusts.

(6) In this section—
'disposition' has the same meaning as in the Law of Property Act 1925;
'interest in land' means any estate, interest or charge in or over land . . .;
'regulated mortgage contract' must be read with—
    (a) section 22 of the Financial Services and Markets Act 2000,
    (b) any relevant order under that section, and
    (c) Schedule 2 of that Act.

(7) Nothing in this section shall apply in relation to contracts made before this section comes into force.

(8) Section 40 of the Law of Property Act 1925 (which is superseded by this section) shall cease to have effect.

3. Abolition of rule in *Bain v Fothergill*

The rule of law known as the rule in *Bain v Fothergill* is abolished in relation to contracts made after this section comes into force.

5. Commencement

(1) The provisions of this Act to which this subsection applies shall come into force on such day as the Lord Chancellor may by order made by statutory instrument appoint.

(2) The provisions to which subsection (1) above applies are—
    (a) section 1 above; and
    (b) section 4 above, except so far as it relates to section 40 of the Law of Property Act 1925.

(3) The provisions of this Act to which this subsection applies shall come into force at the end of the period of two months beginning with the day on which this Act is passed.

(4)   The provisions of this Act to which subsection (3) above applies are—

(a)   sections 2 and 3 above; and

(b)   section 4 above, so far as it relates to section 40 of the Law of Property Act 1925.

ACCESS TO NEIGHBOURING LAND ACT 1992
(1992, c. 23)

1.   Access orders

(1)   A person—

(a)   who, for the purpose of carrying out works to any land (the 'dominant land'), desires to enter upon any adjoining or adjacent land (the 'servient land'), and

(b)   who needs, but does not have, the consent of some other person to that entry,

may make an application to the court for an order under this section ('an access order') against that other person.

(2)   On application under this section, the court shall make an access order if, and only if, it is satisfied—

(a)   that the works are reasonably necessary for the preservation of the whole or any part of the dominant land; and

(b)   that they cannot be carried out, or would be substantially more difficult to carry out, without entry upon the servient land;

but this subsection is subject to subsection (3) below.

(3)   The court shall not make an access order in any case where it is satisfied that, were it to make such an order—

(a)   the respondent or any other person would suffer interference with, or disturbance of, his use or enjoyment of the servient land, or

(b)   the respondent, or any other person (whether of full age or capacity or not) in occupation of the whole or any part of the servient land, would suffer hardship,

to such a degree by reason of the entry (notwithstanding any requirement of this Act or any term or condition that may be imposed under it) that it would be unreasonable to make the order.

(4)   Where the court is satisfied on an application under this section that it is reasonably necessary to carry out any basic preservation works to the dominant land, those works shall be taken for the purposes of this Act to be reasonably necessary for the preservation of the land; and in this subsection 'basic preservation works' means any of the following, that is to say—

(a)   the maintenance, repair or renewal of any part of a building or other structure comprised in, or situate on, the dominant land;

(b)   the clearance, repair or renewal of any drain, sewer, pipe or cable so comprised or situate;

(c)   the treatment, cutting back, felling, removal or replacement of any hedge, tree, shrub or other growing thing which is so comprised and which is, or is in danger of becoming, damaged, diseased, dangerous, insecurely rooted or dead;

(d)   the filling in, or clearance, of any ditch so comprised;

but this subsection is without prejudice to the generality of the works which may, apart from it, be regarded by the court as reasonably necessary for the preservation of any land.

(5)   If the court considers it fair and reasonable in all the circumstances of the case, works may be regarded for the purposes of this Act as being reasonably necessary for the preservation of any land (or, for the purposes of subsection (4) above, as being basic preservation works which it is reasonably necessary to carry out to any land) notwithstanding that the works incidentally involve—

(a)   the making of some alteration, adjustment or improvement to the land, or

(b)   the demolition of the whole or any part of a building or structure comprised in or situate upon the land.

(6)   Where any works are reasonably necessary for the preservation of the whole or any part of the dominant land, the doing to the dominant land of anything which is requisite for, incidental to, or consequential on, the carrying out of those works shall be treated for the purposes of this Act as the carrying out of works which are reasonably necessary for the preservation of that land; and references in this Act to works, or to the carrying out of works, shall be construed accordingly.

(7)   Without prejudice to the generality of subsection (6) above, if it is reasonably necessary for a person to inspect the dominant land—

(a)   for the purpose of ascertaining whether any works may be reasonably necessary for the preservation of the whole or any part of that land,

(b)   for the purpose of making any map or plan, or ascertaining the course of any drain, sewer, pipe or cable, in preparation for, or otherwise in connection with, the carrying out of works which are so reasonably necessary, or

(c)   otherwise in connection with the carrying out of any such works,

the making of such an inspection shall be taken for the purposes of this Act to be the carrying out to the dominant land of works which are reasonably necessary for the preservation of that land; and references in this Act to works, or to the carrying out of works, shall be construed accordingly.

2.   Terms and conditions of access orders

(1)   An access order shall specify—

(a)   the works to the dominant land that may be carried out by entering upon the servient land in pursuance of the order;

(b)   the particular area of servient land that may be entered upon by virtue of the order for the purpose of carrying out those works to the dominant land; and

(c)   the date on which, or the period during which, the land may be so entered upon;

and in the following provisions of this Act any reference to the servient land is a reference to the area specified in the order in pursuance of paragraph (b) above.

(2)   An access order may impose upon the applicant or the respondent such terms and conditions as appear to the court to be reasonably necessary for the purpose of avoiding or restricting—

(a)   any loss, damage, or injury which might otherwise be caused to the respondent or any other person by reason of the entry authorised by the order; or

(b)   any inconvenience or loss of privacy that might otherwise be so caused to the respondent or any other person.

(3)   Without prejudice to the generality of subsection (2) above, the terms and conditions which may be imposed under that subsection include provisions with respect to—

(a)   the manner in which the specified works are to be carried out;

(b)   the days on which, and the hours between which, the work involved may be executed;

(c)   the persons who may undertake the carrying out of the specified works or enter upon the servient land under or by virtue of the order;

(d)   the taking of any such precautions by the applicant as may be specified in the order.

(4)   An access order may also impose terms and conditions—

(a)   requiring the applicant to pay, or to secure that such person connected with him as may be specified in the order pays, compensation for—

(i)   any loss, damage or injury, or

(ii)   any substantial loss of privacy or other substantial inconvenience,

which will, or might, be caused to the respondent or any other person by reason of the entry authorised by the order;

(b)   requiring the applicant to secure that he, or such person connected with him as may be specified in the order, is insured against any such risks as may be so specified; or

(c)   requiring such a record to be made of the condition of the servient land, or of such part of it as may be so specified, as the court may consider expedient with a view to facilitating the determination of any question that may arise concerning damage to that land.

(5) An access order may include provision requiring the applicant to pay the respondent such sum by way of consideration for the privilege of entering the servient land in pursuance of the order as appears to the court to be fair and reasonable having regard to all the circumstances of the case, including, in particular—

(a) the likely financial advantage of the order to the applicant and any persons connected with him; and

(b) the degree of inconvenience likely to be caused to the respondent or any other person by the entry;

but no payment shall be ordered under this subsection if and to the extent that the works which the applicant desires to carry out by means of the entry are works to residential land.

(6) For the purposes of subsection (5)(a) above, the likely financial advantage of an access order to the applicant and any persons connected with him shall in all cases be taken to be a sum of money equal to the greater of the following amounts, that is to say—

(a) the amount (if any) by which so much of any likely increase in the value of any land—

(i) which consists of or includes the dominant land, and

(ii) which is owned or occupied by the same person as the dominant land,

as may reasonably be regarded as attributable to the carrying out of the specified works exceeds the likely cost of carrying out those works with the benefit of the access order; and

(b) the difference (if it would have been possible to carry out the specified works without entering upon the servient land) between—

(i) the likely cost of carrying out those works without entering upon the servient land; and

(ii) the likely cost of carrying them out with the benefit of the access order.

(7) For the purpses of subsection (5) above, 'residential land' means so much of any land as consists of—

(a) a dwelling or part of a dwelling;

(b) a garden, yard, private garage or outbuilding which is used and enjoyed wholly or mainly with a dwelling; or

(c) in the case of a building which includes one or more dwellings, any part of the building which is used and enjoyed wholly or mainly with those dwellings or any of them.

(8) The persons who are to be regarded for the purposes of this section as 'connected with' the applicants are—

(a) the owner of any estate or interest in, or right over, the whole or any part of the dominant land;

(b) the occupier of the whole or any part of the dominant land; and

(c) any person whom the applicant may authorise under section 3(7) below to exercise the power of entry conferred by the access order.

(9) The court may make provision—

(a) for the reimbursement by the applicant of any expenses reasonably incurred by the respondent in connection with the application which are not otherwise recoverable as costs;

(b) for the giving of security by the applicant for any sum that might become payable to the respondent or any other person by virtue of this section or section 3 below.

3. Effect of access order

(1) An access order requires the respondent, so far as he has power to do so, to permit the applicant or any of his associates to do anything which the applicant or associate is authorised or required to do under or by virtue of the order or this section.

(2) Except as otherwise provided by or under this Act, an access order authorises the applicant or any of his associates, without the consent of the respondent,—

(a) to enter upon the servient land for the purpose of carrying out the specified works;

(b) to bring on to that land, leave there during the period permitted by the order and, before the end of that period, remove, such materials, plant and equipment as are reasonably necessary for the carrying out of those works; and

    (c)   to bring on to that land any waste arising from the carrying out of those works, if it is reasonably necessary to do so in the course of removing it from the dominant land;

but nothing in this Act or in any access order shall authorise the applicant or any of his associates to leave anything in, on or over the servient land (otherwise than in discharge of their duty to make good that land) after their entry for the purpose of carrying out works to the dominant land ceases to be authorised under or by virtue of the order.

(3)   An access order requires the applicant—

    (a)   to secure that any waste arising from the carrying out of the specified works is removed from the servient land forthwith;

    (b)   to secure that, before the entry ceases to be authorised under or by virtue of the order, the servient land is, so far as reasonably practicable, made good; and

    (c)   to indemnify the respondent against any damage which may be caused to the servient land or any goods by the applicant or any of his associates which would not have been so caused had the order not been made;

but this subsection is subject to subsections (4) and (5) below.

(4)   In making an access order, the court may vary or exclude, in whole or in part,—

    (a)   any authorisation that would otherwise by conferred by subsection (2)(b) or (c) above; or

    (b)   any requirement that would otherwise by imposed by subsection (3) above.

(5)   Without prejudice to the generality of subsection (4) above, if the court is satisfied that it is reasonably necessary for any such waste as may arise from the carrying out of the specified works to be left on the servient land for some period before removal, the access order may, in place of subsection (3)(a) above, include provision—

    (a)   authorising the waste to be left on that land for such period as may be permitted by the order; and

    (b)   requiring the applicant to secure that the waste is removed before the end of that period.

(6)   Where the applicant or any of his associates is authorised or required under or by virtue of an access order or this section to enter, or do any other thing, upon the servient land, he shall not (as respects that access order) be taken to be a trespasser from the beginning on account of his, or any other person's, subsequent conduct.

(7)   For the purposes of this section, the applicant's 'associates' are such number of persons (whether or not servants or agents of his) whom he may reasonably authorise under this subsection to exercise the power of entry conferred by the access order as may be reasonably necessary for carrying out the specified works.

4.   **Persons bound by access order, unidentified persons and bar on contracting out**

(1)   In addition to the respondent, an access order shall, subject to the provisions of the Land Charges Act 1972 and the Land Registration Act 2002, be binding on—

    (a)   any of his successors in title to the servient land; and

    (b)   any person who has an estate or interest in, or right over, the whole or any part of the servient land which was created after the making of the order and who derives his title to that estate, interest or right under the respondent;

and references to the respondent shall be construed accordingly.

(2)   If and to the extent that the court considers it just and equitable to allow him to do so, a person on whom an access order becomes binding by virtue of subsection (1)(a) or (b) above shall be entitled, as respects anything falling to be done after the order becomes binding on him, to enforce the order or any of its terms or conditions as if he were the respondent, and references to the respondent shall be construed accordingly.

(3)   Rules of court may—

    (a)   provide a procedure which may be followed where the applicant does not know, and cannot reasonably ascertain, the name of any person whom he desires to make respondent to the application; and

    (b)   make provision enabling such an applicant to make such a person respondent by description instead of by name;

and in this subsection 'applicant' includes a person who proposes to make an application for an access order.

(4) Any agreement, whenever made, shall be void if and to the extent that it would, apart from this subsection, prevent a person from applying for an access order or restrict his right to do so.

5.   Registration of access orders and of applications for such orders

. . .

(4) In any case where—
   (a)   an access order is discharged under section 6(1)(a) below, and
   (b)   the order has been protected by an entry registered under the Land Charges Act 1972 or by a notice under the Land Registration Act 2002,
   the court may by order direct that the entry, notice or caution shall be cancelled.

(5) The rights conferred on a person by or under an access order shall not be capable of falling within paragraph 2 of Schedule 1 or 3 to the Land Registration Act 2002 (overriding status of interest of person in actual occupation).

(6) An application for an access order shall be regarded as a pending land action for the purposes of the Land Charges Act 1972 and the Land Registration Act 2002.

6.   Variation of orders and damages for breach

(1) Where an access order or an order under this subsection has been made, the court may, on the application of any party to the proceedings in which the order was made or of any other person on whom the order is binding—
   (a)   discharge or vary the order or any of its terms or conditions;
   (b)   suspend any of its terms or conditions; or
   (c)   revive any term or condition suspended under paragraph (b) above;
   and in the application of subsections (1) and (2) of section 4 above in relation to an access order, any order under this subsection which relates to the access order shall be treated for the purposes of those subsections as included in the access order.

(2) If any person contravenes or fails to comply with any requirement, term or condition imposed upon him by or under this Act, the court may, without prejudice to any other remedy available, make an order for the payment of damages by him to any other person affected by the contravention or failure who makes an application for relief under this subsection.

8.   Interpretation and application

(1) Any reference in this Act to an 'entry' upon any servient land includes a reference to the doing on that land of anything necessary for carrying out the works to the dominant land which are reasonably necessary for its preservation; and 'enter' shall be construed accordingly.

(2) This Act applies in relation to any obstruction of, or other interference with, a right over, or interest in, any land as it applies in relation to an entry upon that land; and 'enter' and 'entry' shall be construed accordingly.

(3) In this Act—
   'access order' has the meaning given by section 1(1) above;
   'applicant' means a person making an applicatiaon for an access order and, subject to section 4 above, 'the respondent' means the respondent, or any of the respondents, to such an application;
   'the court' means the High Court or a county court;
   'the dominant land' and 'the servient land' respectively have the meanings given by section 1(1) above, but subject, in the case of servient land, to section 2(1) above;
   'land' does not include a highway;
   'the specified works' means the works specified in the access order in pursuance of section 2(1)(a) above.

TREASURE ACT 1996
(1996, c. 24)

Meaning of 'treasure'

1. **Meaning of 'treasure'**
   (1)   Treasure is—
         (a)   any object at least 300 years old when found which—
               (i)   is not a coin but has metallic content of which at least 10 per cent by weight is precious metal;
               (ii)   when found, is one of at least two coins in the same find which are at least 300 years old at that time and have that percentage of precious metal; or
               (iii) when found, is one of at least ten coins in the same find which are at least 300 years old at that time;
         (b)   any object at least 200 years old when found which belongs to a class designated under section 2(1);
         (c)   any object which would have been treasure trove if found before the commencement of section 4;
         (d)   any object which, when found, is part of the same find as—
               (i)   an object within paragraph (a), (b) or (c) found at the same time or earlier; or
               (ii)   an object found earlier which would be within paragraph (a) or (b) if it had been found at the same time.
   (2)   Treasure does not include objects which are—
         (a)   unworked natural objects, or
         (b)   minerals as extracted from a natural deposit,
         or which belong to a class designated under section 2(2).

2. **Power to alter meaning**
   (1)   The Secretary of State may by order, for the purposes of section 1(1)(b), designate any class of object which he considers to be of outstanding historical, archaeological or cultural importance.
   (2)   The Secretary of State may by order, for the purposes of section 1(2),
         designate any class of object which (apart from the order) would be treasure.
         . . .

3. **Supplementary**
   (1)   This section supplements section 1.
   (2)   'Coin' includes any metal token which was, or can reasonably be assumed to have been, used or intended for use as or instead of money.
   (3)   'Precious metal' means gold or silver.
   (4)   When an object is found, it is part of the same find as another object if—
         (a)   they are found together,
         (b)   the other object was found earlier in the same place where they had been left together.
         (c)   the other object was found earlier in a different place, but they had been left together and had become separated before being found.
   (5)   If the circumstances in which objects are found can reasonably be taken to indicate that they were together at some time before being found, the objects are to be presumed to have been left together, unless shown not to have been.
   (6)   An object which can reasonably be taken to be at least a particular age is to be presumed to be at least that age, unless shown not to be.
   (7)   An object is not treasure if it is wreck within the meaning of Part IX of the Merchant Shipping Act 1995.

Ownership of treasure

4.   Ownership of treasure which is found

(1)   When treasure is found, it vests, subject to prior interests and rights—

    (a)   in the franchise, if there is one;

    (b)   otherwise, in the Crown.

(2)   Prior interests and rights are any which, or which derive from any which—

    (a)   were held when the treasure was left where it was found, or

    (b)   if the treasure had been moved before being found, were held when it was left where it was before being moved.

(3)   If the treasure would have been treasure trove if found before the commencement of this section, neither the Crown nor any franchisee has any interest in it or right over it except in accordance with this Act.

(4)   This section applies—

    (a)   whatever the nature of the place where the treasure was found, and

    (b)   whatever the circumstances in which it was left (including being lost or being left with no intention of recovery).

5.   Meaning of 'franchisee'

(1)   The franchisee for any treasure is the person who—

    (a)   was, immediately before the commencement of section 4, or

    (b)   apart from this Act, as successor in title, would have been, the franchisee of the Crown in right of treasure trove for the place where the treasure was found.

(2)   It is as franchisees in right of treasure trove that Her Majesty and the Duke of Cornwall are to be treated as having enjoyed the rights to treasure trove which belonged respectively to the Duchy of Lancaster and the Duchy of Cornwall immediately before the commencement of section 4.

6.   Treasure vesting in the Crown

(1)   Treasure vesting in the Crown under this Act is to be treated as part of the hereditary revenues of the Crown to which section 1 of the Civil List Act 1952 applies (surrender of hereditary revenues to the Exchequer).

(2)   Any such treasure may be transferred, or otherwise disposed of, in accordance with directions given by the Secretary of State.

(3)   The Crown's title to any such treasure may be disclaimed at any time by the Secretary of State.

. . .

Coroners' jurisdiction

7.   Jurisdiction of coroners

(1)   The jurisdiction of coroners which is referred to in section 30 of the Coroners Act 1988 (treasure) is exercisable in relation to anything which is treasure for the purposes of this Act.

(2)   That jurisdiction is not exercisable for the purposes of the law relating to treasure trove in relation to anything found after the commencement of section 4.

(3)   The Act of 1988 and anything saved by virtue of section 36(5) of that Act (saving for existing law and practice etc.) has effect subject to this section.

(4)   An inquest held by virtue of this section is to be held without a jury, unless the coroner orders otherwise.

8.   Duty of finder to notify coroner

(1)   A person who finds an object which he believes or has reasonable grounds for believing is treasure must notify the coroner for the district in which the object was found before the end of the notice period.

(2)   The notice period is fourteen days beginning with—

    (a)   the day after the find; or

(b)   if later, the day on which the finder first believes or has reason to believe the object is treasure.

(3)   Any person who fails to comply with subsection (1) is guilty of an offence and liable on summary conviction to—

(a)   imprisonment for a term not exceeding three months;

(b)   a fine of an amount not exceeding level 5 on the standard scale; or

(c)   both.

(4)   In proceedings for an offence under this section, it is a defence for the defendant to show that he had, and has continued to have, a reasonable excuse for failing to notify the coroner.

(5)   If the office of coroner for a district is vacant, the person acting as coroner for that district is the coroner for the purposes of subsection (1).

9.   Procedure for inquests

(1)   In this section, 'inquest' means an inquest held under section 7.

(2)   A coroner proposing to conduct an inquest must notify—

(a)   the British Museum, if his district is in England; or

(b)   the National Museum of Wales, if it is in Wales.

(3)   Before conducting the inquest, the coroner must take reasonable steps to notify—

(a)   any person who it appears to him may have found the treasure; and

(b)   any person who, at the time the treasure was found, occupied land which it appears to him may be where it was found.

(4)   During the inquest the coroner must take reasonable steps to notify any such person not already notified.

(5)   Before or during the inquest, the coroner must take reasonable steps—

(a)   to obtain from any person notified under subsection (3) or (4) the names and addresses of interested persons; and

(b)   to notify any interested person whose name and address he obtains.

(6)   The coroner must take reasonable steps to give any interested person notified under subsection (3), (4) or (5) an opportunity to examine witnesses at the inquest.

(7)   In subsections (5) and (6), 'interested person' means a person who appears to the coroner to be likely to be concerned with the inquest—

(a)   as the finder of the treasure or otherwise involved in the find;

(b)   as the occupier, at the time the treasure was found, of the land where it was found, or

(c)   as having had an interest in that land at that time or since.

Rewards, codes of practice and report

10.   Rewards

(1)   This section applies if treasure—

(a)   has vested in the Crown under section 4; and

(b)   is to be transferred to a museum.

(2)   The Secretary of State must determine whether a reward is to be paid by the museum before the transfer.

(3)   If the Secretary of State determines that a reward is to be paid, he must also determine, in whatever way he thinks fit—

(a)   the treasure's market value:

(b)   the amount of the reward;

(c)   to whom the reward is to be payable; and

(d)   if it is to be payable to more than one person, how much each is to receive.

(4)   The total reward must not exceed the treasure's market value.

(5)   The reward may be payable to—

(a)   the finder or any other person involved in the find:

(b)   the occupier of the land at the time of the find;

(c)   any person who had an interest in the land at that time, or has had such an interest at any time since then.

(6)   Payment of the reward is not enforceable against a museum or the Secretary of State.

(7) In a determination under this section, the Secretary of State must take into account anything relevant in the code of practice issued under section 11.

(8) This section also applies in relation to treasure which has vested in a franchisee under section 4, if the franchisee makes a request to the Secretary of State that it should.

TRUSTS OF LAND AND APPOINTMENT OF TRUSTEES ACT 1996
(1996, c. 47)

PART I
TRUSTS OF LAND

Introductory

1. Meaning of 'trust of land'

(1) In this Act—
  (a) 'trust of land' means (subject to subsection (3)) any trust of property which consists of or includes land, and
  (b) 'trustees of land' means trustees of a trust of land.

(2) The reference in subsection (1)(a) to a trust—
  (a) is to any description of trust (whether express, implied, resulting or constructive), including a trust for sale and a bare trust, and
  (b) includes a trust created, or arising, before the commencement of this Act.

(3) The reference to land in subsection (1)(a) does not include land which (despite section 2) is settled land or which is land to which the Universities and College Estates Act 1925 applies.

Settlements and trusts for sale as trusts of land

2. Trusts in place of settlements

(1) No settlement created after the commencement of this Act is a settlement for the purposes of the Settled Land Act 1925; and no settlement shall be deemed to be made under that Act after that commencement.

(2) Subsection (1) does not apply to a settlement created on the occasion of an alteration in any interest in, or of a person becoming entitled under, a settlement which—
  (a) is in existence at the commencement of this Act, or
  (b) derives from a settlement within paragraph (a) or this paragraph.

(3) But a settlement created as mentioned in subsection (2) is not a settlement for the purposes of the Settled Land Act 1925 if provision to the effect that it is not is made in the instrument, or any of the instruments, by which it is created.

(4) Where at any time after the commencement of this Act there is in the case of any settlement which is a settlement for the purposes of the Settled Land Act 1925 no relevant property which is, or is deemed to be, subject to the settlement, the settlement permanently ceases at that time to be a settlement for the purposes of that Act.
  In this subsection 'relevant property' means land and personal chattels to which section 67(1) of the Settled Land Act 1925 (heirlooms) applies.

(5) No land held on charitable, ecclesiastical or public trusts shall be or be deemed to be settled land after the commencement of this Act, even if it was or was deemed to be settled land before that commencement.

(6) Schedule 1 has effect to make provision consequential on this section (including provision to impose a trust in circumstances in which, apart from this section, there would be a settlement for the purposes of the Settled Land Act 1925 (and there would not otherwise be a trust)).

3. Abolition of doctrine of conversion

(1) Where land is held by trustees subject to a trust for sale, the land is not to be regarded as personal property; and where personal property is subject to a trust for sale in order that the trustees may acquire land, the personal property is not to be regarded as land.

(2)   Subsection (1) does not apply to a trust created by a will if the testator died before the commencement of this Act.

(3)   Subject to that, subsection (1) applies to a trust whether it is created, or arises, before or after that commencement.

4.   Express trusts for sale as trusts of land

(1)   In the case of every trust for sale of land created by a disposition there is to be implied, despite any provision to the contrary made by the disposition, a power for the trustees to postpone sale of the land; and the trustees are not liable in any way for postponing sale of the land, in the exercise of their discretion, for an indefinite period.

(2)   Subsection (1) applies to a trust whether it is created, or arises, before or after the commencement of this Act.

(3)   Subsection (1) does not affect any liability incurred by trustees before that commencement.

5.   Implied trusts for sale as trusts of land

(1)   Schedule 2 has effect in relation to statutory provisions which impose a trust for sale of land in certain circumstances so that in those circumstances there is instead a trust of the land (without a duty to sell).

(2)   Section 1 of the Settled Land Act 1925 does not apply to land held on any trust arising by virtue of that Schedule (so that any such land is subject to a trust of land).

Functions of trustees of land

6.   General powers of trustees

(1)   For the purpose of exercising their functions as trustees, the trustees of land have in relation to the land subject to the trust all the powers of an absolute owner.

(2)   Where in the case of any land subject to a trust of land each of the beneficiaries interested in the land is a person of full age and capacity who is absolutely entitled to the land, the powers conferred on the trustees by subsection (1) include the power to convey the land to the beneficiaries even though they have not required the trustees to do so; and where land is conveyed by virtue of this subsection—

(a)   the beneficiaries shall do whatever is necessary to secure that it vests in them, and

(b)   if they fail to do so, the court may make an order requiring them to do so.

(3)   The trustees of land have power to acquire land under the power conferred by section 8 of the Trustee Act 2000.

(4)   . . .

(5)   In exercising the powers conferred by this section trustees shall have regard to the rights of the beneficiaries.

(6)   The powers conferred by this section shall not be exercised in contravention of, or of any order made in pursuance of, any other enactment or any rule of law or equity.

(7)   The reference in subsection (6) to an order includes an order of any court or of the Charity Commissioners.

(8)   Where any enactment other than this section confers on trustees authority to act subject to any restriction, limitation or condition, trustees of land may not exercise the powers conferred by this section to do any act which they are prevented from doing under the other enactment by reason of the restriction, limitation or condition.

(9)   The duty of care under section 1 of the Trustee Act 2000 applies to trustees of land when exercising the powers conferred by this section.

7.   Partition by trustees

(1)   The trustees of land may, where beneficiaries of full age are absolutely entitled in undivided shares to land subject to the trust, partition the land, or any part of it, and provide (by way of mortgage or otherwise) for the payment of any equality money.

(2)   The trustees shall give effect to any such partition by conveying the partitioned land in severalty (whether or not subject to any legal mortgage created for raising equality money), either absolutely or in trust, in accordance with the rights of those beneficiaries.

(3) Before exercising their powers under subsection (2) the trustees shall obtain the consent of each of those beneficiaries.

(4) Where a share in the land is affected by an incumbrance, the trustees may either give effect to it or provide for its discharge from the property allotted to that share as they think fit.

(5) If a share in the land is absolutely vested in a minor, subsections (1) to (4) apply as if he were of full age, except that the trustees may act on his behalf and retain land or other property representing his share in trust for him.

(6) Subsection (1) is subject to sections 21 (part-unit: interests) and 22 (part-unit: charging) of the Commonhold and Leasehold Reform Act 2002.

8. Exclusion and restriction of powers

(1) Sections 6 and 7 do not apply in the case of a trust of land created by a disposition in so far as provision to the effect that they do not apply is made by the disposition.

(2) If the disposition creating such a trust makes provision requiring any consent to be obtained to the exercise of any power conferred by section 6 or 7, the power may not be exercised without that consent.

(3) Subsection (1) does not apply in the case of charitable, ecclesiastical or public trusts.

(4) Subsections (1) and (2) have effect subject to any enactment which prohibits or restricts the effect of provision of the description mentioned in them.

9. Delegation by trustees

(1) The trustees of land may, by power of attorney, delegate to any beneficiary or beneficiaries of full age and beneficially entitled to an interest in possession in land subject to the trust any of their functions as trustees which relate to the land.

(2) Where trustees purport to delegate to a person by a power of attorney under subsection (1) functions relating to any land and another person in good faith deals with him in relation to the land, he shall be presumed in favour of that other person to have been a person to whom the functions could be delegated unless that other person has knowledge at the time of the transaction that he was not such a person.

And it shall be conclusively presumed in favour of any purchaser whose interest depends on the validity of that transaction that that other person dealt in good faith and did not have such knowledge if that other person makes a statutory declaration to that effect before or within three months after the completion of the purchase.

(3) A power of attorney under subsection (1) shall be given by all the trustees jointly and (unless expressed to be irrevocable and to be given by way of security) may be revoked by any one or more of them; and such a power is revoked by the appointment as a trustee of a person other than those by whom it is given (though not by any of those persons dying or otherwise ceasing to be a trustee).

(4) Where a beneficiary to whom functions are delegated by a power of attorney under subsection (1) ceases to be a person beneficially entitled to an interest in possession in land subject to the trust—

(a) if the functions are delegated to him alone, the power is revoked,

(b) if the functions are delegated to him and to other beneficiaries to be exercised by them jointly (but not separately), the power is revoked if each of the other beneficiaries ceases to be so entitled (but otherwise functions exercisable in accordance with the power are so exercisable by the remaining beneficiary or beneficiaries), and

(c) if the functions are delegated to him and to other beneficiaries to be exercised by them separately (or either separately or jointly), the power is revoked in so far as it relates to him.

(5) A delegation under subsection (1) may be for any period or indefinite.

(6) A power of attorney under subsection (1) cannot be an enduring power within the meaning of the Enduring Powers of Attorney Act 1985.

(7) Beneficiaries to whom functions have been delegated under subsection (1) are, in relation to the exercise of the functions, in the same position as trustees (with the same duties and liabilities); but such beneficiaries shall not be regarded as trustees for any other purposes

(including, in particular, the purposes of any enactment permitting the delegation of functions by trustees or imposing requirements relating to the payment of capital money).

(8) . . .

(9) Neither this section nor the repeal by this Act of section 29 of the Law of Property Act 1925 (which is superseded by this section) affects the operation after the commencement of this Act of any delegation effected before that commencement.

9A.   Duties of trustees in connection with delegation etc.

(1) The duty of care under section 1 of the Trustee Act 2000 applies to trustees of land in deciding whether to delegate any of their functions under section 9.

(2) Subsection (3) applies if the trustees of land—

    (a) delegate any of their functions under section 9, and

    (b) the delegation is not irrevocable.

(3) While the delegation continues, the trustees—

    (a) must keep the delegation under review,

    (b) if circumstances make it appropriate to do so, must consider whether there is a need to exercise any power of intervention that they have, and

    (c) if they consider that there is a need to exercise such a power, must do so.

(4) 'Power of intervention' includes—

    (a) a power to give directions to the beneficiary;

    (b) a power to revoke the delegation.

(5) The duty of care under section 1 of the 2000 Act applies to trustees in carrying out any duty under subsection (3).

(6) A trustee of land is not liable for any act or default of the beneficiary, or beneficiaries, unless the trustee fails to comply with the duty of care in deciding to delegate any of the trustees' functions under section 9 or in carrying out any duty under subsection (3).

(7) Neither this section nor the repeal of section 9(8) by the Trustee Act 2000 affects the operation after the commencement of this section of any delegation effected before that commencement.

Consents and consultation

10.   Consents

(1) If a disposition creating a trust of land requires the consent of more than two persons to the exercise by the trustees of any function relating to the land, the consent of any two of them to the exercise of the function is sufficient in favour of a purchaser.

(2) Subsection (1) does not apply to the exercise of a function by trustees of land held on charitable, ecclesiastical or public trusts.

(3) Where at any time a person whose consent is expressed by a disposition creating a trust of land to be required to the exercise by the trustees of any function relating to the land is not of full age —

    (a) his consent is not, in favour of a purchaser, required to the exercise of the function, but

    (b) the trustees shall obtain the consent of a parent who has parental responsibility for him (within the meaning of the Children Act 1989) or of a guardian of his.

11.   Consultation with beneficiaries

(1) The trustees of land shall in the exercise of any function relating to land subject to the trust—

    (a) so far as practicable, consult the beneficiaries of full age and beneficially entitled to an interest in possession in the land, and

    (b) so far as consistent with the general interest of the trust, give effect to the wishes of those beneficiaries, or (in case of dispute) of the majority (according to the value of their combined interests).

(2) Subsection (1) does not apply—

    (a) in relation to a trust created by a disposition in so far as provision that it does not apply is made by the disposition,

       (b)   in relation to a trust created or arising under a will made before the commencement of this Act, or

       (c)   in relation to the exercise of the power mentioned in section 6(2).

(3)   Subsection (1) does not apply to a trust created before the commencement of this Act by a disposition, or a trust created after that commencement by reference to such a trust, unless provision to the effect that it is to apply is made by a deed executed—

       (a)   in a case in which the trust was created by one person and he is of full capacity, by that person, or

       (b)   in a case in which the trust was created by more than one person, by such of the persons who created the trust as are alive and of full capacity.

(4)   A deed executed for the purposes of subsection (3) is irrevocable.

Right of beneficiaries to occupy trust land

12.   The right to occupy

(1)   A beneficiary who is beneficially entitled to an interest in possession in land subject to a trust of land is entitled by reason of his interest to occupy the land at any time if at that time—

       (a)   the purposes of the trust include making the land available for his occupation (or for the occupation of beneficiaries of a class of which he is a member or of beneficiaries in general), or

       (b)   the land is held by the trustees so as to be so available.

(2)   Subsection (1) does not confer on a beneficiary a right to occupy land if it is either unavailable or unsuitable for occupation by him.

(3)   This section is subject to section 13.

13.   Exclusion and restriction of right to occupy

(1)   Where two or more beneficiaries are (or apart from this subsection would be) entitled under section 12 to occupy land, the trustees of land may exclude or restrict the entitlement of any one or more (but not all) of them.

(2)   Trustees may not under subsection (1)—

       (a)   unreasonably exclude any beneficiary's entitlement to occupy land, or

       (b)   restrict any such entitlement to an unreasonable extent.

(3)   The trustees of land may from time to time impose reasonable conditions on any beneficiary in relation to his occupation of land by reason of his entitlement under section 12.

(4)   The matters to which trustees are to have regard in exercising the powers conferred by this section include—

       (a)   the intentions of the person or persons (if any) who created the trust,

       (b)   the purposes for which the land is held, and

       (c)   the circumstances and wishes of each of the beneficiaries who is (or apart from any previous exercise by the trustees of those powers would be) entitled to occupy the land under section 12.

(5)   The conditions which may be imposed on a beneficiary under subsection (3) include, in particular, conditions requiring him—

       (a)   to pay any outgoings or expenses in respect of the land, or

       (b)   to assume any other obligation in relation to the land or to any activity which is or is proposed to be conducted there.

(6)   Where the entitlement of any beneficiary to occupy land under section 12 has been excluded or restricted, the conditions which may be imposed on any other beneficiary under subsection (3) include, in particular, conditions requiring him to—

       (a)   make payments by way of compensation to the beneficiary whose entitlement has been excluded or restricted, or

       (b)   forgo any payment or other benefit to which he would otherwise be entitled under the trust so as to benefit that beneficiary.

(7)   The powers conferred on trustees by this section may not be exercised—

    (a)   so as prevent any person who is in occupationt of land (whether or not by reason of an entitlement under section 12) from continuing to occupy the land, or

    (b)   in a manner likely to result in any such person ceasing to occupy the land,

unless he consents or the court has given approval.

(8)   The matters to which the court is to have regard in determining whether to give approval under subsection (7) include the matters mentioned in subsection (4)(a) to (c).

Powers of court

14.   Applications for order

(1)   Any person who is a trustee of land or has an interest in property subject to a trust of land may make an application to the court for an order under this section.

(2)   On an application for an order under this section the court may make any such order—

    (a)   relating to the exercise by the trustees of any of their functions (including an order relieving them of any obligation to obtain the consent of, or to consult, any person in connection with the exercise of any of their functions), or

    (b)   declaring the nature or extent of a person's interest in property subject to the trust,

as the court thinks fit.

(3)   The court may not under this section make any order as to the appointment or removal of trustees.

(4)   The powers conferred on the court by this section are exercisable on an application whether it is made before or after the commencement of this Act.

15.   Matters relevant in determining applications

(1)   The matters to which the court is to have regard in determining an application for an order under section 14 include—

    (a)   the intentions of the person or persons (if any) who created the trust,

    (b)   the purposes for which the property subject to the trust is held,

    (c)   the welfare of any minor who occupies or might reasonably be expected to occupy any land subject to the trust as his home, and

    (d)   the interests of any secured creditor of any beneficiary.

(2)   In the case of an application relating to the exercise in relation to any land of the powers conferred on the trustees by section 13, the matters to which the court is to have regard also include the circumstances and wishes of each of the beneficiaries who is (or apart from any previous exercise by the trustees of those powers would be) entitled to occupy the land under section 12.

(3)   In the case of any other application, other than one relating to the exercise of the power mentioned in section 6(2), the matters to which the court is to have regard also include the circumstances and wishes of any beneficiaries of full age and entitled to an interest in possession in property subject to the trust or (in case of dispute) of the majority (according to the value of their combined interests).

(4)   This section does not apply to an application if section 335A of the Insolvency Act 1986 . . . applies to it.

Purchaser protection

16.   Protection of purchasers

(1)   A purchaser of land which is or has been subject to a trust need not be concerned to see that any requirement imposed on the trustees by section 6(5), 7(3) or 11(1) has been complied with.

(2)   Where—

    (a)   trustees of land who convey land which (immediately before it is conveyed) is subject to the trust contravene section 6(6) or (8), but

    (b)   the purchaser of the land from the trustees has no actual notice of the contravention,

the contravention does not invalidate the conveyance.

(3)   Where the powers of trustees of land are limited by virtue of section 8—

(a) the trustees shall take all reasonable steps to bring the limitation to the notice of any purchaser of the land from them, but

(b) the limitation does not invalidate any conveyance by the trustees to a purchaser who has no actual notice of the limitation.

(4) Where trustees of land convey land which (immediately before it is conveyed) is subject to the trust to persons believed by them to be beneficiaries absolutely entitled to the land under the trust and of full age and capacity—

(a) the trustees shall execute a deed declaring that they are discharged from the trust in relation to that land, and

(b) if they fail to do so, the court may make an order requiring them to do so.

(5) A purchaser of land to which a deed under subsection (4) relates is entitled to assume that, as from the date of the deed, the land is not subject to the trust unless he has actual notice that the trustees were mistaken in their belief that the land was conveyed to beneficiaries absolutely entitled to the land under the trust and of full age and capacity.

(6) Subsections (2) and (3) do not apply to land held on charitable, ecclesiastical or public trusts.

(7) This section does not apply to registered land.

Supplementary

17. Applications of provisions to trusts of proceeds of sale

(1) . . .

(2) Section 14 applies in relation to a trust of proceeds of sale of land and trustees of such a trust as in relation to a trust of land and trustees of land.

(3) In this section 'trust of proceeds of sale of land' means (subject to subsection (5)) any trust of property (other than a trust of land) which consists of or includes—

(a) any proceeds of a disposition of land held in trust (including settled land), or

(b) any property representing any such proceeds.

(4) The references in subsection (3) to a trust—

(a) are to any description of trust (whether express, implied, resulting or constructive), including a trust for sale and a bare trust, and

(b) include a trust created, or arising, before the commencement of this Act.

(5) A trust which (despite section 2) is a settlement for the purposes of the Settled Land Act 1925 cannot be a trust of proceeds of sale of land.

(6) In subsection (3)—

(a) 'disposition' includes any disposition made, or coming into operation, before the commencement of this Act, and

(b) the reference to settled land includes personal chattels to which section 67(1) of the Settled Land Act 1925 (heirlooms) applies.

18. Application of Part to personal representatives

(1) The provisions of this Part relating to trustees, other than sections 10, 11 and 14, apply to personal representatives, but with appropriate modifications and without prejudice to the functions of personal representatives for the purposes of administration.

(2) The appropriate modifications include—

(a) the substitution of references to persons interested in the due administration of the estate for references to beneficiaries, and

(b) the substitution of references to the will for references to the disposition creating the trust.

(3) Section 3(1) does not apply to personal representatives if the death occurs before the commencement of this Act.

PART II

APPOINTMENT AND RETIREMENT OF TRUSTEES

19. Appointment and retirement of trustee at instance of beneficiaries

(1) This section applies in the case of a trust where—

       (a)   there is no person nominated for the purpose of appointing new trustees by the instrument, if any, creating the trust, and

       (b) the beneficiaries under the trust are of full age and capacity and (taken together) are absolutely entitled to the property subject to the trust.

(2)   The beneficiaries may give a direction or directions of either or both of the following descriptions—

       (a)   a written direction to a trustee or trustees to retire from the trust, and

       (b) a written direction to the trustees or trustee for the time being (or, if there are none, to the personal representative of the last person who was a trustee) to appoint by writing to be a trustee or trustees the person or persons specified in the direction.

(3)   Where—

       (a)   a trustee has been given a direction under subsection (2)(a),

       (b) reasonable arrangements have been made for the protection of any rights of his in connection with the trust,

       (c)   after he has retired there will be either a trust corporation or at least two persons to act as trustees to perform the trust, and

       (d) either another person is to be appointed to be a new trustee on his retirement (whether in compliance with a direction under subsection (2)(b) or otherwise) or the continuing trustees by deed consent to his retirement,

he shall make a deed declaring his retirement and shall be deemed to have retired and be discharged from the trust.

(4)   Where a trustee retires under subsection (3) he and the continuing trustees (together with any new trustee) shall (subject to any arrangements for the protection of his rights) do anything necessary to vest the trust property in the continuing trustees (or the continuing and new trustees).

(5)   This section has effect subject to the restrictions imposed by the Trustee Act 1925 on the number of trustees.

20.   Appointment of substitute for incapable trustee

(1)   This section applies where—

       (a)   a trustee is incapable by reason of mental disorder of exercising his functions as trustee,

       (b) there is no person who is both entitled and willing and able to appoint a trustee in place of him under section 36(1) of the Trustee Act 1925, and

       (c)   the beneficiaries under the trust are of full age and capacity and (taken together) are absolutely entitled to the property subject to the trust.

(2)   The beneficiaries may give to—

       (a)   a receiver of the trustee,

       (b) an attorney acting for him under the authority of a power of attorney created by an instrument which is registered under section 6 of the Enduring Powers of Attorney Act 1985, or

       (c)   a person authorised for the purpose by the authority having jurisdiction under Part VII of the Mental Health Act 1983,

a written direction to appoint by writing the person or persons specified in the direction to be a trustee or trustees in place of the incapable trustee.

21.   Supplementary

(1)   For the purposes of section 19 or 20 a direction is given by beneficiaries if—

       (a)   a single direction is jointly given by all of them, or

       (b) (subject to subsection (2)) a direction is given by each of them (whether solely or jointly with one or more, but not all, of the others),

and none of them by writing withdraws the direction given by him before it has been complied with.

(2)   Where more than one direction is given each must specify for appointment or retirement the same person or persons.

(3) Subsection (7) of section 36 of the Trustee Act 1925 (powers of trustees appointed under that section) applies to a trustee appointed under section 19 or 20 as if he were appointed under that section.

(4) A direction under section 19 or 20 must not specify a person or persons for appointment if the appointment of that person or those persons would be in contravention of section 35(1) of the Trustee Act 1925 or section 24(1) of the Law of Property Act 1925 (requirements as to identity of trustees).

(5) Sections 19 and 20 do not apply in relation to a trust created by a disposition in so far as provision that they do not apply is made by the disposition.

(6) Sections 19 and 20 do not apply in relation to a trust created before the commencement of this Act by a disposition in so far as provision to the effect that they do not apply is made by a deed executed—

(a) in a case in which the trust was created by one person and he is of full capacity, by that person, or

(b) in a case in which the trust was created by more than one person, by such of the persons who created the trust as are alive and of full capacity.

(7) A deed executed for the purposes of subsection (6) is irrevocable.

(8) Where a deed is executed for the purposes of subsection (6)—

(a) it does not affect anything done before its execution to comply with a direction under section 19 or 20, but

(b) a direction under section 19 or 20 which has been given but not complied with before its execution shall cease to have effect.

PART III
SUPPLEMENTARY

22. Meaning of 'beneficiary'

(1) In this Act 'beneficiary', in relation to a trust, means any person who under the trust has an interest in property subject to the trust (including a person who has such an interest as a trustee or a personal representative).

(2) In this Act references to a beneficiary who is beneficially entitled do not include a beneficiary who has an interest in property subject to the trust only by reason of being a trustee or personal representative.

(3) For the purposes of this Act a person who is a beneficiary only by reason of being an annuitant is not to be regarded as entitled to an interest in possession in land subject to the trust.

23. Other interpretation provisions

(1) In this Act 'purchaser' has the same meaning as in Part I of the Law of Property Act 1925.

(2) Subject to that, where an expression used in this Act is given a meaning by the Law of Property Act 1925 it has the same meaning as in that Act unless the context otherwise requires.

(3) In this Act 'the court' means—

(a) the High Court, or

(b) a county court.

SCHEDULES

Section 2

SCHEDULE 1
PROVISIONS CONSEQUENTIAL ON SECTION 2

Minors

1. (1) Where after the commencement of this Act a person purports to convey a legal estate in land to a minor, or two or more minors, alone, the conveyance—

(a) is not effective to pass the legal estate, but

(b) operates as a declaration that the land is held in trust for the minor or minors (or if he purports to convey it to the minor or minors in trust for any persons, for those persons).

(2)   Where after the commencement of this Act a person purports to convey a legal estate in land to—

(a)   a minor or two or more minors, and

(b)   another person who is, or other persons who are, of full age,

the conveyance operates to vest the land in the other person or persons in trust for the minor or minors and the other person or persons (or if he purports to convey it to them in trust for any persons, for those persons).

(3)   Where immediately before the commencement of this Act a conveyance is operating (by virtue of section 27 of the Settled Land Act 1925) as an agreement to execute a settlement in favour of a minor or minors—

(a)   the agreement ceases to have effect on the commencement of this Act, and

(b)   the conveyance subsequently operates instead as a declaration that the land is held in trust for the minor or minors.

2.   Where after the commencement of this Act a legal estate in land would, by reason of intestacy or in any other circumstances not dealt with in paragraph 1, vest in a person who is a minor if he were a person of full age, the land is held in trust for the minor.

Family charges

3.   Where, by virtue of an instrument coming into operation after the commencement of this Act, land becomes charged voluntarily (or in consideration of marriage or the formation of a civil partnership) or by way of family arrangement, whether immediately or after an interval, with the payment of—

(a)   a rentcharge for the life of a person or a shorter period, or

(b)   capital, annual or periodical sums for the benefit of a person,

the instrument operates as a declaration that the land is held in trust for giving effect to the charge.

Charitable, ecclesiastical and public trusts

4.   (1)   This paragraph applies in the case of land held on charitable, ecclesiastical or public trusts (other than land to which the Universities and College Estates Act 1925 applies).

(2)   Where there is a conveyance of such land—

(a)   if neither section 37(1) nor section 39(1) of the Charities Act 1993 applies to the conveyance, it shall state that the land is held on such trusts, and

(b)   if neither section 37(2) nor section 39(2) of that Act has been complied with in relation to the conveyance and a purchaser has notice that the land is held on such trusts, he must see that any consents or orders necessary to authorise the transaction have been obtained.

(3)   Where any trustees or the majority of any set of trustees have power to transfer or create any legal estate in the land, the estate shall be transferred or created by them in the names and on behalf of the persons in whom it is vested.

Entailed interests

5.   (1)   Where a person purports by an instrument coming into operation after the commencement of this Act to grant to another person an entailed interest in real or personal property, the instrument—

(a)   is not effective to grant an entailed interest, but

(b)   operates instead as a declaration that the property is held in trust absolutely for the person to whom an entailed interest in the property was purportedly granted.

(2)   Where a person purports by an instrument coming into operation after the commencement of this Act to declare himself a tenant in tail of real or personal property, the instrument is not effective to create an entailed interest.

Property held on settlement ceasing to exist

6.   Where a settlement ceases to be a settlement for the purposes of the Settled Land Act 1925 because no relevant property (within the meaning of section 2(4)) is, or is deemed to be, subject to

the settlement, any property which is or later becomes subject to the settlement is held in trust for the persons interested under the settlement.

HUMAN RIGHTS ACT 1998
(1998, c. 42)

Legislation

3.   Interpretation of legislation

(1)   So far as it is possible to do so, primary legislation and subordinate legislation must be read and given effect in a way which is compatible with Convention rights.

(2)   This section—

(a)   applies to primary legislation and subordinate legislation whenever enacted;

(b)   does not affect the validity, continuing operation or enforcement of any incompatible primary legislation; and

(c)   does not affect the validity, continuing operation or enforcement of any incompatible subordinate legislation if (disregarding any possibility of revocation) primary legislation prevents removal of the incompatibility.

SCHEDULES
SCHEDULE 1
THE ARTICLES
PART I
THE CONVENTION RIGHTS AND FREEDOMS

Right to respect for private and family life

Article 8

1.   Everyone has the right to respect for his private and family life, his home and his correspondence.

2.   There shall be no interference by a public authority with the exercise of this right except such as is in accordance with the law and is necessary in a democratic society in the interests of national security, public safety or the economic well-being of the country, for the prevention of disorder or crime, for the protection of health or morals, or for the protection of the rights and freedoms of others.

PART II
THE FIRST PROTOCOL

Protection of property

Article 1

Every natural or legal person is entitled to the peaceful enjoyment of his possessions. No one shall be deprived of his possessions except in the public interest and subject to the conditions provided for by law and by the general principles of international law.

The preceding provisions shall not, however, in any way impair the right of a State to enforce such laws as it deems necessary to control the use of property in accordance with the general interest or to secure the payment of taxes or other contributions or penalties.

TRUSTEE DELEGATION ACT 1999
(1999, c. 15)

Attorney of trustee with beneficial interest in land

1.   Exercise of trustee functions by attorney

(1)   The donee of a power of attorney is not prevented from doing an act in relation to—

(a)   land,

    (b)   capital proceeds of a conveyance of land, or

    (c)   income from land,

by reason only that the act involves the exercise of a trustee function of the donor if, at the time when the act is done, the donor has a beneficial interest in the land, proceeds or income.

  (2)   In this section—

    (a)   'conveyance' has the same meaning as in the Law of Property Act 1925, and

    (b)   references to a trustee function of the donor are to a function which the donor has as trustee (either alone or jointly with any other person or persons).

  (3)   Subsection (1) above—

    (a)   applies only if and so far as a contrary intention is not expressed in the instrument creating the power of attorney, and

    (b)   has effect subject to the terms of that instrument.

  (4)   The donor of the power of attorney—

    (a)   is liable for the acts or defaults of the donee in exercising any function by virtue of subsection (1) above in the same manner as if they were acts or defaults of the donor, but

    (b)   is not liable by reason only that a function is exercised by the donee by virtue of that subsection.

  (5)   Subsections (1) and (4) above—

    (a)   apply only if and so far as a contrary intention is not expressed in the instrument (if any) creating the trust, and

    (b)   have effect subject to the terms of such an instrument.

  (6)   The fact that it appears that, in dealing with any shares or stock, the donee of the power of attorney is exercising a function by virtue of subsection (1) above does not affect with any notice of any trust a person in whose books the shares are, or stock is, registered or inscribed.

  (7)   In any case where (by way of exception to section 3(1) of the Trusts of Land and Appointment of Trustees Act 1996) the doctrine of conversion continues to operate, any person who, by reason of the continuing operation of that doctrine, has a beneficial interest in the proceeds of sale of land shall be treated for the purposes of this section and section 2 below as having a beneficial interest in the land.

  (8)   The donee of a power of attorney is not to be regarded as exercising a trustee function by virtue of subsection (1) above if he is acting under a trustee delegation power; and for this purpose a trustee delegation power is a power of attorney given under—

    (a)   a statutory provision, or

    (b)   a provision of the instrument (if any) creating a trust,

under which the donor of the power is expressly authorised to delegate the exercise of all or any of his trustee functions by power of attorney.

  (9)   Subject to section 4(6) below, this section applies only to powers of attorney created after the commencement of this Act.

2.   Evidence of beneficial interest

  (1)   This section applies where the interest of a purchaser depends on the donee of a power of attorney having power to do an act in relation to any property by virtue of section 1(1) above. In this subsection 'purchaser' has the same meaning as in Part I of the Law of Property Act 1925.

  (2)   Where this section applies an appropriate statement is, in favour of the purchaser, conclusive evidence of the donor of the power having a beneficial interest in the property at the time of the doing of the act.

  (3)   In this section 'an appropriate statement' means a signed statement made by the donee—

    (a)   when doing the act in question, or

    (b)   at any other time within the period of three months beginning with the day on which the act is done,

that the donor has a beneficial interest in the property at the time of the donee doing the act.

(4) If an appropriate statement is false, the donee is liable in the same way as he would be if the statement were contained in a statutory declaration.

4. Enduring powers

(1) Section 3(3) of the Enduring Powers of Attorney Act 1985 (which entitles the donee of an enduring power to exercise any of the donor's functions as trustee and to give receipt for capital money etc.) does not apply to enduring powers created after the commencement of this Act.

(2) Section 3(3) of the Enduring Powers of Attorney Act 1985 ceases to apply to enduring powers created before the commencement of this Act—

    (a) where subsection (3) below applies, in accordance with that subsection, and

    (b) otherwise, at the end of the period of one year from that commencement.

(3) Where an application for the registration of the instrument creating such an enduring power is made before the commencement of this Act, or during the period of one year from that commencement, section 3(3) of the Enduring Powers of Attorney Act 1985 ceases to apply to the power—

    (a) if the instrument is registered pursuant to the application (whether before commencement or during or after that period), when the registration of the instrument is cancelled, and

    (b) if the application is finally refused during or after that period, when the application is finally refused.

(4) In subsection (3) above—

    (a) 'registration' and 'registered' mean registration and registered under section 6 of the Enduring Powers of Attorney Act 1985, and

    (b) 'cancelled' means cancelled under section 8(4) of that Act.

(5) For the purposes of subsection (3)(b) above an application is finally refused—

    (a) if the application is withdrawn or any appeal is abandoned, when the application is withdrawn or the appeal is abandoned, and

    (b) otherwise, when proceedings on the application (including any proceedings on, or in consequence of, an appeal) have been determined and any time for appealing or further appealing has expired.

(6) Section 1 above applies to an enduring power created before the commencement of this Act from the time when (in accordance with subsections (2) to (5) above) section 3(3) of the Enduring Powers of Attorney Act 1985 ceases to apply to it.

Miscellaneous provisions about attorney acting for trustee

7. Two-trustee rules

(1) A requirement imposed by an enactment—

    (a) that capital money be paid to, or dealt with as directed by, at least two trustees or that a valid receipt for capital money be given otherwise than by a sole trustee, or

    (b) that, in order for an interest or power to be overreached, a conveyance or deed be executed by at least two trustees,

is not satisfied by money being paid to or dealt with as directed by, or a receipt for money being given by, a relevant attorney or by a conveyance or deed being executed by such an attorney.

(2) In this section 'relevant attorney' means a person (other than a trust corporation within the meaning of the Trustee Act 1925) who is acting either—

    (a) both as a trustee and as attorney for one or more other trustees, or

    (b) as attorney for two or more trustees,

and who is not acting together with any other person or persons.

(3) This section applies whether a relevant attorney is acting under a power created before or after the commencement of this Act (but in the case of such an attorney acting under an enduring power created before that commencement is without prejudice to any continuing application of section 3(3) of the Enduring Powers of Attorney Act 1985 to the enduring power after that commencement in accordance with section 4 above).

Authority of attorney to act in relation to land

10. **Extent of attorney's authority to act in relation to land**

(1) Where the donee of a power of attorney is authorised by the power to do an act of any description in relation to any land, his authority to do an act of that description at any time includes authority to do it with respect to any estate or interest in the land which is held at that time by the donor (whether alone or jointly with any other person or persons).

(2) Subsection (1) above—

(a) applies only if and so far as a contrary intention is not expressed in the instrument creating the power of attorney, and

(b) has effect subject to the terms of that instrument.

(3) This section applies only to powers of attorney created after the commencement of this Act.

Supplementary

11. **Interpretation**

(1) In this Act—

'land' has the same meaning as in the Trustee Act 1925, and

'enduring power' has the same meaning as in the Enduring Powers of Attorney Act 1985.

(2) References in this Act to the creation of a power of attorney are to the execution by the donor of the instrument creating it.

CONTRACTS (RIGHTS OF THIRD PARTIES) ACT 1999
(1999, c. 31)

1. **Right of third party to enforce contractual term**

(1) Subject to the provisions of this Act, a person who is not a party to a contract (a 'third party') may in his own right enforce a term of the contract if—

(a) the contract expressly provides that he may, or

(b) subject to subsection (2), the term purports to confer a benefit on him.

(2) Subsection (1)(b) does not apply if on a proper construction of the contract it appears that the parties did not intend the term to be enforceable by the third party.

(3) The third party must be expressly identified in the contract by name, as a member of a class or as answering a particular description but need not be in existence when the contract is entered into.

(4) This section does not confer a right on a third party to enforce a term of a contract otherwise than subject to and in accordance with any other relevant terms of the contract.

(5) For the purpose of exercising his right to enforce a term of the contract, there shall be available to the third party any remedy that would have been available to him in an action for breach of contract if he had been a party to the contract (and the rules relating to damages, injunctions, specific performance and other relief shall apply accordingly).

(6) Where a term of a contract excludes or limits liability in relation to any matter references in this Act to the third party enforcing the term shall be construed as references to his availing himself of the exclusion or limitation.

(7) In this Act, in relation to a term of a contract which is enforceable by a third party—

'the promisor' means the party to the contract against whom the term is enforceable by the third party, and

'the promisee' means the party to the contract by whom the term is enforceable against the promisor.

TRUSTEE ACT 2000
(2000, c. 29)

PART I
THE DUTY OF CARE

1.   The duty of care
  (1)   Whenever the duty under this subsection applies to a trustee, he must exercise such care and skill as is reasonable in the circumstances, having regard in particular—
  (a)   to any special knowledge or experience that he has or holds himself out as having, and
  (b)   if he acts as trustee in the course of a business or profession, to any special knowledge or experience that it is reasonable to expect of a person acting in the course of that kind of business or profession.
  (2)   In this Act the duty under subsection (1) is called 'the duty of care'.

2.   Application of duty of care
Schedule 1 makes provision about when the duty of care applies to a trustee.

PART II
INVESTMENT

3.   General power of investment
  (1)   Subject to the provisions of this Part, a trustee may make any kind of investment that he could make if he were absolutely entitled to the assets of the trust.
  (2)   In this Act the power under subsection (1) is called 'the general power of investment'.
  (3)   The general power of investment does not permit a trustee to make investments in land other than in loans secured on land (but see also section 8).
  (4)   A person invests in a loan secured on land if he has rights under any contract under which—
  (a)   one person provides another with credit, and
  (b)   the obligation of the borrower to repay is secured on land.
  (5)   'Credit' includes any cash loan or other financial accommodation.
  (6)   'Cash' includes money in any form.

4.   Standard investment criteria
  (1)   In exercising any power of investment, whether arising under this Part or otherwise, a trustee must have regard to the standard investment criteria.
  (2)   A trustee must from time to time review the investments of the trust and consider whether, having regard to the standard investment criteria, they should be varied.
  (3)   The standard investment criteria, in relation to a trust, are—
  (a)   the suitability to the trust of investments of the same kind as any particular investment proposed to be made or retained and of that particular investment as an investment of that kind, and
  (b)   the need for diversification of investments of the trust, in so far as is appropriate to the circumstances of the trust.

5.   Advice
  (1)   Before exercising any power of investment, whether arising under this Part or otherwise, a trustee must (unless the exception applies) obtain and consider proper advice about the way in which, having regard to the standard investment criteria, the power should be exercised.
  (2)   When reviewing the investments of the trust, a trustee must (unless the exception applies) obtain and consider proper advice about whether, having regard to the standard investment criteria, the investments should be varied.
  (3)   The exception is that a trustee need not obtain such advice if he reasonably concludes that in all the circumstances it is unnecessary or inappropriate to do so.
  (4)   Proper advice is the advice of a person who is reasonably believed by the trustee to be qualified to give it by his ability in and practical experience of financial and other matters relating to the proposed investment.

6.   Restriction or exclusion of this Part etc.

(1)   The general power of investment is—

(a)   in addition to powers conferred on trustees otherwise than by this Act, but

(b)   subject to any restriction or exclusion imposed by the trust instrument or by any enactment or any provision of subordinate legislation.

(2)   For the purposes of this Act, an enactment or a provision of subordinate legislation is not to be regarded as being, or as being part of, a trust instrument.

(3)   In this Act 'subordinate legislation' has the same meaning as in the Interpretation Act 1978.

7.   Existing trusts

(1)   This Part applies in relation to trusts whether created before or after its commencement.

(2)   No provision relating to the powers of a trustee contained in a trust instrument made before 3rd August 1961 is to be treated (for the purposes of section 6(1)(b)) as restricting or excluding the general power of investment.

(3)   A provision contained in a trust instrument made before the commencement of this Part which—

(a)   has effect under section 3(2) of the Trustee Investments Act 1961 as a power to invest under that Act, or

(b)   confers power to invest under that Act,

is to be treated as conferring the general power of investment on a trustee.

PART III
ACQUISTION OF LAND

8.   Power to acquire freehold and leasehold land

(1)   A trustee may acquire freehold or leasehold land in the United Kingdom—

(a)   as an investment,

(b)   for occupation by a beneficiary, or

(c)   for any other reason.

(2)   'Freehold or leasehold land' means—

(a)   in relation to England and Wales, a legal estate in land.

(b)   in relation to Scotland—

(i)   the estate or interest of the proprietor of the dominium utile or, in the case of land not held on feudal tenure, the estate or interest of the owner, or

(ii)   a tenancy, and

(c)   in relation to Northern Ireland, a legal estate in land, including land held under a fee farm grant.

(3)   For the purpose of exercising his functions as a trustee, a trustee who acquires land under this section has all the powers of an absolute owner in relation to the land.

9.   Restriction or exclusion of this Part etc.

The powers conferred by this Part are—

(a)   in addition to powers conferred on trustees otherwise than by this Part, but

(b)   subject to any restriction or exclusion imposed by the trust instrument or by any enactment or any provision of subordinate legislation.

10.   Existing trusts

(1)   This Part does not apply in relation to—

(a)   a trust of property which consists of or includes land which (despite section 2 of the Trusts of Land and Appointment of Trustees Act 1996) is settled land, or

(b)   a trust to which the Universities and College Estates Act 1925 applies.

(2)   Subject to subsection (1), this Part applies in relation to trusts whether created before or after its commencement.

PART IV
AGENTS, NOMINEES AND CUSTODIANS

Agents

11.   Power to employ agents

(1)   Subject to the provisions of this Part, the trustees of a trust may authorise any person to exercise any or all of their delegable functions as their agent.

(2)   In the case of a trust other than a charitable trust, the trustees' delegable functions consist of any function other than—

(a)   any function relating to whether or in what way any assets of the trust should be distributed,

(b)   any power to decide whether any fees or other payment due to be made out of the trust funds should be made out of income or capital.

(c)   any power to appoint a person to be a trustee of the trust, or

(d)   any power conferred by any other enactment or the trust instrument which permits the trustees to delegate any of their functions or to appoint a person to act as a nominee or custodian.

(3)   In the case of a charitable trust, the trustees' delegable functions are—

(a)   any function consisting of carrying out a decision that the trustees have taken;

(b)   any function relating to the investment of assets subject to the trust (including, in the case of land held as an investment, managing the land and creating or disposing of an interest in the land);

(c)   any function relating to the raising of funds for the trust otherwise than by means of profits of a trade which is an integral part of carrying out the trust's charitable purpose;

(d)   any other function prescribed by an order made by the Secretary of State.

(4)   For the purposes of subsection (3)(c) a trade is an integral part of carrying out a trust's charitable purpose if, whether carried on in the United Kingdom or elsewhere, the profits are applied solely to the purposes of the trust and either—

(a)   the trade is exercised in the course of the actual carrying out of a primary purpose of the trust, or

(b)   the work in connection with the trade is mainly carried out by beneficiaries of the trust.

(5)   The power to make an order under subsection (3)(d) is exercisable by statutory instrument which shall be subject to annulment in pursuance of a resolution of either House of Parliament.

12.   Persons who may act as agents

(1)   Subject to subsection (2), the persons whom the trustees may under section 11 authorise to exercise functions as their agent include one or more of their number.

(2)   The trustees may not authorise two (or more) persons to exercise the same function unless they are to exercise the function jointly.

(3)   The trustees may not under section 11 authorise a beneficiary to exercise any function as their agent (even if the beneficiary is also a trustee).

(4)   The trustees may under section 11 authorise a person to exercise functions as their agent even though he is also appointed to act as their nominee or custodian (whether under section 16, 17 or 18 or any other power).

13.   Linked functions etc.

(1)   Subject to subsections (2) and (5), a person who is authorised under section 11 to exercise a function is (whatever the terms of the agency) subject to any specific duties or restrictions attached to the function.

For example, a person who is authorised under section 11 to exercise the general power of investment is subject to the duties under section 4 in relation to that power.

(2)   A person who is authorised under section 11 to exercise a power which is subject to a requirement to obtain advice is not subject to the requirement if he is the kind of person

from whom it would have been proper for the trustees, in compliance with the requirement, to obtain advice.

(3) Subsections (4) and (5) apply to a trust to which section 11(1) of the Trusts of Land and Appointment of Trustees Act 1996 (duties to consult beneficiaries and give effect to their wishes) applies.

(4) The trustees may not under section 11 authorise a person to exercise any of their functions on terms that prevent them from complying with section 11(1) of the 1996 Act.

(5) A person who is authorised under section 11 to exercise any function relating to land subject to the trust is not subject to section 11(1) of the 1996 Act.

14. Terms of agency

(1) Subject to subsection (2) and sections 15(2) and 29 to 32, the trustees may authorise a person to exercise functions as their agent on such terms as to remuneration and other matters as they may determine.

(2) The trustees may not authorise a person to exercise functions as their agent on any of the terms mentioned in subsection (3) unless it is reasonably necessary for them to do so.

(3) The terms are—
    (a) a term permitting the agent to appoint a substitute;
    (b) a term restricting the liability of the agent or his substitute to the trustees or any beneficiary;
    (c) a term permitting the agent to act in circumstances capable of giving rise to a conflict of interest.

15. Asset management: special restrictions

(1) The trustees may not authorise a person to exercise any of their asset management functions as their agent except by an agreement which is in or evidenced in writing.

(2) The trustees may not authorise a person to exercise any of their asset management functions as their agent unless—
    (a) they have prepared a statement that gives guidance as to how the functions should be exercised ('a policy statement'), and
    (b) the agreement under which the agent is to act includes a term to the effect that he will secure compliance with—
        (i) the policy statement, or
        (ii) if the policy statement is revised or replaced under section 22, the revised or replacement policy statement.

(3) The trustees must formulate any guidance given in the policy statement with a view to ensuring that the functions will be exercised in the best interests of the trust.

(4) The policy statement must be in or evidenced in writing.

(5) The asset management functions of trustees are their functions relating to—
    (a) the investment of assets subject to the trust.
    (b) the acquisition of property which is to be subject to the trust, and
    (c) managing property which is subject to the trust and disposing of, or creating or disposing of an interest in, such property.

Nominees and custodians

16. Power to appoint nominees

(1) Subject to the provisions of this Part, the trustees of a trust may—
    (a) appoint a person to act as their nominee in relation to such of the assets of the trust as they determine (other than settled land), and
    (b) take such steps as are necessary to secure that those assets are vested in a person so appointed.

(2) An appointment under this section must be in or evidenced in writing.

(3) This section does not apply to any trust having a custodian trustee or in relation to any assets vested in the official custodian for charities.

17.   Power to appoint custodians

(1)   Subject to the provisions of this Part, the trustees of a trust may appoint a person to act as a custodian in relation to such of the assets of the trust as they may determine.

(2)   For the purposes of this Act a person is a custodian in relation to assets if he undertakes the safe custody of the assets or of any documents or records concerning the assets.

(3)   An appointment under this section must be in or evidenced in writing.

(4)   This section does not apply to any trust having a custodian trustee or in relation to any assets vested in the official custodian for charities.

18.   Investment in bearer securities

(1)   If trustees retain or invest in securities payable to bearer, they must appoint a person to act as a custodian of the securities.

(2)   Subsection (1) does not apply if the trust instrument or any enactment or provision of subordinate legislation contains provision which (however expressed) permits the trustees to retain or invest in securities payable to bearer without appointing a person to act as a custodian.

(3)   An appointment under this section must be in or evidenced in writing.

(4)   This section does not apply to any trust having a custodian trustee or in relation to any securities vested in the official custodian for charities.

19.   Persons who may be appointed as nominees or custodians

(1)   A person may not be appointed under section 16, 17 or 18 as a nominee or custodian unless one of the relevant conditions is satisfied.

(2)   The relevant conditions are that—

(a)   the person carries on a business which consists of or includes acting as a nominee or custodian;

(b)   the person is a body corporate which is controlled by the trustees;

(c)   the person is a body corporate recognised under section 9 of the Administration of Justice Act 1985.

(3)   The question whether a body corporate is controlled by trustees is to be determined in accordance with section 840 of the Income and Corporation Taxes Act 1988.

(4)   The trustees of a charitable trust which is not an exempt charity must act in accordance with any guidance given by the Charity Commissioners concerning the selection of a person for appointment as a nominee or custodian under section 16, 17 or 18.

(5)   Subject to subsections (1) and (4), the persons whom the trustees may under section 16, 17 or 18 appoint as a nominee or custodian include—

(a)   one of their number, if that one is a trust corporation, or

(b)   two (or more) of their number, if they are to act as joint nominees or joint custodians.

(6)   The trustees may under section 16 appoint a person to act as their nominee even though he is also—

(a)   appointed to act as their custodian (whether under section 17 or 18 or any other power), or

(b)   authorised to exercise functions as their agent (whether under section 11 or any other power).

(7)   Likewise, the trustees may under section 17 or 18 appoint a person to act as their custodian even though he is also—

(a)   appointed to act as their nominee (whether under section 16 or any other power), or

(b)   authorised to exercise functions as their agent (whether under section 11 or any other power).

20.   Terms of appointment of nominees and custodians

(1)   Subject to subsection (2) and sections 29 to 32, the trustees may under section 16, 17 or 18 appoint a person to act as a nominee or custodian on such terms as to remuneration and other matters as they may determine.

(2)   The trustees may not under section 16, 17 or 18 appoint a person to act as a nominee or custodian on any of the terms mentioned in subsection (3) unless it is reasonably necessary for them to do so.

(3)   The terms are—

    (a)   a term permitting the nominee or custodian to appoint a substitute;

    (b)   a term restricting the liability of the nominee or custodian or his substitute to the trustees or to any beneficiary;

    (c)   a term permitting the nominee or custodian to act in circumstances capable of giving rise to a conflict of interest.

Review of and liability for agents, nominees and custodians etc.

21.   Application of sections 22 and 23

(1)   Sections 22 and 23 apply in a case where trustees have, under section 11, 16, 17 or 18—

    (a)   authorised a person to exercise functions as their agent, or

    (b)   appointed a person to act as a nominee or custodian.

(2)   Subject to subsection (3), sections 22 and 23 also apply in a case where trustees have, under any power conferred on them by the trust instrument or by any enactment or any provision of subordinate legislation

    (a)   authorised a person to exercise functions as their agent, or

    (b)   appointed a person to act as a nominee or custodian.

(3)   If the application of section 22 or 23 is inconsistent with the terms of the trust instrument or the enactment or provision of subordinate legislation, the section in question does not apply.

22.   Review of agents, nominees and custodians etc.

(1)   While the agent, nominee or custodian continues to act for the trust, the trustees—

    (a)   must keep under review the arrangements under which the agent, nominee or custodian acts and how those arrangements are being put into effect,

    (b)   if circumstances make it appropriate to do so, must consider whether there is a need to exercise any power of intervention that they have, and

    (c)   if they consider that there is a need to exercise such a power, must do so.

(2)   If the agent has been authorised to exercise asset management functions, the duty under subsection (1) includes, in particular—

    (a)   a duty to consider whether there is any need to revise or replace the policy statement made for the purposes of section 15,

    (b)   if they consider that there is a need to revise or replace the policy statement. a duty to do so, and

    (c)   a duty to assess whether the policy statement (as it has effect for the time being) is being complied with.

(3)   Subsections (3) and (4) of section 15 apply to the revision or replacement of a policy statement under this section as they apply to the making of a policy statement under that section.

(4)   'Power of intervention' includes—

    (a)   a power to give directions to the agent, nominee or custodian;

    (b)   a power to revoke the authorisation or appointment.

23.   Liability for agents, nominees and custodians etc.

(1)   A trustee is not liable for any act or default of the agent, nominee or custodian unless he has failed to comply with the duty of care applicable to him, under paragraph 3 of Schedule 1—

    (a)   when entering into the arrangements under which the person acts as agent, nominee or custodian, or

    (b)   when carrying out his duties under section 22.

(2)   If a trustee has agreed a term under which the agent, nominee or custodian is permitted to appoint a substitute, the trustee is not liable for any act or default of the substitute unless he has failed to comply with the duty of care applicable to him, under paragraph 3 of Schedule 1—

    (a)   when agreeing that term, or

    (b)   when carrying out his duties under section 22 in so far as they relate to the use of the substitute.

Supplementary

24. Effect of trustees exceeding their powers

A failure by the trustees to act within the limits of the powers conferred by this Part—

    (a)   in authorising a person to exercise a function of theirs as an agent, or

    (b)   in appointing a person to act as a nominee or custodian, does not invalidate the authorisation or appointment.

25. Sole trustees

(1)   Subject to subsection (2), this Part applies in relation to a trust having a sole trustee as it applies in relation to other trusts (and references in this Part to trustees — except in sections 12(1) and (3) and 19(5) — are to be read accordingly).

(2)   Section 18 does not impose a duty on a sole trustee if that trustee is a trust corporation.

26. Restriction or exclusion of this Part etc.

The powers conferred by this Part are—

    (a)   in addition to powers conferred on trustees otherwise than by this Act, but

    (b)   subject to any restriction or exclusion imposed by the trust instrument or by any enactment or any provision of subordinate legislation.

27. Existing trusts

This Part applies in relation to trusts whether created before or after its commencement.

PART V

REMUNERATION

28. Trustee's entitlement to payment under trust instrument

(1)   Except to the extent (if any) to which the trust instrument makes inconsistent provision, subsections (2) to (4) apply to a trustee if—

    (a)   there is a provision in the trust instrument entitling him to receive payment out of trust funds in respect of services provided by him to or on behalf of the trust, and

    (b)   the trustee is a trust corporation or is acting in a professional capacity.

(2)   The trustee is to be treated as entitled under the trust instrument to receive payment in respect of services even if they are services which are capable of being provided by a lay trustee.

(3)   Subsection (2) applies to a trustee of a charitable trust who is not a trust corporation only—

    (a)   if he is not a sole trustee, and

    (b)   to the extent that a majority of the other trustees have agreed that it should apply to him.

(4)   Any payments to which the trustee is entitled in respect of services are to be treated as remuneration for services (and not as a gift) for the purposes of—

    (a)   section 15 of the Wills Act 1837 (gifts to an attesting witness to be void), and

    (b)   section 34(3) of the Administration of Estates Act 1925 (order in which estate to be paid out).

(5)   For the purposes of this Part, a trustee acts in a professional capacity if he acts in the course of a profession or business which consists of or includes the provision of services in connection with—

    (a)   the management or administration of trusts generally or a particular kind of trust, or

    (b)   any particular aspect of the management or administration of trusts generally or a particular kind of trust,

and the services he provides to or on behalf of the trust fall within that description.

(6)   For the purposes of this Part, a person acts as a lay trustee if he—

    (a)   is not a trust corporation, and

    (b)   does not act in a professional capacity.

29.   Remuneration of certain trustees

(1)   Subject to subsection (5), a trustee who—

    (a)   is a trust corporation, but

    (b)   is not a trustee of a charitable trust,

is entitled to receive reasonable remuneration out of the trust funds for any services that the trust corporation provides to or on behalf of the trust.

(2)   Subject to subsection (5), a trustee who—

    (a)   acts in a professional capacity, but

    (b)   is not a trust corporation, a trustee of a charitable trust or a sole trustee,

is entitled to receive reasonable remuneration out of the trust funds for any services that he provides to or on behalf of the trust if each other trustee has agreed in writing that he may be remunerated for the services.

(3)   'Reasonable remuneration' means, in relation to the provision of services by a trustee such remuneration as is reasonable in the circumstances for the provision of those services to or on behalf of that trust by that trustee and for the purposes of subsection (1) includes, in relation to the provision of services by a trustee who is an authorised institution under the Banking Act 1987 and provides the services in that capacity, the institution's reasonable charges for the provision of such services.

(4)   A trustee is entitled to remuneration under this section even if the services in question are capable of being provided by a lay trustee.

(5)   A trustee is not entitled to remuneration under this section if any provision about his entitlement to remuneration has been made—

    (a)   by the trust instrument, or

    (b)   by any enactment or any provision of subordinate legislation.

(6)   This section applies to a trustee who has been authorised under a power conferred by Part IV or the trust instrument—

    (a)   to exercise functions as an agent of the trustees, or

    (b)   to act as a nominee or custodian,

as it applies to any other trustee.

30.   Remuneration of trustees of charitable trusts

(1)   The Secretary of State may by regulations make provision for the remuneration of trustees of charitable trusts who are trust corporations or act in a professional capacity.

(2)   The power under subsection (1) includes power to make provision for the remuneration of a trustee who has been authorised under a power conferred by Part IV or any other enactment or any provision of subordinate legislation, or by the trust instrument—

    (a)   to exercise functions as an agent of the trustees, or

    (b)   to act as a nominee or custodian.

(3)   Regulations under this section may—

    (a)   make different provision for different cases:

    (b)   contain such supplemental, incidental, consequential and transitional provision as the Secretary of State considers appropriate.

(4)   The power to make regulations under this section is exercisable by statutory instrument, but no such instrument shall be made unless a draft of it has been laid before Parliament and approved by a resolution of each House of Parliament.

31.   Trustees' expenses

(1)   A trustee—

    (a)   is entitled to be reimbursed from the trust funds, or

    (b)   may pay out of the trust funds,

expenses properly incurred by him when acting on behalf of the trust.

(2)   This section applies to a trustee who has been authorised under a power conferred by Part IV or any other enactment or any provision of subordinate legislation, or by the trust instrument—

    (a)   to exercise functions as an agent of the trustees, or

(b)   to act as a nominee or custodian,

as it applies to any other trustee.

32.   Remuneration and expenses of agents, nominees and custodians

(1)   This section applies if, under a power conferred by Part IV or any other enactment or any provision of subordinate legislation, or by the trust instrument, a person other than a trustee has been—

(a)   authorised to exercise functions as an agent of the trustees, or

(b)   appointed to act as a nominee or custodian.

(2)   The trustees may remunerate the agent, nominee or custodian out of the trust funds for services if—

(a)   he is engaged on terms entitling him to be remunerated for those services, and

(b)   the amount does not exceed such remuneration as is reasonable in the circumstances for the provision of those services by him to or on behalf of that trust.

(3)   The trustees may reimburse the agent, nominee or custodian out of the trust funds for any expenses properly incurred by him in exercising functions as an agent, nominee or custodian.

33.   Application

(1)   Subject to subsection (2), sections 28, 29, 31 and 32 apply in relation to services provided to or on behalf of, or (as the case may be) expenses incurred on or after their commencement on behalf of, trusts whenever created.

(2)   Nothing in section 28 or 29 is to be treated as affecting the operation of—

(a)   section 15 of the Wills Act 1837, or

(b)   section 34(3) of the Administration of Estates Act 1925,

in relation to any death occurring before the commencement of section 28 or (as the case may be) section 29.

PART VI
MISCELLANEOUS AND SUPPLEMENTARY

35.   Personal representatives

(1)   Subject to the following provisions of this section, this Act applies in relation to a personal representative administering an estate according to the law as it applies to a trustee carrying out a trust for beneficiaries.

(2)   For this purpose this Act is to be read with the appropriate modifications and in particular—

(a)   references to the trust instrument are to be read as references to the will,

(b)   references to a beneficiary or to beneficiaries, apart from the reference to a beneficiary in section 8(1)(b), are to be read as references to a person or the persons interested in the due administration of the estate, and

(c)   the reference to a beneficiary in section 8(1)(b) is to be read as a reference to a person who under the will of the deceased or under the law relating to intestacy is beneficially interested in the estate.

(3)   Remuneration to which a personal representative is entitled under section 28 or 29 is to be treated as an administration expense for the purposes of—

(a)   section 34(3) of the Administration of Estates Act 1925 (order in which estate to be paid out), and

(b)   any provision giving reasonable administration expenses priority over the preferential debts listed in Schedule 6 to the Insolvency Act 1986.

(4)   Nothing in subsection (3) is to be treated as affecting the operation of the provisions mentioned in paragraphs (a) and (b) of that subsection in relation to any death occurring before the commencement of this section.

36.   Pension schemes

(1)   In this section 'pension scheme' means an occupational pension scheme (within the meaning of the Pension Schemes Act 1993) established under a trust and subject to the law of England and Wales.

(2) Part I does not apply in so far as it imposes a duty of care in relation to—

    (a) the functions described in paragraphs 1 and 2 of Schedule 1, or

    (b) the functions described in paragraph 3 of that Schedule to the extent that they relate to trustees—

        (i) authorising a person to exercise their functions with respect to investment, or

        (ii) appointing a person to act as their nominee or custodian.

(3) Nothing in Part II or III applies to the trustees of any pension scheme.

(4) Part IV applies to the trustees of a pension scheme subject to the restrictions in subsections (5) to (8).

(5) The trustees of a pension scheme may not under Part IV authorise any person to exercise any functions relating to investment as their agent.

(6) The trustees of a pension scheme may not under Part IV authorise a person who is—

    (a) an employer in relation to the scheme, or

    (b) connected with or an associate of such an employer,

to exercise any of their functions as their agent.

(7) For the purposes of subsection (6)—

    (a) 'employer', in relation to a scheme, has the same meaning as in the Pensions Act 1995;

    (b) sections 249 and 435 of the Insolvency Act 1986 apply for the purpose of determining whether a person is connected with or an associate of an employer.

39. Interpretation

(1) In this Act—

'asset' includes any right or interest;

'charitable trust' means a trust under which property is held for charitable purposes and 'charitable purposes' has the same meaning as in the Charities Act 1993;

'custodian trustee' has the same meaning as in the Public Trustee Act 1906;

'enactment' includes any provision of a Measure of the Church Assembly or of the General Synod of the Church of England;

'exempt charity' has the same meaning as in the Charities Act 1993;

'functions' includes powers and duties;

'legal mortgage' has the same meaning as in the Law of Property Act 1925;

'personal representative' has the same meaning as in the Trustee Act 1925;

'settled land' has the same meaning as in the Settled Land Act 1925;

'trust corporation' has the same meaning as in the Trustee Act 1925;

'trust funds' means income or capital funds of the trust.

. . .

LAND REGISTRATION ACT 2002
(2002, c. 9)

PART 1
PRELIMINARY

1. Register of title

(1) There is to continue to be a register of title kept by the registrar.

(2) Rules may make provision about how the register is to be kept and may, in particular, make provision about—

    (a) the information to be included in the register,

    (b) the form in which information included in the register is to be kept, and

    (c) the arrangement of that information.

2. Scope of title registration

This Act makes provision about the registration of title to—

    (a) unregistered legal estates which are interests of any of the following kinds—

(i)   an estate in land,

(ii)   a rentcharge,

(iii)   a franchise,

(iv)   a profit a prendre in gross, and

(v)   any other interest or charge which subsists for the benefit of, or is a charge on, an interest the title to which is registered; and

(b) interests capable of subsisting at law which are created by a disposition of an interest the title to which is registered.

PART 2

FIRST REGISTRATION OF TITLE

CHAPTER 1

FIRST REGISTRATION

Voluntary registration

3.   When title may be registered

(1) This section applies to any unregistered legal estate which is an interest of any of the following kinds—

(a)   an estate in land,

(b)   a rentcharge,

(c)   a franchise, and

(d)   a profit a prendre in gross.

(2) Subject to the following provisions, a person may apply to the registrar to be registered as the proprietor of an unregistered legal estate to which this section applies if—

(a)   the estate is vested in him, or

(b)   he is entitled to require the estate to be vested in him.

(3) Subject to subsection (4), an application under subsection (2) in respect of a leasehold estate may only be made if the estate was granted for a term of which more than seven years are unexpired.

(4) In the case of an estate in land, subsection (3) does not apply if the right to possession under the lease is discontinuous.

(5) A person may not make an application under subsection (2)(a) in respect of a leasehold estate vested in him as a mortgagee where there is a subsisting right of redemption.

(6) A person may not make an application under subsection (2)(b) if his entitlement is as a person who has contracted to buy under a contract.

(7) If a person holds in the same right both—

(a)   a lease in possession, and

(b)   a lease to take effect in possession on, or within a month of, the end of the lease in possession, then, to the extent that they relate to the same land, they are to be treated for the purposes of this section as creating one continuous term.

Compulsory registration

4.   When title must be registered

(1) The requirement of registration applies on the occurrence of any of the following events—

(a)   the transfer of a qualifying estate—

(i)   for valuable or other consideration, by way of gift or in pursuance of an order of any court, or

(ii)   by means of an assent (including a vesting assent);

(b)   the transfer of an unregistered legal estate in land in circumstances where section 171A of the Housing Act 1985 applies (disposal by landlord which leads to a person no longer being a secure tenant);

(c)   the grant out of a qualifying estate of an estate in land—

(i)   for a term of years absolute of more than seven years from the date of the grant, and

(ii)   for valuable or other consideration, by way of gift or in pursuance of an order of any court;

(d)   the grant out of a qualifying estate of an estate in land for a term of years absolute to take effect in possession after the end of the period of three months beginning with the date of the grant;

(e)   the grant of a lease in pursuance of Part 5 of the Housing Act 1985 (the right to buy) out of an unregistered legal estate in land;

(f)   the grant of a lease out of an unregistered legal estate in land in such circumstances as are mentioned in paragraph (b);

(g)   the creation of a protected first legal mortgage of a qualifying estate.

(2)   For the purposes of subsection (1), a qualifying estate is an unregistered legal estate which is—

(a)   a freehold estate in land, or

(b)   a leasehold estate in land for a term which, at the time of the transfer, grant or creation, has more than seven years to run.

(3)   In subsection (1)(a), the reference to transfer does not include transfer by operation of law.

(4)   Subsection (1)(a) does not apply to—

(a)   the assignment of a mortgage term, or

(b)   the assignment or surrender of a lease to the owner of the immediate reversion where the term is to merge in that reversion.

(5)   Subsection (1)(c) does not apply to the grant of an estate to a person as a mortgagee.

(6)   For the purposes of subsection (1)(a) and (c), if the estate transferred or granted has a negative value, it is to be regarded as transferred or granted for valuable or other consideration.

(7)   In subsection (1)(a) and (c), references to transfer or grant by way of gift include transfer or grant for the purpose of—

(a)   constituting a trust under which the settlor does not retain the whole of the beneficial interest, or

(b)   uniting the bare legal title and the beneficial interest in property held under a trust under which the settlor did not, on constitution, retain the whole of the beneficial interest.

(8)   For the purposes of subsection (1)(g)—

(a)   a legal mortgage is protected if it takes effect on its creation as a mortgage to be protected by the deposit of documents relating to the mortgaged estate, and

(b)   a first legal mortgage is one which, on its creation, ranks in priority ahead of any other mortgages then affecting the mortgaged estate.

(9)   In this section—

'land' does not include mines and minerals held apart from the surface;

'vesting assent' has the same meaning as in the Settled Land Act 1925.

5.   Power to extend section 4

(1)   The Lord Chancellor may by order—

(a)   amend section 4 so as to add to the events on the occurrence of which the requirement of registration applies such relevant event as he may specify in the order, and

(b)   make such consequential amendments of any provision of, or having effect under, any Act as he thinks appropriate.

(2)   For the purposes of subsection (1)(a), a relevant event is an event relating to an unregistered legal estate which is an interest of any of the following kinds—

(a)   an estate in land,

(b)   a rentcharge,

(c)   a franchise, and

(d)   a profit a prendre in gross.

(3)   The power conferred by subsection (1) may not be exercised so as to require the title to an estate granted to a person as a mortgagee to be registered.

(4)   Before making an order under this section the Lord Chancellor must consult such persons as he considers appropriate.

6.   Duty to apply for registration of title

(1)   If the requirement of registration applies, the responsible estate owner, or his successor in title, must, before the end of the period for registration, apply to the registrar to be registered as the proprietor of the registrable estate.

(2)   If the requirement of registration applies because of section 4(1)(g)—

    (a)   the registrable estate is the estate charged by the mortgage, and

    (b)   the responsible estate owner is the owner of that estate.

(3)   If the requirement of registration applies otherwise than because of section 4(1)(g)—

    (a)   the registrable estate is the estate which is transferred or granted, and

    (b)   the responsible estate owner is the transferee or grantee of that estate.

(4)   The period for registration is 2 months beginning with the date on which the relevant event occurs, or such longer period as the registrar may provide under subsection (5).

(5)   If on the application of any interested person the registrar is satisfied that there is good reason for doing so, he may by order provide that the period for registration ends on such later date as he may specify in the order.

(6)   Rules may make provision enabling the mortgagee under any mortgage falling within section 4(1)(g) to require the estate charged by the mortgage to be registered whether or not the mortgagor consents.

7.   Effect of non-compliance with section 6

(1)   If the requirement of registration is not complied with, the transfer, grant or creation becomes void as regards the transfer, grant or creation of a legal estate.

(2)   On the application of subsection (1)—

    (a)   in a case falling within section 4(1)(a) or (b), the title to the legal estate reverts to the transferor who holds it on a bare trust for the transferee, and

    (b)   in a case falling within section 4(1)(c) to (g), the grant or creation has effect as a contract made for valuable consideration to grant or create the legal estate concerned.

(3)   If an order under section 6(5) is made in a case where subsection (1) has already applied, that application of the subsection is to be treated as not having occurred.

(4)   The possibility of reverter under subsection (1) is to be disregarded for the purposes of determining whether a fee simple is a fee simple absolute.

8.   Liability for making good void transfers etc

If a legal estate is retransferred, regranted or recreated because of a failure to comply with the requirement of registration, the transferee, grantee or, as the case may be, the mortgagor—

    (a)   is liable to the other party for all the proper costs of and incidental to the retransfer, regrant or recreation of the legal estate, and

    (b)   is liable to indemnify the other party in respect of any other liability reasonably incurred by him because of the failure to comply with the requirement of registration.

Classes of title

9.   Titles to freehold estates

(1)   In the case of an application for registration under this Chapter of a freehold estate, the classes of title with which the applicant may be registered as proprietor are—

    (a)   absolute title,

    (b)   qualified title, and

    (c)   possessory title; and the following provisions deal with when each of the classes of title is available.

(2)   A person may be registered with absolute title if the registrar is of the opinion that the person's title to the estate is such as a willing buyer could properly be advised by a competent professional adviser to accept.

(3)   In applying subsection (2), the registrar may disregard the fact that a person's title appears to him to be open to objection if he is of the opinion that the defect will not cause the holding under the title to be disturbed.

(4)   A person may be registered with qualified title if the registrar is of the opinion that the person's title to the estate has been established only for a limited period or subject to certain reservations which cannot be disregarded under subsection (3).

(5)   A person may be registered with possessory title if the registrar is of the opinion—

(a)   that the person is in actual possession of the land, or in receipt of the rents and profits of the land, by virtue of the estate, and

(b)   that there is no other class of title with which he may be registered.

10.   Titles to leasehold estates

(1)   In the case of an application for registration under this Chapter of a leasehold estate, the classes of title with which the applicant may be registered as proprietor are—

(a)   absolute title,

(b)   good leasehold title,

(c)   qualified title, and

(d)   possessory title; and the following provisions deal with when each of the classes of title is available.

(2)   A person may be registered with absolute title if—

(a)   the registrar is of the opinion that the person's title to the estate is such as a willing buyer could properly be advised by a competent professional adviser to accept, and

(b)   the registrar approves the lessor's title to grant the lease.

(3)   A person may be registered with good leasehold title if the registrar is of the opinion that the person's title to the estate is such as a willing buyer could properly be advised by a competent professional adviser to accept.

(4)   In applying subsection (2) or (3), the registrar may disregard the fact that a person's title appears to him to be open to objection if he is of the opinion that the defect will not cause the holding under the title to be disturbed.

(5)   A person may be registered with qualified title if the registrar is of the opinion that the person's title to the estate, or the lessor's title to the reversion, has been established only for a limited period or subject to certain reservations which cannot be disregarded under subsection (4).

(6)   A person may be registered with possessory title if the registrar is of the opinion—

(a)   that the person is in actual possession of the land, or in receipt of the rents and profits of the land, by virtue of the estate, and

(b)   that there is no other class of title with which he may be registered.

Effect of first registration

11.   Freehold estates

(1)   This section is concerned with the registration of a person under this Chapter as the proprietor of a freehold estate.

(2)   Registration with absolute title has the effect described in subsections (3) to (5).

(3)   The estate is vested in the proprietor together with all interests subsisting for the benefit of the estate.

(4)   The estate is vested in the proprietor subject only to the following interests affecting the estate at the time of registration—

(a)   interests which are the subject of an entry in the register in relation to the estate,

(b)   unregistered interests which fall within any of the paragraphs of Schedule 1, and

(c)   interests acquired under the Limitation Act 1980 of which the proprietor has notice.

(5)   If the proprietor is not entitled to the estate for his own benefit, or not entitled solely for his own benefit, then, as between himself and the persons beneficially entitled to the estate, the estate is vested in him subject to such of their interests as he has notice of.

(6) Registration with qualified title has the same effect as registration with absolute title, except that it does not affect the enforcement of any estate, right or interest which appears from the register to be excepted from the effect of registration.

(7) Registration with possessory title has the same effect as registration with absolute title, except that it does not affect the enforcement of any estate, right or interest adverse to, or in derogation of, the proprietor's title subsisting at the time of registration or then capable of arising.

12.   Leasehold estates

(1) This section is concerned with the registration of a person under this Chapter as the proprietor of a leasehold estate.

(2) Registration with absolute title has the effect described in subsections (3) to (5).

(3) The estate is vested in the proprietor together with all interests subsisting for the benefit of the estate.

(4) The estate is vested subject only to the following interests affecting the estate at the time of registration—
   (a)   implied and express covenants, obligations and liabilities incident to the estate,
   (b)   interests which are the subject of an entry in the register in relation to the estate,
   (c)   unregistered interests which fall within any of the paragraphs of Schedule 1, and
   (d)   interests acquired under the Limitation Act 1980 of which the proprietor has notice.

(5) If the proprietor is not entitled to the estate for his own benefit, or not entitled solely for his own benefit, then, as between himself and the persons beneficially entitled to the estate, the estate is vested in him subject to such of their interests as he has notice of.

(6) Registration with good leasehold title has the same effect as registration with absolute title, except that it does not affect the enforcement of any estate, right or interest affecting, or in derogation of, the title of the lessor to grant the lease.

(7) Registration with qualified title has the same effect as registration with absolute title except that it does not affect the enforcement of any estate, right or interest which appears from the register to be excepted from the effect of registration.

(8) Registration with possessory title has the same effect as registration with absolute title, except that it does not affect the enforcement of any estate, right or interest adverse to, or in derogation of, the proprietor's title subsisting at the time of registration or then capable of arising.

Dependent estates

13.   Appurtenant rights and charges

Rules may—
   (a)   make provision for the registration of the proprietor of a registered estate as the proprietor of an unregistered legal estate which subsists for the benefit of the registered estate;
   (b)   make provision for the registration of a person as the proprietor of an unregistered legal estate which is a charge on a registered estate.

Supplementary

14.   Rules about first registration

Rules may—
   (a)   make provision about the making of applications for registration under this Chapter;
   (b)   make provision about the functions of the registrar following the making of such an application, including provision about—
      (i)   the examination of title, and
      (ii)   the entries to be made in the register where such an application is approved;
   (c)   make provision about the effect of any entry made in the register in pursuance of such an application.

CHAPTER 2
CAUTIONS AGAINST FIRST REGISTRATION

15.   **Right to lodge**

(1)   A person may lodge a caution against the registration of title to an unregistered legal estate if he claims to be—

    (a)   the owner of a qualifying estate, or

    (b)   entitled to an interest affecting a qualifying estate.

(2)   For the purposes of subsection (1), a qualifying estate is a legal estate which—

    (a)   relates to land to which the caution relates, and

    (b)   is an interest of any of the following kinds—

       (i)   an estate in land,

       (ii)   a rentcharge,

       (iii)   a franchise, and

       (iv)   a profit a prendre in gross.

(3)   . . .

(4)   The right under subsection (1) is exercisable by application to the registrar.

16.   **Effect**

(1)   Where an application for registration under this Part relates to a legal estate which is the subject of a caution against first registration, the registrar must give the cautioner notice of the application and of his right to object to it.

(2)   The registrar may not determine an application to which subsection (1) applies before the end of such period as rules may provide, unless the cautioner has exercised his right to object to the application or given the registrar notice that he does not intend to do so.

(3)   Except as provided by this section, a caution against first registration has no effect and, in particular, has no effect on the validity or priority of any interest of the cautioner in the legal estate to which the caution relates.

(4)   For the purposes of subsection (1), notice given by a person acting on behalf of an applicant for registration under this Part is to be treated as given by the registrar if—

    (a)   the person is of a description provided by rules, and

    (b)   notice is given in such circumstances as rules may provide.

17.   **Withdrawal**

The cautioner may withdraw a caution against first registration by application to the registrar.

18.   **Cancellation**

(1)   A person may apply to the registrar for cancellation of a caution against first registration if he is—

    (a)   the owner of the legal estate to which the caution relates, or

    (b)   a person of such other description as rules may provide.

(2)   Subject to rules, no application under subsection (1)(a) may be made by a person who—

    (a)   consented in such manner as rules may provide to the lodging of the caution, or

    (b)   derives title to the legal estate by operation of law from a person who did so.

(3)   Where an application is made under subsection (1), the registrar must give the cautioner notice of the application and of the effect of subsection (4).

(4)   If the cautioner does not exercise his right to object to the application before the end of such period as rules may provide, the registrar must cancel the caution.

19.   **Cautions register**

(1)   The registrar must keep a register of cautions against first registration.

(2)   Rules may make provision about how the cautions register is to be kept and may, in particular, make provision about—

    (a)   the information to be included in the register,

    (b)   the form in which information included in the register is to be kept, and

    (c)   the arrangement of that information.

20. Alteration of register by court

(1) The court may make an order for alteration of the cautions register for the purpose of—

    (a) correcting a mistake, or

    (b) bringing the register up to date.

(2) An order under subsection (1) has effect when served on the registrar to impose a duty on him to give effect to it.

(3) Rules may make provision about—

    (a) the circumstances in which there is a duty to exercise the power under subsection (1),

    (b) the form of an order under that subsection, and

    (c) service of such an order.

21. Alteration of register by registrar

(1) The registrar may alter the cautions register for the purpose of—

    (a) correcting a mistake, or

    (b) bringing the register up to date.

(2) Rules may make provision about—

    (a) the circumstances in which there is a duty to exercise the power under subsection (1),

    (b) how the cautions register is to be altered in exercise of that power,

    (c) applications for the exercise of that power, and

    (d) procedure in relation to the exercise of that power, whether on application or otherwise.

(3) Where an alteration is made under this section, the registrar may pay such amount as he thinks fit in respect of any costs reasonably incurred by a person in connection with the alteration.

22. Supplementary

In this Chapter, 'the cautioner', in relation to a caution against first registration, means the person who lodged the caution, or such other person as rules may provide.

PART 3

DISPOSITIONS OF REGISTERED LAND

Powers of disposition

23. Owner's powers

(1) Owner's powers in relation to a registered estate consist of—

    (a) power to make a disposition of any kind permitted by the general law in relation to an interest of that description, other than a mortgage by demise or sub-demise, and

    (b) power to charge the estate at law with the payment of money.

(2) Owner's powers in relation to a registered charge consist of—

    (a) power to make a disposition of any kind permitted by the general law in relation to an interest of that description, other than a legal sub-mortgage, and

    (b) power to charge at law with the payment of money indebtedness secured by the registered charge.

(3) In subsection (2)(a), 'legal sub-mortgage' means—

    (a) a transfer by way of mortgage,

    (b) a sub-mortgage by sub-demise, and

    (c) a charge by way of legal mortgage.

24. Right to exercise owner's powers

A person is entitled to exercise owner's powers in relation to a registered estate or charge if he is—

(a) the registered proprietor, or

(b) entitled to be registered as the proprietor.

25. Mode of exercise

(1) A registrable disposition of a registered estate or charge only has effect if it complies with such requirements as to form and content as rules may provide.

(2)   Rules may apply subsection (1) to any other kind of disposition which depends for its effect on registration.

26.   Protection of disponees

(1)   Subject to subsection (2), a person's right to exercise owner's powers in relation to a registered estate or charge is to be taken to be free from any limitation affecting the validity of a disposition.

(2)   Subsection (1) does not apply to a limitation—

     (a)   reflected by an entry in the register, or

     (b)   imposed by, or under, this Act.

(3)   This section has effect only for the purpose of preventing the title of a disponee being questioned (and so does not affect the lawfulness of a disposition).

Registrable dispositions

27.   Dispositions required to be registered

(1)   If a disposition of a registered estate or registered charge is required to be completed by registration, it does not operate at law until the relevant registration requirements are met.

(2)   In the case of a registered estate, the following are the dispositions which are required to be completed by registration—

     (a)   a transfer,

     (b)   where the registered estate is an estate in land, the grant of a term of years absolute—

         (i)   for a term of more than seven years from the date of the grant,

         (ii)   to take effect in possession after the end of the period of three months beginning with the date of the grant,

         (iii)   under which the right to possession is discontinuous,

         (iv)   in pursuance of Part 5 of the Housing Act 1985 (the right to buy), or

         (v)   in circumstances where section 171A of that Act applies (disposal by landlord which leads to a person no longer being a secure tenant),

     (c)   where the registered estate is a franchise or manor, the grant of a lease,

     (d)   the express grant or reservation of an interest of a kind falling within section 1(2)(a) of the Law of Property Act 1925, other than one which is capable of being registered under the Commons Registration Act 1965,

     (e)   the express grant or reservation of an interest of a kind falling within section 1(2)(b) or (e) of the Law of Property Act 1925, and

     (f)   the grant of a legal charge.

(3)   In the case of a registered charge, the following are the dispositions which are required to be completed by registration—

     (a)   a transfer, and

     (b)   the grant of a sub-charge.

(4)   Schedule 2 to this Act (which deals with the relevant registration requirements) has effect.

(5)   This section applies to dispositions by operation of law as it applies to other dispositions, but with the exception of the following—

     (a)   a transfer on the death or bankruptcy of an individual proprietor,

     (b)   a transfer on the dissolution of a corporate proprietor, and

     (c)   the creation of a legal charge which is a local land charge.

(6)   Rules may make provision about applications to the registrar for the purpose of meeting registration requirements under this section.

(7)   In subsection (2)(d), the reference to express grant does not include grant as a result of the operation of section 62 of the Law of Property Act 1925.

Effect of dispositions on priority

28.   Basic rule

(1)   Except as provided by sections 29 and 30, the priority of an interest affecting a registered estate or charge is not affected by a disposition of the estate or charge.

(2)   It makes no difference for the purposes of this section whether the interest or disposition is registered.

29.   Effect of registered dispositions: estates

(1)   If a registrable disposition of a registered estate is made for valuable consideration, completion of the disposition by registration has the effect of postponing to the interest under the disposition any interest affecting the estate immediately before the disposition whose priority is not protected at the time of registration.

(2)   For the purposes of subsection (1), the priority of an interest is protected—

    (a)   in any case, if the interest—

        (i)   is a registered charge or the subject of a notice in the register,

        (ii)   falls within any of the paragraphs of Schedule 3, or

        (iii)   appears from the register to be excepted from the effect of registration, and

    (b)   in the case of a disposition of a leasehold estate, if the burden of the interest is incident to the estate.

(3)   Subsection (2)(a)(ii) does not apply to an interest which has been the subject of a notice in the register at any time since the coming into force of this section.

(4)   Where the grant of a leasehold estate in land out of a registered estate does not involve a registrable disposition, this section has effect as if—

    (a)   the grant involved such a disposition, and

    (b)   the disposition were registered at the time of the grant.

30.   Effect of registered dispositions: charges

(1)   If a registrable disposition of a registered charge is made for valuable consideration, completion of the disposition by registration has the effect of postponing to the interest under the disposition any interest affecting the charge immediately before the disposition whose priority is not protected at the time of registration.

(2)   For the purposes of subsection (1), the priority of an interest is protected—

    (a)   in any case, if the interest—

        (i)   is a registered charge or the subject of a notice in the register,

        (ii)   falls within any of the paragraphs of Schedule 3, or

        (iii)   appears from the register to be excepted from the effect of registration, and

    (b)   in the case of a disposition of a charge which relates to a leasehold estate, if the burden of the interest is incident to the estate.

(3)   Subsection (2)(a)(ii) does not apply to an interest which has been the subject of a notice in the register at any time since the coming into force of this section.

31.   Inland Revenue charges

The effect of a disposition of a registered estate or charge on a charge under section 237 of the Inheritance Tax Act 1984 (charge for unpaid tax) is to be determined, not in accordance with sections 28 to 30 above, but in accordance with sections 237(6) and 238 of that Act (under which a purchaser in good faith for money or money's worth takes free from the charge in the absence of registration).

PART 4
NOTICES AND RESTRICTIONS

Notices

32.   Nature and effect

(1)   A notice is an entry in the register in respect of the burden of an interest affecting a registered estate or charge.

(2)   The entry of a notice is to be made in relation to the registered estate or charge affected by the interest concerned.

(3)   The fact that an interest is the subject of a notice does not necessarily mean that the interest is valid, but does mean that the priority of the interest, if valid, is protected for the purposes of sections 29 and 30.

33.   Excluded interests

No notice may be entered in the register in respect of any of the following—

(a)   an interest under—

    (i)   a trust of land, or

    (ii)   a settlement under the Settled Land Act 1925,

(b)   a leasehold estate in land which—

    (i)   is granted for a term of years of three years or less from the date of the grant, and

    (ii)   is not required to be registered,

(c)   a restrictive covenant made between a lessor and lessee, so far as relating to the demised premises,

(d)   an interest which is capable of being registered under the Commons Registration Act 1965, and

(e)   an interest in any coal or coal mine, the rights attached to any such interest and the rights of any person under section 38, 49 or 51 of the Coal Industry Act 1994.

34.   Entry on application

(1)   A person who claims to be entitled to the benefit of an interest affecting a registered estate or charge may, if the interest is not excluded by section 33, apply to the registrar for the entry in the register of a notice in respect of the interest.

(2)   Subject to rules, an application under this section may be for—

    (a)   an agreed notice, or

    (b)   a unilateral notice.

(3)   The registrar may only approve an application for an agreed notice if—

    (a)   the applicant is the relevant registered proprietor, or a person entitled to be registered as such proprietor,

    (b)   the relevant registered proprietor, or a person entitled to be registered as such proprietor, consents to the entry of the notice, or

    (c)   the registrar is satisfied as to the validity of the applicant's claim.

(4)   In subsection (3), references to the relevant registered proprietor are to the proprietor of the registered estate or charge affected by the interest to which the application relates.

35.   Unilateral notices

(1)   If the registrar enters a notice in the register in pursuance of an application under section 34(2)(b) ('a unilateral notice'), he must give notice of the entry to—

    (a)   the proprietor of the registered estate or charge to which it relates, and

    (b)   such other persons as rules may provide.

(2)   A unilateral notice must—

    (a)   indicate that it is such a notice, and

    (b)   identify who is the beneficiary of the notice.

(3)   The person shown in the register as the beneficiary of a unilateral notice, or such other person as rules may provide, may apply to the registrar for the removal of the notice from the register.

36.   Cancellation of unilateral notices

(1)   A person may apply to the registrar for the cancellation of a unilateral notice if he is—

    (a)   the registered proprietor of the estate or charge to which the notice relates, or

    (b)   a person entitled to be registered as the proprietor of that estate or charge.

(2)   Where an application is made under subsection (1), the registrar must give the beneficiary of the notice notice of the application and of the effect of subsection (3).

(3)   If the beneficiary of the notice does not exercise his right to object to the application before the end of such period as rules may provide, the registrar must cancel the notice.

(4)   In this section—

'beneficiary', in relation to a unilateral notice, means the person shown in the register as the beneficiary of the notice, or such other person as rules may provide;

'unilateral notice' means a notice entered in the register in pursuance of an application under section 34(2)(b).

37. **Unregistered interests**

(1) If it appears to the registrar that a registered estate is subject to an unregistered interest which—

(a) falls within any of the paragraphs of Schedule 1, and

(b) is not excluded by section 33, he may enter a notice in the register in respect of the interest.

(2) The registrar must give notice of an entry under this section to such persons as rules may provide.

38. **Registrable dispositions**

Where a person is entered in the register as the proprietor of an interest under a disposition falling within section 27(2)(b) to (e), the registrar must also enter a notice in the register in respect of that interest.

39. **Supplementary**

Rules may make provision about the form and content of notices in the register.

Restrictions

40. **Nature**

(1) A restriction is an entry in the register regulating the circumstances in which a disposition of a registered estate or charge may be the subject of an entry in the register.

(2) A restriction may, in particular—

(a) prohibit the making of an entry in respect of any disposition, or a disposition of a kind specified in the restriction;

(b) prohibit the making of an entry—

(i) indefinitely,

(ii) for a period specified in the restriction, or

(iii) until the occurrence of an event so specified.

(3) Without prejudice to the generality of subsection (2)(b)(iii), the events which may be specified include—

(a) the giving of notice,

(b) the obtaining of consent, and

(c) the making of an order by the court or registrar.

(4) The entry of a restriction is to be made in relation to the registered estate or charge to which it relates.

41. **Effect**

(1) Where a restriction is entered in the register, no entry in respect of a disposition to which the restriction applies may be made in the register otherwise than in accordance with the terms of the restriction, subject to any order under subsection (2).

(2) The registrar may by order—

(a) disapply a restriction in relation to a disposition specified in the order or dispositions of a kind so specified, or

(b) provide that a restriction has effect, in relation to a disposition specified in the order or dispositions of a kind so specified, with modifications so specified.

(3) The power under subsection (2) is exercisable only on the application of a person who appears to the registrar to have a sufficient interest in the restriction.

42. **Power of registrar to enter**

(1) The registrar may enter a restriction in the register if it appears to him that it is necessary or desirable to do so for the purpose of—

(a) preventing invalidity or unlawfulness in relation to dispositions of a registered estate or charge,

(b) securing that interests which are capable of being overreached on a disposition of a registered estate or charge are overreached, or

(c) protecting a right or claim in relation to a registered estate or charge.

(2)	No restriction may be entered under subsection (1)(c) for the purpose of protecting the priority of an interest which is, or could be, the subject of a notice.

(3)	The registrar must give notice of any entry made under this section to the proprietor of the registered estate or charge concerned, except where the entry is made in pursuance of an application under section 43.

(4)	For the purposes of subsection (1)(c), a person entitled to the benefit of a charging order relating to an interest under a trust shall be treated as having a right or claim in relation to the trust property.

## 43.	Applications

(1)	A person may apply to the registrar for the entry of a restriction under section 42(1) if—

(a)	he is the relevant registered proprietor, or a person entitled to be registered as such proprietor,

(b)	the relevant registered proprietor, or a person entitled to be registered as such proprietor, consents to the application, or

(c)	he otherwise has a sufficient interest in the making of the entry.

(2)	Rules may—

(a)	require the making of an application under subsection (1) in such circumstances, and by such person, as the rules may provide;

(b)	make provision about the form of consent for the purposes of subsection (1)(b);

(c)	provide for classes of person to be regarded as included in subsection (1)(c);

(d)	specify standard forms of restriction.

(3)	If an application under subsection (1) is made for the entry of a restriction which is not in a form specified under subsection (2)(d), the registrar may only approve the application if it appears to him—

(a)	that the terms of the proposed restriction are reasonable, and

(b)	that applying the proposed restriction would—

(i)	be straightforward, and

(ii)	not place an unreasonable burden on him.

(4)	In subsection (1), references to the relevant registered proprietor are to the proprietor of the registered estate or charge to which the application relates.

## 44.	Obligatory restrictions

(1)	If the registrar enters two or more persons in the register as the proprietor of a registered estate in land, he must also enter in the register such restrictions as rules may provide for the purpose of securing that interests which are capable of being overreached on a disposition of the estate are overreached.

(2)	Where under any enactment the registrar is required to enter a restriction without application, the form of the restriction shall be such as rules may provide.

## 45.	Notifiable applications

(1)	Where an application under section 43(1) is notifiable, the registrar must give notice of the application, and of the right to object to it, to—

(a)	the proprietor of the registered estate or charge to which it relates, and

(b)	such other persons as rules may provide.

(2)	The registrar may not determine an application to which subsection (1) applies before the end of such period as rules may provide, unless the person, or each of the persons, notified under that subsection has exercised his right to object to the application or given the registrar notice that he does not intend to do so.

(3)	For the purposes of this section, an application under section 43(1) is notifiable unless it is—

(a)	made by or with the consent of the proprietor of the registered estate or charge to which the application relates, or a person entitled to be registered as such proprietor,

(b)	made in pursuance of rules under section 43(2)(a), or

(c)	an application for the entry of a restriction reflecting a limitation under an order of the court or registrar, or an undertaking given in place of such an order.

46. Power of court to order entry

(1) If it appears to the court that it is necessary or desirable to do so for the purpose of protecting a right or claim in relation to a registered estate or charge, it may make an order requiring the registrar to enter a restriction in the register.

(2) No order under this section may be made for the purpose of protecting the priority of an interest which is, or could be, the subject of a notice.

(3) The court may include in an order under this section a direction that an entry made in pursuance of the order is to have overriding priority.

(4) If an order under this section includes a direction under subsection (3), the registrar must make such entry in the register as rules may provide.

(5) The court may make the exercise of its power under subsection (3) subject to such terms and conditions as it thinks fit.

47. Withdrawal

A person may apply to the registrar for the withdrawal of a restriction if—

(a) the restriction was entered in such circumstances as rules may provide, and

(b) he is of such a description as rules may provide.

PART 5
CHARGES

Relative priority

48. Registered charges

(1) Registered charges on the same registered estate, or on the same registered charge, are to be taken to rank as between themselves in the order shown in the register.

(2) Rules may make provision about—

(a) how the priority of registered charges as between themselves is to be shown in the register, and

(b) applications for registration of the priority of registered charges as between themselves.

49. Tacking and further advances

(1) The proprietor of a registered charge may make a further advance on the security of the charge ranking in priority to a subsequent charge if he has not received from the subsequent chargee notice of the creation of the subsequent charge.

(2) Notice given for the purposes of subsection (1) shall be treated as received at the time when, in accordance with rules, it ought to have been received.

(3) The proprietor of a registered charge may also make a further advance on the security of the charge ranking in priority to a subsequent charge if—

(a) the advance is made in pursuance of an obligation, and

(b) at the time of the creation of the subsequent charge the obligation was entered in the register in accordance with rules.

(4) The proprietor of a registered charge may also make a further advance on the security of the charge ranking in priority to a subsequent charge if—

(a) the parties to the prior charge have agreed a maximum amount for which the charge is security, and

(b) at the time of the creation of the subsequent charge the agreement was entered in the register in accordance with rules.

(5) Rules may—

(a) disapply subsection (4) in relation to charges of a description specified in the rules, or

(b) provide for the application of that subsection to be subject, in the case of charges of a description so specified, to compliance with such conditions as may be so specified.

(6) Except as provided by this section, tacking in relation to a charge over registered land is only possible with the agreement of the subsequent chargee.

50.   Overriding statutory charges: duty of notification

If the registrar enters a person in the register as the proprietor of a charge which—

(a)   is created by or under an enactment, and

(b)   has effect to postpone a charge which at the time of registration of the statutory charge is—

    (i)   entered in the register, or

    (ii)   the basis for an entry in the register,

he must in accordance with rules give notice of the creation of the statutory charge to such person as rules may provide.

Powers as chargee

51.   Effect of completion by registration

On completion of the relevant registration requirements, a charge created by means of a registrable disposition of a registered estate has effect, if it would not otherwise do so, as a charge by deed by way of legal mortgage.

52.   Protection of disponees

(1)   Subject to any entry in the register to the contrary, the proprietor of a registered charge is to be taken to have, in relation to the property subject to the charge, the powers of disposition conferred by law on the owner of a legal mortgage.

(2)   Subsection (1) has effect only for the purpose of preventing the title of a disponee being questioned (and so does not affect the lawfulness of a disposition).

53.   Powers as sub-chargee

The registered proprietor of a sub-charge has, in relation to the property subject to the principal charge or any intermediate charge, the same powers as the sub-chargor.

Realisation of security

54.   Proceeds of sale: chargee's duty

For the purposes of section 105 of the Law of Property Act 1925 (mortgagee's duties in relation to application of proceeds of sale), in its application to the proceeds of sale of registered land, a person shall be taken to have notice of anything in the register immediately before the disposition on sale.

55.   Local land charges

A charge over registered land which is a local land charge may only be realised if the title to the charge is registered.

Miscellaneous

56.   Receipt in case of joint proprietors

Where a charge is registered in the name of two or more proprietors, a valid receipt for the money secured by the charge may be given by—

(a)   the registered proprietors,

(b)   the survivors or survivor of the registered proprietors, or

(c)   the personal representative of the last survivor of the registered proprietors.

57.   Entry of right of consolidation

Rules may make provision about entry in the register of a right of consolidation in relation to a registered charge.

PART 6
REGISTRATION: GENERAL

Registration as proprietor

58.   Conclusiveness

(1)   If, on the entry of a person in the register as the proprietor of a legal estate, the legal estate would not otherwise be vested in him, it shall be deemed to be vested in him as a result of the registration.

(2)   Subsection (1) does not apply where the entry is made in pursuance of a registrable disposition in relation to which some other registration requirement remains to be met.

59.   Dependent estates

(1)   The entry of a person in the register as the proprietor of a legal estate which subsists for the benefit of a registered estate must be made in relation to the registered estate.

(2)   The entry of a person in the register as the proprietor of a charge on a registered estate must be made in relation to that estate.

(3)   The entry of a person in the register as the proprietor of a sub-charge on a registered charge must be made in relation to that charge.

Boundaries

60.   Boundaries

(1)   The boundary of a registered estate as shown for the purposes of the register is a general boundary, unless shown as determined under this section.

(2)   A general boundary does not determine the exact line of the boundary.

(3)   Rules may make provision enabling or requiring the exact line of the boundary of a registered estate to be determined and may, in particular, make provision about—

(a)   the circumstances in which the exact line of a boundary may or must be determined,

(b)   how the exact line of a boundary may be determined,

(c)   procedure in relation to applications for determination, and

(d)   the recording of the fact of determination in the register or the index maintained under section 68.

(4)   Rules under this section must provide for applications for determination to be made to the registrar.

61.   Accretion and diluvion

(1)   The fact that a registered estate in land is shown in the register as having a particular boundary does not affect the operation of accretion or diluvion.

(2)   An agreement about the operation of accretion or diluvion in relation to a registered estate in land has effect only if registered in accordance with rules.

Quality of title

62.   Power to upgrade title

(1)   Where the title to a freehold estate is entered in the register as possessory or qualified, the registrar may enter it as absolute if he is satisfied as to the title to the estate.

(2)   Where the title to a leasehold estate is entered in the register as good leasehold, the registrar may enter it as absolute if he is satisfied as to the superior title.

(3)   Where the title to a leasehold estate is entered in the register as possessory or qualified the registrar may—

(a)   enter it as good leasehold if he is satisfied as to the title to the estate, and

(b)   enter it as absolute if he is satisfied both as to the title to the estate and as to the superior title.

(4)   Where the title to a freehold estate in land has been entered in the register as possessory for at least twelve years, the registrar may enter it as absolute if he is satisfied that the proprietor is in possession of the land.

(5)   Where the title to a leasehold estate in land has been entered in the register as possessory for at least twelve years, the registrar may enter it as good leasehold if he is satisfied that the proprietor is in possession of the land.

(6)   None of the powers under subsections (1) to (5) is exercisable if there is outstanding any claim adverse to the title of the registered proprietor which is made by virtue of an estate, right or interest whose enforceability is preserved by virtue of the existing entry about the class of title.

(7)   The only persons who may apply to the registrar for the exercise of any of the powers under subsections (1) to (5) are—

(a)   the proprietor of the estate to which the application relates,

(b)   a person entitled to be registered as the proprietor of that estate,

(c)   the proprietor of a registered charge affecting that estate, and

(d)   a person interested in a registered estate which derives from that estate.

(8)   In determining for the purposes of this section whether he is satisfied as to any title, the registrar is to apply the same standards as those which apply under section 9 or 10 to first registration of title.

(9)   The Lord Chancellor may by order amend subsection (4) or (5) by substituting for the number of years for the time being specified in that subsection such number of years as the order may provide.

63.   Effect of upgrading title

(1)   On the title to a registered freehold or leasehold estate being entered under section 62 as absolute, the proprietor ceases to hold the estate subject to any estate, right or interest whose enforceability was preserved by virtue of the previous entry about the class of title.

(2)   Subsection (1) also applies on the title to a registered leasehold estate being entered under section 62 as good leasehold, except that the entry does not affect or prejudice the enforcement of any estate, right or interest affecting, or in derogation of, the title of the lessor to grant the lease.

64.   Use of register to record defects in title

(1)   If it appears to the registrar that a right to determine a registered estate in land is exercisable, he may enter the fact in the register.

(2)   Rules may make provision about entries under subsection (1) and may, in particular, make provision about—

(a)   the circumstances in which there is a duty to exercise the power conferred by that subsection,

(b)   how entries under that subsection are to be made, and

(c)   the removal of such entries.

Alteration of register

65.   Alteration of register

Schedule 4 (which makes provision about alteration of the register) has effect.

Information etc.

66.   Inspection of the registers etc

(1)   Any person may inspect and make copies of, or of any part of—

(a)   the register of title,

(b)   any document kept by the registrar which is referred to in the register of title,

(c)   any other document kept by the registrar which relates to an application to him, or

(d)   the register of cautions against first registration.

(2)   The right under subsection (1) is subject to rules which may, in particular—

(a)   provide for exceptions to the right, and

(b)   impose conditions on its exercise, including conditions requiring the payment of fees.

67.   Official copies of the registers etc

(1)   An official copy of, or of a part of—

(a)   the register of title,

(b)   any document which is referred to in the register of title and kept by the registrar,

(c)   any other document kept by the registrar which relates to an application to him, or

(d)   the register of cautions against first registration, is admissible in evidence to the same extent as the original.

(2)   A person who relies on an official copy in which there is a mistake is not liable for loss suffered by another by reason of the mistake.

(3)   Rules may make provision for the issue of official copies and may, in particular, make provision about—

(a)   the form of official copies,

(b)   who may issue official copies,

(c)   applications for official copies, and

(d)   the conditions to be met by applicants for official copies, including conditions requiring the payment of fees.

68.   Index

(1)   The registrar must keep an index for the purpose of enabling the following matters to be ascertained in relation to any parcel of land—

(a)   whether any registered estate relates to the land,

(b)   how any registered estate which relates to the land is identified for the purposes of the register,

(c)   whether the land is affected by any, and, if so what, caution against first registration, and

(d)   such other matters as rules may provide.

(2)   Rules may—

(a)   make provision about how the index is to be kept and may, in particular, make provision about—

(i)   the information to be included in the index,

(ii)   the form in which information included in the index is to be kept, and

(iii) the arrangement of that information;

(b)   make provision about official searches of the index.

69.   Historical information

(1)   The registrar may on application provide information about the history of a registered title.

(2)   Rules may make provision about applications for the exercise of the power conferred by subsection (1).

(3)   The registrar may—

(a)   arrange for the provision of information about the history of registered titles, and

(b)   authorise anyone who has the function of providing information under paragraph (a) to have access on such terms as the registrar thinks fit to any relevant information kept by him.

70.   Official searches

Rules may make provision for official searches of the register, including searches of pending applications for first registration, and may, in particular, make provision about—

(a)   the form of applications for searches,

(b)   the manner in which such applications may be made,

(c)   the form of official search certificates, and

(d)   the manner in which such certificates may be issued.

Applications

71.   Duty to disclose unregistered interests

Where rules so provide—

(a)   a person applying for registration under Chapter 1 of Part 2 must provide to the registrar such information as the rules may provide about any interest affecting the estate to which the application relates which—

(i)   falls within any of the paragraphs of Schedule 1, and

(ii)   is of a description specified by the rules;

(b)   a person applying to register a registrable disposition of a registered estate must provide to the registrar such information as the rules may provide about any unregistered interest affecting the estate which—

(i)   falls within any of the paragraphs of Schedule 3, and

(ii)   is of description specified by the rules.

72.   Priority protection

    (1)   For the purposes of this section, an application for an entry in the register is protected if—

        (a)   it is one to which a priority period relates, and

        (b)   it is made before the end of that period.

    (2)   Where an application for an entry in the register is protected, any entry made in the register during the priority period relating to the application is postponed to any entry made in pursuance of it.

    (3)   Subsection (2) does not apply if—

        (a)   the earlier entry was made in pursuance of a protected application, and

        (b)   the priority period relating to that application ranks ahead of the one relating to the application for the other entry.

    (4)   Subsection (2) does not apply if the earlier entry is one to which a direction under section 46(3) applies.

    (5)   The registrar may defer dealing with an application for an entry in the register if it appears to him that subsection (2) might apply to the entry were he to make it.

    (6)   Rules may—

        (a)   make provision for priority periods in connection with—

            (i)   official searches of the register, including searches of pending applications for first registration, or

            (ii)   the noting in the register of a contract for the making of a registrable disposition of a registered estate or charge;

        (b)   make provision for the keeping of records in relation to priority periods and the inspection of such records.

    (7)   Rules under subsection (6)(a) may, in particular, make provision about—

        (a)   the commencement and length of a priority period,

        (b)   the applications for registration to which such a period relates,

        (c)   the order in which competing priority periods rank, and

        (d)   the application of subsections (2) and (3) in cases where more than one priority period relates to the same application.

73.   Objections

    (1)   Subject to subsections (2) and (3), anyone may object to an application to the registrar.

    (2)   In the case of an application under section 18, only the person who lodged the caution to which the application relates, or such other person as rules may provide, may object.

    (3)   In the case of an application under section 36, only the person shown in the register as the beneficiary of the notice to which the application relates, or such other person as rules may provide, may object.

    (4)   The right to object under this section is subject to rules.

    (5)   Where an objection is made under this section, the registrar—

        (a)   must give notice of the objection to the applicant, and

        (b)   may not determine the application until the objection has been disposed of.

    (6)   Subsection (5) does not apply if the objection is one which the registrar is satisfied is groundless.

    (7)   If it is not possible to dispose by agreement of an objection to which subsection (5) applies, the registrar must refer the matter to the adjudicator.

    (8)   Rules may make provision about references under subsection (7).

74.   Effective date of registration

An entry made in the register in pursuance of—

    (a)   an application for registration of an unregistered legal estate, or

    (b)   an application for registration in relation to a disposition required to be completed by registration,

has effect from the time of the making of the application.

Proceedings before the registrar

75.   Production of documents

(1)   The registrar may require a person to produce a document for the purposes of proceedings before him.

(2)   The power under subsection (1) is subject to rules.

(3)   A requirement under subsection (1) shall be enforceable as an order of the court.

(4)   A person aggrieved by a requirement under subsection (1) may appeal to a county court, which may make any order which appears appropriate.

76.   Costs

(1)   The registrar may make orders about costs in relation to proceedings before him.

(2)   The power under subsection (1) is subject to rules which may, in particular, make provision about—

    (a)   who may be required to pay costs,

    (b)   whose costs a person may be required to pay,

    (c)   the kind of costs which a person may be required to pay, and

(d)   the assessment of costs.

(3)   Without prejudice to the generality of subsection (2), rules under that subsection may include provision about—

    (a)   costs of the registrar, and

    (b)   liability for costs thrown away as the result of neglect or delay by a legal representative of a party to proceedings.

(4)   An order under subsection (1) shall be enforceable as an order of the court.

(5)   A person aggrieved by an order under subsection (1) may appeal to a county court, which may make any order which appears appropriate.

Miscellaneous

77.   Duty to act reasonably

(1)   A person must not exercise any of the following rights without reasonable cause—

    (a)   the right to lodge a caution under section 15,

    (b)   the right to apply for the entry of a notice or restriction, and

    (c)   the right to object to an application to the registrar.

(2)   The duty under this section is owed to any person who suffers damage in consequence of its breach.

78.   Notice of trust not to affect registrar

The registrar shall not be affected with notice of a trust.

PART 7
SPECIAL CASES

The Crown

79.   Voluntary registration of demesne land

(1)   Her Majesty may grant an estate in fee simple absolute in possession out of demesne land to Herself.

(2)   The grant of an estate under subsection (1) is to be regarded as not having been made unless an application under section 3 is made in respect of the estate before the end of the period for registration.

(3)   The period for registration is two months beginning with the date of the grant, or such longer period as the registrar may provide under subsection (4).

(4)   If on the application of Her Majesty the registrar is satisfied that there is a good reason for doing so, he may by order provide that the period for registration ends on such later date as he may specify in the order.

(5)   If an order under subsection (4) is made in a case where subsection (2) has already applied, that application of the subsection is to be treated as not having occurred.

80. Compulsory registration of grants out of demesne land

(1) Section 4(1) shall apply as if the following were included among the events listed—

    (a) the grant by Her Majesty out of demesne land of an estate in fee simple absolute in possession, otherwise than under section 79;

    (b) the grant by Her Majesty out of demesne land of an estate in land—

        (i) for a term of years absolute of more than seven years from the date of the grant, and

        (ii) for valuable or other consideration, by way of gift or in pursuance of an order of any court.

(2) In subsection (1)(b)(ii), the reference to grant by way of gift includes grant for the purpose of constituting a trust under which Her Majesty does not retain the whole of the beneficial interest.

(3) Subsection (1) does not apply to the grant of an estate in mines and minerals held apart from the surface.

(4) The Lord Chancellor may by order—

    (a) amend this section so as to add to the events in subsection (1) such events relating to demesne land as he may specify in the order, and

    (b) make such consequential amendments of any provision of, or having effect under, any Act as he thinks appropriate.

(5) In its application by virtue of subsection (1), section 7 has effect with the substitution for subsection (2) of—

'(2) On the application of subsection (1), the grant has effect as a contract made for valuable consideration to grant the legal estate concerned'.

81. Demesne land: cautions against first registration

(1) Section 15 shall apply as if demesne land were held by Her Majesty for an unregistered estate in fee simple absolute in possession.

(2) The provisions of this Act relating to cautions against first registration shall, in relation to cautions lodged by virtue of subsection (1), have effect subject to such modifications as rules may provide.

82. Escheat etc

(1) Rules may make provision about—

    (a) the determination of a registered freehold estate in land, and

    (b) the registration of an unregistered freehold legal estate in land in respect of land to which a former registered freehold estate in land related.

(2) Rules under this section may, in particular—

    (a) make provision for determination to be dependent on the meeting of such registration requirements as the rules may specify;

    (b) make provision for entries relating to a freehold estate in land to continue in the register, notwithstanding determination, for such time as the rules may provide;

    (c) make provision for the making in the register in relation to a former freehold estate in land of such entries as the rules may provide;

    (d) make provision imposing requirements to be met in connection with an application for the registration of such an unregistered estate as is mentioned in subsection (1)(b).

83. Crown and Duchy land: representation

(1) With respect to a Crown or Duchy interest, the appropriate authority—

    (a) may represent the owner of the interest for all purposes of this Act,

    (b) is entitled to receive such notice as that person is entitled to receive under this Act, and

    (c) may make such applications and do such other acts as that person is entitled to make or do under this Act.

(2) In this section—

'the appropriate authority' means—

    (a) in relation to an interest belonging to Her Majesty in right of the Crown and forming part of the Crown Estate, the Crown Estate Commissioners;

(b)   in relation to any other interest belonging to Her Majesty in right of the Crown, the government department having the management of the interest or, if there is no such department, such person as Her Majesty may appoint in writing under the Royal Sign Manual;

(c)   in relation to an interest belonging to Her Majesty in right of the Duchy of Lancaster, the Chancellor of the Duchy;

(d)   in relation to an interest belonging to the Duchy of Cornwall, such person as the Duke of Cornwall, or the possessor for the time being of the Duchy of Cornwall, appoints;

(e)   in relation to an interest belonging to a government department, or held in trust for Her Majesty for the purposes of a government department, that department;

'Crown interest' means an interest belonging to Her Majesty in right of the Crown, or belonging to a government department, or held in trust for Her Majesty for the purposes of a government department;

'Duchy interest' means an interest belonging to Her Majesty in right of the Duchy of Lancaster, or belonging to the Duchy of Cornwall;

'interest' means any estate, interest or charge in or over land and any right or claim in relation to land.

84.   Disapplication of requirements relating to Duchy land

Nothing in any enactment relating to the Duchy of Lancaster or the Duchy of Cornwall shall have effect to impose any requirement with respect to formalities or enrolment in relation to a disposition by a registered proprietor.

85.   Bona vacantia

Rules may make provision about how the passing of a registered estate or charge as bona vacantia is to be dealt with for the purposes of this Act.

Pending actions etc.

86.   Bankruptcy

(1)   In this Act, references to an interest affecting an estate or charge do not include a petition in bankruptcy or bankruptcy order.

(2)   As soon as practicable after registration of a petition in bankruptcy as a pending action under the Land Charges Act 1972, the registrar must enter in the register in relation to any registered estate or charge which appears to him to be affected a notice in respect of the pending action.

(3)   Unless cancelled by the registrar in such manner as rules may provide, a notice entered under subsection (2) continues in force until—

(a)   a restriction is entered in the register under subsection (4), or

(b)   the trustee in bankruptcy is registered as proprietor.

(4)   As soon as practicable after registration of a bankruptcy order under the Land Charges Act 1972, the registrar must, in relation to any registered estate or charge which appears to him to be affected by the order, enter in the register a restriction reflecting the effect of the Insolvency Act 1986.

(5)   Where the proprietor of a registered estate or charge is adjudged bankrupt, the title of his trustee in bankruptcy is void as against a person to whom a registrable disposition of the estate or charge is made if—

(a)   the disposition is made for valuable consideration,

(b)   the person to whom the disposition is made acts in good faith, and

(c)   at the time of the disposition—

(i)   no notice or restriction is entered under this section in relation to the registered estate or charge, and

(ii)   the person to whom the disposition is made has no notice of the bankruptcy petition or the adjudication.

(6)   Subsection (5) only applies if the relevant registration requirements are met in relation to the disposition, but, when they are met, has effect as from the date of the disposition.

(7) Nothing in this section requires a person to whom a registrable disposition is made to make any search under the Land Charges Act 1972.

87. Pending land actions, writs, orders and deeds of arrangement

(1) Subject to the following provisions, references in this Act to an interest affecting an estate or charge include—

(a) a pending land action within the meaning of the Land Charges Act 1972,

(b) a writ or order of the kind mentioned in section 6(1)(a) of that Act (writ or order affecting land issued or made by any court for the purposes of enforcing a judgment or recognisance),

(c) an order appointing a receiver or sequestrator, and

(d) a deed of arrangement.

(2) No notice may be entered in the register in respect of—

(a) an order appointing a receiver or sequestrator, or

(b) a deed of arrangement.

(3) None of the matters mentioned in subsection (1) shall be capable of falling within paragraph 2 of Schedule 1 or 3.

(4) In its application to any of the matters mentioned in subsection (1), this Act shall have effect subject to such modifications as rules may provide.

(5) In this section, 'deed of arrangement' has the same meaning as in the Deeds of Arrangement Act 1914.

Miscellaneous

88. Incorporeal hereditaments

In its application to—

(a) rentcharges,

(b) franchises,

(c) profits a prendre in gross, or

(d) manors,

this Act shall have effect subject to such modification as rules may provide.

89. Settlements

(1) Rules may make provision for the purposes of this Act in relation to the application to registered land of the enactments relating to settlements under the Settled Land Act 1925 (c. 18).

(2) Rules under this section may include provision modifying any of those enactments in its application to registered land.

(3) In this section, 'registered land' means an interest the title to which is, or is required to be, registered.

90. PPP leases relating to transport in London

(1) No application for registration under section 3 may be made in respect of a leasehold estate in land under a PPP lease.

(2) The requirement of registration does not apply on the grant or transfer of a leasehold estate in land under a PPP lease.

(3) For the purposes of section 27, the following are not dispositions requiring to be completed by registration—

(a) the grant of a term of years absolute under a PPP lease;

(b) the express grant of an interest falling within section 1(2) of the Law of Property Act 1925, where the interest is created for the benefit of a leasehold estate in land under a PPP lease.

(4) No notice may be entered in the register in respect of an interest under a PPP lease.

(5) Schedules 1 and 3 have effect as if they included a paragraph referring to a PPP lease.

(6) In this section, 'PPP lease' has the meaning given by section 218 of the Greater London Authority Act 1999 (which makes provision about leases created for public-private partnerships relating to transport in London).

PART 8
ELECTRONIC CONVEYANCING

91.   Electronic dispositions: formalities

(1)   This section applies to a document in electronic form where—

    (a)   the document purports to effect a disposition which falls within subsection (2), and

    (b)   the conditions in subsection (3) are met.

(2)   A disposition falls within this subsection if it is—

    (a)   a disposition of a registered estate or charge,

    (b)   a disposition of an interest which is the subject of a notice in the register, or

    (c)   a disposition which triggers the requirement of registration, which is of a kind specified by rules.

(3)   The conditions referred to above are that—

    (a)   the document makes provision for the time and date when it takes effect,

    (b)   the document has the electronic signature of each person by whom it purports to be authenticated,

    (c)   each electronic signature is certified, and

    (d)   such other conditions as rules may provide are met.

(4)   A document to which this section applies is to be regarded as—

    (a)   in writing, and

    (b)   signed by each individual, and sealed by each corporation, whose electronic signature it has.

(5)   A document to which this section applies is to be regarded for the purposes of any enactment as a deed.

(6)   If a document to which this section applies is authenticated by a person as agent, it is to be regarded for the purposes of any enactment as authenticated by him under the written authority of his principal.

(7)   If notice of an assignment made by means of a document to which this section applies is given in electronic form in accordance with rules, it is to be regarded for the purposes of any enactment as given in writing.

(8)   The right conferred by section 75 of the Law of Property Act 1925 (purchaser's right to have the execution of a conveyance attested) does not apply to a document to which this section applies.

(9)   If subsection (4) of section 36A of the Companies Act 1985 (execution of documents) applies to a document because of subsection (4) above, subsection (6) of that section (presumption of due execution) shall have effect in relation to the document with the substitution of 'authenticated' for 'signed' (and subsection (8) of that section, in so far as it relates to the document, shall be read accordingly).

(9A) If subsection (3) of section 29C of the Industrial and Provident Societies Act 1965 (execution of documents) applies to a document because of subsection (4) above, subsection (5) of that section (presumption of due execution) shall have effect in relation to the document with the substitution of 'authenticated' for 'signed'.

(10) In this section, references to an electronic signature and to the certification of such a signature are to be read in accordance with section 7(2) and (3) of the Electronic Communications Act 2000.

92.   Land registry network

(1)   The registrar may provide, or arrange for the provision of, an electronic communications network for use for such purposes as he thinks fit relating to registration or the carrying on of transactions which—

    (a)   involve registration, and

    (b)   are capable of being effected electronically.

(2)   Schedule 5 (which makes provision in connection with a network provided under subsection (1) and transactions carried on by means of such a network) has effect.

93.   Power to require simultaneous registration

(1)   This section applies to a disposition of—

    (a)   a registered estate or charge, or

    (b)   an interest which is the subject of a notice in the register, where the disposition is of a description specified by rules.

(2)   A disposition to which this section applies, or a contract to make such a disposition, only has effect if it is made by means of a document in electronic form and if, when the document purports to take effect—

    (a)   it is electronically communicated to the registrar, and

    (b)   the relevant registration requirements are met.

(3)   For the purposes of subsection (2)(b), the relevant registration requirements are—

    (a)   in the case of a registrable disposition, the requirements under Schedule 2, and

    (b)   in the case of any other disposition, or a contract, such requirements as rules may provide.

(4)   Section 27(1) does not apply to a disposition to which this section applies.

(5)   Before making rules under this section the Lord Chancellor must consult such persons as he considers appropriate.

(6)   In this section, 'disposition', in relation to a registered charge, includes postponement. 94 Electronic settlement The registrar may take such steps as he thinks fit for the purpose of securing the provision of a system of electronic settlement in relation to transactions involving registration.

95.   Supplementary

Rules may—

(a)   make provision about the communication of documents in electronic form to the registrar;

(b)   make provision about the electronic storage of documents communicated to the registrar in electronic form.

PART 9

ADVERSE POSSESSION

96.   Disapplication of periods of limitation

(1)   No period of limitation under section 15 of the Limitation Act 1980 (time limits in relation to recovery of land) shall run against any person, other than a chargee, in relation to an estate in land or rentcharge the title to which is registered.

(2)   No period of limitation under section 16 of that Act (time limits in relation to redemption of land) shall run against any person in relation to such an estate in land or rentcharge.

(3)   Accordingly, section 17 of that Act (extinction of title on expiry of time limit) does not operate to extinguish the title of any person where, by virtue of this section, a period of limitation does not run against him.

97.   Registration of adverse possessor

Schedule 6 (which makes provision about the registration of an adverse possessor of an estate in land or rentcharge) has effect.

98.   Defences

(1)   A person has a defence to an action for possession of land if—

    (a)   on the day immediately preceding that on which the action was brought he was entitled to make an application under paragraph 1 of Schedule 6 to be registered as the proprietor of an estate in the land, and

    (b)   had he made such an application on that day, the condition in paragraph 5(4) of that Schedule would have been satisfied.

(2)   A judgment for possession of land ceases to be enforceable at the end of the period of two years beginning with the date of the judgment if the proceedings in which the judgment is given were commenced against a person who was at that time entitled to make an application under paragraph 1 of Schedule 6.

(3)   A person has a defence to an action for possession of land if on the day immediately preceding that on which the action was brought he was entitled to make an application under paragraph 6 of Schedule 6 to be registered as the proprietor of an estate in the land.

(4)   A judgment for possession of land ceases to be enforceable at the end of the period of two years beginning with the date of the judgment if, at the end of that period, the person against whom the judgment was given is entitled to make an application under paragraph 6 of Schedule 6 to be registered as the proprietor of an estate in the land.

(5)   Where in any proceedings a court determines that—

(a)   a person is entitled to a defence under this section, or

(b)   a judgment for possession has ceased to be enforceable against a person by virtue of subsection (4), the court must order the registrar to register him as the proprietor of the estate in relation to which he is entitled to make an application under Schedule 6.

(6)   The defences under this section are additional to any other defences a person may have.

(7)   Rules may make provision to prohibit the recovery of rent due under a rentcharge from a person who has been in adverse possession of the rentcharge.

PART 10
LAND REGISTRY

Administration

99.   The land registry

(1)   There is to continue to be an office called Her Majesty's Land Registry which is to deal with the business of registration under this Act.

(2)   The land registry is to consist of—

(a)   the Chief Land Registrar, who is its head, and

(b)   the staff appointed by him; and references in this Act to a member of the land registry are to be read accordingly.

(3)   The Lord Chancellor shall appoint a person to be the Chief Land Registrar.

(4)   Schedule 7 (which makes further provision about the land registry) has effect.

100.   Conduct of business

(1)   Any function of the registrar may be carried out by any member of the land registry who is authorised for the purpose by the registrar.

(2)   The Lord Chancellor may by regulations make provision about the carrying out of functions during any vacancy in the office of registrar.

(3)   The Lord Chancellor may by order designate a particular office of the land registry as the proper office for the receipt of applications or a specified description of application.

(4)   The registrar may prepare and publish such forms and directions as he considers necessary or desirable for facilitating the conduct of the business of registration under this Act.

101.   Annual report

(1)   The registrar must make an annual report on the business of the land registry to the Lord Chancellor.

(2)   The registrar must publish every report under this section and may do so in such manner as he thinks fit.

(3)   The Lord Chancellor must lay copies of every report under this section before Parliament.

Fees and indemnities

102.   Fee orders

The Lord Chancellor may with the advice and assistance of the body referred to in section 127(2) (the Rule Committee), and the consent of the Treasury, by order—

(a)   prescribe fees to be paid in respect of dealings with the land registry, except under section 69(3)(b) or 105;

(b)   make provision about the payment of prescribed fees.

103. **Indemnities**

Schedule 8 (which makes provision for the payment of indemnities by the registrar) has effect.

Miscellaneous

104. **General information about land**

The registrar may publish information about land in England and Wales if it appears to him to be information in which there is legitimate public interest.

105. **Consultancy and advisory services**

(1) The registrar may provide, or arrange for the provision of, consultancy or advisory services about the registration of land in England and Wales or elsewhere.

(2) The terms on which services are provided under this section by the registrar, in particular terms as to payment, shall be such as he thinks fit.

106. **Incidental powers: companies**

(1) If the registrar considers it expedient to do so in connection with his functions under section 69(3)(a), 92(1), 94 or 105(1) or paragraph 10 of Schedule 5, he may—

(a) form, or participate in the formation of, a company, or

(b) purchase, or invest in, a company.

(2) In this section—

'company' means a company within the meaning of the Companies Act 1985;

'invest' means invest in any way (whether by acquiring assets, securities or rights or otherwise).

(3) This section is without prejudice to any powers of the registrar exercisable otherwise than by virtue of this section.

PART 11

ADJUDICATION

107. **The adjudicator**

(1) The Lord Chancellor shall appoint a person to be the Adjudicator to Her Majesty's Land Registry.

(2) To be qualified for appointment under subsection (1), a person must have a 10 year general qualification (within the meaning of section 71 of the Courts and Legal Services Act 1990).

(3) Schedule 9 (which makes further provision about the adjudicator) has effect.

108. **Jurisdiction**

(1) The adjudicator has the following functions—

(a) determining matters referred to him under section 73(7), and

(b) determining appeals under paragraph 4 of Schedule 5.

(2) Also, the adjudicator may, on application, make any order which the High Court could make for the rectification or setting aside of a document which—

(a) effects a qualifying disposition of a registered estate or charge,

(b) is a contract to make such a disposition, or

(c) effects a transfer of an interest which is the subject of a notice in the register.

(3) For the purposes of subsection (2)(a), a qualifying disposition is—

(a) a registrable disposition, or

(b) a disposition which creates an interest which may be the subject of a notice in the register.

(4) The general law about the effect of an order of the High Court for the rectification or setting aside of a document shall apply to an order under this section.

109. **Procedure**

(1) Hearings before the adjudicator shall be held in public, except where he is satisfied that exclusion of the public is just and reasonable.

(2) Subject to that, rules may regulate the practice and procedure to be followed with respect to proceedings before the adjudicator and matters incidental to or consequential on such proceedings.

(3) Rules under subsection (2) may, in particular, make provision about—

   (a) when hearings are to be held,

   (b) requiring persons to attend hearings to give evidence or to produce documents,

   (c) the form in which any decision of the adjudicator is to be given,

   (d) payment of costs of a party to proceedings by another party to the proceedings, and

   (e) liability for costs thrown away as the result of neglect or delay by a legal representative of a party to proceedings.

110. Functions in relation to disputes

(1) In proceedings on a reference under section 73(7), the adjudicator may, instead of deciding a matter himself, direct a party to the proceedings to commence proceedings within a specified time in the court for the purpose of obtaining the court's decision on the matter.

(2) Rules may make provision about the reference under subsection (1) of matters to the court and may, in particular, make provision about—

   (a) adjournment of the proceedings before the adjudicator pending the outcome of the proceedings before the court, and

   (b) the powers of the adjudicator in the event of failure to comply with a direction under subsection (1).

(3) Rules may make provision about the functions of the adjudicator in consequence of a decision on a reference under section 73(7) and may, in particular, make provision enabling the adjudicator to determine, or give directions about the determination of—

   (a) the application to which the reference relates, or

   (b) such other present or future application to the registrar as the rules may provide.

(4) If, in the case of a reference under section 73(7) relating to an application under paragraph 1 of Schedule 6, the adjudicator determines that it would be unconscionable because of an equity by estoppel for the registered proprietor to seek to dispossess the applicant, but that the circumstances are not such that the applicant ought to be registered as proprietor, the adjudicator—

   (a) must determine how the equity due to the applicant is to be satisfied, and

   (b) may for that purpose make any order that the High Court could make in the exercise of its equitable jurisdiction.

111. Appeals

(1) Subject to subsection (2), a person aggrieved by a decision of the adjudicator may appeal to the High Court.

(2) In the case of a decision on an appeal under paragraph 4 of Schedule 5, only appeal on a point of law is possible.

(3) If on an appeal under this section relating to an application under paragraph 1 of Schedule 6 the court determines that it would be unconscionable because of an equity by estoppel for the registered proprietor to seek to dispossess the applicant, but that the circumstances are not such that the applicant ought to be registered as proprietor, the court must determine how the equity due to the applicant is to be satisfied.

112. Enforcement of orders etc.

A requirement of the adjudicator shall be enforceable as an order of the court.

113. Fees

The Lord Chancellor may by order—

(a) prescribe fees to be paid in respect of proceedings before the adjudicator;

(b) make provision about the payment of prescribed fees.

PART 12

MISCELLANEOUS AND GENERAL

Miscellaneous

115. Rights of pre-emption

(1)   A right of pre-emption in relation to registered land has effect from the time of creation as an interest capable of binding successors in title (subject to the rules about the effect of dispositions on priority).

(2)   This section has effect in relation to rights of pre-emption created on or after the day on which this section comes into force.

116. Proprietary estoppel and mere equities

It is hereby declared for the avoidance of doubt that, in relation to registered land, each of the following—

(a)   an equity by estoppel, and

(b)   a mere equity,

has effect from the time the equity arises as an interest capable of binding successors in title (subject to the rules about the effect of dispositions on priority).

117. Reduction in unregistered interests with automatic protection

(1)   Paragraphs 10 to 14 of Schedules 1 and 3 shall cease to have effect at the end of the period of ten years beginning with the day on which those Schedules come into force.

(2)   If made before the end of the period mentioned in subsection (1), no fee may be charged for—

(a)   an application to lodge a caution against first registration by virtue of an interest falling within any of paragraphs 10 to 14 of Schedule 1, or

(b)   an application for the entry in the register of a notice in respect of an interest falling within any of paragraphs 10 to 14 of Schedule 3.

118. Power to reduce qualifying term

(1)   The Lord Chancellor may by order substitute for the term specified in any of the following provisions—

(a)   section 3(3),

(b)   section 4(1)(c)(i) and (2)(b),

(c)   section 15(3)(a)(ii),

(d)   section 27(2)(b)(i),

(e)   section 80(1)(b)(i),

(f)   paragraph 1 of Schedule 1,

(g)   paragraphs 4(1), 5(1) and 6(1) of Schedule 2, and

(h)   paragraph 1 of Schedule 3, such shorter term as he thinks fit.

(2)   An order under this section may contain such transitional provision as the Lord Chancellor thinks fit.

(3)   Before making an order under this section, the Lord Chancellor must consult such persons as he considers appropriate.

119. Power to deregister manors

On the application of the proprietor of a registered manor, the registrar may remove the title to the manor from the register.

120. Conclusiveness of filed copies etc.

(1)   This section applies where—

(a)   a disposition relates to land to which a registered estate relates, and

(b)   an entry in the register relating to the registered estate refers to a document kept by the registrar which is not an original.

(2)   As between the parties to the disposition, the document kept by the registrar is to be taken—

(a)   to be correct, and

(b)   to contain all the material parts of the original document.

(3)   No party to the disposition may require production of the original document.

(4)   No party to the disposition is to be affected by any provision of the original document which is not contained in the document kept by the registrar.

121.   Forwarding of applications to registrar of companies

The Lord Chancellor may by rules make provision about the transmission by the registrar to the registrar of companies (within the meaning of the Companies Act 1985) of applications under—

(a)   Part 12 of that Act (registration of charges), or

(b)   Chapter 3 of Part 23 of that Act (corresponding provision for oversea companies).

Offences etc.

123.   Suppression of information

(1)   A person commits an offence if in the course of proceedings relating to registration under this Act he suppresses information with the intention of—

(a)   concealing a person's right or claim, or

(b)   substantiating a false claim.

(2)   A person guilty of an offence under this section is liable—

(a)   on conviction on indictment, to imprisonment for a term not exceeding two years or to a fine;

(b)   on summary conviction, to imprisonment for a term not exceeding six months or to a fine not exceeding the statutory maximum, or to both.

124.   Improper alteration of the registers

(1)   A person commits an offence if he dishonestly induces another—

(a)   to change the register of title or cautions register, or

(b)   to authorise the making of such a change.

(2)   A person commits an offence if he intentionally or recklessly makes an unauthorised change in the register of title or cautions register.

(3)   A person guilty of an offence under this section is liable—

(a)   on conviction on indictment, to imprisonment for a term not exceeding 2 years or to a fine;

(b)   on summary conviction, to imprisonment for a term not exceeding six months or to a fine not exceeding the statutory maximum, or to both.

(4)   In this section, references to changing the register of title include changing a document referred to in it.

125.   Privilege against self-incrimination

(1)   The privilege against self-incrimination, so far as relating to offences under this Act, shall not entitle a person to refuse to answer any question or produce any document or thing in any legal proceedings other than criminal proceedings.

(2)   No evidence obtained under subsection (1) shall be admissible in any criminal proceedings under this Act against the person from whom it was obtained or that person's spouse or civil partner.

Land registration rules

126.   Miscellaneous and general powers

Schedule 10 (which contains miscellaneous and general land registration rule-making powers) has effect.

127.   Exercise of powers

(1)   Power to make land registration rules is exercisable by the Lord Chancellor with the advice and assistance of the Rule Committee.

. . .

Supplementary

129. Crown application

This Act binds the Crown.

130. Application to internal waters

This Act applies to land covered by internal waters of the United Kingdom which are—

(a) within England or Wales, or

(b) adjacent to England or Wales and specified for the purposes of this section by order made by the Lord Chancellor.

131. 'Proprietor in possession'

(1) For the purposes of this Act, land is in the possession of the proprietor of a registered estate in land if it is physically in his possession, or in that of a person who is entitled to be registered as the proprietor of the registered estate.

(2) In the case of the following relationships, land which is (or is treated as being) in the possession of the second-mentioned person is to be treated for the purposes of subsection (1) as in the possession of the first-mentioned person—

(a) landlord and tenant;

(b) mortgagor and mortgagee;

(c) licensor and licensee;

(d) trustee and beneficiary.

(3) In subsection (1), the reference to entitlement does not include entitlement under Schedule 6.

132. General interpretation

(1) In this Act—

'adjudicator' means the Adjudicator to Her Majesty's Land Registry;

'caution against first registration' means a caution lodged under section 15;

'cautions register' means the register kept under section 19(1);

'charge' means any mortgage, charge or lien for securing money or money's worth;

'demesne land' means land belonging to Her Majesty in right of the Crown which is not held for an estate in fee simple absolute in possession;

'land' includes—

(a) buildings and other structures,

(b) land covered with water, and

(c) mines and minerals, whether or not held with the surface;

'land registration rules' means any rules under this Act, other than rules under section 93, Part 11, section 121 or paragraph 1, 2 or 3 of Schedule 5;

'legal estate' has the same meaning as in the Law of Property Act 1925;

'legal mortgage' has the same meaning as in the Law of Property Act 1925;

'mines and minerals' includes any strata or seam of minerals or substances in or under any land, and powers of working and getting any such minerals or substances;

'registrar' means the Chief Land Registrar;

'register' means the register of title, except in the context of cautions against first registration;

'registered' means entered in the register;

'registered charge' means a charge the title to which is entered in the register;

'registered estate' means a legal estate the title to which is entered in the register, other than a registered charge;

'registered land' means a registered estate or registered charge;

'registrable disposition' means a disposition which is required to be completed by registration under section 27;

'requirement of registration' means the requirement of registration under section 4;

'sub-charge' means a charge under section 23(2)(b);

'term of years absolute' has the same meaning as in the Law of Property Act 1925;

'valuable consideration' does not include marriage consideration or a nominal consideration in money.

(2) In subsection (1), in the definition of 'demesne land', the reference to land belonging to Her Majesty does not include land in relation to which a freehold estate in land has determined, but in relation to which there has been no act of entry or management by the Crown.

(3) In this Act—

    (a) references to the court are to the High Court or a county court,

    (b) references to an interest affecting an estate or charge are to an adverse right affecting the title to the estate or charge, and

    (c) references to the right to object to an application to the registrar are to the right under section 73.

Final provisions

133. Minor and consequential amendments

Schedule 11 (which makes minor and consequential amendments) has effect.

134. Transition

(1) The Lord Chancellor may by order make such transitional provisions and savings as he thinks fit in connection with the coming into force of any of the provisions of this Act.

(2) Schedule 12 (which makes transitional provisions and savings) has effect.

(3) Nothing in Schedule 12 affects the power to make transitional provisions and savings under subsection (1); and an order under that subsection may modify any provision made by that Schedule.

135. Repeals

The enactments specified in Schedule 13 (which include certain provisions which are already spent) are hereby repealed to the extent specified there.

136. Short title, commencement and extent

(1) This Act may be cited as the Land Registration Act 2002.

(2) This Act shall come into force on such day as the Lord Chancellor may by order appoint, and different days may be so appointed for different purposes.

(3) Subject to subsection (4), this Act extends to England and Wales only.

(4) Any amendment or repeal by this Act of an existing enactment, other than—

    (a) section 37 of the Requisitioned Land and War Works Act 1945, and

    (b) Schedule 2A to the Building Societies Act 1986,

has the same extent as the enactment amended or repealed.

SCHEDULES

SCHEDULE 1

UNREGISTERED INTERESTS WHICH OVERRIDE FIRST REGISTRATION

Leasehold estates in land

1. A leasehold estate in land granted for a term not exceeding seven years from the date of the grant, except for a lease the grant of which falls within section 4(1) (d), (e) or (f).

Interests of persons in actual occupation

2. An interest belonging to a person in actual occupation, so far as relating to land of which he is in actual occupation, except for an interest under a settlement under the Settled Land Act 1925.

Easements and profits a prendre

3. A legal easement or profit a prendre.

Customary and public rights

4. A customary right.

5. A public right.

Local land charges

6.   A local land charge.

Mines and minerals

7.   An interest in any coal or coal mine, the rights attached to any such interest and the rights of any person under section 38, 49 or 51 of the Coal Industry Act 1994.
8.   In the case of land to which title was registered before 1898, rights to mines and minerals (and incidental rights) created before 1898.
9.   In the case of land to which title was registered between 1898 and 1925 inclusive, rights to mines and minerals (and incidental rights) created before the date of registration of the title.

Miscellaneous

10.   A franchise.
11.   A manorial right.
12.   A right to rent which was reserved to the Crown on the granting of any freehold estate (whether or not the right is still vested in the Crown).
13.   A non-statutory right in respect of an embankment or sea or river wall.
14.   A right to payment in lieu of tithe.
15.   A right acquired under the Limitation Act 1980 before the coming into force of this Schedule.
16.   A right in respect of the repair of a church chancel.

SCHEDULE 2
REGISTRABLE DISPOSITIONS: REGISTRATION REQUIREMENTS

PART 1
REGISTERED ESTATES

Introductory

1.   This Part deals with the registration requirements relating to those dispositions of registered estates which are required to be completed by registration.

Transfer

2.   (1)   In the case of a transfer of whole or part, the transferee, or his successor in title, must be entered in the register as the proprietor.
         (2)   In the case of a transfer of part, such details of the transfer as rules may provide must be entered in the register in relation to the registered estate out of which the transfer is made.

Lease of estate in land

3.   (1)   This paragraph applies to a disposition consisting of the grant out of an estate in land of a term of years absolute.
         (2)   In the case of a disposition to which this paragraph applies—
               (a)   the grantee, or his successor in title, must be entered in the register as the proprietor of the lease, and
               (b)   a notice in respect of the lease must be entered in the register.

Lease of franchise or manor

4.   (1)   This paragraph applies to a disposition consisting of the grant out of a franchise or manor of a lease for a term of more than seven years from the date of the grant.
         (2)   In the case of a disposition to which this paragraph applies—
               (a)   the grantee, or his successor in title, must be entered in the register as the proprietor of the lease, and
               (b)   a notice in respect of the lease must be entered in the register.
5.   (1)   This paragraph applies to a disposition consisting of the grant out of a franchise or manor of a lease for a term not exceeding seven years from the date of the grant.
         (2)   In the case of a disposition to which this paragraph applies, a notice in respect of the lease must be entered in the register.

Creation of independently registrable legal interest

6.   (1)   This paragraph applies to a disposition consisting of the creation of a legal rentcharge or profit a prendre in gross, other than one created for, or for an interest equivalent to, a term of years absolute not exceeding seven years from the date of creation.

       (2)   In the case of a disposition to which this paragraph applies—

           (a)   the grantee, or his successor in title, must be entered in the register as the proprietor of the interest created, and

           (b)   a notice in respect of the interest created must be entered in the register.

       (3)   In sub-paragraph (1), the reference to a legal rentcharge or profit a prendre in gross is to one falling within section 1(2) of the Law of Property Act 1925.

Creation of other legal interest

7.   (1)   This paragraph applies to a disposition which—

           (a)   consists of the creation of an interest of a kind falling within section 1(2)(a), (b) or (e) of the Law of Property Act 1925, and

           (b)   is not a disposition to which paragraph 4, 5 or 6 applies.

       (2)   In the case of a disposition to which this paragraph applies—

           (a)   a notice in respect of the interest created must be entered in the register, and

           (b)   if the interest is created for the benefit of a registered estate, the proprietor of the registered estate must be entered in the register as its proprietor.

       (3)   Rules may provide for sub-paragraph (2) to have effect with modifications in relation to a right of entry over or in respect of a term of years absolute.

Creation of legal charge

8.   In the case of the creation of a charge, the chargee, or his successor in title, must be entered in the register as the proprietor of the charge.

PART 2
REGISTERED CHARGES

Introductory

9.   This Part deals with the registration requirements relating to those dispositions of registered charges which are required to be completed by registration.

Transfer

10.   In the case of a transfer, the transferee, or his successor in title, must be entered in the register as the proprietor.

Creation of sub-charge

11.   In the case of the creation of a sub-charge, the sub-chargee, or his successor in title, must be entered in the register as the proprietor of the sub-charge.

SCHEDULE 3
UNREGISTERED INTERESTS WHICH OVERRIDE REGISTERED DISPOSITIONS

Leasehold estates in land

1.   A leasehold estate in land granted for a term not exceeding seven years from the date of the grant, except for—

    (a)   a lease the grant of which falls within section 4(1)(d), (e) or (f);

    (b)   a lease the grant of which constitutes a registrable disposition.

Interests of persons in actual occupation

2.   An interest belonging at the time of the disposition to a person in actual occupation, so far as relating to land of which he is in actual occupation, except for—

    (a)   an interest under a settlement under the Settled Land Act 1925;

(b)   an interest of a person of whom inquiry was made before the disposition and who failed to disclose the right when he could reasonably have been expected to do so;

(c)   an interest—

    (i)   which belongs to a person whose occupation would not have been obvious on a reasonably careful inspection of the land at the time of the disposition, and

    (ii)   of which the person to whom the disposition is made does not have actual knowledge at that time;

(d)   a leasehold estate in land granted to take effect in possession after the end of the period of three months beginning with the date of the grant and which has not taken effect in possession at the time of the disposition.

2A.   (1)   An interest which, immediately before the coming into force of this Schedule, was an overriding interest under section 70(1)(g) of the Land Registration Act 1925 by virtue of a person's receipt of rents and profits, except for an interest of a person of whom inquiry was made before the disposition and who failed to disclose the right when he could reasonably have been expected to do so.

    (2)   Sub-paragraph (1) does not apply to an interest if at any time since the coming into force of this Schedule it has been an interest which, had the Land Registration Act 1925 continued in force, would not have been an overriding interest under section 70(1)(g) of that Act by virtue of a person's receipt of rents and profits.

Easements and profits a prendre

3.   (1)   A legal easement or profit a prendre, except for an easement, or a profit a prendre which is not registered under the Commons Registration Act 1965, which at the time of the disposition—

    (a)   is not within the actual knowledge of the person to whom the disposition is made, and

    (b)   would not have been obvious on a reasonably careful inspection of the land over which the easement or profit is exercisable.

    (2)   The exception in sub-paragraph (1) does not apply if the person entitled to the easement or profit proves that it has been exercised in the period of one year ending with the day of the disposition.

Customary and public rights

4.   A customary right.

5.   A public right.

Local land charges

6.   A local land charge.

Mines and minerals

7.   An interest in any coal or coal mine, the rights attached to any such interest and the rights of any person under section 38, 49 or 51 of the Coal Industry Act 1994.

8.   In the case of land to which title was registered before 1898, rights to mines and minerals (and incidental rights) created before 1898.

9.   In the case of land to which title was registered between 1898 and 1925 inclusive, rights to mines and minerals (and incidental rights) created before the date of registration of the title.

Miscellaneous

10.   A franchise.

11.   A manorial right.

12.   A right to rent which was reserved to the Crown on the granting of any freehold estate (whether or not the right is still vested in the Crown).

13.   A non-statutory right in respect of an embankment or sea or river wall.

14.   A right to payment in lieu of tithe.

15.   A right under paragraph 18(1) of Schedule 12.

16.   A right in respect of the repair of a church chancel.

SCHEDULE 4
ALTERATION OF THE REGISTER

Introductory

1. In this Schedule, references to rectification, in relation to alteration of the register, are to alteration which—
    (a) involves the correction of a mistake, and
    (b) prejudicially affects the title of a registered proprietor.

Alteration pursuant to a court order

2. (1) The court may make an order for alteration of the register for the purpose of—
        (a) correcting a mistake,
        (b) bringing the register up to date, or
        (c) giving effect to any estate, right or interest excepted from the effect of registration.
    (2) An order under this paragraph has effect when served on the registrar to impose a duty on him to give effect to it.

3. (1) This paragraph applies to the power under paragraph 2, so far as relating to rectification.
    (2) If alteration affects the title of the proprietor of a registered estate in land, no order may be made under paragraph 2 without the proprietor's consent in relation to land in his possession unless—
        (a) he has by fraud or lack of proper care caused or substantially contributed to the mistake, or
        (b) it would for any other reason be unjust for the alteration not to be made.
    (3) If in any proceedings the court has power to make an order under paragraph 2, it must do so, unless there are exceptional circumstances which justify its not doing so.
    (4) In sub-paragraph (2), the reference to the title of the proprietor of a registered estate in land includes his title to any registered estate which subsists for the benefit of the estate in land.

4. Rules may—
    (a) make provision about the circumstances in which there is a duty to exercise the power under paragraph 2, so far as not relating to rectification;
    (b) make provision about the form of an order under paragraph 2;
    (c) make provision about service of such an order.

Alteration otherwise than pursuant to a court order

5. The registrar may alter the register for the purpose of—
    (a) correcting a mistake,
    (b) bringing the register up to date,
    (c) giving effect to any estate, right or interest excepted from the effect of registration, or
    (d) removing a superfluous entry.

6. (1) This paragraph applies to the power under paragraph 5, so far as relating to rectification.
    (2) No alteration affecting the title of the proprietor of a registered estate in land may be made under paragraph 5 without the proprietor's consent in relation to land in his possession unless—
        (a) he has by fraud or lack of proper care caused or substantially contributed to the mistake, or
        (b) it would for any other reason be unjust for the alteration not to be made.
    (3) If on an application for alteration under paragraph 5 the registrar has power to make the alteration, the application must be approved, unless there are exceptional circumstances which justify not making the alteration.
    (4) In sub-paragraph (2), the reference to the title of the proprietor of a registered estate in land includes his title to any registered estate which subsists for the benefit of the estate in land.

7. Rules may—
    (a) make provision about the circumstances in which there is a duty to exercise the power under paragraph 5, so far as not relating to rectification;
    (b) make provision about how the register is to be altered in exercise of that power;

(c)   make provision about applications for alteration under that paragraph, including provision requiring the making of such applications;

(d)   make provision about procedure in relation to the exercise of that power, whether on application or otherwise.

Rectification and derivative interests

8.   The powers under this Schedule to alter the register, so far as relating to rectification, extend to changing for the future the priority of any interest affecting the registered estate or charge concerned.

Costs in non-rectification cases

9.   (1)   If the register is altered under this Schedule in a case not involving rectification, the registrar may pay such amount as he thinks fit in respect of any costs or expenses reasonably incurred by a person in connection with the alteration which have been incurred with the consent of the registrar.

            (2)   The registrar may make a payment under sub-paragraph (1) notwithstanding the absence of consent if—

                (a)   it appears to him—

                     (i)   that the costs or expenses had to be incurred urgently, and

                     (ii)   that it was not reasonably practicable to apply for his consent, or

                (b)   he has subsequently approved the incurring of the costs or expenses.

SCHEDULE 5
LAND REGISTRY NETWORK

Access to network

1.   (1)   A person who is not a member of the land registry may only have access to a land registry network under authority conferred by means of an agreement with the registrar.

            (2)   An agreement for the purposes of sub-paragraph (1) ('network access agreement') may authorise access for—

                (a)   the communication, posting or retrieval of information,

                (b)   the making of changes to the register of title or cautions register,

                (c)   the issue of official search certificates,

                (d)   the issue of official copies, or

                (e)   such other conveyancing purposes as the registrar thinks fit.

            (3)   Rules may regulate the use of network access agreements to confer authority to carry out functions of the registrar.

            (4)   The registrar must, on application, enter into a network access agreement with the applicant if the applicant meets such criteria as rules may provide.

Terms of access

2.   (1)   The terms on which access to a land registry network is authorised shall be such as the registrar thinks fit, subject to sub-paragraphs (3) and (4), and may, in particular, include charges for access.

            (2)   The power under sub-paragraph (1) may be used, not only for the purpose of regulating the use of the network, but also for—

                (a)   securing that the person granted access uses the network to carry on such qualifying transactions as may be specified in, or under, the agreement,

                (b)   such other purpose relating to the carrying on of qualifying transactions as rules may provide, or

                (c)   enabling network transactions to be monitored.

            (3)   It shall be a condition of a network access agreement which enables the person granted access to use the network to carry on qualifying transactions that he must comply with any rules for the time being in force under paragraph 5.

            (4)   Rules may regulate the terms on which access to a land registry network is authorised.

Termination of access

3. (1) The person granted access by a network access agreement may terminate the agreement at any time by notice to the registrar.

    (2) Rules may make provision about the termination of a network access agreement by the registrar and may, in particular, make provision about—
    (a) the grounds of termination,
    (b) the procedure to be followed in relation to termination, and
    (c) the suspension of termination pending appeal.

    (3) Without prejudice to the generality of sub-paragraph (2)(a), rules under that provision may authorise the registrar to terminate a network access agreement if the person granted access—
    (a) fails to comply with the terms of the agreement,
    (b) ceases to be a person with whom the registrar would be required to enter into a network access agreement conferring the authority which the agreement confers, or
    (c) does not meet such conditions as the rules may provide.

Appeals

4. (1) A person who is aggrieved by a decision of the registrar with respect to entry into, or termination of, a network access agreement may appeal against the decision to the adjudicator.

    (2) On determining an appeal under this paragraph, the adjudicator may give such directions as he considers appropriate to give effect to his determination.

    (3) Rules may make provision about appeals under this paragraph.

Network transaction rules

5. (1) Rules may make provision about how to go about network transactions.

    (2) Rules under sub-paragraph (1) may, in particular, make provision about dealings with the land registry, including provision about—
    (a) the procedure to be followed, and
    (b) the supply of information (including information about unregistered interests).

Overriding nature of network access obligations

6. To the extent that an obligation not owed under a network access agreement conflicts with an obligation owed under such an agreement by the person granted access, the obligation not owed under the agreement is discharged.

Do-it-yourself conveyancing

7. (1) If there is a land registry network, the registrar has a duty to provide such assistance as he thinks appropriate for the purpose of enabling persons engaged in qualifying transactions who wish to do their own conveyancing to do so by means of the network.

    (2) The duty under sub-paragraph (1) does not extend to the provision of legal advice.

Presumption of authority

8. Where—
    (a) a person who is authorised under a network access agreement to do so uses the network for the making of a disposition or contract, and
    (b) the document which purports to effect the disposition or to be the contract—
    (i) purports to be authenticated by him as agent, and
    (ii) contains a statement to the effect that he is acting under the authority of his principal,
    he shall be deemed, in favour of any other party, to be so acting.

Management of network transactions

9. (1) The registrar may use monitoring information for the purpose of managing network transactions and may, in particular, disclose such information to persons authorised to use

the network, and authorise the further disclosure of information so disclosed, if he considers it is necessary or desirable to do so.

(2)   The registrar may delegate his functions under sub-paragraph (1), subject to such conditions as he thinks fit.

(3)   In sub-paragraph (1), 'monitoring information' means information provided in pursuance of provision in a network access agreement included under paragraph 2(2)(c).

Supplementary

10.   The registrar may provide, or arrange for the provision of, education and training in relation to the use of a land registry network.

11.   (1)   Power to make rules under paragraph 1, 2 or 3 is exercisable by the Lord Chancellor.

(2)   Before making such rules, the Lord Chancellor must consult such persons as he considers appropriate.

(3)   In making rules under paragraph 1 or 3(2)(a), the Lord Chancellor must have regard, in particular, to the need to secure—

(a)   the confidentiality of private information kept on the network,

(b)   competence in relation to the use of the network (in particular for the purpose of making changes), and

(c)   the adequate insurance of potential liabilities in connection with use of the network.

12.   In this Schedule—

'land registry network' means a network provided under section 92(1);

'network access agreement' has the meaning given by paragraph 1(2);

'network transaction' means a transaction carried on by means of a land registry network;

'qualifying transaction' means a transaction which—

(a)   involves registration, and

(b)   is capable of being effected electronically.

SCHEDULE 6
REGISTRATION OF ADVERSE POSSESSOR

Note. In relation to registered rentcharges see the Land Registration Rules 2003, Sch 8.

Right to apply for registration

1.   (1)   A person may apply to the registrar to be registered as the proprietor of a registered estate in land if he has been in adverse possession of the estate for the period of ten years ending on the date of the application.

(2)   A person may also apply to the registrar to be registered as the proprietor of a registered estate in land if—

(a)   he has in the period of six months ending on the date of the application ceased to be in adverse possession of the estate because of eviction by the registered proprietor, or a person claiming under the registered proprietor,

(b)   on the day before his eviction he was entitled to make an application under sub-paragraph (1), and

(c)   the eviction was not pursuant to a judgment for possession.

(3)   However, a person may not make an application under this paragraph if—

(a)   he is a defendant in proceedings which involve asserting a right to possession of the land, or

(b)   judgment for possession of the land has been given against him in the last two years.

(4)   For the purposes of sub-paragraph (1), the estate need not have been registered throughout the period of adverse possession.

Notification of application

2.   (1)   The registrar must give notice of an application under paragraph 1 to—

(a)   the proprietor of the estate to which the application relates,

(b)   the proprietor of any registered charge on the estate,

(c)   where the estate is leasehold, the proprietor of any superior registered estate,

(d) any person who is registered in accordance with rules as a person to be notified under this paragraph, and

(e) such other persons as rules may provide.

(2) Notice under this paragraph shall include notice of the effect of paragraph 4.

Treatment of application

3. (1) A person given notice under paragraph 2 may require that the application to which the notice relates be dealt with under paragraph 5.

(2) The right under this paragraph is exercisable by notice to the registrar given before the end of such period as rules may provide.

4. If an application under paragraph 1 is not required to be dealt with under paragraph 5, the applicant is entitled to be entered in the register as the new proprietor of the estate.

5. (1) If an application under paragraph 1 is required to be dealt with under this paragraph, the applicant is only entitled to be registered as the new proprietor of the estate if any of the following conditions is met.

(2) The first condition is that—

(a) it would be unconscionable because of an equity by estoppel for the registered proprietor to seek to dispossess the applicant, and

(b) the circumstances are such that the applicant ought to be registered as the proprietor.

(3) The second condition is that the applicant is for some other reason entitled to be registered as the proprietor of the estate.

(4) The third condition is that—

(a) the land to which the application relates is adjacent to land belonging to the applicant,

(b) the exact line of the boundary between the two has not been determined under rules under section 60,

(c) for at least ten years of the period of adverse possession ending on the date of the application, the applicant (or any predecessor in title) reasonably believed that the land to which the application relates belonged to him, and

(d) the estate to which the application relates was registered more than one year prior to the date of the application.

(5) In relation to an application under paragraph 1(2), this paragraph has effect as if the reference in sub-paragraph (4)(c) to the date of the application were to the day before the date of the applicant's eviction.

Right to make further application for registration

6. (1) Where a person's application under paragraph 1 is rejected, he may make a further application to be registered as the proprietor of the estate if he is in adverse possession of the estate from the date of the application until the last day of the period of two years beginning with the date of its rejection.

(2) However, a person may not make an application under this paragraph if—

(a) he is a defendant in proceedings which involve asserting a right to possession of the land,

(b) judgment for possession of the land has been given against him in the last two years, or

(c) he has been evicted from the land pursuant to a judgment for possession.

7. If a person makes an application under paragraph 6, he is entitled to be entered in the register as the new proprietor of the estate.

Restriction on applications

8. (1) No one may apply under this Schedule to be registered as the proprietor of an estate in land during, or before the end of twelve months after the end of, any period in which the existing registered proprietor is for the purposes of the Limitation (Enemies and War Prisoners) Act 1945—

(a) an enemy, or

(b) detained in enemy territory.

(2)   No-one may apply under this Schedule to be registered as the proprietor of an estate in land during any period in which the existing registered proprietor is—

     (a)   unable because of mental disability to make decisions about issues of the kind to which such an application would give rise, or

     (b)   unable to communicate such decisions because of mental disability or physical impairment.

(3)   For the purposes of sub-paragraph (2), 'mental disability' means a disability or disorder of the mind or brain, whether permanent or temporary, which results in an impairment or disturbance of mental functioning.

(4)   Where it appears to the registrar that sub-paragraph (1) or (2) applies in relation to an estate in land, he may include a note to that effect in the register.

Effect of registration

9.   (1)   Where a person is registered as the proprietor of an estate in land in pursuance of an application under this Schedule, the title by virtue of adverse possession which he had at the time of the application is extinguished.

     (2)   Subject to sub-paragraph (3), the registration of a person under this Schedule as the proprietor of an estate in land does not affect the priority of any interest affecting the estate.

     (3)   Subject to sub-paragraph (4), where a person is registered under this Schedule as the proprietor of an estate, the estate is vested in him free of any registered charge affecting the estate immediately before his registration.

     (4)   Sub-paragraph (3) does not apply where registration as proprietor is in pursuance of an application determined by reference to whether any of the conditions in paragraph 5 applies.

Apportionment and discharge of charges

10.   (1)   Where—

     (a)   a registered estate continues to be subject to a charge notwithstanding the registration of a person under this Schedule as the proprietor, and

     (b)   the charge affects property other than the estate, the proprietor of the estate may require the chargee to apportion the amount secured by the charge at that time between the estate and the other property on the basis of their respective values.

     (2)   The person requiring the apportionment is entitled to a discharge of his estate from the charge on payment of—

     (a)   the amount apportioned to the estate, and

     (b)   the costs incurred by the chargee as a result of the apportionment.

     (3)   On a discharge under this paragraph, the liability of the chargor to the chargee is reduced by the amount apportioned to the estate.

     (4)   Rules may make provision about apportionment under this paragraph, in particular, provision about—

     (a)   procedure,

     (b)   valuation,

     (c)   calculation of costs payable under sub-paragraph (2)(b), and

     (d)   payment of the costs of the chargor.

Meaning of "adverse possession"

11.   (1)   A person is in adverse possession of an estate in land for the purposes of this Schedule if, but for section 96, a period of limitation under section 15 of the Limitation Act 1980 would run in his favour in relation to the estate.

     (2)   A person is also to be regarded for those purposes as having been in adverse possession of an estate in land—

     (a)   where he is the successor in title to an estate in the land, during any period of adverse possession by a predecessor in title to that estate, or

     (b)   during any period of adverse possession by another person which comes between, and is continuous with, periods of adverse possession of his own.

(3) In determining whether for the purposes of this paragraph a period of limitation would run under section 15 of the Limitation Act 1980, there are to be disregarded—

    (a) the commencement of any legal proceedings, and

    (b) paragraph 6 of Schedule 1 to that Act.

Trusts

12. A person is not to be regarded as being in adverse possession of an estate for the purposes of this Schedule at any time when the estate is subject to a trust, unless the interest of each of the beneficiaries in the estate is an interest in possession.

Crown foreshore

13. (1) Where—

    (a) a person is in adverse possession of an estate in land,

    (b) the estate belongs to Her Majesty in right of the Crown or the Duchy of Lancaster or to the Duchy of Cornwall, and

    (c) the land consists of foreshore, paragraph 1(1) is to have effect as if the reference to ten years were to sixty years.

(2) For the purposes of sub-paragraph (1), land is to be treated as foreshore if it has been foreshore at any time in the previous ten years.

(3) In this paragraph, 'foreshore' means the shore and bed of the sea and of any tidal water, below the line of the medium high tide between the spring and neap tides.

Rentcharges

14. Rules must make provision to apply the preceding provisions of this Schedule to registered rentcharges, subject to such modifications and exceptions as the rules may provide.

Procedure

15. Rules may make provision about the procedure to be followed pursuant to an application under this Schedule.

SCHEDULE 8
INDEMNITIES

Entitlement

1. (1) A person is entitled to be indemnified by the registrar if he suffers loss by reason of—

    (a) rectification of the register,

    (b) a mistake whose correction would involve rectification of the register,

    (c) a mistake in an official search,

    (d) a mistake in an official copy,

    (e) a mistake in a document kept by the registrar which is not an original and is referred to in the register,

    (f) the loss or destruction of a document lodged at the registry for inspection or safe custody,

    (g) a mistake in the cautions register, or

    (h) failure by the registrar to perform his duty under section 50.

(2) For the purposes of sub-paragraph (1)(a)—

    (a) any person who suffers loss by reason of the change of title under section 62 is to be regarded as having suffered loss by reason of rectification of the register, and

    (b) the proprietor of a registered estate or charge claiming in good faith under a forged disposition is, where the register is rectified, to be regarded as having suffered loss by reason of such rectification as if the disposition had not been forged.

(3) No indemnity under sub-paragraph (1)(b) is payable until a decision has been made about whether to alter the register for the purpose of correcting the mistake; and the loss suffered by reason of the mistake is to be determined in the light of that decision.

Mines and minerals

2.   No indemnity is payable under this Schedule on account of—

    (a)   any mines or minerals, or

    (b)   the existence of any right to work or get mines or minerals,

unless it is noted in the register that the title to the registered estate concerned includes the mines or minerals.

Costs

3.   (1)   In respect of loss consisting of costs or expenses incurred by the claimant in relation to the matter, an indemnity under this Schedule is payable only on account of costs or expenses reasonably incurred by the claimant with the consent of the registrar.

    (2)   The requirement of consent does not apply where—

        (a)   the costs or expenses must be incurred by the claimant urgently, and

        (b)   it is not reasonably practicable to apply for the registrar's consent.

    (3)   If the registrar approves the incurring of costs or expenses after they have been incurred, they shall be treated for the purposes of this paragraph as having been incurred with his consent.

4.   (1)   If no indemnity is payable to a claimant under this Schedule, the registrar may pay such amount as he thinks fit in respect of any costs or expenses reasonably incurred by the claimant in connection with the claim which have been incurred with the consent of the registrar.

    (2)   The registrar may make a payment under sub-paragraph (1) notwithstanding the absence of consent if—

        (a)   it appears to him—

            (i)   that the costs or expenses had to be incurred urgently, and

            (ii)   that it was not reasonably practicable to apply for his consent, or

        (b)   he has subsequently approved the incurring of the costs or expenses.

Claimant's fraud or lack of care

5.   (1)   No indemnity is payable under this Schedule on account of any loss suffered by a claimant—

        (a)   wholly or partly as a result of his own fraud, or

        (b)   wholly as a result of his own lack of proper care.

    (2)   Where any loss is suffered by a claimant partly as a result of his own lack of proper care, any indemnity payable to him is to be reduced to such extent as is fair having regard to his share in the responsibility for the loss.

    (3)   For the purposes of this paragraph any fraud or lack of care on the part of a person from whom the claimant derives title (otherwise than under a disposition for valuable consideration which is registered or protected by an entry in the register) is to be treated as if it were fraud or lack of care on the part of the claimant.

Valuation of estates etc.

6.   Where an indemnity is payable in respect of the loss of an estate, interest or charge, the value of the estate, interest or charge for the purposes of the indemnity is to be regarded as not exceeding—

    (a)   in the case of an indemnity under paragraph 1(1)(a), its value immediately before rectification of the register (but as if there were to be no rectification), and

    (b)   in the case of an indemnity under paragraph 1(1)(b), its value at the time when the mistake which caused the loss was made.

Determination of indemnity by court

7.   (1)   A person may apply to the court for the determination of any question as to—

        (a)   whether he is entitled to an indemnity under this Schedule, or

        (b)   the amount of such an indemnity.

(2) Paragraph 3(1) does not apply to the costs of an application to the court under this paragraph or of any legal proceedings arising out of such an application.

Time limits

8. For the purposes of the Limitation Act 1980—
(a) a liability to pay an indemnity under this Schedule is a simple contract debt, and
(b) the cause of action arises at the time when the claimant knows, or but for his own default might have known, of the existence of his claim.

Interest

9. Rules may make provision about the payment of interest on an indemnity under this Schedule, including—
(a) the circumstances in which interest is payable, and
(b) the periods for and rates at which it is payable.

Recovery of indemnity by registrar

10. (1) Where an indemnity under this Schedule is paid to a claimant in respect of any loss, the registrar is entitled (without prejudice to any other rights he may have)—
(a) to recover the amount paid from any person who caused or substantially contributed to the loss by his fraud, or
(b) for the purpose of recovering the amount paid, to enforce the rights of action referred to in sub-paragraph (2).
(2) Those rights of action are—
(a) any right of action (of whatever nature and however arising) which the claimant would have been entitled to enforce had the indemnity not been paid, and
(b) where the register has been rectified, any right of action (of whatever nature and however arising) which the person in whose favour the register has been rectified would have been entitled to enforce had it not been rectified.
(3) References in this paragraph to an indemnity include interest paid on an indemnity under rules under paragraph 9.

Interpretation

11. (1) For the purposes of this Schedule, references to a mistake in something include anything mistakenly omitted from it as well as anything mistakenly included in it.
(2) In this Schedule, references to rectification of the register are to alteration of the register which—
(a) involves the correction of a mistake, and
(b) prejudicially affects the title of a registered proprietor.

SCHEDULE 10
MISCELLANEOUS AND GENERAL POWERS

PART 1
MISCELLANEOUS

Dealings with estates subject to compulsory first registration

1. (1) Rules may make provision—
(a) applying this Act to a pre-registration dealing with a registrable legal estate as if the dealing had taken place after the date of first registration of the estate, and
(b) about the date on which registration of the dealing is effective.
(2) For the purposes of sub-paragraph (1)—
(a) a legal estate is registrable if a person is subject to a duty under section 6 to make an application to be registered as the proprietor of it, and
(b) a pre-registration dealing is one which takes place before the making of such an application.

Regulation of title matters between sellers and buyers

2.   (1)   Rules may make provision about the obligations with respect to—
            (a)   proof of title, or
            (b)   perfection of title, of the seller under a contract for the transfer, or other disposition, for valuable consideration of a registered estate or charge.
       (2)   Rules under this paragraph may be expressed to have effect notwithstanding any stipulation to the contrary.

Implied covenants

3.   Rules may—
       (a)   make provision about the form of provisions extending or limiting any covenant implied by virtue of Part 1 of the Law of Property (Miscellaneous Provisions) Act 1994 (c. 36) (implied covenants for title) on a registrable disposition;
       (b)   make provision about the application of section 77 of the Law of Property Act 1925 (c. 20) (implied covenants in conveyance subject to rents) to transfers of registered estates;
       (c)   make provision about reference in the register to implied covenants, including provision for the state of the register to be conclusive in relation to whether covenants have been implied.

Land certificates

4.   Rules may make provision about—
       (a)   when a certificate of registration of title to a legal estate may be issued,
       (b)   the form and content of such a certificate, and
       (c)   when such a certificate must be produced or surrendered to the registrar.

PART 2
GENERAL

Notice

5.   (1)   Rules may make provision about the form, content and service of notice under this Act.
       (2)   Rules under this paragraph about the service of notice may, in particular—
            (a)   make provision requiring the supply of an address for service and about the entry of addresses for service in the register;
            (b)   make provision about—
                (i)   the time for service,
                (ii)   the mode of service, and
                (iii)   when service is to be regarded as having taken place.

Applications

6.   Rules may—
       (a)   make provision about the form and content of applications under this Act;
       (b)   make provision requiring applications under this Act to be supported by such evidence as the rules may provide;
       (c)   make provision about when an application under this Act is to be taken as made;
       (d)   make provision about the order in which competing applications are to be taken to rank;
       (e)   make provision for an alteration made by the registrar for the purpose of correcting a mistake in an application or accompanying document to have effect in such circumstances as the rules may provide as if made by the applicant or other interested party or parties.

Statutory statements

7.   Rules may make provision about the form of any statement required under an enactment to be included in an instrument effecting a registrable disposition or a disposition which triggers the requirement of registration.

Residual power

8. Rules may make any other provision which it is expedient to make for the purposes of carrying this Act into effect, whether similar or not to any provision which may be made under the other powers to make land registration rules.

SCHEDULE 12
TRANSITION

Existing entries in the register

1. Nothing in the repeals made by this Act affects the validity of any entry in the register.
2. (1) This Act applies to notices entered under the Land Registration Act 1925 as it applies to notices entered in pursuance of an application under section 34(2)(a).

    (2) This Act applies to restrictions and inhibitions entered under the Land Registration Act 1925 as it applies to restrictions entered under this Act.

    (3) Notwithstanding their repeal by this Act, sections 55 and 56 of the Land Registration Act 1925 shall continue to have effect so far as relating to cautions against dealings lodged under that Act.

    (4) Rules may make provision about cautions against dealings entered under the Land Registration Act 1925.

    (5) In this paragraph, references to the Land Registration Act 1925 include a reference to any enactment replaced (directly or indirectly) by that Act.
3. An entry in the register which, immediately before the repeal of section 144(1)(xi) of the Land Registration Act 1925, operated by virtue of rule 239 of the Land Registration Rules as a caution under section 54 of that Act shall continue to operate as such a caution.

Existing cautions against first registration

4. Notwithstanding the repeal of section 56(3) of the Land Registration Act 1925, that provision shall continue to have effect in relation to cautions against first registration lodged under that Act, or any enactment replaced (directly or indirectly) by that Act.

Pending applications

5. Notwithstanding the repeal of the Land Registration Act 1925, that Act shall continue to have effect in relation to an application for the entry in the register of a notice, restriction, inhibition or caution against dealings which is pending immediately before the repeal of the provision under which the application is made.
6. Notwithstanding the repeal of section 53 of the Land Registration Act 1925, subsections (1) and (2) of that section shall continue to have effect in relation to an application to lodge a caution against first registration which is pending immediately before the repeal of those provisions.

Former overriding interests

7. For the period of three years beginning with the day on which Schedule 1 comes into force, it has effect with the insertion after paragraph 14 of—

    '15. A right acquired under the Limitation Act 1980 before the coming into force of this Schedule.'
8. Schedule 3 has effect with the insertion after paragraph 2 of—

    '2A (1) An interest which, immediately before the coming into force of this Schedule, was an overriding interest under section 70(1)(g) of the Land Registration Act 1925 by virtue of a person's receipt of rents and profits, except for an interest of a person of whom inquiry was made before the disposition and who failed to disclose the right when he could reasonably have been expected to do so.

    (2) Sub-paragraph (1) does not apply to an interest if at any time since the coming into force of this Schedule it has been an interest which, had the Land Registration Act 1925 continued in force, would not have been an overriding interest under section 70(1)(g) of that Act by virtue of a person's receipt of rents and profits.'

9.   (1)   This paragraph applies to an easement or profit a prendre which was an overriding interest in relation to a registered estate immediately before the coming into force of Schedule 3, but which would not fall within paragraph 3 of that Schedule if created after the coming into force of that Schedule.

        (2)   In relation to an interest to which this paragraph applies, Schedule 3 has effect as if the interest were not excluded from paragraph 3.

10.   For the period of three years beginning with the day on which Schedule 3 comes into force, paragraph 3 of the Schedule has effect with the omission of the exception.

11.   For the period of three years beginning with the day on which Schedule 3 comes into force, it has effect with the insertion after paragraph 14 of—

            '15. A right under paragraph 18(1) of Schedule 12.'

12.   Paragraph 1 of each of Schedules 1 and 3 shall be taken to include an interest which immediately before the coming into force of the Schedule was an overriding interest under section 70(1)(k) of the Land Registration Act 1925.

13.   Paragraph 6 of each of Schedules 1 and 3 shall be taken to include an interest which immediately before the coming into force of the Schedule was an overriding interest under section 70(1)(i) of the Land Registration Act 1925 and whose status as such was preserved by section 19(3) of the Local Land Charges Act 1975 (transitional provision in relation to change in definition of 'local land charge').

Cautions against first registration

14.   (1)   For the period of two years beginning with the day on which section 15 comes into force, it has effect with the following omissions—

            (a)   in subsection (1), the words 'Subject to subsection (3),', and

            (b)   subsection (3).

        (2)   Any caution lodged by virtue of sub-paragraph (1) which is in force immediately before the end of the period mentioned in that sub-paragraph shall cease to have effect at the end of that period, except in relation to applications for registration made before the end of that period.

        (3)   This paragraph does not apply to section 15 as applied by section 81.

15.   (1)   As applied by section 81, section 15 has effect for the period of ten years beginning with the day on which it comes into force, or such longer period as rules may provide, with the omission of subsection (3)(a)(i).

        (2)   Any caution lodged by virtue of sub-paragraph (1) which is in force immediately before the end of the period mentioned in that sub-paragraph shall cease to have effect at the end of that period, except in relation to applications for registration made before the end of that period.

16.   This Act shall apply as if the definition of 'caution against first registration' in section 132 included cautions lodged under section 53 of the Land Registration Act 1925.

Applications under section 34 or 43 by cautioners

17.   Where a caution under section 54 of the Land Registration Act 1925 is lodged in respect of a person's estate, right, interest or claim, he may only make an application under section 34 or 43 above in respect of that estate, right, interest or claim if he also applies to the registrar for the withdrawal of the caution.

Adverse possession

18.   (1)   Where a registered estate in land is held in trust for a person by virtue of section 75(1) of the Land Registration Act 1925 immediately before the coming into force of section 97, he is entitled to be registered as the proprietor of the estate.

        (2)   A person has a defence to any action for the possession of land (in addition to any other defence he may have) if he is entitled under this paragraph to be registered as the proprietor of an estate in the land.

        (3)   Where in an action for possession of land a court determines that a person is entitled to a defence under this paragraph, the court must order the registrar to register him as the

proprietor of the estate in relation to which he is entitled under this paragraph to be registered.

(4)   Entitlement under this paragraph shall be disregarded for the purposes of section 131(1).

(5)   Rules may make transitional provision for cases where a rentcharge is held in trust under section 75(1) of the Land Registration Act 1925 immediately before the coming into force of section 97.

Indemnities

19.   (1)   Schedule 8 applies in relation to claims made before the commencement of that Schedule which have not been settled by agreement or finally determined by that time (as well as to claims for indemnity made after the commencement of that Schedule).

(2)   But paragraph 3(1) of that Schedule does not apply in relation to costs and expenses incurred in respect of proceedings, negotiations or other matters begun before 27 April 1997.

Implied indemnity covenants on transfers of pre-1996 leases

Note. See the Land Registration Rules 2003, r 60(2).

20.   (1)   On a disposition of a registered leasehold estate by way of transfer, the following covenants are implied in the instrument effecting the disposition, unless the contrary intention is expressed—

    (a)   in the case of a transfer of the whole of the land comprised in the registered lease, the covenant in sub-paragraph (2), and

    (b)   in the case of a transfer of part of the land comprised in the lease—

        (i)   the covenant in sub-paragraph (3), and

        (ii)   where the transferor continues to hold land under the lease, the covenant in sub-paragraph (4).

(2)   The transferee covenants with the transferor that during the residue of the term granted by the registered lease the transferee and the persons deriving title under him will—

    (a)   pay the rent reserved by the lease,

    (b)   comply with the covenants and conditions contained in the lease, and

    (c)   keep the transferor and the persons deriving title under him indemnified against all actions, expenses and claims on account of any failure to comply with paragraphs (a) and (b).

(3)   The transferee covenants with the transferor that during the residue of the term granted by the registered lease the transferee and the persons deriving title under him will—

    (a)   where the rent reserved by the lease is apportioned, pay the rent apportioned to the part transferred,

    (b)   comply with the covenants and conditions contained in the lease so far as affecting the part transferred, and

    (c)   keep the transferor and the persons deriving title under him indemnified against all actions, expenses and claims on account of any failure to comply with paragraphs (a) and (b).

(4)   The transferor covenants with the transferee that during the residue of the term granted by the registered lease the transferor and the persons deriving title under him will—

    (a)   where the rent reserved by the lease is apportioned, pay the rent apportioned to the part retained,

    (b)   comply with the covenants and conditions contained in the lease so far as affecting the part retained, and

    (c)   keep the transferee and the persons deriving title under him indemnified against all actions, expenses and claims on account of any failure to comply with paragraphs (a) and (b).

(5)   This paragraph does not apply to a lease which is a new tenancy for the purposes of section 1 of the Landlord and Tenant (Covenants) Act 1995.

COMMONHOLD AND LEASEHOLD REFORM ACT 2002
(2002, c. 15)

PART 1
COMMONHOLD

Nature of commonhold

1.   Commonhold land

(1)   Land is commonhold land if—

(a)   the freehold estate in the land is registered as a freehold estate in commonhold land,

(b)   the land is specified in the memorandum of association of a commonhold association as the land in relation to which the association is to exercise functions, and

(c)   a commonhold community statement makes provision for rights and duties of the commonhold association and unit-holders (whether or not the statement has come into force).

(2)   In this Part a reference to a commonhold is a reference to land in relation to which a commonhold association exercises functions.

(3)   In this Part—

'commonhold association' has the meaning given by section 34,

'commonhold community statement' has the meaning given by section 31,

'commonhold unit' has the meaning given by section 11,

'common parts' has the meaning given by section 25, and

'unit-holder' has the meaning given by sections 12 and 13.

(4)   Sections 7 and 9 make provision for the vesting in the commonhold association of the fee simple in possession in the common parts of a commonhold.

Registration

2.   Application

(1)   The Registrar shall register a freehold estate in land as a freehold estate in commonhold land if—

(a)   the registered freeholder of the land makes an application under this section, and

(b)   no part of the land is already commonhold land.

(2)   An application under this section must be accompanied by the documents listed in Schedule 1.

(3)   A person is the registered freeholder of land for the purposes of this Part if—

(a)   he is registered as the proprietor of a freehold estate in the land with absolute title, or

(b)   he has applied, and the Registrar is satisfied that he is entitled, to be registered as mentioned in paragraph (a).

3.   Consent

(1)   An application under section 2 may not be made in respect of a freehold estate in land without the consent of anyone who—

(a)   is the registered proprietor of the freehold estate in the whole or part of the land,

(b)   is the registered proprietor of a leasehold estate in the whole or part of the land granted for a term of more than than 21 years,

(c)   is the registered proprietor of a charge over the whole or part of the land, or

(d)   falls within any other class of person which may be prescribed.

(2)   Regulations shall make provision about consent for the purposes of this section; in particular, the regulations may make provision—

(a)   prescribing the form of consent;

(b)   about the effect and duration of consent (including provision for consent to bind successors);

(c)   about withdrawal of consent (including provision preventing withdrawal in specified circumstances);

    (d)   for consent given for the purpose of one application under section 2 to have effect for the purpose of another application;

    (e)   for consent to be deemed to have been given in specified circumstances;

    (f)   enabling a court to dispense with a requirement for consent in specified circumstances.

(3)   An order under subsection (2)(f) dispensing with a requirement for consent—

    (a)   may be absolute or conditional, and

    (b)   may make such other provision as the court thinks appropriate.

4. Land which may not be commonhold

Schedule 2 (which provides that an application under section 2 may not relate wholly or partly to land of certain kinds) shall have effect.

5. Registered details

(1)   The Registrar shall ensure that in respect of any commonhold land the following are kept in his custody and referred to in the register—

    (a)   the prescribed details of the commonhold association;

    (b)   the prescribed details of the registered freeholder of each commonhold unit;

    (c)   a copy of the commonhold community statement;

    (d)   a copy of the memorandum and articles of association of the commonhold association.

(2)   The Registrar may arrange for a document or information to be kept in his custody and referred to in the register in respect of commonhold land if the document or information—

    (a)   is not mentioned in subsection (1), but

    (b)   is submitted to the Registrar in accordance with a provision made by or by virtue of this Part.

(3)   Subsection (1)(b) shall not apply during a transitional period within the meaning of section 8.

6. Registration in error

(1)   This section applies where a freehold estate in land is registered as a freehold estate in commonhold land and—

    (a)   the application for registration was not made in accordance with section 2,

    (b)   the certificate under paragraph 7 of Schedule 1 was inaccurate, or

    (c)   the registration contravened a provision made by or by virtue of this Part.

(2)   The register may not be altered by the Registrar under Schedule 4 to the Land Registration Act 2002 (alteration of register).

(3)   The court may grant a declaration that the freehold estate should not have been registered as a freehold estate in commonhold land.

(4)   A declaration under subsection (3) may be granted only on the application of a person who claims to be adversely affected by the registration.

(5)   On granting a declaration under subsection (3) the court may make any order which appears to it to be appropriate.

(6)   An order under subsection (5) may, in particular—

    (a)   provide for the registration to be treated as valid for all purposes;

    (b)   provide for alteration of the register;

    (c)   provide for land to cease to be commonhold land;

    (d)   require a director or other specified officer of a commonhold association to take steps to alter or amend a document;

    (e)   require a director or other specified officer of a commonhold association to take specified steps;

    (f)   make an award of compensation (whether or not contingent upon the occurrence or non-occurrence of a specified event) to be paid by one specified person to another;

    (g)   apply, disapply or modify a provision of Schedule 8 to the Land Registration Act 2002 (indemnity).

Effect of registration

7.   Registration without unit-holders

(1)   This section applies where—

  (a)   a freehold estate in land is registered as a freehold estate in commonhold land in pursuance of an application under section 2, and

  (b)   the application is not accompanied by a statement under section 9(1)(b).

(2)   On registration—

  (a)   the applicant shall continue to be registered as the proprietor of the freehold estate in the commonhold land, and

  (b)   the rights and duties conferred and imposed by the commonhold community statement shall not come into force (subject to section 8(2)(b)).

(3)   Where after registration a person other than the applicant becomes entitled to be registered as the proprietor of the freehold estate in one or more, but not all, of the commonhold units—

  (a)   the commonhold association shall be entitled to be registered as the proprietor of the freehold estate in the common parts,

  (b)   the Registrar shall register the commonhold association in accordance with paragraph (a) (without an application being made),

  (c)   the rights and duties conferred and imposed by the commonhold community statement shall come into force, and

  (d)   any lease of the whole or part of the commonhold land shall be extinguished by virtue of this section.

(4)   For the purpose of subsection (3)(d) 'lease' means a lease which—

  (a)   is granted for any term, and

  (b)   is granted before the commonhold association becomes entitled to be registered as the proprietor of the freehold estate in the common parts.

8.   Transitional period

(1)   In this Part 'transitional period' means the period between registration of the freehold estate in land as a freehold estate in commonhold land and the event mentioned in section 7(3).

(2)   Regulations may provide that during a transitional period a relevant provision—

  (a)   shall not have effect, or

  (b)   shall have effect with specified modifications.

(3)   In subsection (2) 'relevant provision' means a provision made—

  (a)   by or by virtue of this Part,

  (b)   by a commonhold community statement, or

  (c)   by the memorandum or articles of the commonhold association.

(4)   The Registrar shall arrange for the freehold estate in land to cease to be registered as a freehold estate in commonhold land if the registered proprietor makes an application to the Registrar under this subsection during the transitional period.

(5)   The provisions about consent made by or under sections 2 and 3 and Schedule 1 shall apply in relation to an application under subsection (4) as they apply in relation to an application under section 2.

(6)   A reference in this Part to a commonhold association exercising functions in relation to commonhold land includes a reference to a case where a commonhold association would exercise functions in relation to commonhold land but for the fact that the time in question falls in a transitional period.

9.   Registration with unit-holders

(1)   This section applies in relation to a freehold estate in commonhold land if—

  (a)   it is registered as a freehold estate in commonhold land in pursuance of an application under section 2, and

  (b)   the application is accompanied by a statement by the applicant requesting that this section should apply.

(2)   A statement under subsection (1)(b) must include a list of the commonhold units giving in relation to each one the prescribed details of the proposed initial unit-holder or joint unit-holders.

(3)   On registration—

(a)   the commonhold association shall be entitled to be registered as the proprietor of the freehold estate in the common parts,

(b)   a person specified by virtue of subsection (2) as the initial unit-holder of a commonhold unit shall be entitled to be registered as the proprietor of the freehold estate in the unit,

(c)   a person specified by virtue of subsection (2) as an initial joint unit-holder of a commonhold unit shall be entitled to be registered as one of the proprietors of the freehold estate in the unit,

(d)   the Registrar shall make entries in the register to reflect paragraphs (a) to (c) (without applications being made),

(e)   the rights and duties conferred and imposed by the commonhold community statement shall come into force, and

(f)   any lease of the whole or part of the commonhold land shall be extinguished by virtue of this section.

(4)   For the purpose of subsection (3)(f) 'lease' means a lease which—

(a)   is granted for any term, and

(b)   is granted before the commonhold association becomes entitled to be registered as the proprietor of the freehold estate in the common parts.

10.   Extinguished lease: liability

(1)   This section applies where—

(a)   a lease is extinguished by virtue of section 7(3)(d) or 9(3)(f), and

(b)   the consent of the holder of that lease was not among the consents required by section 3 in respect of the application under section 2 for the land to become commonhold land.

(2)   If the holder of a lease superior to the extinguished lease gave consent under section 3, he shall be liable for loss suffered by the holder of the extinguished lease.

(3)   If the holders of a number of leases would be liable under subsection (2), liability shall attach only to the person whose lease was most proximate to the extinguished lease.

(4)   If no person is liable under subsection (2), the person who gave consent under section 3 as the holder of the freehold estate out of which the extinguished lease was granted shall be liable for loss suffered by the holder of the extinguished lease.

Commonhold unit

11.   Definition

(1)   In this Part 'commonhold unit' means a commonhold unit specified in a commonhold community statement in accordance with this section.

(2)   A commonhold community statement must—

(a)   specify at least two parcels of land as commonhold units, and

(b)   define the extent of each commonhold unit.

(3)   In defining the extent of a commonhold unit a commonhold community statement—

(a)   must refer to a plan which is included in the statement and which complies with prescribed requirements,

(b)   may refer to an area subject to the exclusion of specified structures, fittings, apparatus or appurtenances within the area,

(c)   may exclude the structures which delineate an area referred to, and

(d)   may refer to two or more areas (whether or not contiguous).

(4)   A commonhold unit need not contain all or any part of a building.

12.   Unit-holder

A person is the unit-holder of a commonhold unit if he is entitled to be registered as the proprietor of the freehold estate in the unit (whether or not he is registered).

13.   Joint unit-holders

(1)   Two or more persons are joint unit-holders of a commonhold unit if they are entitled to be registered as proprietors of the freehold estate in the unit (whether or not they are registered).

(2)   In the application of the following provisions to a unit with joint unit-holders a reference to a unit-holder is a reference to the joint unit-holders together—

(b)   section 15(1),

(d)   section 20(1),

(e)   section 23(1),

(f)   section 35(1)(b), and

(i)   section 47(2).

(3)   In the application of the following provisions to a unit with joint unit-holders a reference to a unit-holder includes a reference to each joint unit-holder and to the joint unit-holders together—

(a)   section 1(1)(c),

(aa)   section 14(3),

(ab)   section 15(3),

(b)   section 16,

(ba)   section 19(2) and (3),

(c)   section 31(1)(b), (3)(b), (5)(j) and (7),

(d)   section 32(4)(a) and (c),

(e)   section 35(1)(a), (2) and (3),

(f)   section 37(2),

(fa)   section 38(1),

(fb)   section 39(2),

(g)   section 40(1), and

(h)   section 58(3)(a).

(4)   Regulations under this Part which refer to a unit-holder shall make provision for the construction of the reference in the case of joint unit-holders.

(5)   Regulations may amend subsection (2) or (3).

(6)   Regulations may make provision for the construction in the case of joint unit-holders of a reference to a unit-holder in—

(a)   an enactment,

(b)   a commonhold community statement,

(c)   the memorandum or articles of association of a commonhold association, or

(d)   another document.

14.   Use and maintenance

(1)   A commonhold community statement must make provision regulating the use of commonhold units.

(2)   A commonhold community statement must make provision imposing duties in respect of the insurance, repair and maintenance of each commonhold unit.

(3)   A duty under subsection (2) may be imposed on the commonhold association or the unit-holder.

15.   Transfer

(1)   In this Part a reference to the transfer of a commonhold unit is a reference to the transfer of a unit-holder's freehold estate in a unit to another person—

(a)   whether or not for consideration,

(b)   whether or not subject to any reservation or other terms, and

(c)   whether or not by operation of law.

(2)   A commonhold community statement may not prevent or restrict the transfer of a commonhold unit.

(3)   On the transfer of a commonhold unit the new unit-holder shall notify the commonhold association of the transfer.

(4)   Regulations may—

    (a)   prescribe the form and manner of notice under subsection (3);

    (b)   prescribe the time within which notice is to be given;

    (c)   make provision (including provision requiring the payment of money) about the effect of failure to give notice.

16.   Transfer: effect

(1)   A right or duty conferred or imposed—

    (a)   by a commonhold community statement, or

    (b)   in accordance with section 20, shall affect a new unit-holder in the same way as it affected the former unit-holder.

(2)   A former unit-holder shall not incur a liability or acquire a right—

    (a)   under or by virtue of the commonhold community statement, or

    (b)   by virtue of anything done in accordance with section 20.

(3)   Subsection (2)—

    (a)   shall not be capable of being disapplied or varied by agreement, and

    (b)   is without prejudice to any liability or right incurred or acquired before a transfer takes effect.

(4)   In this section—

'former unit-holder' means a person from whom a commonhold unit has been transferred (whether or not he has ceased to be the registered proprietor), and

'new unit-holder' means a person to whom a commonhold unit is transferred (whether or not he has yet become the registered proprietor).

17.   Leasing: residential

(1)   It shall not be possible to create a term of years absolute in a residential commonhold unit unless the term satisfies prescribed conditions.

(2)   The conditions may relate to—

    (a)   length;

    (b)   the circumstances in which the term is granted;

    (c)   any other matter.

(3)   Subject to subsection (4), an instrument or agreement shall be of no effect to the extent that it purports to create a term of years in contravention of subsection (1).

(4)   Where an instrument or agreement purports to create a term of years in contravention of subsection (1) a party to the instrument or agreement may apply to the court for an order—

    (a)   providing for the instrument or agreement to have effect as if it provided for the creation of a term of years of a specified kind;

    (b)   providing for the return or payment of money;

    (c)   making such other provision as the court thinks appropriate.

(5)   A commonhold unit is residential if provision made in the commonhold community statement by virtue of section 14(1) requires it to be used only—

    (a)   for residential purposes, or

    (b)   for residential and other incidental purposes.

18.   Leasing: non-residential

An instrument or agreement which creates a term of years absolute in a commonhold unit which is not residential (within the meaning of section 17) shall have effect subject to any provision of the commonhold community statement.

19.   Leasing: supplementary

(1)   Regulations may—

    (a)   impose obligations on a tenant of a commonhold unit;

(b)   enable a commonhold community statement to impose obligations on a tenant of a commonhold unit.

(2)   Regulations under subsection (1) may, in particular, require a tenant of a commonhold unit to make payments to the commonhold association or a unit-holder in discharge of payments which—

(a)   are due in accordance with the commonhold community statement to be made by the unit-holder, or

(b)   are due in accordance with the commonhold community statement to be made by another tenant of the unit.

(3)   Regulations under subsection (1) may, in particular, provide—

(a)   for the amount of payments under subsection (2) to be set against sums owed by the tenant (whether to the person by whom the payments were due to be made or to some other person);

(b)   for the amount of payments under subsection (2) to be recovered from the unit-holder or another tenant of the unit.

(4)   Regulations may modify a rule of law about leasehold estates (whether deriving from the common law or from an enactment) in its application to a term of years in a commonhold unit.

(5)   Regulations under this section—

(a)   may make provision generally or in relation to specified circumstances, and

(b)   may make different provision for different descriptions of commonhold land or commonhold unit.

20.   Other transactions

(1)   A commonhold community statement may not prevent or restrict the creation, grant or transfer by a unit-holder of—

(a)   an interest in the whole or part of his unit, or

(b)   a charge over his unit.

(2)   Subsection (1) is subject to sections 17 to 19 (which impose restrictions about leases).

(3)   It shall not be possible to create an interest of a prescribed kind in a commonhold unit unless the commonhold association—

(a)   is a party to the creation of the interest, or

(b)   consents in writing to the creation of the interest.

(4)   A commonhold association may act as described in subsection (3)(a) or (b) only if—

(a)   the association passes a resolution to take the action, and

(b)   at least 75 per cent. of those who vote on the resolution vote in favour.

(5)   An instrument or agreement shall be of no effect to the extent that it purports to create an interest in contravention of subsection (3).

(6)   In this section 'interest' does not include—

(a)   a charge, or

(b)   an interest which arises by virtue of a charge.

21.   Part-unit: interests

(1)   It shall not be possible to create an interest in part only of a commonhold unit.

(2)   But subsection (1) shall not prevent—

(a)   the creation of a term of years absolute in part only of a residential commonhold unit where the term satisfies prescribed conditions,

(b)   the creation of a term of years absolute in part only of a non-residential commonhold unit, or

(c)   the transfer of the freehold estate in part only of a commonhold unit where the commonhold association consents in writing to the transfer.

(3)   An instrument or agreement shall be of no effect to the extent that it purports to create an interest in contravention of subsection (1).

(4)   Subsection (5) applies where—

(a)   land becomes commonhold land or is added to a commonhold unit, and

(b)   immediately before that event there is an interest in the land which could not be created after that event by reason of subsection (1).

(5)   The interest shall be extinguished by virtue of this subsection to the extent that it could not be created by reason of subsection (1).

(6)   Section 17(2) and (4) shall apply (with any necessary modifications) in relation to subsection (2)(a) and (b) above.

(7)   Where part only of a unit is held under a lease, regulations may modify the application of a provision which—

(a)   is made by or by virtue of this Part, and

(b)   applies to a unit-holder or a tenant or both.

(8)   Section 20(4) shall apply in relation to subsection (2)(c) above.

(9)   Where the freehold interest in part only of a commonhold unit is transferred, the part transferred—

(a)   becomes a new commonhold unit by virtue of this subsection, or

(b)   in a case where the request for consent under subsection (2)(c) states that this paragraph is to apply, becomes part of a commonhold unit specified in the request.

(10)   Regulations may make provision, or may require a commonhold community statement to make provision, about—

(a)   registration of units created by virtue of subsection (9);

(b)   the adaptation of provision made by or by virtue of this Part or by or by virtue of a commonhold community statement to a case where units are created or modified by virtue of subsection (9).

22.   Part-unit: charging

(1)   It shall not be possible to create a charge over part only of an interest in a commonhold unit.

(2)   An instrument or agreement shall be of no effect to the extent that it purports to create a charge in contravention of subsection (1).

(3)   Subsection (4) applies where—

(a)   land becomes commonhold land or is added to a commonhold unit, and

(b)   immediately before that event there is a charge over the land which could not be created after that event by reason of subsection (1).

(4)   The charge shall be extinguished by virtue of this subsection to the extent that it could not be created by reason of subsection (1).

23.   Changing size

(1)   An amendment of a commonhold community statement which redefines the extent of a commonhold unit may not be made unless the unit-holder consents—

(a)   in writing, and

(b)   before the amendment is made.

(2)   But regulations may enable a court to dispense with the requirement for consent on the application of a commonhold association in prescribed circumstances.

24.   Changing size: charged unit

(1)   This section applies to an amendment of a commonhold community statement which redefines the extent of a commonhold unit over which there is a registered charge.

(2)   The amendment may not be made unless the registered proprietor of the charge consents—

(a)   in writing, and

(b)   before the amendment is made.

(3)   But regulations may enable a court to dispense with the requirement for consent on the application of a commonhold association in prescribed circumstances.

(4)   If the amendment removes land from the commonhold unit, the charge shall by virtue of this subsection be extinguished to the extent that it relates to the land which is removed.

(5)   If the amendment adds land to the unit, the charge shall by virtue of this subsection be extended so as to relate to the land which is added.

(6)   Regulations may make provision—

(a) requiring notice to be given to the Registrar in circumstances to which this section applies;

(b) requiring the Registrar to alter the register to reflect the application of subsection (4) or (5).

Common parts

25. Definition

(1) In this Part 'common parts' in relation to a commonhold means every part of the commonhold which is not for the time being a commonhold unit in accordance with the commonhold community statement.

(2) A commonhold community statement may make provision in respect of a specified part of the common parts (a 'limited use area') restricting—

(a) the classes of person who may use it;

(b) the kind of use to which it may be put.

(3) A commonhold community statement—

(a) may make provision which has effect only in relation to a limited use area, and

(b) may make different provision for different limited use areas.

26. Use and maintenance

A commonhold community statement must make provision—

(a) regulating the use of the common parts;

(b) requiring the commonhold association to insure the common parts;

(c) requiring the commonhold association to repair and maintain the common parts.

27. Transactions

(1) Nothing in a commonhold community statement shall prevent or restrict—

(a) the transfer by the commonhold association of its freehold estate in any part of the common parts, or

(b) the creation by the commonhold association of an interest in any part of the common parts.

(2) In this section 'interest' does not include—

(a) a charge, or

(b) an interest which arises by virtue of a charge.

28. Charges: general prohibition

(1) It shall not be possible to create a charge over common parts.

(2) An instrument or agreement shall be of no effect to the extent that it purports to create a charge over common parts.

(3) Where by virtue of section 7 or 9 a commonhold association is registered as the proprietor of common parts, a charge which relates wholly or partly to the common parts shall be extinguished by virtue of this subsection to the extent that it relates to the common parts.

(4) Where by virtue of section 30 land vests in a commonhold association following an amendment to a commonhold community statement which has the effect of adding land to the common parts, a charge which relates wholly or partly to the land added shall be extinguished by virtue of this subsection to the extent that it relates to that land.

(5) This section is subject to section 29 (which permits certain mortgages).

29. New legal mortgages

(1) Section 28 shall not apply in relation to a legal mortgage if the creation of the mortgage is approved by a resolution of the commonhold association.

(2) A resolution for the purposes of subsection (1) must be passed—

(a) before the mortgage is created, and

(b) unanimously.

(3) In this section 'legal mortgage' has the meaning given by section 205(1)(xvi) of the Law of Property Act 1925 (interpretation).

30.   Additions to common parts

(1)   This section applies where an amendment of a commonhold community statement—

    (a)   specifies land which forms part of a commonhold unit, and

    (b)   provides for that land (the 'added land') to be added to the common parts.

(2)   The amendment may not be made unless the registered proprietor of any charge over the added land consents—

    (a)   in writing, and

    (b)   before the amendment is made.

(3)   But regulations may enable a court to dispense with the requirement for consent on the application of a commonhold association in specified circumstances.

(4)   On the filing of the amended statement under section 33—

    (a)   the commonhold association shall be entitled to be registered as the proprietor of the freehold estate in the added land, and

    (b)   the Registrar shall register the commonhold association in accordance with paragraph (a) (without an application being made).

Commonhold community statement

31.   Form and content: general

(1)   A commonhold community statement is a document which makes provision in relation to specified land for—

    (a)   the rights and duties of the commonhold association, and

    (b)   the rights and duties of the unit-holders.

(2)   A commonhold community statement must be in the prescribed form.

(3)   A commonhold community statement may—

    (a)   impose a duty on the commonhold association;

    (b)   impose a duty on a unit-holder;

    (c)   make provision about the taking of decisions in connection with the management of the commonhold or any other matter concerning it.

(4)   Subsection (3) is subject to—

    (a)   any provision made by or by virtue of this Part, and

    (b)   any provision of the memorandum or articles of the commonhold association.

(5)   In subsection (3)(a) and (b) 'duty' includes, in particular, a duty—

    (a)   to pay money;

    (b)   to undertake works;

    (c)   to grant access;

    (d)   to give notice;

    (e)   to refrain from entering into transactions of a specified kind in relation to a commonhold unit;

    (f)   to refrain from using the whole or part of a commonhold unit for a specified purpose or for anything other than a specified purpose;

    (g)   to refrain from undertaking works (including alterations) of a specified kind;

    (h)   to refrain from causing nuisance or annoyance;

    (i)   to refrain from specified behaviour;

    (j)   to indemnify the commonhold association or a unit-holder in respect of costs arising from the breach of a statutory requirement.

(6)   Provision in a commonhold community statement imposing a duty to pay money (whether in pursuance of subsection (5)(a) or any other provision made by or by virtue of this Part) may include provision for the payment of interest in the case of late payment.

(7)   A duty conferred by a commonhold community statement on a commonhold association or a unit-holder shall not require any other formality.

(8)   A commonhold community statement may not provide for the transfer or loss of an interest in land on the occurrence or non-occurrence of a specified event.

(9)   Provision made by a commonhold community statement shall be of no effect to the extent that—

      (a)   it is prohibited by virtue of section 32,

      (b)   it is inconsistent with any provision made by or by virtue of this Part,

      (c)   it is inconsistent with anything which is treated as included in the statement by virtue of section 32, or

      (d)   it is inconsistent with the memorandum or articles of association of the commonhold association.

32.   **Regulations**

(1)   Regulations shall make provision about the content of a commonhold community statement.

(2)   The regulations may permit, require or prohibit the inclusion in a statement of—

      (a)   specified provision, or

      (b)   provision of a specified kind, for a specified purpose or about a specified matter.

(3)   The regulations may—

      (a)   provide for a statement to be treated as including provision prescribed by or determined in accordance with the regulations;

      (b)   permit a statement to make provision in place of provision which would otherwise be treated as included by virtue of paragraph (a).

(4)   The regulations may—

      (a)   make different provision for different descriptions of commonhold association or unit-holder;

      (b)   make different provision for different circumstances;

      (c)   make provision about the extent to which a commonhold community statement may make different provision for different descriptions of unit-holder or common parts.

(5)   The matters to which regulations under this section may relate include, but are not limited to—

      (a)   the matters mentioned in sections 11, 14, 15, 20, 21, 25, 26, 27, 38, 39 and 58, and

      (b)   any matter for which regulations under section 37 may make provision.

33.   **Amendment**

(1)   Regulations under section 32 shall require a commonhold community statement to make provision about how it can be amended.

(2)   The regulations shall, in particular, make provision under section 32(3)(a) (whether or not subject to provision under section 32(3)(b)).

(3)   An amendment of a commonhold community statement shall have no effect unless and until the amended statement is registered in accordance with this section.

(4)   If the commonhold association makes an application under this subsection the Registrar shall arrange for an amended commonhold community statement to be kept in his custody, and referred to in the register, in place of the unamended statement.

(5)   An application under subsection (4) must be accompanied by a certificate given by the directors of the commonhold association that the amended commonhold community statement satisfies the requirements of this Part.

(6)   Where an amendment of a commonhold community statement redefines the extent of a commonhold unit, an application under subsection (4) must be accompanied by any consent required by section 23(1) or 24(2) (or an order of a court dispensing with consent).

(7)   Where an amendment of a commonhold community statement has the effect of changing the extent of the common parts, an application under subsection (4) must be accompanied by any consent required by section 30(2) (or an order of a court dispensing with consent).

(8)   Where the Registrar amends the register on an application under subsection (4) he shall make any consequential amendments to the register which he thinks appropriate.

Commonhold association

34.   **Constitution**

(1)   A commonhold association is a private company limited by guarantee the memorandum of which—

     (a)   states that an object of the company is to exercise the functions of a commonhold association in relation to specified commonhold land, and

     (b)   specifies £1 as the amount required to be specified in pursuance of section 2(4) of the Companies Act 1985 (members' guarantee).

(2)   Schedule 3 (which makes provision about the constitution of a commonhold association) shall have effect.

35. Duty to manage

(1)   The directors of a commonhold association shall exercise their powers so as to permit or facilitate so far as possible—

     (a)   the exercise by each unit-holder of his rights, and

     (b)   the enjoyment by each unit-holder of the freehold estate in his unit.

(2)   The directors of a commonhold association shall, in particular, use any right, power or procedure conferred or created by virtue of section 37 for the purpose of preventing, remedying or curtailing a failure on the part of a unit-holder to comply with a requirement or duty imposed on him by virtue of the commonhold community statement or a provision of this Part.

(3)   But in respect of a particular failure on the part of a unit-holder (the 'defaulter') the directors of a commonhold association—

     (a)   need not take action if they reasonably think that inaction is in the best interests of establishing or maintaining harmonious relationships between all the unit-holders, and that it will not cause any unit-holder (other than the defaulter) significant loss or significant disadvantage, and

     (b)   shall have regard to the desirability of using arbitration, mediation or conciliation procedures (including referral under a scheme approved under section 42) instead of legal proceedings wherever possible.

(4)   A reference in this section to a unit-holder includes a reference to a tenant of a unit.

36. Voting

(1)   This section applies in relation to any provision of this Part (a 'voting provision') which refers to the passing of a resolution by a commonhold association.

(2)   A voting provision is satisfied only if every member is given an opportunity to vote in accordance with any relevant provision of the memorandum or articles of association or the commonhold community statement.

(3)   A vote is cast for the purposes of a voting provision whether it is cast in person or in accordance with a provision which—

     (a)   provides for voting by post, by proxy or in some other manner, and

     (b)   is contained in the memorandum or articles of association or the commonhold community statement.

(4)   A resolution is passed unanimously if every member who casts a vote votes in favour.

Termination: voluntary winding-up

43. Winding-up resolution

(1)   A winding-up resolution in respect of a commonhold association shall be of no effect unless—

     (a)   the resolution is preceded by a declaration of solvency,

     (b)   the commonhold association passes a termination-statement resolution before it passes the winding-up resolution, and

     (c)   each resolution is passed with at least 80 per cent. of the members of the association voting in favour.

(2)   In this Part—

'declaration of solvency' means a directors' statutory declaration made in accordance with section 89 of the Insolvency Act 1986,

'termination-statement resolution' means a resolution approving the terms of a termination statement (within the meaning of section 47), and 'winding-up resolution' means a resolution for voluntary winding-up within the meaning of section 84 of that Act.

44.   100 per cent. agreement

(1)   This section applies where a commonhold association—

    (a)   has passed a winding-up resolution and a termination-statement resolution with 100 per cent. of the members of the association voting in favour, and

    (b)   has appointed a liquidator under section 91 of the Insolvency Act 1986.

(2)   The liquidator shall make a termination application within the period of six months beginning with the day on which the winding-up resolution is passed.

(3)   If the liquidator fails to make a termination application within the period specified in subsection (2) a termination application may be made by—

    (a)   a unit-holder, or

    (b)   a person falling within a class prescribed for the purposes of this subsection.

45.   80 per cent. agreement

(1)   This section applies where a commonhold association—

    (a)   has passed a winding-up resolution and a termination-statement resolution with at least 80 per cent. of the members of the association voting in favour, and

    (b)   has appointed a liquidator under section 91 of the Insolvency Act 1986.

(2)   The liquidator shall within the prescribed period apply to the court for an order determining—

    (a)   the terms and conditions on which a termination application may be made, and

    (b)   the terms of the termination statement to accompany a termination application.

(3)   The liquidator shall make a termination application within the period of three months starting with the date on which an order under subsection (2) is made.

(4)   If the liquidator fails to make an application under subsection (2) or (3) within the period specified in that subsection an application of the same kind may be made by—

    (a)   a unit-holder, or

    (b)   a person falling within a class prescribed for the purposes of this subsection.

46.   Termination application

(1)   A 'termination application' is an application to the Registrar that all the land in relation to which a particular commonhold association exercises functions should cease to be commonhold land.

(2)   A termination application must be accompanied by a termination statement.

(3)   On receipt of a termination application the Registrar shall note it in the register.

47.   Termination statement

(1)   A termination statement must specify—

    (a)   the commonhold association's proposals for the transfer of the commonhold land following acquisition of the freehold estate in accordance with section 49(3), and

    (b)   how the assets of the commonhold association will be distributed.

(2)   A commonhold community statement may make provision requiring any termination statement to make arrangements—

    (a)   of a specified kind, or

    (b)   determined in a specified manner, about the rights of unit-holders in the event of all the land to which the statement relates ceasing to be commonhold land.

(3)   A termination statement must comply with a provision made by the commonhold community statement in reliance on subsection (2).

(4)   Subsection (3) may be disapplied by an order of the court—

    (a)   generally,

    (b)   in respect of specified matters, or

    (c)   for a specified purpose.

(5)   An application for an order under subsection (4) may be made by any member of the commonhold association.

48.   The liquidator

(1)   This section applies where a termination application has been made in respect of particular commonhold land.

(2)   The liquidator shall notify the Registrar of his appointment.

(3)   In the case of a termination application made under section 44 the liquidator shall either—

    (a)   notify the Registrar that the liquidator is content with the termination statement submitted with the termination application, or

    (b)   apply to the court under section 112 of the Insolvency Act 1986 to determine the terms of the termination statement.

(4)   The liquidator shall send to the Registrar a copy of a determination made by virtue of subsection (3)(b).

(5)   Subsection (4) is in addition to any requirement under section 112(3) of the Insolvency Act 1986.

(6)   A duty imposed on the liquidator by this section is to be performed as soon as possible.

(7)   In this section a reference to the liquidator is a reference—

    (a)   to the person who is appointed as liquidator under section 91 of the Insolvency Act 1986, or

    (b)   in the case of a members' voluntary winding up which becomes a creditors' voluntary winding up by virtue of sections 95 and 96 of that Act, to the person acting as liquidator in accordance with section 100 of that Act.

49.   Termination

(1)   This section applies where a termination application is made under section 44 and—

    (a)   a liquidator notifies the Registrar under section 48(3)(a) that he is content with a termination statement, or

    (b)   a determination is made under section 112 of the Insolvency Act 1986 by virtue of section 48(3)(b).

(2)   This section also applies where a termination application is made under section 45.

(3)   The commonhold association shall by virtue of this subsection be entitled to be registered as the proprietor of the freehold estate in each commonhold unit.

(4)   The Registrar shall take such action as appears to him to be appropriate for the purpose of giving effect to the termination statement.

Termination: winding-up by court

50.   Introduction

(1)   Section 51 applies where a petition is presented under section 124 of the Insolvency Act 1986 for the winding up of a commonhold association by the court.

(2)   For the purposes of this Part—

    (a)   an 'insolvent commonhold association' is one in relation to which a winding-up petition has been presented under section 124 of the Insolvency Act 1986,

    (b)   a commonhold association is the 'successor commonhold association' to an insolvent commonhold association if the land specified for the purpose of section 34(1)(a) is the same for both associations, and

    (c)   a 'winding-up order' is an order under section 125 of the Insolvency Act 1986 for the winding up of a commonhold association.

51.   Succession order

(1)   At the hearing of the winding-up petition an application may be made to the court for an order under this section (a 'succession order') in relation to the insolvent commonhold association.

(2)   An application under subsection (1) may be made only by—

    (a)   the insolvent commonhold association,

    (b)   one or more members of the insolvent commonhold association, or

    (c)   a provisional liquidator for the insolvent commonhold association appointed under section 135 of the Insolvency Act 1986.

(3)   An application under subsection (1) must be accompanied by—

    (a)   prescribed evidence of the formation of a successor commonhold association, and

    (b)   a certificate given by the directors of the successor commonhold association that its memorandum and articles of association comply with regulations under paragraph 2(1) of Schedule 3.

(4)   The court shall grant an application under subsection (1) unless it thinks that the circumstances of the insolvent commonhold association make a succession order inappropriate.

52.   Assets and liabilities

(1)   Where a succession order is made in relation to an insolvent commonhold association this section applies on the making of a winding-up order in respect of the association.

(2)   The successor commonhold association shall be entitled to be registered as the proprietor of the freehold estate in the common parts.

(3)   The insolvent commonhold association shall for all purposes cease to be treated as the proprietor of the freehold estate in the common parts.

(4)   The succession order—

    (a)   shall make provision as to the treatment of any charge over all or any part of the common parts;

    (b)   may require the Registrar to take action of a specified kind;

    (c)   may enable the liquidator to require the Registrar to take action of a specified kind;

    (d)   may make supplemental or incidental provision.

53.   Transfer of responsibility

(1)   Where a succession order is made in relation to an insolvent commonhold association this section applies on the making of a winding-up order in respect of the association.

(2)   The successor commonhold association shall be treated as the commonhold association for the commonhold in respect of any matter which relates to a time after the making of the winding-up order.

(3)   On the making of the winding-up order the court may make an order requiring the liquidator to make available to the successor commonhold association specified—

    (a)   records;

    (b)   copies of records;

    (c)   information.

(4)   An order under subsection (3) may include terms as to—

    (a)   timing;

    (b)   payment.

54.   Termination of commonhold

(1)   This section applies where the court—

    (a)   makes a winding-up order in respect of a commonhold association, and

    (b)   has not made a succession order in respect of the commonhold association.

(2)   The liquidator of a commonhold association shall as soon as possible notify the Registrar of—

    (a)   the fact that this section applies,

    (b)   any directions given under section 168 of the Insolvency Act 1986 (liquidator: supplementary powers),

    (c)   any notice given to the court and the registrar of companies in accordance with section 172(8) of that Act (liquidator vacating office after final meeting),

    (d)   any notice given to the Secretary of State under section 174(3) of that Act (completion of winding-up),

    (e)   any application made to the registrar of companies under section 202(2) of that Act (insufficient assets: early dissolution),

    (f)   any notice given to the registrar of companies under section 205(1)(b) of that Act (completion of winding-up), and

    (g)   any other matter which in the liquidator's opinion is relevant to the Registrar.

(3)   Notification under subsection (2)(b) to (f) must be accompanied by a copy of the directions, notice or application concerned.

(4)   The Registrar shall—

(a)   make such arrangements as appear to him to be appropriate for ensuring that the freehold estate in land in respect of which a commonhold association exercises functions ceases to be registered as a freehold estate in commonhold land as soon as is reasonably practicable after he receives notification under subsection (2)(c) to (f), and

(b)   take such action as appears to him to be appropriate for the purpose of giving effect to a determination made by the liquidator in the exercise of his functions.

SCHEDULES

SCHEDULE 1
APPLICATION FOR REGISTRATION: DOCUMENTS

Introduction

1.   This Schedule lists the documents which are required by section 2 to accompany an application for the registration of a freehold estate as a freehold estate in commonhold land.

Commonhold association documents

2.   The commonhold association's certificate of incorporation under section 13 of the Companies Act 1985.

3.   Any altered certificate of incorporation issued under section 28 of that Act.

4.   The memorandum and articles of association of the commonhold association.

Commonhold community statement

5.   The commonhold community statement.

Consent

6.   (1)   Where consent is required under or by virtue of section 3—

(a)   the consent,

(b)   an order of a court by virtue of section 3(2)(f) dispensing with the requirement for consent, or

(c)   evidence of deemed consent by virtue of section 3(2)(e).

(2)   In the case of a conditional order under section 3(2)(f), the order must be accompanied by evidence that the condition has been complied with.

Certificate

7.   A certificate given by the directors of the commonhold association that—

(a)   the memorandum and articles of association submitted with the application comply with regulations under paragraph 2(1) of Schedule 3,

(b)   the commonhold community statement submitted with the application satisfies the requirements of this Part,

(c)   the application satisfies Schedule 2,

(d)   the commonhold association has not traded, and

(e)   the commonhold association has not incurred any liability which has not been discharged.

SCHEDULE 2
LAND WHICH MAY NOT BE COMMONHOLD LAND

"Flying freehold"

1.   (1)   Subject to sub-paragraph (2), an application may not be made under section 2 wholly or partly in relation to land above ground level ('raised land') unless all the land between the ground and the raised land is the subject of the same application.

(2)   An application for the addition of land to a commonhold in accordance with section 41 may be made wholly or partly in relation to raised land if all the land between the ground and the raised land forms part of the commonhold to which the raised land is to be added.

Agricultural land

2.   An application may not be made under section 2 wholly or partly in relation to land if—

(a)   it is agricultural land within the meaning of the Agriculture Act 1947,

(b)   it is comprised in a tenancy of an agricultural holding within the meaning of the Agricultural Holdings Act 1986, or

(c)   it is comprised in a farm business tenancy for the purposes of the Agricultural Tenancies Act 1995.

Contingent title

3.   (1)   An application may not be made under section 2 if an estate in the whole or part of the land to which the application relates is a contingent estate.

(2)   An estate is contingent for the purposes of this paragraph if (and only if)—

(a)   it is liable to revert to or vest in a person other than the present registered proprietor on the occurrence or non-occurrence of a particular event, and

(b)   the reverter or vesting would occur by operation of law as a result of an enactment listed in sub-paragraph (3).

(3)   The enactments are—

(a)   the School Sites Act 1841 (conveyance for use as school),

(b)   the Lands Clauses Acts (compulsory purchase),

(c)   the Literary and Scientific Institutions Act 1854 (sites for institutions), and

(d)   the Places of Worship Sites Act 1873 (sites for places of worship).

(4)   Regulations may amend sub-paragraph (3) so as to—

(a)   add an enactment to the list, or

(b)   remove an enactment from the list.

SCHEDULE 3
COMMONHOLD ASSOCIATION

PART 1
MEMORANDUM AND ARTICLES OF ASSOCIATION

Introduction

1.   In this Schedule—

(a)   'memorandum' means the memorandum of association of a commonhold association, and

(b)   'articles' means the articles of association of a commonhold association.

Form and content

2.   (1)   Regulations shall make provision about the form and content of the memorandum and articles.

(2)   A commonhold association may adopt provisions of the regulations for its memorandum or articles.

(3)   The regulations may include provision which is to have effect for a commonhold association whether or not it is adopted under sub-paragraph (2).

(4)   A provision of the memorandum or articles shall have no effect to the extent that it is inconsistent with the regulations.

(5)   Regulations under this paragraph shall have effect in relation to a memorandum or articles—

(a)   irrespective of the date of the memorandum or articles, but

(b)   subject to any transitional provision of the regulations.

Alteration

3.   (1)   An alteration of the memorandum or articles of association shall have no effect until the altered version is registered in accordance with this paragraph.

(2)   If the commonhold association makes an application under this sub-paragraph the Registrar shall arrange for an altered memorandum or altered articles to be kept in his custody, and referred to in the register, in place of the unaltered version.

(3) An application under sub-paragraph (2) must be accompanied by a certificate given by the directors of the commonhold association that the altered memorandum or articles comply with regulations under paragraph 2(1).

(4) Where the Registrar amends the register on an application under sub-paragraph (2) he shall make any consequential amendments to the register which he thinks appropriate.

Disapplication of Companies Act 1985

4. (1) The following provisions of the Companies Act 1985 shall not apply to a commonhold association—
    (a) sections 2(7) and 3 (memorandum), and
    (b) section 8 (articles of association).

(2) No application may be made under paragraph 3(2) for the registration of a memorandum altered by special resolution in accordance with section 4(1) of the Companies Act 1985 (objects) unless—
    (a) the period during which an application for cancellation of the alteration may be made under section 5(1) of that Act has expired without an application being made,
    (b) any application made under that section has been withdrawn, or
    (c) the alteration has been confirmed by the court under that section.

PART 2
MEMBERSHIP

Pre-commonhold period

5. During the period beginning with incorporation of a commonhold association and ending when land specified in its memorandum becomes commonhold land, the subscribers (or subscriber) to the memorandum shall be the sole members (or member) of the association.

Transitional period

6. (1) This paragraph applies to a commonhold association during a transitional period.
(2) The subscribers (or subscriber) to the memorandum shall continue to be members (or the member) of the association.
(3) A person who for the time being is the developer in respect of all or part of the commonhold is entitled to be entered in the register of members of the association.

Unit-holders

7. A person is entitled to be entered in the register of members of a commonhold association if he becomes the unit-holder of a commonhold unit in relation to which the association exercises functions—
    (a) on the unit becoming commonhold land by registration with unit-holders under section 9, or
    (b) on the transfer of the unit.

Joint unit-holders

8. (1) This paragraph applies where two or more persons become joint unit-holders of a commonhold unit—
    (a) on the unit becoming commonhold land by registration with unit-holders under section 9, or
    (b) on the transfer of the unit.

(2) If the joint unit-holders nominate one of themselves for the purpose of this sub-paragraph, he is entitled to be entered in the register of members of the commonhold association which exercises functions in relation to the unit.

(3) A nomination under sub-paragraph (2) must—
    (a) be made in writing to the commonhold association, and
    (b) be received by the association before the end of the prescribed period.

(4) If no nomination is received by the association before the end of the prescribed period the person whose name appears first in the proprietorship register is on the expiry of that period entitled to be entered in the register of members of the association.

(5) On the application of a joint unit-holder the court may order that a joint unit-holder is entitled to be entered in the register of members of a commonhold association in place of a person who is or would be entitled to be registered by virtue of sub-paragraph (4).

(6) If joint unit-holders nominate one of themselves for the purpose of this sub-paragraph, the nominated person is entitled to be entered in the register of members of the commonhold association in place of the person entered by virtue of—

(a) sub-paragraph (2),

(b) sub-paragraph (5), or

(c) this sub-paragraph.

Self-membership

9. A commonhold association may not be a member of itself.

No other members

10. A person may not become a member of a commonhold association otherwise than by virtue of a provision of this Schedule.

Effect of registration

11. A person who is entitled to be entered in the register of members of a commonhold association becomes a member when the company registers him in pursuance of its duty under section 352 of the Companies Act 1985 (duty to maintain register of members).

Termination of membership

12. Where a member of a commonhold association ceases to be a unit-holder or joint unit-holder of a commonhold unit in relation to which the association exercises functions—

(a) he shall cease to be a member of the commonhold association, but

(b) paragraph (a) does not affect any right or liability already acquired or incurred in respect of a matter relating to a time when he was a unit-holder or joint unit-holder.

13. A member of a commonhold association may resign by notice in writing to the association if (and only if) he is a member by virtue of paragraph 5 or 6 of this Schedule (and not also by virtue of any other paragraph).

Register of members

14. (1) Regulations may make provision about the performance by a commonhold association of its duty under section 352 of the Companies Act 1985 (duty to maintain register of members) where a person—

(a) becomes entitled to be entered in the register by virtue of paragraphs 5 to 8, or

(b) ceases to be a member by virtue of paragraph 12 or on resignation.

(2) The regulations may in particular require entries in the register to be made within a specified period.

(3) A period specified under sub-paragraph (2) may be expressed to begin from—

(a) the date of a notification under section 15(3),

(b) the date on which the directors of the commonhold association first become aware of a specified matter, or

(c) some other time.

(4) A requirement by virtue of this paragraph shall be treated as a requirement of section 352 for the purposes of section 352(5) (fines).

Companies Act 1985

15. (1) Section 22(1) of the Companies Act 1985 (initial members) shall apply to a commonhold association subject to this Schedule.

(2)   Sections 22(2) and 23 of that Act (members: new members and holding company) shall not apply to a commonhold association.

CHARITIES BILL

PART 1
MEANING OF 'CHARITY' AND 'CHARITABLE PURPOSE'

1.   Meaning of 'charity'

(1)   For the purposes of the law of England and Wales, 'charity' means an institution which—
    (a)   is established for charitable purposes only, and
    (b)   falls to be subject to the control of the High Court in the exercise of its jurisdiction with respect to charities.

(2)   The definition of 'charity' in subsection (1) does not apply for the purposes of an enactment if a different definition of that term applies for those purposes by virtue of that or any other enactment.

(3)   A reference in any enactment or document to a charity within the meaning of the Charitable Uses Act 1601 or the preamble to it is to be construed as a reference to a charity as defined by subsection (1).

(4)   In this section 'institution' includes a trust or undertaking, whether incorporated or not.

2.   Meaning of 'charitable purpose'

(1)   For the purposes of the law of England and Wales, a charitable purpose is a purpose which—
    (a)   falls within subsection (2), and
    (b)   is for the public benefit (see section 3).

(2)   A purpose falls within this subsection if it falls within any of the following descriptions of purposes—
    (a)   the prevention or relief of poverty;
    (b)   the advancement of education;
    (c)   the advancement of religion;
    (d)   the advancement of health or the saving of lives;
    (e)   the advancement of citizenship or community development;
    (f)   the advancement of the arts, culture, heritage or science;
    (g)   the advancement of amateur sport;
    (h)   the advancement of human rights, conflict resolution or reconciliation or the promotion of religious or racial harmony or equality and diversity;
    (i)   the advancement of environmental protection or improvement;
    (j)   the relief of those in need by reason of youth, age, ill-health, disability, financial hardship or other disadvantage;
    (k)   the advancement of animal welfare;
    (l)   any other purposes within subsection (4).

(3)   In subsection (2)—
    (a)   in paragraph (d) 'the advancement of health' includes the prevention or relief of sickness, disease or human suffering;
    (b)   paragraph (e) includes—
        (i)   rural or urban regeneration, and
        (ii)   the promotion of civic responsibility, volunteering, the voluntary sector or the effectiveness or efficiency of charities;
    (c)   in paragraph (g) 'sport' means sport which involves physical skill and exertion; and
    (d)   paragraph (j) includes relief given by the provision of accommodation or care to the persons mentioned in that paragraph.

(4)   The purposes within this subsection (see subsection (2)(l)) are—
    (a)   any purposes not within paragraphs (a) to (k) of subsection (2) but recognised as charitable purposes under existing charity law or by virtue of section 1 of the Recreational Charities Act 1958;

     (b)   any purposes that may reasonably be regarded as analogous to, or within the spirit of, any purposes falling within any of those paragraphs or paragraph (a) above; and

     (c)   any purposes that may reasonably be regarded as analogous to, or within the spirit of, any purposes which have been recognised under charity law as falling within paragraph (b) above or this paragraph.

(5)   Where any of the terms used in any of paragraphs (a) to (k) of subsection (2), or in subsection (3), has a particular meaning under charity law, the term is to be taken as having the same meaning where it appears in that provision.

(6)   In this section—

'charity law' means the law relating to charities in England and Wales; and

'existing charity law' means charity law as in force immediately before the day on which this section comes into force.

3.   The 'public benefit' test

(1)   This section applies in connection with the requirement in section 2(1)(b) that a purpose falling within section 2(2) must be for the public benefit if it is to be a charitable purpose.

(2)   In determining whether that requirement is satisfied in relation to any such purpose, it is not to be presumed that a purpose of a particular description is for the public benefit.

(3)   In this Part any reference to the public benefit is a reference to the public benefit as that term is understood for the purposes of the law relating to charities in England and Wales.

(4)   Subsection (3) applies subject to subsection (2).

4.   Guidance as to operation of public benefit requirement

(1)   The Charity Commission for England and Wales (see section 6 of this Act) must issue guidance in pursuance of its public benefit objective.

(2)   That objective is to promote awareness and understanding of the operation of the requirement mentioned in section 3(1) (see section 1B(3) and (4) of the Charities Act 1993, as inserted by section 7 of this Act).

(3)   The Commission may from time to time revise any guidance issued under this section.

(4)   The Commission must carry out such public and other consultation as it considers appropriate—

     (a)   before issuing any guidance under this section, or

     (b)   (unless it considers that it is unnecessary to do so) before revising any such guidance.

(5)   The Commission must publish any guidance issued or revised under this section in such manner as it considers appropriate.

5.   Special provisions about recreational charities, sports clubs etc.

(1)   The Recreational Charities Act 1958 is amended in accordance with subsections (2) and (3).

(2)   In section 1 (certain recreational and similar purposes deemed to be charitable) for subsection (2) substitute—

'(2)   The requirement in subsection (1) that the facilities are provided in the interests of social welfare cannot be satisfied if the basic conditions are not met.

(2A)   The basic conditions are—

     (a)   that the facilities are provided with the object of improving the conditions of life for the persons for whom the facilities are primarily intended; and

     (b)   that either—

        (i)   those persons have need of the facilities by reason of their youth, age, infirmity or disability, poverty, or social and economic circumstances, or

        (ii)   the facilities are to be available to members of the public at large or to male, or to female, members of the public at large.'

(3)   Section 2 (miners' welfare trusts) is omitted.

(4)   A registered sports club established for charitable purposes is to be treated as not being so established, and accordingly cannot be a charity.

(5)   In subsection (4) a 'registered sports club' means a club for the time being registered under Schedule 18 to the Finance Act 2002 (relief for community amateur sports club).

INDEX